DIVINISING EXPERIENCE

Essays in the History of Religious Experience from Origen to Ricœur

EDITED BY

LIEVEN BOEVE

&

LAURENCE P. HEMMING

PEETERS
LEUVEN – PARIS – DUDLEY, MA
2004

Library of Congress Cataloging-in-Publication Data

Divinising experience: essays in the history of religious experience from Origen to Ricœur
/ Lieven Boeve & Laurence P. Hemming, ed[itor]s.
    p. cm -- (Studies in philosophical theology; 23)
    Includes bibliographical references.
    ISBN 90-429-1383-5 (alk. paper)
    1. Experience (Religion)--History of doctrines. I. Boeve, L. (Lieven) II. Hemming,
Laurence Paul. III. Series.

BR110.D58 2003
204'.2--dc22

                                                                    2003062384

© 2004 – Peeters – Bondgenotenlaan 153 – 3000 Leuven – Belgium.

ISBN 90-429-1383-5
D. 2003/0602/135

CONTENTS

INTRODUCTION

There is hardly a category more prominent in modern and postmodern reflection on religion than that of religious experience. This is particularly true in philosophical and theological approaches which emphasise questions of methodology and epistemology in the study of religion. In classical overviews of the history of the development of theology, the appeal to experience holds out the offer of a renewed way to account for the truth claims of religion. And yet as a formal category of enquiry, religious experience arises specifically out of the philosophical subjectivity of the Enlightenment. The slow preparation for and emergence of this discourse, with roots in neo-Platonism, in the mysticism of Pseudo-Dionysius Areopagita, in Eckhart's 'divine spark' in the soul, in Tauler, and together with the *coincidentia oppositorum* of Nicholas of Cusa, and Luther's doctrine of the Christian as *simul iustus et peccator* all, in different ways, prepare the ground for a consideration of God and the religious as directly accessible to experience and so to knowledge.

It is above all René Descartes who ushers in a radical transformation of the philosophical understanding of human experience, whereby there is always a self established *prior* to everything the self knows. This is a most radical step in the history of philosophy, a fundamental transformation which is now so constitutive of how we understand the being of being-human that it is taken almost automatically to be true – that I *am* before anything that I might know *is*. It stands opposed to the understanding of the ancients, for whom all self-knowledge is consequent upon and occurs together with, and at the same time, as what the self knows. Descartes' formulation 'I think, therefore I am' represents a transformation of the basis of selfhood, from being based on something which *lies ahead of me* – a thing in the world of the possible experience to a basis such that there is always something which is 'already there' and so lies in the past for me, namely the subject, the already-underlying (*sub-iectum*), the presupposition for all experience and knowledge.

The Cartesian and Enlightenment self, taking the self as already given prior to discovering things in the world, takes itself as an entity prior to anything it knows (it precedes what is known and so exists, not from the future, but the past). How then does the Cartesian subject relate to God? For Descartes, God is taken to be an *already constitutive* aspect of this *already existent* self. One need look no further than Descartes' *Medita-tions* to understand how the self, having established itself as the *one* thing it may indubitably know, discovers itself to *be* independently of anything else that *is*. Descartes describes this independent, certain, already-existing self as a finite substance. He then proceeds to ask, *before* establishing the self as living in a world of dubitable things, what more perfect, *infi-nite*, substance could have given such a self existence and replies that only God could have authored such a self (i.e. precisely *not* the realm of the things the self ordinarily knows by experience, and so can doubt): "I understand by the name of God a substance at once infinite, inde-pendent ... by which I myself, and all others – if some other exists, inas-much as it exists – have been created ... For although the idea of sub-stance would surely be in me from thence that I be a substance, this idea would therefore not be the idea of an infinite substance, since I be finite, unless it did not proceed from some other substance which indeed truly were infinite."[1]

Religious experience from now on appears to be of a different order to ordinary sense-experience, in a way that it could never have been for the ancient mind. It appears in the structure of the Cartesian self that religious experience is a unique category of experience which helps make sense of the world of things, rather than religious experience being in some way mediated by the realm of ordinary experience.

The full consequences of this transformation, made systematic in Descartes in a remarkable way for the first time, were pursued in differ-ent directions by the empiricists, the rationalists, and above all by Kant's transcendental idealism and what followed it in Hegel and Nietzsche. The enquiry into religious experience not only sought to provide a legitimate realm for religion, *ad extra*, in a reaction against all approaches to reli-gion which were too scientistic, functionalist, and reductive. In the same vein this enquiry challenged, *ad intra*, dogmatist and moralist conceptions of religion. If one name in the history of ideas emerges with particular sig-nificance for the development of an understanding of religious experience, it is that of Friedrich Schleiermacher. In a variety of ways his ideas on reli-gious experience were received and further developed in liberal protestant

---

[1] René Descartes, *Meditationes de prima philosophia*, ed. Charles Adam and Paul Tan-nery, vol. VII (Paris: Vrin, 1996) Meditation III, 45: "Dei nomine intelligo substantiam quandam inifinitam, independentem ... a quâ tum ego ipse, tum aliud omne, si quid aliud extat, quodcumque extat, est creatum ... Nam quamvis substantiæ quidem idea in me sit ex hoc ipso sim substantia, non tamen idcirco esset idea substantiæ infinitæ, cùm sim fini-tus, nisi ab aliquâ substantia, quæ revera esset infinita, procederet."

theology, and after the Second Vatican Council, in Catholic theology as well. His ideas and those that follow on from him have occurred in constant discussion with a host of critical voices in working out the role of experience in Christian faith and tradition. The focus on experience might very well be called the specific hallmark of 'modern' theology. The way in which experience functions among so-called pluralist contemporary theological viewpoints – as an attempt to find a unifying element beyond the diversity of particular religious traditions – is only one current example.

These developments – the taking for granted of the establishment of a 'prior' self – the subject – to any experience it had the effect of laying the basis for enquiring into what kind of experience this subject may have. Postmodern emphases on the 'decentring' of the subject have not managed to get beyond or outside this question. Even the 'decentred' subject is always understood to exist in some manner prior to what it is he, or she, might know. The work of Judith Butler is a case in point here. Butler is largely unconcerned with questions of religious experience. However, she has certainly developed an understanding of the subject as decentred. For her, even the 'normalising' and legitimating form of the subject, the male heterosexual, is himself a construct arising out of an understanding of subjectivity that demands that something lies *behind* and so *prior* to his very appearance or the appearances of the other gendered identities that are deflected from him: she notes "the parodic repetition of 'the original' ... reveals the original to be nothing other than a parody of the *idea* of the natural and original".[2] In other words even though for her subjectivity is always gendered, and every appearance of what is gendered is in some sense parodic of something occurring somewhere else (the heterosexual matrix), nevertheless its appearance depends on that something *already existing, even as an idea*, and so lying prior to and functioning as an underlying (*sub-iectum*) subjectivity.

Only in the philosophy of Martin Heidegger and in a handful of thinkers who have understood his radical critique of subjectivity has there been an attempt to understand human experience as constituted in its unity by what is to be known and experienced, thus raising questions about whether or not Descartes' fundamental descriptions of the self and its relation to the world and to God are correctly formulated and described. Heidegger, to some extent following a hermeneutical path opened by Schleiermacher, points to the way in which subjectivity can be thrown

---

[2] Judith Butler, *Gender Trouble: Feminism and the Subversion of Identity* (London: Routledge, 1990) 31.

into relief by asking about who it is that actually conducts an enquiry. Therefore, even with regard to religious experience, the fundamental question emerges: not just what is it that this experience is, and how is it to be understood, but *to whom* does it occur, and how can this 'to whom' be understood in its concrete, historical appearing.

The way in which a particular thinker or theologian conceives of the relation between religion (Christian faith in particular) and experience could almost be said to be determinative for the manner in which he or she will read the history of theology, and the history of reflexive approaches to Christian faith. Religious experience as a formal category of thinking is now so much taken for granted that it becomes a key, it seems, with which to read the past. Some of the essays in this book certainly take that view – taking an understanding of religious experience as developed out a philosophy of subjectivity as a presupposition with which to understand pre-Enlightenment figures. Other essays either make this commitment more explicit, or proceeding the other way about, challenge it directly.

However, once the category of religious experience is established, then for many thinkers the appeal to experience in theology can also function to develop their intuition that faith has to do with the concrete lives of believers and their communities. The truth of faith stands in a relation to the way in which faith makes a difference to human existence and what it means to reflect on it. From this point of view experience is not only a concept with which only modern theology is to be approached but can for some serve as a hermeneutical matrix to explore the history of theology as a whole. Many questions come to the surface in an endeavour of this kind, informing the investigation of any particular theological paradigm, any theologian, any theological text. What is experience? And what is religious experience? Has it to do with experiencing God, or precisely not experiencing God? What about experience in terms of 'experienced' or 'lived faith', and does it have close links with spirituality? How is it possible to distinguish experience in religious matters from other kinds of experiences? And further, from a more methodological viewpoint, what is the place of experience in answering the question of religious truth? What is the relation of experience to tradition, and should one take precedence over the other? Does experience offer opportunities to bring tradition right up to date? And if so, what are the conditions required? Or is the distinction between experience and tradition already a confusing one, as some would claim?

Evidently the current volume does not pretend to diagnose and unravel the entire history of (religious) experience as it has been discussed in

Christian theology, nor does it answer all the questions just raised. We have sought to investigate from quite different perspectives the theological approaches of twelve authors. Each of the investigations in itself suggests a different approach to and analysis of 'experience' as a category. The book therefore presents almost a 'double movement' not only as an enquiry into specific thinkers, but also what it means for them to be thought about. And is not experience itself like this – or rather are we not seeing performed here in these very texts not just an explanation of the category of religious experience, but also how that explanation can be received, and so experienced? The essays arrange the thinkers in chronological order: Origen, St. Augustine, St. Thomas Aquinas, St. Ignatius of Loyola, Friedrich Schleiermacher, William James, Wolfhard Pannenberg, Paul Tillich, John Henry Newman, Edward Schillebeeckx, Hans Urs von Balthasar and Paul Ricoeur. We are well aware that many other theologians and religious thinkers – among them several women – could have been equally well selected to feature in this volume; nevertheless an investigation, with religious experience as a reading key, of these thinkers proved a challenging and fruitful enquiry. In their own way, the twelve essays of *Divinising Experience* provide a kind of introductory reader in the question of religious experience.

The present volume is the outcome of one of the research activities by a research group whose work has been unified under the title *Theology in a Postmodern Context*, at the Faculty of Theology, K. U. Leuven. Both junior and senior members of this research group, together with other colleagues in the Dogmatic Theology department engaged in research, contributed to a series of lectures, of which the present collection of essays is the result. This series is part of a more extensive research project on religious experience and theological epistemology, sponsored by the *Fund for Scientific Research – Flanders* and the *Research Fund of the K.U. Leuven*. Particular thanks are due to Hans Geybels, our project assistant, for his much appreciated help in organising the lecture series and preparing this volume. We also owe a debt of thanks to Rita Corstjens, Frederiek Depoortere, Gillian Paterson and Tom Jacobs for their part in the editorial preparation of this text.

Lieven Boeve
Laurence Paul Hemming

ORIGEN: SPIRITUAL LIFE, OR WHAT THEOLOGY
IS ALL ABOUT

JACQUES HAERS

When one starts studying Origen's understanding of spiritual experiences, one cannot but be struck by the importance he gives to the spiritual life in his homilies and commentaries. In his perspective, being Christian is fundamentally about the encounter with God in Christ. I suggest that the structure of spiritual experiences, as Origen understands them, is in fact also the core structure of his theological discourse and endeavour. It seems to me that, in a reflection on the interaction between Origen's theology and his understanding of religious experiences and spiritual life, three crucial issues have to be addressed:[1] (1) Origen's work lies at the origins of some of the most important mystical vocabulary; (2) Origen, particularly in his homilies, likes to link biblical texts to the spiritual and religious experiences of his hearers; (3) the structure of spiritual experience as the mystery of the encounter with God, structuring human life and its interactions with created reality, constitutes the backbone and interpretative framework for Origen's theology. In fact, this third feature provides a hermeneutical key to read Origen's work and to situate his more systematic book *De Principiis*,[2] in a perspective that does justice to some

---

[1] By highlighting precisely these three issues, I show my dependence on the interpretation of Origen's work by Henri de Lubac and Henri Crouzel. For more information on the various interpretative traditions of Origen's writings, see Ulrich Berner, *Origenes*, Erträge der Forschung, 147 (Darmstadt: Wissenschaftliche Buchhandlung, 1981); and also: H. Crouzel, "Les études sur Origène des douze dernières années," *Etudes théologiques et religieuses* 58 (1983) 97-107. The main biography on Origen is still: H. Crouzel, *Origen*, translated from the French by A.S. Worall (Edinburgh: T. & T. Clark, 1989). For the bibliography on Origen, see three volumes published by H. Crouzel: *Bibliographie critique d'Origène*, Instrumenta patristica, VIII (Steenbrugge: Sint Pietersabdij and Den Haag: Martinus Nijhoff, 1971); *Bibliographie critique d'Origène. Supplément I*, Instrumenta patristica, VIIIA (Steenbrugge: Sint Pietersabdij and Den Haag: Martinus Nijhoff, 1982); *Bibliographie critique d'Origène. Supplément II*, Instrumenta patristica, VIIIB (Steenbrugge: Sint Pietersabdij and Turnhout: Brepols, 1996). See also the regular "Chroniques Origéniennes" in *Bulletin de littérature ecclésiastique*.

[2] When reference is made to works of Origen, usually I refer to the critical editions of the series *Sources chrétiennes*. The abbreviations are straightforward when one remembers that 'hom' stands for 'homilies' and 'com' for 'commentary'. *DP* is the abbreviation for *De Principiis*. *CC* is the abbreviation for *Contra Celsum*.

of its controversial theological claims, such as the pre-existence of the souls and the subordination of the Son. I will clarify the third issue by offering an analysis of Origen's understanding of the idea of creation as linked to his biblical hermeneutics, his understanding of theology, and his anthropological views, based foremost on Saint Paul. But before doing so, I will comment on the first two issues.

1. Origen and Mystical Discourse

In Origen's writings one finds the very early expression of language and metaphors that later in the course of history will become standard discourse for describing and articulating mystical experiences. By the latter I mean overwhelming experiences of intimacy with a God who reveals Himself directly to a human being who, in the very experience, discovers its ultimate passivity and personhood, de-centered from its 'I' that attempts to control the world and order reality according to its own wishes.[3] Theologians will emphasize that such mystical experiences are not a way to flee reality or to induce some absolute dualism between a perfect higher world and the broken human and creational reality. Indeed, mystics point out that, because of their encounter with the God who loves creation, they are invited to commit themselves lovingly to this creation. Mystics are oriented towards the world as they recognize and come to share God's salvific love for it. Their descriptions of the world and their interactions with it, as well as their anthropological perspectives, are patterned by the structure of their encounter with God. Their descriptive language provides a framework for a theological discourse. This theological observation is important with regard to the often discussed question whether or not Origen himself was a mystic. Indeed, I am not sure whether I would share Henri Crouzel's opinion,[4] when he argues in favour of Origen being a mystic by referring to his first homily on the Song of Songs[5] and to the

---

[3] For this approach to mysticism and mystical experiences, I rely on the research of Paul Mommaers, as exemplified in *Wat is mystiek?*, Spiritualiteit, 12 (Nijmegen: B. Gottmer and Brugge: Emmaüs, 1977) and "The Problem of the I," *Bijdragen* 56 (1995) 257-285.

[4] E.g. "Origène," in *Dictionnaire de spiritualité* XI (1981-1982) cols. 933-961, 959-960. See also Crouzel, *Origen*, 118-119.

[5] *HomSS* I,7: "The Bride then beholds the Bridegroom; and He, as soon as she has seen Him, goes away. He does this frequently throughout the Song; and that is something nobody can understand who has not suffered it himself. God is my witness that I have often perceived the Bridegroom drawing near me and being most intensely present with me; then

fact that it is highly improbable that a non-mystic would have been able to develop the mystical language he used. It seems to me that it is somewhat anachronistic to use the qualification "mystic" for Origen as it was developed only much later in the course of history.[6] I prefer to see Origen as a theologian, with a deep longing for the encounter with God,[7] using his faith in the reality of such encounter as the structuring principle of his whole theology. Here lies also the meaning I want to give to "spiritual theology" in this article: a theology is spiritual in so far as it articulates the belief that encounter with God is possible and, therefore, structures theological discourse. In that sense, Origen's theological endeavour is comparable to that of Karl Rahner when unfolding in his *Grundkurs des Glaubens*, the idea of a transcendental experience of God.[8]

But whether he himself was a mystic or not, Origen clearly lies at the origin of some of the most powerful language used to describe mystical experiences based on biblical texts. His influence on the Christian mystical and spiritual traditions has been very deep and lasting.[9] In his homilies and commentary on the Song of Songs he uses nuptial metaphors to

suddenly He has withdrawn and I could not find Him, though I sought to do so." The English translations of the homilies on the Song of Song used in this article are by R.P. Lawson, in Origen, *The Song of Songs: Commentary and Homilies*, Ancient Christian Writers, 26 (Westminster, MD: The Newman Press and London: Longmans, Green, and Co., 1957).

[6] The concept of mysticism, as it is used today, dates from the beginning of the fifteenth century, when Jean Gerson delivered his lectures "De mystica theologia" in Paris. See Albert Deblaere, "Mystique. II: Théories de la mystique chrétienne. A: La littérature mystique au Moyen-Age," in *Dictionnaire de spiritualité* X (1980) cols. 1902-1919, 1903.

[7] E.g. Rowan Williams, *The Wound of Knowledge: Christian Spirituality from the New Testament to St John of the Cross* (London: Darton, Longman, and Todd, 1987) 8. Eric Junod writes: "Si l'idéal d'O. est de type mystique, on ne trouve pas dans son oeuvre d'attestation claire d'une expérience mystique ou d'une extase" ("Origène," *Dictionnaire critique de la théologie*, ed. Jean-Yves Lacoste (Paris: Quadrige and PUF, 2002) 832-834, 833), but to my taste he distinguishes too sharply between "le théologien" and "le spirituel".

[8] *Grundkurs des Glaubens: Einführung in den Begriff des Christentums* (Freiburg, Basel, and Wien: Herder, 1977) 31-32: "Das subjekthafte, unthematische und in jedwedem geistigen Erkenntnisakt mitgegebene, notwendige und unaufgebare Mitbewusstsein des erkennenden Subjekts und seine Entschranktheit auf die unbegrenzte Weite aller möglichen Wirklichkeit nennen wir transzendentale Erfahrung."

[9] E.g., see the many references in Kurt Ruh, *Geschichte der abendländischen Mystik. Band I: Die Grundlegung durch die Kirchenväter und die Monchstheologie des 12. Jahrhunderts* (München: C.H. Beck, 1990). Particularly with regard to Paul Verdeyen's studies on William of St. Thierry, see e.g. "La théologie mystique de Guillaume de Saint-Thierry," *Ons Geestelijk Erf* 51 (1977) 327-366; 52 (1978) 152-178, 257-295. W.A. Bienert and U. Kühneweg (eds.), *Origeniana Septima: Origenes in den Auseinandersetzungen des 4. Jahrhunderts*, BETL, 137 (Leuven: University Press and Peeters, 1999) presents abundant material to study the influence of Origen.

describe both the relationship between the individual soul and Christ, and the relationship between the Church and Christ, without neglecting the historical or surface level of the Song of Songs as a love song. He also turns a seemingly boring travel account of Israel through the desert into a powerful description of the adventure of spiritual and mystical growth.[10] In his article on Origen in *Dictionnaire de spiritualité*,[11] H. Crouzel mentions the following themes: the mystical espousals, the dart and wound of love, the birth and growth of Christ in the soul,[12] the climbing of the mountain,[13] light, life, spiritual food,[14] wine, the five spiritual senses,[15] and the discernment of the spirits.

2. Growth and Discernment in Origen's Thought

For our purposes, Origen's emphasis on spiritual growth and the spiritual discernment necessary to it, are central features in his understanding of spiritual life. They also characterise his theological style. Although he is systematic, in his theoretical works as well as in his commentaries and homilies, he never claims to have the last word and likes bold hypotheses or contradictions which fuel thought. The criteria he uses to gauge his theological and spiritual claims are very much on the side of the intellect, but they never fail to include also a keen sense for the existential human situation.[16]

---

[10] Homily XXVII on the Book of Numbers, explaining Nu 33.

[11] Cf. ftn. 4. For a close analysis of many spiritual themes in Origen's writings, see Mathijs Rutten, *Om mijn oorsprong vechtend: Origenes ofwel het optimisme van een mysticus*, Serie Mystieke teksten en thema's, 5 (Kampen: Kok and Averbode: Altiora, 1991).

[12] E.g. Hugo Rahner, "Die Gottesgeburt: Die Lehre der Kirchenväter von der Geburt Christi im Herzen der Gläubigen," *Zeitschrift für katholische Theologie* 59 (1935) 333-418.

[13] E.g. José Fernandez Lago, "La montaña, en las homilias de Orígenes," Collectanea Scientifica Compostellana, 7 (Santiago de Compostela: Instituto Teológico Compostelano, 1993).

[14] E.g. Virginia L. Noel, "Nourishment in Origen's *On Prayer*," *Origeniana Quinta: Papers of the 5th International Origenes Congress, Boston College, 14-18 August 1989*, ed. Robert J. Daly, BETL, 105 (Leuven: University Press and Peeters, 1992) 481-487.

[15] E.g. Karl Rahner, "Le début d'une doctrine des cinq sens spirituels chez Origène," *Revue d'ascétique et de mystique* 13 (1932) 113-145.

[16] Dominique Bertrand emphasizes the importance from Origen's move from Alexandria to Caesarea: it was also a move from a more intellectual environment to a pastoral situation in which, inevitably, Origen had to take into account the lives of the people he ministered to ("Le creuset alexandrin du discernement des esprits," *Théophilyon* 8 (2003) 387-516).

Origen's anthropology is an articulation of the human spiritual condition more than an exercise in metaphysics or psychology.[17] Therefore, it relies more on scriptural ideas – particularly the writings of Saint Paul – than on philosophical, cosmological and metaphysical categories, be these (middle-)platonic, stoic, or aristotelian. Origen refers to Paul's polarity between the interior (inner) and the exterior (outer) being (2 Cor 4:16), as well as to his trichotomy of spirit (pneuma, spiritus), soul (psychè, anima), and body (sôma, corpus) (1 Thes 5:23). Interestingly, as we shall see further on, the interplay between polarity and trichotomy parallells Origen's hermeneutics as the interplay between, on the one side, the polarity of superficial and deeper levels of meaning in Scripture, and, on the other side, the trichotomy of historical, moral and spiritual senses. We will see that the same parallelisms exist with regard to Origen's concept of creation and the structure of his theological discourse. This indicates that we touch here a fundamental structure of Origen's thought. In fact, the trichotomies express the movement and growth that is present in the tension of the polarities.

Origen's anthropology goes one step further in articulating the interplay of the polar and trichotomous views in the idea of the fall. Indeed, a further distinction is made between trichotomies, so as to clarify the tensions between creation before and after the fall. The trichotomy that we have mentioned above is, in fact, the one after the fall. Then, the soul is a battlefield between the intelligence (nous, mens) as attraction towards God, and the attraction away from God towards the flesh (sarx, caro), the body in as far as it conflicts with the call towards God. Before the fall, the spiritual battle that takes place in the soul only after the fall, did not yet exist, and the soul is then totally intellect. Moreover, the body, when falling, becomes more heavy as it looses its ease in the relationship with

---

[17] H. Crouzel writes, referring to Henri De Lubac: "Le P. De Lubac a bien vu le sens de l'anthropologie d'Origène: elle est orientée par la perspective du combat spirituel. Origène n'est pas premièrement un métaphysicien ni même un théologien: sa métaphysique et sa théologie ne sont guère exposées pour elles-mêmes, mais contenues dans sa doctrine spirituelle. Il est avant tout un auteur spirituel, qui a directement en vue la montée vers Dieu de son auditeur ou de son lecteur et qui cherche dans l'Ecriture les principes de cette ascension. Aussi son anthropologie est-elle plutôt d'ordre tendantiel que d'ordre substantiel: ce ne sont pas les problèmes de nature qui l'intéressent au premier chef, mais les problèmes d'action" ("L'anthropologie d'Origène dans la perspective du combat spirituel," *Revue d'ascétique et de mystique* 31 (1955) 364-385, 365). A key reference is Henri De Lubac, *Histoire et esprit: L'intelligence de l'Ecriture d'après Origène*, Théologie, 16 (Paris: Aubier and Editions Montaigne, 1950). Useful syntheses can be found in Crouzel, *Origen*, 87-98 and Rutten, *Om mijn oorsprong vechtend*, 26-33.

God.[18] The process of discernment as it takes place in the soul, mirrors the tension between the situation before the fall and the situation after the fall. Therefore, as we shall see further on, it also reflects the situation between the first and the second creation. A first figure helps to clarify the situation.[19]

To illustrate these spiritual tensions at work in Origen's anthropology, one may refer to a crucial text of *De Principiis*:

> Certain careful investigators have concluded that an interpretation of no slight importance is suggested by the very meaning of the word soul (anima) as indicated in the Greek form. For a divine saying speaks of God as fire, saying, 'Our God is a consuming fire' (Heb 12:29; Dt 4:24; 9:3). ... As therefore God is 'fire' (ignis) and the angels 'a flame of fire' (Ex 3:2), and the saints are all 'fervent in spirit' (Rom 12:11), so on the contrary those who have fallen away (decidere) from the love of/for God (dilectione dei), must undoubtedly be said to have cooled in their affection (caritas) for Him and to have become cold (frigidus). ... If therefore the things which are holy are termed fire and light (lumen) and fervent things (ferventia), while their opposites are termed cold and the affection of sinners is said to grow cold (refrigescere) (Mt 24,12), we must ask whether perhaps even the word 'soul', which in Greek is psychè, was not formed from psychesthai, with the idea of growing cold after having been in a diviner and better state, and whether it was not derived from thence because the soul seems to have grown cold by the loss of its first natural and divine warmth and on that account to have been placed in its present state with its present designation.[20]

The battlefield of the soul concerns, therefore, the quality of the relationship with God. Here we touch the core "spiritual" structure of Origen's theology as a whole. This quality of the relationship with God is what his theological concepts attempt to articulate, as we will further illustrate when focusing on his understanding of creation.

---

[18] It would lead too far to present a detailed analysis of Origen's understanding of matter. It is crucial to remember that only the triune God is immaterial. There is no created reality that is not bodily. Corporeality is the one feature that distinguishes between Creator and creation. Cf. *DP* I,6,4; II,2,2; IV,3,15; IV,4,8; *HomEx* VI,5. This means that also the spiritual or rational natures have bodies. One has to take into account, however, that bodies may change and evolve, e.g. becoming heavier after the fall. It is, therefore, possible to speak about spiritual and heavy bodies. These distinctions indicate spiritual tensions, i.e. differences or changes in the relationship to God. Related to the issue of the changing body is also the interpretation given by Origen to the interaction between the verses 1:27, 2:7, and 3:21 of *Genesis*. See Manlio Simonetti, "Alcune osservazioni sull'interpretazione origeniana di Genesi 2,7 e 3,21," *Aevum* 36 (1962) 370-381; Henri Crouzel, "Le thème platonicien du 'véhicule de l'âme' chez Origène," *Didaskalia* 7 (1977) 225-237.

[19] See fig 1. I rely also on Rutten, *Om mijn oorsprong vechtend*.

[20] *DP* II,8,3. The translations from *De Principiis* are taken from G.W. Butterworth, *Origen on First Principles* (Gloucester, MA: Peter Smith, 1973).

The spiritual tension provokes a dynamism which may be characterised as a journey of growth. I will illustrate this rapidly, using one of Origen's less well known texts, his small treatise on Easter.[21] Origen concentrates on the meaning of the Hebrew verb "pasach", which he translates in Greek as "diabainô"[22] – referring to the crossing of a river, and calling to mind the Exodus story as passing through the Red Sea – or "hyperbainô"[23] – in the sense of passing by, referring to God's gracious intervention on behalf of his people during the Passover night in Egypt. Easter, therefore, refers to a journey in which the initiative and action of God appear on the foreground. Origen provides an allegorical and spiritual interpretation, throwing light on the human spiritual journey. The journey starts in Egypt, the land of Pharaoh, i.e. the land of trouble in the human heart, caused by estrangement resulting from the fall, interpreted as the act of moving away from God.[24] In the midst of this situation of estrangement, human beings are called to the holy land of God's nearness.[25] Origen conceives of this journey in a very concrete way: there will be need for discernement between good and evil, and for asceticism.[26] Further, in Origen's perspective, Easter refers not to the cross, but to Jesus Christ himself.[27] It contains a call to follow Christ,[28] who saves us from the estrangement and leads us on the journey to God. The spiritual journey, therefore, is decidedly christological.[29] We will recognize the same features

---

[21] See, for more detail, my article "Origenes' verhandeling over Pasen: Eschatologie midden in het leven van mensen," *Hoop en opstanding: Feestbundel bij het emeritaat van Herman-Emiel Mertens*, ed. G. De Schrijver, R. Michiels, and L. Boeve (Leuven and Amersfoort: Acco, 1993) 279-293. Origen's treatise has been published as: Origenes, *Sur la Pâque: Traité inédit publiée d'après un papyrus de Toura par Octave Guéraud et Pierre Nautin*, Christianisme antique, 2 (Paris: Beauchesne, 1979). I refer to the treatise as *PP* (*Peri Pascha*).

[22] *PP* 1,8.22; 2,17; 4,18.20.22.

[23] *PP* 45,14; 47,33.34.

[24] *PP* 4,27; 34,16-20; 39,15-17; 43,8-9.10-21.28-29; 44,29-30; 46,8.22; 49,23-24.29.

[25] *PP* 3,25-26; 34,10-18; 37,18; 46,23.

[26] *PP* 34,23-24; 35,4-39,6. Here we find a chain of allegorical interpretations.

[27] *PP* 13,1-3.10-14; 14,22-24.

[28] *PP* 23,6; 31,30ff.

[29] *PP* 4,5-28; 45,7-29; 47,33-48,10; 48,18-31. Origen is a very christological thinker, who cultivates a strong intimacy with Jesus Christ (*PP* 3,18-23; 18,9-19,1), up to the point that he becomes suspect of subordinationism. See J. Nigel Rowe, *Origen's Doctrine of Subordination: A Study in Origen's Christology*, European University Studies, Ser. 23, Theology, 272 (Bern, Frankfurt, New York, NY, and Paris: Peter Lang, 1987); Michel Fédou, *La sagesse et le monde: Le Christ d'Origène*, Jésus et Jésus-Christ, 64 (Paris: Desclée, 1994). See, for a sympathetic approach to Origen's subordinationism: Wolfgang Marcus, *Der Subordinatianismus als historiologisches Phänomen: Ein Beitrag zu unserer Kenntnis von der Entstehung der altchristlichen "Theologie" und Kultur unter besonderer Berücksichtigung der Begriffe "Oikonomia" und "Theologia"* (München: Huber, 1963).

later on when discussing Origen's understanding of creation, seen also as a journey, christologically focused.

In such process of growth as described above, as well as in the tensions that structure Origen's anthropology, discernment is inevitable,[30] not only as the ability to distinguish between good and evil,[31] or between true and false prophets,[32] but also as awareness of the "forces" that influence us in our thoughts and actions. In Origen's writings these forces are personified as angels and demons.[33] Although Origen does not offer a full and explicit theory of discernment, the idea nevertheless is very much present, expressed by the words "diakrinomai – diakrisis" (discernere – discretio), and by his frequent use of pauline texts such as 1 Cor 12:10. Origen may, therefore, be thought of as one of the foundational thinkers with regard to discernment. Indeed, discernment lies at the heart of the spiritual struggle, which characterizes Origen's thought and spirituality.

3. Origen's Writings as an Appeal to the Spiritual Experience of his Hearers

Another issue of discernment in Origen's work concerns his interpretation of Scripture. There can be no doubt about the exegetical skills of the editor of the Hexapla. His allegorical method, however, has received much criticism.[34] As in the tension between polarity and trichotomy in his anthropology, we can also, here, distinguish between the main concern of

---

[30] See, with regard to the idea of discernment in Origen's thought: Gustave Bardy, "Discernement. II: Chez les Pères," *Dictionnaire de spiritualité* III (1957) 1247-1254, cols. 1248-1249; Jean Daniélou, "Démon. II: Dans la littérature ecclésiastique jusqu'à Origène. 5: Le combat spirituel chez Origène," *Dictionnaire de spiritualité* III (1957) 182-189; Manuel Ruiz Jurado, *El discernimiento espiritual: Teología. Historia. Práctica,* B.A.C., 544 (Madrid: B.A.C., 1994) 71-73; Lothar Lies, "Die Lehre der Unterscheidung der Geister bei Origenes und Ignatius von Loyola," *Origeniana Septima,* 717-732; Dominique Bertrand, "Le creuset alexandrin du discernement des esprits," *Théophilyon* 8 (2003) 487-516. I am not sure that I would agree fully with Lies's remark that, whereas Ignatius's understanding of discernment is oriented towards concrete and practical life, Origen's use of discernment aims at the experience of intimacy with God. This seems to me to separate too clearly the intimacy with God from the practical commitment.

[31] *PP* 34,23-24; *HomGen* I,2; I,8.

[32] *HomEz* II.

[33] *DP* III,2,4.

[34] E.g. R.P.C. Hanson, *Allegory and Event: A Study of the Sources and Significance of Origen's Interpretation of Scripture* (London: SCM Press, 1959) 371: "He had in his hand a panacea for all biblical intransigence, allegory. Where the Bible did not obviously mean what he thought it ought to mean, or even where it obviously did not mean what he thought it ought to mean, he had only to turn the magic ring of allegory, and – hey presto!

allegory expressed as the tension between the text and its existential meaning today, and the dynamism of the allegorical method, expressed as one of two trichotomies of surface, moral and spiritual layers. The polar view, the search for the existential and spiritual depth of Scripture is most straightforwardly found in the homilies and commentaries.

In his Panegyric addressed to Origen, Gregory Thaumaturgus[35] describes how Origen, as a friend and a teacher, guides his students through philosophy and theology into the encounter with God. By his own example, offering his own experience of God, Origen invites others to engage on a similar spiritual journey. His own practice is, therefore, a narrative one very similar to that in the *Spiritual Exercises*. According to Roland Barthes' sharp analysis,[36] Ignatius Loyola shares his own experience of God to invite the one who walks the path of the exercises into a similar encounter with God.[37] In the case of Origen, as explained by Gregory, this move into an encounter with God involves also a sustained intellectual effort in the confrontation with existing culture and worldviews. This is mystagogy at its best: the introduction into a mystery – God's presence in human life and in the world – that always remains, as opposed to a secret knowledge,[38] to be fathomed in its depth. It entails a process of discernment concerning both people's concrete lives and the biblical texts that contain in narrative form the traces of the early encounters with God in Jesus Christ.

We begin by unwrapping the allegorical method in its existential polar significance, as it is found mainly in the homilies and commentaries. In her perceptive analysis of the hermeneutical techniques used by Origen in his approach to biblical texts, more particularly in his homilies, Karen Jo Torjesen writes: "The corresponding theological structure which determines Origen's exegetical procedure consists of two levels: the original, historical pedagogy of the Logos represented in the literal sense of Scripture, and a contemporary pedagogy of the Logos directed toward the hearer given in the spiritual sense. ... Exegesis is the mediation of Christ's redemptive teaching activity to the hearer."[39] In fact, we have here a

---

– the desired meaning appeared." Origen defends himself and the allegorical method by founding it in Scripture itself. A nice example is *PP* 26-30 referring to Ex 12:8-9.

[35] Published by H. Crouzel as *Sources chrétiennes* no. 148 (Paris: Éditions du Cerf, 1969).

[36] Roland Barthes, *Sade, Fourier, Loyola*, Points, 116 (Paris: Éditions du Seuil, 1971).

[37] It is also a risky process, both for the one who offers as for the one who receives. See my own "A Risk Observed," *Louvain Studies* 21 (1996) 46-60.

[38] Cf. Andrew Louth's remark in *Discerning the Mystery: An Essay on the Nature of Theology* (Oxford: Clarendon, 1999), 112ff., e.g. p. 113: "We are not concerned with a technique for solving problems but with an art for discerning the mystery."

[39] Karen Jo Torjesen, *Hermeneutical Procedure and Theological Method in Origen's Exegesis*, Patristische Texte und Studien, 28 (Berlin and New York, NY: Walter de Gruyter,

description of one aspect of the allegorical method, showing its underlying polar dynamism: from the surface – the story of a text or a biblical passage – to its spiritual depth for the hearer today. In his theoretical works, particularly in *De Principiis*, Origen develops the allegorical dynamism in three steps, in which the pivotal role is played by Christ as the one to whom the text ultimately refers, and as the one who calls to follow him. The allegorical method, in the homilies and commentaries as well as in *De Principiis* is, therefore, not primarily a method to provide a theologically plausible interpretation or content for some difficult and recalcitrant biblical text. It is, rather, a literary device that helps to unleash an existential dynamism that allows the faithful to probe more deeply into their own faith and its significance in concrete life.

Most homilies of Origen would serve to illustrate the point. I will provide a few examples[40] of the literary technique used by Origen in his homilies on the Song of Songs, when he switches from a descriptive, analytical style to an involved "we", or starts addressing his audience with a challenging "you". After a description of the various actors involved in the Song of Songs – the bride and her maidens, the bridegroom and his companions – follows the invitation: "When you have grasped this, listen to the Song of Songs and make haste to understand it and to join with the Bride in saying what she says, so that you may hear also what she heard. And, if you are unable to join the Bride in her words, then, so that you may hear the things that are said to her, make haste at least to join the Bridegroom's companions. And if they also are beyond you, then be with the maidens who stay in the Bride's retinue and share her pleasures."[41] Analysing various meanings of the verse "your eyes are doves" (1:15), he continues by a triple move, addressing his hearers directly, switching from the eyes of the flesh to the eyes of the heart, and giving the whole a definite christological perspective: "So please do not understand what I have said only with reference to eyes of the flesh, although it may not be

1986) 13-14. See also Rendtorff's remark: "Die umfangreiche, wenig erforschte Literatur der praktischen Schriftauslegung hat die Allegorie als Mittel zur Vergegenwärtigung der biblischen Botschaft reichlich verwendet, um den Abstand zwischen den heilsgeschichtlichen Ereignissen und der Gegenwart zu überbrücken, um den Anruf Gottes hörbar zu machen und um den Leser in seiner persönlichen Existenz anzusprechen" ("Allegorie," *RGG* I (1957) 240).

[40] For a more detailed analysis, see my "Over theologische stijl: Origenes' mystagogische theologie in de homilieën op het Hooglied," *Geloven als toekomst: Godsdienstpedagogische visies en bijdragen aangeboden aan Professor Jozef Bulckens bij zijn emeritaat*, ed. Lambert Leijssen, Herman Lombaerts, and Bert Roebben (Leuven and Amersfoort: Acco, 1995) 51-66.

[41] *HomSS* I,1.

unprofitable to include these. Enter rather into your own inmost heart and seek diligently with your mind for other eyes … If you understand the Law spiritually, your eyes are those of a dove; so too if you understand the Gospel as the Gospel means itself to be understood and preached, seeing Jesus as healing all manner of sickness and infirmity not only at the time when those things happened in the flesh, but also at the present day, and realizing that He not only came down to men, but comes down and is present here to-day."[42]

In a last example, we see how Origen stresses the gradualness and the difficulties of the encounter with God in Christ. He probes into what keeps us from an intimate relationship with God. He refers to verse 2:4a of the Song of Songs: "'Bring ye me into the house of wine'. The Bridegroom stood without, and was received by the Bride; that is to say, He reposed between her breasts. The many maidens are not such as to deserve to have the Bridegroom as their guest; to the multitude that is without, He speaks in parables (Mk 4:11). How much I fear lest perhaps we ourselves should be these many maidens! 'Bring ye me into the house of wine'. Why do I stay so long outside? Behold, I stand at the gate and knock; if any man shall … open to me, I will come in to him, and will sup with him, and he with me (Ap 3:20). 'Bring ye me in'. And now the Divine Word says the same; see, it is Christ who says: 'Bring ye me in'. He speaks to the catechumens also: 'Bring ye me in' – not only 'into the house', but 'into the house of wine'! Let your soul be filled with the wine of gladness, the wine of the Holy Spirit, and so bring the Bridegroom, the Word, Wisdom and Truth, into your house. For 'bring ye me into the house of wine' can be said also to those who are not yet perfect."[43]

We discover a similar dynamism in the commentary on the Song of Songs. Of course, as a commentary, it is less parænetic and direct than the homilies: it is concerned more with the unwrapping of the deeper layers of significance of the Song of Songs with regard to the Church and the soul as an anthropological or philosophical reality. Nevertheless, it also reveals at times the existential switch to the "we", in which the biblical text is linked, through Christ, to the individual's life adventure. In the third chapter of the prologue to the commentary, we encounter the switch from the more neutral third singular to the involved first plural of the verbs: "If, then, a man has completed his course in the first subject, as taught in the Proverbs, by amending his behaviour and keeping his

---

[42] *HomSS* II,4.
[43] *HomSS* II,7.

commandments, and thereafter, having seen how empty is the world and
realized the brittleness of transitory things, has come to renounce the
world and all that is therein, he will follow on from that point to con-
template and to desire the things that are not seen, and that are eternal.
To attain to these, however, we need God's mercy; so that, having beheld
the beauty of the Word of God, we may be kindled with a saving love
for Him, and He Himself may deign to love the soul, whose longing for
Himself He has perceived."[44] Again, in a passage discussing the verse
"Set ye in order charity in me" (2:4b LXX), Origen switches from general observations, to the concrete commitments of his community, talking immediately to his reader or using the first person plural.[45] A last
example shows how Origen links up the theme of the mountain, Christ
and his readers all in one. He is referring to verse 2:8 of the Song of
Songs: "Behold, he cometh leaping upon the mountains, skipping over
the hills." He comments: "I believe that it was for this reason that Jesus
Himself, when He came to be transfigured, was not on some plain, nor
in a valley, but went up a mountain and was there transfigured; you are
to understand from this that He always appears on mountains or hills, to
teach you too, lest you should ever seek Him elsewhere than on the mountains of the Law and the Prophets."[46]

These few examples show the search for existential relevance in Origen's application of the allegorical method. He wants to effectuate the
switch from the biblical texts to the here and now of "us", himself and
his hearers or readers. We also remark how deeply this switch has a christological perspective. In and through Christ the biblical texts are connected to us. The similarities with what was said about the *Peri Pascha*
are striking. Therefore, the accent lies not so much on the defense of doctrine (although that is present also) but on the attempt to relate Scripture
to the life of its readers. This is a spiritual attitude, which emphasizes the
existential impact of the texts under study. Indeed, it assumes a dialogue
between Scripture and reader, similar to the prayerful assimilation of biblical texts that brings about a relationship between God and the faithful.

It is not easy to discover in an equally clear way the same existential
dimensions of the allegorical method in the more systematic work *De
Principiis*. Here a more doctrinal type of allegory seems to prevail, as an

---

[44] *ComSS* Prol 4,22-23.
[45] *ComSS* III,7.
[46] *ComSS* III,12,5. There is a difference in counting between the *Sources chrétiennes* edition (no. 376), which I follow, and R.P. Lawson's translation (referring to *ComSS* III,11).

attempt to unveil the hidden doctrines or insights underneath the scriptural texts. Origen's hermeneutical treatise in the fourth book of *De Principiis* is well known, also in its *Philocalia* version. It is introduced in the preface to *De Principiis* with a view on allegory that contains clear existential overtones: "Then there is the doctrine that the Scriptures were composed through the Spirit of God and that they have not only that meaning which is obvious (in manifesto), but also another which is hidden (latere) from the majority of readers. For the contents of Scripture are the forms of certain mysteries and the images of divine things. On this point the entire Church is unanimous, that while the whole law is spiritual, the inspired meaning is not recognized by all, but only by those who are gifted with the grace of the Holy Spirit in the word of wisdom and knowledge."[47]

This doctrinal allegory is elaborated on in Origen's hermeneutical treatise, which begins by an attempt to prove that Scripture is divinely inspired.[48] It is because of this divine inspiration that a closer scrutiny of the text is necessary. Referring to Pr 22:20-21, in which a threefold enquiry into Scripture is urged, and assuming the existence of three types of faithful according to their understanding of faith and Scripture, Origen distinguishes between body (sarx, corpus), soul (psyche, anima), and spirit (pneuma, spiritus) of the text.[49]

The existence of such layers of meaning in the biblical texts sometimes forces itself upon the reader, when the literal interpretation of what is written lacks sense.[50] This lack of sense is a signpost urging the reader to look for more and to discover the dynamics of revelation at work in Scripture. We face here a dynamism of revelation that cleverly uses the tension between visible and hidden. The Spirit sheds light on the divine mysteries,[51] but at times also hides them, as not all readers of Scripture are capable of deeper understanding.[52] Readers are, therefore, invited to grow in understanding.

Understanding, indeed. There are clear intellectual overtones in Origen's treatise on hermeneutics. Sharing in the divine mysteries means communion in the doctrines contained in the Scriptures. Furthermore, the

---

[47] *DP* I,praef,8.
[48] *DP* IV,1.
[49] *DP* IV,2,4.
[50] *DP* IV,2,9.
[51] *DP* IV,2,7.
[52] *DP* IV,2,8.

enumeration of these doctrines in itself offers a summary of *De Principiis*.[53] The mysteries are the intellectual insights acquired after studying *De Principiis*. The allegorical method seems to provide legitimation for the philosophical and cosmological convictions held by Origen.

To compare *De Principiis* and the homilies, De Lubac[54] points out that also in the homilies one may recognize a trichotomous dynamism for allegory, urging the hearer towards a spiritual experience. Two types of trichotomy, then, seem to exist side by side in Origen. The first, stressing the dynamism "history, moral sense, mystical sense" aims at uncovering the Christ oriented meaning of scriptural passages. The second, "history, meaning with respect to Christ and the Church, spiritual sense as related to the soul", aims at challenging human beings to a process of change and conversion. This second type connects well with the general spiritual dynamism of the homilies, as also there christology was pivotal. In *De Principiis* very often, though, allegory is used to reach the mystical doctrines, the mysteries of Christ and the Church, whereas in the homilies these deeper meanings are invitations to the combat of the soul and the discernment between good and evil, between true and false prophets, between angels and demons.

By way of conclusion, one may say that there seems to be a double focus in Origen's use of allegory. On the one side, he emphasizes, particularly in his homilies and also in his commentaries, the existential link between the biblical texts and the concrete lives of his hearers and readers. On the other side, allegory seems to be to him a hermeneutical tool to uncover various levels of interpretation of scriptural texts, so as to allow more precise and in-depth knowledge of the mystery of God's presence as hidden in the text. In his mind both aspects are most probably intimately connected: more depth in the understanding of the biblical texts to him also means a better understanding of one's own life and a deeper aweress of the intimacy of the relationship with God. Also, out of that intimacy with God, expressed as the presence of the Spirit, it becomes possible better to unlock the deeper meanings of Scripture and better to discover how, in Scripture, God reveals Himself.

---

[53] *DP* IV,2,7. For a summary of *De Principiis*, see also *DP* I,Praef.

[54] "'Typologie' et 'allégorie'," *Recherches de science religieuse* 34 (1947) 180-226; *Histoire et esprit*.

4. The Structuring Principle of Origen's Theology as Illustrated in his Thought on Creation

The spiritual features of Origen's thought, his emphasis on spiritual struggle, on spiritual growth, on the relationship with Jesus Christ, ... all of these profoundly permeate his understanding of creation.[55] In fact, in my opinion, they provide the key to understand his protological schemes correctly against the inclination to read them as a mere cosmological discourse, a tendency we find to a certain extent even in H. Crouzel's *Origen*. We also indicated the strong parallelism between the allegorical methods for interpreting Scripture and Origen's anthropology. We will link both of these to Origen's understanding of creation. The resulting triple parallelism provides a strong argument in favour of using a spiritual key to understand Origen's theology, i.e. to understand it, essentially, as the articulation of the relation with God. Origen's theology, then, will have a spiritual structure, articulating God's self-revelation as it comes to the fore in the encounter with God. This encounter takes place as an inner spiritual experience, but for Origen it is always also mediated by the encounter with Christ in the Church.

When reading *De Principiis* and attempting to understand creation and how it takes place, one finds oneself involved in a cosmology. At least, that is the general opinion and, at first sight, seems to be correct. Origen appears to propose clear knowledge about how the world has come about, such as it is now. He presents a sequence of steps, spread out in time, logically flowing one out of the other, fitting in a systematic pattern, moving from the creation of the world of the rational natures characterized by free will, through their fall, to the creation of a new world materially structured so as to accommodate the consequences of the fall. The following passage of *De Principiis* illustrates this approach and it is, indeed, difficult not to interpret it as a cosmology, situated in the context of fierce theological and philosophical disputes, as well as flavoured with a psychology of free will:

---

[55] For an introduction to Origen's thought on creation, see Gerald Bostock, "Origen's Philosophy of Creation," *Origeniana Quinta*, 253-269.

[56] *DP* II,9,6. Many scholars point to the importance of free will as the key to Origen's system of thought. The most detailed and balanced account of this perspective, taking into account its christological and spiritual dimensions, seems to me Eberhard Schockenhoff, *Zum Fest der Freiheit: Theologie des christlichen Handelns bei Origenes*, Tübinger Theologische Studien, 33 (Mainz: Grünewald, 1990).

We have frequently shown in the preceding chapters, by declarations which we were able to quote from the divine scriptures, that God the Creator of the Universe is good and just and omnipotent. Now when 'in the beginning' he created (creare) what he wished to create, that is rational beings (rationabiles naturae), he had no other reason (causa) for creating them except himself, that is, his goodness. As therefore he himself, in whom was neither variation nor change nor lack of power, was the cause (causa) of all that was to be created, he created all his creatures equal and alike (aequales ac similes), because there was to him no cause for variety and diversity. But since these rational creatures, as we have frequently shown and will show yet again in its proper place, were endowed with the power of free will (facultas arbitrii liberi), it was this freedom of one's will which induced each one either to make progress through the imitation of God (profectus per imitationem dei) or to deteriorate through negligence (defectus per neglegentiam). This, as we have said before, was the cause of the diversity among rational creatures, a cause that takes its origin not from the will or judgement of the Creator, but from the decision (arbitrium) of the creature's own freedom. God, however, who then felt it just (iustus) to arrange his creation according to merit (pro merito), gathered the diversities of minds (mens) into the harmony of a single world (consonantia unius mundi), so as to furnish, as it were, out of these diverse vessels or souls (anima) or minds, one house, in which there must be 'not only vessels of gold and silver, but also of wood and of earth, and some unto honour and some unto dishonour'. These were the reasons, as I think, which gave rise to the diversity of this world, wherein divine providence governs each according to the variation in their movements and in their minds and in their mode of conduct. For this reason the Creator will not appear to be unjust, as he has given everybody his place according to merit in keeping with antecedent reasons; nor will the happiness or unhappiness of anyone's birth, or any condition whatever that may fall to his lot, be supposed to be due to chance; nor will it be believed that there are different creators or souls that are diverse by nature.[56]

Obviously, such a text suggests a cosmological reading. It proposes a sequence of events to explain how the differentiated and ambiguous world in which human beings live, has come about. It is embedded in a context of fierce philosophical discussions about dualism, determinism, anthropological categories and views of God. It gives rise to problems that will haunt the legacy of Origen: the reasons for God to create the world and the theodicy that attempts to put the burden of evil and sin not on God but on the rational natures and the human beings; the status of the rational creatures – "noi" or "logikoi" in Greek – that belong to the first creation; the tension between creation as a whole and creational diversity; the interaction, in the second creation, between life and matter, the latter created to allow for a more or less harmonious world after the fall; the intellectualism and anthropocentrism of a thought that focuses on rational creatures; the entrapments of meritocracy, sometimes understood as an early form of arianism; the issue how to understand Jesus Christ as a saviour without pushing him into a subordinate position.[57]

Clearly, all these issues have to be addressed and they will lead scholars into complicated philosophical and cosmological areas of research. Nevertheless, I am convinced that in doing so, we merely scratch the surface of Origen's thought, its outer dress so to say. The *De Principiis* text above also contains some triggers – such as the emphasis on human responsibility and free will, or relational expressions as "imitation of God" and "negligence" to describe sin – that suggest a different key for its interpretation, a more spiritual key, taking into account the spiritual struggle of human beings in the midst of their broken reality and their difficulties to relate to God. When one admits that perspective, Origen is no longer seen as describing a cosmological sequence of events, but rather as unwrapping the various levels of the spiritual experience of human beings, i.e. of their relationship with God, in its intimacy and in its distancing. The second creation in the cosmological scheme, then, corresponds to the surface level of reality: the intricacies of the world in which human beings live, its history, its diversity, its beauty and ugliness, its goodness and evil, its joys and sufferings. This is a world in which human beings become aware of their own ambiguities, the evil they are capable of and the evil that holds them prisoner, but also of the great things that they bring about, the love they are capable of and the commitment to just causes. They know about their responsibility and accountability for what happens. At this stage a journey starts for them to uncover the deeper layers of their existence, layers that ultimately concern their relationship to a God who calls them to life in a relationship with Him. Here, in their deepest structures of existence, all human beings are equal to one another: their deepest reality, indeed, is their relationship with God. That, they do share. This is where they are called rational natures, logikoi or noi, resembling the Logos, Jesus Christ. Here is revealed the in-depth structure of the universe they inhabit, the structure (or logos) of their world. What is at stake in our complex world is precisely the simplicity of the relationship with God, whether one inhabits that relationship or whether one turns away from it.

---

[57] Recently H. Crouzel voiced the following judgement on the condemnations of Origen: "Quand sont attribuées à un théologien dans une condamnation conciliaire des doctrines qui ne sont pas les siennes, mais celles de lointains héritiers et que d'autre part les propositions condamnées ne découlent pas d'une étude complète et précise de sa doctrine on peut dire que la condamnation canonique est sans valeur" ("Les condamnations subies par Origène et sa doctrine," *Origeniana Septima*, 311-315, 315).

Therefore, it may well be that Origen – while talking about a cosmological sequence of several creations, starting with the creation of the rational natures (C_1) as God has planned and wished them $(C_0,$ as the ideas and plans of God), and continuing in the creation of a world adapted to the fallen situation (C_2) – is in fact unwrapping the existential tensions that human beings are subjected to. In these tensions, human beings experience both their deeper or spiritual nature as oriented towards God and their fallen or broken nature, as turned away from God and neglecting their most fundamental relationship. They are related to God and to one another and live the challenge to cherish and foster those relationships with God. They also perceive their distance from God and their fellow human beings; they know about the evil in which they take part. Origen's cosmology indicates these various levels of human reality and, in fact, he is attempting to uncover the deeper layers of human relatedness to God. Cosmology is, so to speak, an allegory for existential relatedness to God. Origen seems to suggest using the allegorical method on his own theological texts so as to discover the mystery not only in the biblical stories but also in theological discourse.

Not surprisingly, Origen is a humble theologian, systematic in his own way, faithful to the rule of faith, decidedly biblical in his argumentation, and open to ever deeper enquiry in the issues at hand.[58] He ends his systematic work *De Principiis* with a reflection on the kinship between God and human beings. One may compare with the effect of allegory, while remembering the broad meaning of the word "intellectual" as referring, indeed, to the capacity to relate to God:

> Moreover, the marks of the divine image in man may be clearly discerned, not in the form of his body, which goes to corruption, but in the prudence of his mind, in his righteousness, his self-control, his courage, his wisdom, his discipline, in fact, in the whole company of virtues; which exist in God essentially, and may exist in man as a result of his own efforts and his imitation of God ... We see, therefore that men have a kind of blood-relationship with God; and since God knows all things and not a single intellectual truth can escape His notice ... it is possible that a rational mind (rationabilis mens) also, by advancing from a knowledge of small to a knowledge of greater things and from things visible to things invisible, may attain to an increasingly perfect understanding. For it has been placed in a body, and of necessity advances from things of sense, which are bodily, to things beyond sense perception, which are incorporeal and intellectual. But in case it should appear mistaken to say as we have done that intellectual things are beyond sense perception we will quote as an illustration the saying of Solomon:

---

58 See H. Crouzel, *Origen*, 163-169, referring on pp. 163-164 to *DP* I,Praef,1-3.

'You will find also a divine sense' (Pr 2:5 LXX). By this he shows that intellectual things are to be investigated not by bodily sense but by some other which he calls divine.[59]

If our interpretation of Origen's way of doing theology and of his concept of creation, as expounded in *De Principiis* is correct, then there are profound similarities between Origen's fundamental theology, his concept of creation, his anthropology and his biblical hermeneutics. I have brought these elements together in figure 2 at the end of the article. At this stage, I want to strengthen this position by referring to the first homily on the book of Genesis: here, much more clearly than in *De Principiis*, while put in a paranetic and nearly conversational style, appear the spiritual features of Origen's understanding of creation. I can only highlight some examples of Origen's ideas and will have to leave some very interesting theological concepts aside.

In the first homily on Genesis – but this is true also for many other homilies – two basic tensions are found. The first, which I will indicate by T_a, is the tension of allegory as such. The literal meaning (secundum litteram) stands over against the spiritual understanding (secundum spiritalem intelligentiam)[60] and the application of the text to one's own life (sed iterum referamus et ad nos).[61] The literal meaning of the biblical text contrasts with its allegorical depth (per allegoriam).[62] Origen's hearers are challenged to discover the deeper layers of the creation narratives and to use the story of the creation of the universe as a hermeneutical key to understand their own lives. The spiritual structure of the cosmos and the spiritual structure of human beings are similar, parallel.

The second tension, T_b, expresses the dual structure of reality: things are not any more and/or not yet what they really are. They have a past to which they relate (T_{b1}), and a future to which they relate (T_{b2}): the first creation (C_1) is both the past and the future of the second creation (C_2), the fallen world as it is now and unfolds in time. This dynamism is illustrated in figure 3, at the end of the article. In the homily itself, T_b is illustrated by such tensions as between "firmament" and "heaven", or between "waters of the deep" and "spiritual waters", or between "crawling animals" and "birds".[63] When interpreted anthropologically through

---

[59] *DP* IV,4,10.
[60] *HomGen* I,1; I,11.
[61] *HomGen* I,3. The switch to "we", as we illustrated it in the homilies and commentary on the Song of Songs.
[62] *HomGen* I,14-15.
[63] *HomGen* I,1-2; I,8.

an allegorical effort (T_a), as for example in the tension between "external being" and "spiritual being", there is a clear indebtedness to Saint Paul.[64] The tension between C_1 and C_2, thus, also articulates the existential tension that characterizes human beings as created beings: they never seem able to develop their full potential, although that lies in their past and in their future. There exists, therefore, an affinity between T_a and T_b, as is also literally illustrated by the double use of the word "spiritual".

The tension between heaven (H) and firmament (F) provides a first example to illustrate the interlocked tensions.[65] The firmament is the corporeal heaven; to be and to become heaven is what the firmament is ultimately about. Firmament and heaven, then, are not opposite entities, totally distinct and separate from one another. Rather, they are different viewpoints on a same reality, and because of the tensional difference between them, they produce a dynamism and a process of change and growth. Moreover, the firmament can also truly be called heaven, as it defines the borderline between the corporeal and spiritual realms. This seemingly "fuzzy" use of vocabulary once more indicates that the opposition between firmament and heaven is not a mere opposition. The firmament is the heaven, in as far as the former is pointing towards the latter as its ultimate reality. Origen thus seems to conceive, in this case, of T_{b2} as a vector from F to H: $F \rightarrow H$. This vectorial tension reflects the tension between C_2 and C_1. And that is precisely what the one creation is all about: C_2 is called to become what it really is meant to be and originally was, C_1. C_1 can, therefore, be called the blueprint of C_2.[66]

Now, Origen goes on with an allegorical explanation of the tension between firmament and heaven, giving it an anthropological twist. He provides an anthropological reading of the creation narrative: the tension between firmament and heaven, which reflects the tension between the first and second creation, indicates the tension between the exterior (or earthly) and the interior (or spiritual) human being. Those who can discern (dividere and discernere) between the different levels of reality can truly be called celestial beings (cf. 1 Cor 15:47). The ultimate goal of a

---

[64] *HomGen* I,2. References to 2 Cor 2:16 and 1 Cor 2:15.

[65] *HomGen* I,2.

[66] Origen likes to illustrate the tension between the first and second creation, as separated by the fall, with the tension between dry land and earth. See *DP* II,9,1; *Contra Celsum* VI,9; VII,30f.; *HomNum* XXVI,5f. In the last text, paradise is associated with earth and earth is also the word to indicate the promised and future world. The tension here is also applied anthropologically, so that, again, the tension between first and second creation has an anthropological parallel.

human being is at the same time what it has been created to be: to participate in the celestial, spiritual nature, so as to become truly celestial. This is what is at stake in the tension between the first and the second creation.

Another allegory in the same homily illustrates the christological backbone of the tension T_{b2}. The fact that in Gn 1:11 God speaks about fruit containing its own seed, is considered by Origen as an allegory for the orientation towards virtue, in the heart of human beings.[67] These fruits result from God's Word building its roots in our hearts. Our fruits have to be sown not alongside the path, but on the path itself, i.e. on Him who says "I am the Way": our fruits thus consist in our orientation towards Christ.[68]

That Jesus Christ is the central reference point around which to articulate one's life, becomes even clearer when the sun and the moon are said to refer allegorically to the importance of Jesus Christ and the Church in the lives of the faithful.[69] As the sun and the moon give light to our bodies, so do Christ and the Church illuminate our spirits. Origen is keen to stress this as a gradual process: God approaches and draws human beings nearer to Himself and to what they ultimately and profoundly are, in the measure that they open up to his light. A process of growth, therefore, forms an integral part of Origen's anthropology and by parallellism one can suppose the same to be true also of his notion of creation.

A last example will do to illustrate both T_a and T_b. Out of the waters of the sea come the crawling animals or reptiles and the birds, as the bad and good thoughts pour out of the spirit and heart of human beings.[70] They bring them before God, who will judge them and in doing so allow human beings to discern the good from the bad and to discard the evil. In God's presence, human beings discern what moves them. Origen is analyzing the tension T_b, here not on the level of exterior acts, but on the level of inner motion and disposition, as a process of discernment. The existential tension within human beings, between their being created in God's image and their being pulled away from God, forces them to discern and to search the way to God.

The tensions within the human being, its profound calling to become a celestial being and to respect its being created in the image of God –

---

[67] *HomGen* I,4.
[68] Origen plays on the expression "hè hodos" in Lk 8:4-8 and Jn 14:6.
[69] *HomGen* I,5-7.
[70] *HomGen* I,8.

the image of God being Christ[71] – reappear when Origen discusses the creation of the human being. That human beings are made according to God's image is a crucial idea in Origen's thought on creation and in his anthropology.[72] There are, so to speak, two layers of image. Indeed, "kath'eikona theou" means that human beings are made in the resemblance of God's image (homo ad similitudinem imaginis Dei factus), and, hence, are not, strictly speaking, God's image. The image of God is the Saviour, the First-born of creation, the "in the beginning" of all creation. Human beings can take on this image, or reject it and take on the image of the devil (imago maligni, imago diaboli). This is the essence of sin. Because of this turning away from what they are (fall), human beings are in need of restoring their resemblance to God's image. This is made possible by the fact that the Saviour takes on the image of human beings (imago hominis): this is the incarnation. It is then, by turning towards the Saviour, as the Apostles did to a high degree, that human beings reorient themselves in the direction of the image in which they were made. They can then, with the help of the Saviour, of God's Word, grow in the recovery of the form in which they have been created:

> If human beings, made in the image of God, by sinning looked, against their own nature, at the image of the devil, and were made similar to the devil, how much more will they not receive through the Word and his strength, the form that was given them according to their nature, when seeing God's image in which resemblance they were made by God.

---

[71] The tension between "image" and "in the image" and its christological importance, are well attested in Origen's writings. E.g. *CC* VI,63: "Then Celsus failed to see the difference between what is 'in the image of God' and His image. He did not realize that the image of God is the firstborn of all creation, the very logos and truth, and, further, the very wisdom Himself, being the 'image of his goodness', whereas man was made 'in the image of God', and, furthermore, every man of whom Christ is head is 'God's image and glory'. Moreover, he failed to understand to what characteristic of man the words 'in the image of God' apply, and that this exists in the soul which either has not possessed or possesses no longer 'the old man with his deeds', and which, as a result of not possessing this, is said to be in the image of the Creator. ... that which is made in the image of God is to be understood of the inward man, as we call it, which is renewed and has the power to be formed in the image of the Creator, when a man becomes perfect as his heavenly Father is perfect and when he hears: 'Be holy because I the Lord your God am holy', and when he learns the saying: 'Become imitators of God' and assumes into his own virtuous soul the characteristics of God. Then also the body of the man who has assumed the characteristics of God, in that part which is made in the image of God, is a temple, since he possesses a soul of this character and has God in his soul because of that which is in His image" (translation taken from *Contra Celsum*, trans. H. Chadwick [Cambridge: Cambridge University Press, 1980]). See also: *HomJer* II,1; *HomLk* XXXIX,5-7; *HomEz* XIII,2; *ComJn* XX,xxii (182-183). Origen also uses the tension between "image" and "likeness". Cf. *CC* IV,30.

[72] *HomGen* I,13.

The tension T_{b2} between C_2 and C_1 has now become the tension between the image of the devil and the image of God in human beings. The return to the original image I_G from the fallen image I_d happens through Christ. One touches again the process of discernment that was analyzed earlier on. The choice between the image of the devil and the image of God has to be made, not only on the level of corporeal nature and external being,[73] but also on the level of the thoughts and motions present in the human spirit, arising from the depths of the human heart.[74] To do this, one needs the light of Christ and the light of the Church, which refracts Christ's light. Illuminated by Christ one becomes light oneself, capable of insight and of gradual nearness to Christ, a process which ultimately leads to the Father.[75] Human beings are, therefore, invited to live towards Jesus Christ, to sow on the path that is Jesus Christ, to look for the things from above, where Christ is seated at the right hand of the Father,[76] to receive in their hearts the triune God.[77]

By way of a conclusion, one could say that Origen's first homily on the book of Genesis, shows a parallel between anthropological tensions and the tension between the first and second creations, separated by the fall. These tensions represent a dynamism of growth, fueled by strong christological "image" references that ultimately point to the intimate relationship with God. In that sense one may speak about a spiritual dynamism that is unfolded at the depth of a cosmological framework. This frame helps us to better understand the systematic cosmological presentation of *De Principiis* as a surface that has to be scratched to discover its deeper layers of significance.

5. Conclusions

In the foregoing we have attempted to discuss spiritual experiences and spiritual life in Origen's works. We have shown Origen's importance in the history of the development of mystical vocabulary, although we have avoided calling him a mystic himself. We have then provided some examples illustrating Origen's concern in his homilies and commentaries to stimulate a spiritual journey in the lives of his readers and listeners. This

---

[73] *HomGen* I,11.
[74] *HomGen* I,8-10.
[75] *HomGen* I,4.
[76] *HomGen* I,2.
[77] *HomGen* I,17.

spiritual journey is a process of growth characterized by an effort of discernment which is essentially focused on Christ and the Church. Finally, through an analysis of Origen's understanding of creation, both in his more theoretical *De Principiis* and in his homilies on the book of Genesis, we have clarified how allegorical method, concept of creation, anthropological views and fundamental theology are closely knit together precisely because they share a common structure which is also the structure of spiritual life itself, as the endeavour to enter into an intimate encounter with God. We do not lightly use the word "spiritual" to characterize Origen's theology. We end with a passage from H. Crouzel's Origen biography, in which the full weight of the significance of the word "spirit" (pneuma, spiritus) as intimate relationship with God is addressed: "The spirit is the divine element present in man and thus it has real continuity with the Hebrew *ruach*. ... It is the pedagogue of the soul, or rather of the intellect, training the latter in the practice of the virtues, for it is in the spirit that the moral consciousness is found; and training it also in the knowledge of God and in prayer. Distinguished from the Holy Spirit, it is nonetheless a kind of created participation in the latter and the latter's seat when He is present in man. ... it is found in every man and not simply in the baptised ... it does not quit man when he sins."[78]

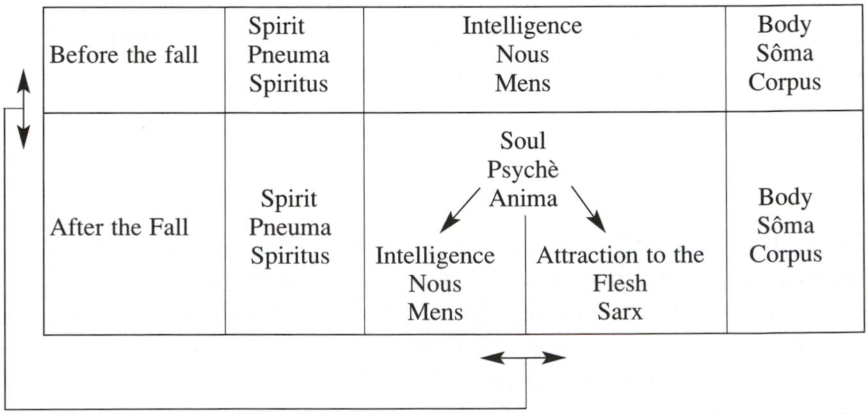

	Spirit Pneuma Spiritus	Intelligence Nous Mens		Body Sôma Corpus
Before the fall				
After the Fall	Spirit Pneuma Spiritus	Soul Psychè Anima ↙ Intelligence Nous Mens	↘ Attraction to the Flesh Sarx	Body Sôma Corpus

Fig. 1: Origen's anthropology

---

[78] Crouzel, *Origen*, 88.

	Biblical Hermeneutics	Anthropology	Creation	Theology
Polar	**Surface of the text** **Depth layers of the text**	**Outer human being** **Inner human being**	C_2 C_0 / C_1	**Cosmology / system** **Spiritual**
Trichotomy	**Surface (history) layer** **Moral layer** **Spiritual layer**	**Sôma** **Psychè (nous)** **Pneuma**	C_2 C_1 C_0	**Material life and sense** **Discernment (moral sense)** **Spiritual (God's presence)**

One has to take into account that the trichotomies may take slightly different forms, as they mainly clarify the dynamic and research element as it is present in the polar view.

Fig. 2: Some powerfull parallellisms

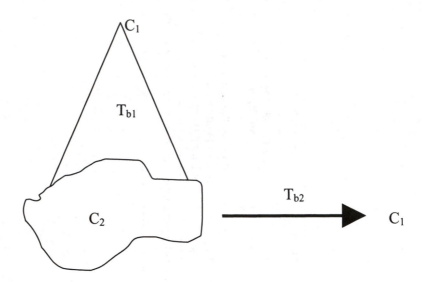

$$C_1$$

$$T_{b1}$$

$$C_2$$

$$T_{b2}$$

$$C_1$$

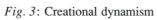

Fig. 3: Creational dynamism

EXPERIENCE SEARCHING FOR THEOLOGY & THEOLOGY INTERPRETING EXPERIENCE: AUGUSTINE'S HERMENEUTICS OF RELIGIOUS EXPERIENCE

HANS GEYBELS[1]

> *Give me one who loves, and he feels what I am saying.*
> *Give me one who desires, give me one who hungers,*
> *give me one traveling and thirsting in this solitude*
> *and sighing for the fountain of an eternal homeland,*
> *give me such a one, and he knows what I am saying.*
> *But if I speak to someone coldly unresponsive,*
> *He knows not what I speak.*
> Augustine[2]

Religious experience has become a major theme in contemporary theology, perhaps in consequence of the importance the concept has assumed in the contemporary perception of religion as a subjective or personal matter. In this essay, we focus on the importance of the concept in Augustine's theology, keeping in mind that religious experience as many understand it now (as a personal and emotional involvement in religion), is a nineteenth-century notion. Therefore, we start with a theoretical discussion of how the bishop of Hippo looks at religious experience (the grammar of religious experience in the context of his ideas on language) and the object of that experience. Next, we consider the example of aesthetic experience and, finally, we conclude by addressing the question of whether or not Augustine could justifiably be called a mystic.

Three things become clear immediately. First, human existential experience plays a very important role in Augustine's theology, although, at first sight, he seems to be one who privileges the intellect and is unconcerned with the senses or the consequences of experience.[3] Second, his

---

[1] I would like to express my sincere gratitude to my co-promoter, prof. M. Lamberigts, who corrected earlier versions of this text and suggested numerous improvements.

[2] Page reference of the original texts are from CCSL (Corpus Christianorum. Series Latina), in this case CCSL 36 (1954) 262. Translation: St. Augustine, *Tractates on the Gospel of John 11-27* [*In Johannis evangelium tractatus*], ed. J.W. Rettig, The Fathers of the Church, 79 (Washington, DC: Catholic University of America Press, 1988) 263.

[3] At first sight, Augustine is only busy with the intellectual side of conversion (Maurice Testard, "La raison et la grace chez Augustin," *Revue des études latines* 46 (1968) 68-83,

own existential experiences as a human being do not appear to be a direct source for his knowledge about God. Third, we recognise two variants of religious experience, as we understand it, in his writings, though Augustine never uses this terminology. First, Augustine's own human, existential experiences are described in theological terms in e.g. the *Confessiones* (theology informs experience).[4] Second, he speaks about theology as experiential knowledge: for a right understanding of what one confesses, one has to experience the Scriptures and doctrine (experience 'informs' theology). For a right understanding of theology, though, it has to be experienced, though not necessarily in a mystical way.

In what follows, we will concentrate on some early works of the church father (the period until the *Confessiones*, ca. 400 AD), but whenever necessary, we will draw on later periods in his work.

1. Preliminary Remark

In the ancient Graeco-Roman world, philosophy was more than an academic way of thinking. Above all, it was a spiritual way of life. A clear example is the community of the Pythagoreans.[5] Experiences could be called religious if they included the search for the determining characteristics of the divine: Truth, Beauty, and Goodness. Carol Harrison observes: "Religious experience, therefore, could just as meaningfully be had and described in relation to the philosopher, to one seeking to live a virtuous life, or to one encountering ordered beauty and harmony, as in relation to the adherent of a particular religious sect."[6] When we look at the early writings of Augustine in the Cassiciacum-period (*De beata vita*, *Contra academicos*, *Soliloquia*), we find that he searches, above all,

a view confirmed by Goulven Madec in "La conversion d'Augustin," *Lumen Vitae* 42 (1987) 184-194 and by Tarsicius Van Bavel in "De la Raison à la Foi: La conversion d'Augustin," *Augustiniana* 36 (1986) 5-27.

[4] *Confessiones* will be abbreviated as *Conf.*

[5] Pierre Hadot, *Exercices spirituels et philosophie antique,* Études augustiniennes (Paris: Études augustiniennes, 1981). Also Kees Waaijman, "Wijsgerige verstandigheid en onderscheiding der geesten," *Tegenwoordigheid van Geest: Opstellen over spiritualiteit en mensbeschouwing,* ed. Gerben Groenewoud *et al.* (Zoetermeer: Meinema, 2001) 135-152, 135-136; and Kees Waaijman, *Spiritualiteit: Vormen, grondslagen, methoden* (Kampen: Kok, 2000) 395 [English translation: *Spirituality: Form, Foundations, Methods* (New York, NY: Crossroad, 2002)] and Gillian Rosemary Evans, *Philosophy & Theology in the Middle Ages* (London and New York, NY: Routledge, 1993) 10-16.

[6] Carol Harrison, "Augustine and Religious Experience," *Louvain Studies* 27 (2002) 99-118, 99.

for the Truth, which he finally finds in 'Catholic' christianity, rather than in Manicheism, in neo-Platonism, or in Scepticism.[7]

2. Grammar of Language

In her book on Augustine's aesthetics, Carol Harison makes use of the grammar of language to delineate Augustine's aesthetic views, and it is instructive to dwell upon the principle which lies behind Augustine's views on language.[8] That principle is of the utmost importance for understanding the status of religious experience in Augustine. In order to do this we will make use of a rather early work of Augustine, *De doctrina christiana* (abbreviated as *Doctr.*), of which the first three books appeared about circa 397 AD (the last part of the third book and the fourth book only to be completed some thirty years after[9]). Significant portions of *Doctr.* deal with the proper hermeneutical approach to the Scriptures. In the first three books, Augustine talks about acquiring knowledge and gaining insight into the Christian articles of faith in order to understand the Scriptures better. A correct understanding of the Bible that permits the deduction of Christian truths from it is the only guarantee for an effective Christian *paideia*.[10]

---

[7] Harrison, "Augustine and Religious Experience," 100. Harrison is right in believing that there is no big gap in Augustine's writings before and after 396 (composition of the *Confessiones* and letter to Simplicianus). To a certain extent his experience remains the same after his last conversion, only his vocabulary changes. In the early period, Augustine's work is more 'existential' than doctrinal, a fact to which Pelagius later objects, according to Augustine in *De natura et gratia* (pp. 101 and 104). In sum, Harrison notices a continuity in Augustine's thought based on continuity of experience, but the language in which this experience is manifested developed under the influence of his increasing familiarity with Scriptures and the Christian tradition. It is easy to see how Augustine integerated the thought systems he studied into his own theology, e.g. in his teachings on grace: see for instance V.H. Drecoll, *Die Entstehung der Gnadelehre Augustins,* Beiträge zur historischen Theologie, 109 (Tübingen: Mohr Siebeck, 1999) and on the virtues: see J. Wang Tch'ang-tche, *Saint Augustin et les vertus des païens,* Études de théologie historique (Paris: Beauchesne, 1938).

[8] Carol Harrison, *Beauty and Revelation in the Thought of Saint Augustine,* Oxford Theological Monographs, 11 (Oxford: Clarendon, 1992). Harrison overemphasizes the distinctions between the different intellectual periods in Augustine's biography. Augustine could be better compared to a sponge: he exploited the best of the different religious and philosophical systems he met, and incorporated them in his concept of Christianity.

[9] On the circumstances of composition: James O'Donnell, "De doctrina christiana," *Augustine Through the Ages: An Encyclopedia*, ed. Allan D. Fitzgerald (Grand Rapids, MI and Cambridge: Eerdmans, 1999) 278-280.

[10] See the introduction to Augustinus, *Wat betekent de bijbel?*, ed. Jan Den Boeft and Ineke Sluiter (Amsterdam: Ambo-klassiek and Leuven: Kritak, 1999) 14-16. For an

Augustine describes his subject within the wider context of the status of human knowledge in relation to revelation. Revelation can override all the limitations of human reason in its search for Truth. Left to its own devices, human reason is in need of an epistemological system, since it would be untenable if human reason invented its own foundation for its truth claims: reason can indicate, but it cannot indicate that it is indicating. Reason only helps one to see that the foundation of metaphysics cannot objectively be based on reason itself. This is part of the domain of wisdom, or *sapientia*.[11] The insight which is resigned to itself, passes inner certainty and is at the same time the anchorage of faith. Augustine confesses that he cannot find God outside of his memory (*memoria*).[12] He discovers God, Truth itself, inside himself (*Conf.* 10,24,35).[13]

The guarantee for absolute certainty has a transcendent foundation in God, which is technically elucidated in *Doctr.*, where Augustine lingers over the semantic functioning of language and – in that respect also – of the epistemological status of experiences in general. Each linguistic utterance contains a reference to a non-linguistic reality (referent), but that reality in its turn functions as a *signum* to an always elusive *res*. The tree which we read that Moses throws into the bitter waters to make them drinkable, or the stone which Jacob places under his head, or the sheep which Abraham sacrified in place of his son. These are things, but they are at the same time signs of other things (*Doctr.* 1,2,2).[14]

interesting essay on *signum* and the theory of signification, see J. Norris, "Augustine and Sign in Tractatus in Ioannis Evangelium," *Augustine: Biblical Exegete*, ed. Frederick Van Fleteren and Joseph C. Schnaubelt, Collectanea augustiniana, 5 (New York, NY: Lang, 2001) 215-231 and also Michael Cameron, "Sign," *Augustine Through the Ages*, 793-798 (Here, Cameron also pays attention to the way in which Augustine's thought on signs evolved over the course of his life).

[11] General study: H. Hasso, *The Patristic Conception of Wisdom in the Light of Biblical and Rabbinical Research*, Studia patristica, 4 (Texte und Untersuchungen, 79) (Berlin: Akademie Verlag, 1961). Exhaustive studies on this topic include Fulbert Cayré, "La notion de sagesse chez saint Augustin," *L'année théologique* 4 (1943) 433-456 and Henri-Irénée Marrou, *Saint Augustin et la fin de la culture antique* (Paris: de Boccard, 1943) [republication in 1983] 368-380 and Appendice, note B, p. 561-569. *Sapientia* is both human and divine. Human *sapientia* participates in God's *sapientia*, in which human wisdom finds its origin and its goal. *Sapientia* points towards the most superior action of the *mens*, by which the mind contemplates God and divine truths.

[12] Memory deals as well with all temporal images, as with all intelligible concepts. Memory is able to remember God: e.g. the beauty of creation is a sign, pointing our mind to eternal and immutable Beauty (see *infra*).

[13] Original CCSL 27 (1981) 174. Translation: Saint Augustine, *Confessions*, ed. Henry Chadwick (New York, NY: Oxford University Press, 1991) 200.

[14] On *signa*: Gustave Combès and Albert Farges, *Le magistère chrétien*, Bibliothèque augustinienne, 11 (Paris: Desclee de Brouwer, 1949) 563-567.

In Augustine's own words: *"Res per signa discuntur"*. These are the two pivots in Augustine's process of knowing.[15] Augustine demonstrates the continually referential character of language by using the terminology *res et signum datum* or *signum translatum*. *Signa data* are given to things felt or understood by a subject: here the relationship between sign and referent is clear. *Signa translata* are rather ambiguous because they have to be understood in a figurative way, not a literal (*propria*) one: *transferre* is the translation of μεταφέρειν and each language consequently comes to be regarded as metaphorical. Therefore, we use the word 'ox' (*bos*) in its proper sense (*"propria dicuntur", Doctr.* 22,10,15) to refer to a head of cattle. The signs remain metaphorical or figurative even when the realities themselves that are indicated by that word refer to something else. 'Ox' refers to a herd animal, but at the same time, through that animal we also understand the evangelist Luke (*Doctr.* 2,10,15; referring to 1 Cor 9:9, quoting Dt 25:4). Augustine does not only apply the mechanism of language to the scheme *signum/res* but also applies them to the referents themselves! One *res* becomes a symbol of another *res*.[16] In this respect, the whole Bible is an accumulation of words functioning as signs with the primary purposes of pointing to realities beyond themselves, even when those signs can never represent the things signified in their entirety. Scripture's images lift the mind into the presence of the transcendent: *"Hoc est ut de corporalibus temporalibusque rebus aeterna et spiritalia capiamus"* (*Doctr.* 1,4,4).[17]

Augustine makes use not only of a system of multiple semiotic reference to linguistic signs, but also to the objects themselves, to historical

---

[15] Cornelius Mayer, "Res per signa: Der Grundgedanke des Prologs in Augustins Schrift De doctrina christiana und das Problem seiner Datierung," *Revue des études augustiniennes* 20 (1974) 100-112, 100. This text parallels the *De magistro* 7,19 where Augustine contends that things are learned by means of signs, an activity that prompts the soul to remember what it knows or stimulates its desire to know more. In the same treatise (*De magistro* 8,24) Augustine posits the rule that the sign compels the attention of the mind to the thing signified.

[16] Cf. his example of the wine: *Doctr.* 4,21,45. *Doctr.* 1,2,2 provides another example of how the text of the Bible functions as a sign, pointing both to literal and figurative realities. In Ex 15, Moses throws a piece of wood in the water of Marah, to make it drinkable. The text refers to the actual deed of Moses, but the piece of wood is also a sign for the salvific force of Christ's cross. The things signified are also signs of themselves.

[17] CCSL 32 (1962) 8. See also *Doctr.* 2,2,3 where Augustine explains that the biblical text consists of signs given by God but pointed out to us by men: *"Signa diuinitus data, quae scripturis sanctis continentur, sed per homines nobis indicata sunt."* Quoted by Michael Cameron, "The Christological Substructure of Augustine's Figurative Exegesis," *Augustine and the Bible,* ed. Pamela Bright, The Bible Through the Ages, 2 (Notre Dame, IN: University of Notre Dame Press, 1997) 52-73, 59 and 66.

facts and to human experiences and their matching psychological capabilities (*mens, notitia, intellectus* and *uoluntas*). In that way, he ends up with a system where all created things become referents for everything, eventually canceling out every meaning (Augustine thinks hierarchically, everything in creation pointing towards the top of the pyramid.) To escape from that vicious circle, there has to be an ultimate referent, to which all created referents refer, namely God, the *res* which is no longer a *signum* of something else. Every language and every created thing include a reference to the ultimate *res*. In interpreting the Scriptures, one has to keep an eye on that *res* as a *telos*, because that *res* determines when a passage has to be interpreted literally or allegorically; an idea which comprises the primary theme of the third book of *Doctr*. More examples of *res* are given in the *Conf.* (books 10-13): language and science, prophecy, gospel and sacraments, Jesus in the flesh...

Human, existential experiences only reveal themselves completely if they are aware of their counter-character, if they do not refer to themselves, but to divine reality or to any other kind of otherness (e.g. love of neighbour can be an example of *frui* for Augustine). To enjoy something (*frui*) is to hold fast to it in love for its own sake, and not for the sake of something else (*uti*). Language, experience and reality belong to the sphere of *uti* and serve exclusively to bring up God, the only object of *frui* (*Doctr.* 1,4,4 and 5).[18] The things which are to be enjoyed are the Father, the Son, and the Holy Spirit.

It is impossible to speak of God totally and efficiently, because a human being remains in the *uti*-structure of language and experience. God will always be indescribable, even if we say something by uttering that! Augustine is aware of this paradox (*Doctr.* 1,6). In spite of the changeability and the instability of his knowledge, he experiences the existence of a transcendent *res*, which goes beyond that instability and functions as an ultimate referent that has established all meaning.[19]

In his early work *De genesi aduersus manichaeos* (2,3-6), Augustine gives a theological answer to the question of why eventually it is necessary to turn to referring signs. Beginning with an allegory on Gn 2:5*ss.*,

---

[18] On *uti/frui* see Raymond Canning, *The Unity of Love for God and Neighbour in Saint Augustine* (Leuven: Augustinian Historical Institute, 1993) 79-115; Rudolf Lorenz, "Fruitio Dei bei Augustin," *Zeitschrift für Kirchengeschichte* 63 (1950-1951) 75-132 and Tarsicius Jan Van Bavel, "Fruitio, delectatio and voluptas in Augustine," *Augustinus* 37 (1993) 499-510 and especially C. Mayer, "Delectatio (delectare)," *Augustinus-lexikon* 2 (1996) 267-285.

[19] A similar argument is possible concerning *Conf.* 11,28,38 (CCSL 27 (1981) 214).

Augustine describes how, since the fall, mankind has to fall back on the function of signs if it is to acquire knowledge concerning the transcendental. The linguistic communication of humans is a consequence of the sin that is characterized by *superbia*, i.e. arrogance. Since direct communication from one soul to another has become impossible because of pride, *caritas* (love) makes the inevitable detour of the *signa* (signs).

In order to increase insight in the meaning of *signum* (sign), it is necessary to add to his concept the notion of *sacramentum* (sacrament), to which Augustine pays attention in early works. *Sacramentum* is the translation of the Greek μυστήριον, identified by Augustine as sacred signs (*signa sacra*)[20] or symbols of God's salutary presence (*Doctr.* 3,9,13), and used in many of his works. Signs or sacraments are material references to a deeper and higher transcendence. The external or visible becomes a sign of the internal or invisible (*s.* 272), and this is a crucial idea in order to understand Augustine's concept of religious experience (see *infra*). Sacraments are helpful for walking on the inward way (*via interior*). Both Church and tradition are the authorities from which sacraments arise (*inq. Jan.* 54,1).[21] In this same letter to Januarius (*inq. Jan.* 55,2-3), Augustine states that a sacrament is a special kind of sign, because a sacrament moves from the visible or external to the invisible or internal or spiritual, or from ordinary experience to spiritual reality. For this reason, Easter is called a sacrament, because Easter, received by the Church, is the time when a Christian finds oneness with Christ; the Easter event is a feast which locates the Easter mystery in the history of salvation.[22]

Another way to circumscribe the notion of religious experience is to link two already mentioned concepts: *memoria* and *via interior* (linked to the image doctrine). The grammar of language pointed towards the use of

---

[20] E.g. later documents like *Epistula* 138,7 and *De civitate Dei* 10,5, where Augustine explicitly uses the characterization *signum sacrum* to indicate sacraments.

[21] In a later work (*In Johannis evangelium tractatus* 15,8) than letter 55 to Januarius, Augustine argues that the power of each sacrament originates in the Word of God, for which it is a sign, and that the Church continues that Word in faith. Sacraments are ecclesiologicially and christologically God's Word in action.

[22] In this letter to Januarius, Augustine recognises sacraments which are not derived from scripture, but from tradition, ordained or recommended by the Apostles or by plenary councils, such as the annual commemorations of the Lord's Passion, Resurrection and Ascension. See, e.g., Carolo Couturier, "Sacramentum et mysterium dans l'œuvre de saint Augustin," *Études augustiniennes*, ed. Henri Rondet *et al.* (Paris: Institut d'études augustiniennes, 1953) 161-274 and H.-M. Féret, "Sacramentum-Res dans la langue théologique de saint Augustin," *Revue des sciences philosophiques et théologiques* 29 (1940) 218-243.

signa/sacramenta, i.e. material signs with a spiritual meaning, helping
Christians to walk the interior way. External signs point to internal truths,
and internal truths point to the highest Truth. Thus the dynamic is from
an outer world to an inner world, and from this inner world to the highest world. The link is the extremely rich concept of *memoria*, one which
Augustine would continue to work on for the rest of his life. In *Conf.* 10
the main ideas are already present (exhaustively elaborated in *De trinitate*).
Memory contains images brought in from the senses and it contains its
own imaginative creations. Memory also retains ideas acquired through
teaching and it stores up emotions and passions of the mind, its experiences and opinions. This means that memory is equal to self-awareness
(*Conf.* 10,8,12-10,17,26). God cannot be in human memory, since God is
not an image, nor a passion nor a self-reflection of the mind. Though God
is not in the the mind, we know Him, because we seek truth and happiness. There is but one solution: the mind – built according to the image
of God and structured in a trinitarian way – must remember God, because,
from the very moment God is in the human memory, God is known. From
this very moment onwards, the interior way turns into an ascent, or – in
other words – knowing oneself and knowing God are indissolubly inter-
connected.[23] If carried out correctly, the experience of the self can be experience of God.

3. Grammar of Experience

Augustine's grammar of experience is best explained in his mystagogical teachings. Within the broader context of his pastoral writings, Augustine's catechetical (mystagogical) activity deserves particular attention
when discussing religious experience.[24] In Milan, Augustine was exposed
to Ambrose's *disciplina arcani*, the pastoral doctrine which presumes
that mysteries have to be existentially experienced because they cannot
totally be explained in words.[25] This principle makes clear how religious

---

[23] On this complex topic: John A. Mourant, *St. Augustine on Memory* (Villanova, PA:
Villanova University Press, 1979) and Aimé Solignac, "Memoria dans la tradition augustinienne," *Dictionnaire de spiritualité* X (1980) 995-999.

[24] Frederick Van Fleteren, Joseph C. Schnaubelt, and Joseph Reino, *Augustine: Mystic and Mystagogue*, Collectanea augustiniana, 3 (New York, NY: Lang) 1994.

[25] Augustine probably derived his theory of signification from Ambrose, who inferred
knowledge of God from the Scriptures in a figurative way. See e.g. M. Zelser, "Zur
Sprache des Ambrosiaster," *Wiener Studien* 83 (1970) 196-213.

language and tradition are constitutive for religious experience. Applying the techniques of symbolism, a religious text is explained by means of images, which only the Christian – living a religious life – can understand existententially. In his sermons, Augustine often addresses a mixed audience of baptised Christians and catechumens. When he preaches, he does not talk about the secrets of faith to catechumens, but he does encourage their participation. More than anybody else, he is convinced that faith cannot be passed on by mere words (*In Ioannis euangelium tractatus* 2,3). Each will believe as much as he or she can bear (*De magistro* 11,38). That is the essence of the process of awakening, of becoming conscious, the event which takes places in Christian initiation.[26] The most remarkable and the most elaborate example of *disciplina arcani* is situated in *Sermo* 132,1,1, probably a later sermon, but one which expresses very well the early thoughts of *De magistro*:

> As we heard when the Holy Gospel was being read, the Lord Jesus Christ exhorted us by the promise of eternal life to eat His flesh and to drink His blood. You heard these words, but you have not all understood them. For, he baptised and the faithful know what He meant. But those among you who are yet called catechumens, or hearers, could be hearers when it was being read, but could they be understanders too? Accordingly, our discourse is directed to both. Let them who already eat the flesh of the Lord and drink His blood, think what it is they eat and drink, so that, as the apostle says, they eat and drink judgement to themselves. But they who do not yet eat and drink, let them hurry when invited to such a banquet. These days the teachers feed you; Christ fed you daily. His table is ever ordered before you. What is the reason, O hearers, that you see the table and come not to the banquet? And just now, when the gospel was being read, you said in your hearts: "We are thinking what it is that He said, my flesh is meat indeed, and my blood is drink indeed. How is the flesh of the Lord eaten, and the blood of the Lord drunk? We are wondering what He said." Who had closed it against you, that you did not know this? There is a veil over it, but if you will, the veil will be taken away. Come to the profession, and you have resolved the difficulty. For what the Lord Jesus said, the faithful know well already. But you are called a catechumen, a hearer, and are deaf. For you have the ears of the body open, seeing that you heard the words which were spoken; but you have the ears of the heart still closed, seeing that you don't understand what was spoken.[27]

---

[26] Tjeu Van Den Berk, *Mystagogie: Inwijding in het symbolisch bewustzijn* (Zoetermeer: Meinema, 1999) 95-99.

[27] Original: PL, 38, col. 734. Based on the translation: *Sermons on Selected Lessons of the New Testament by S. Augustine, Bishop of Hippo*, A Library of the Fathers of the Holy Catholic Church anterior to the Division of the East and West, 20 (Oxford: Parker, 1845) 593-594.

The catechumens are indeed called *audientes* in the sermon, but in fact they are deaf. They think they know, but they do not understand what they hear. They do have knowledge, but they do not have experiential knowledge of Christian teachings. If they believed, they would really know in their hearts what they are now professing only verbally. In *De magistro* 2,38 Augustine further elaborates his answer to this mystery. The truth is not conveyed by external words, but by the mind that leads inwards, to God who lives in us and who instructs us from that place, each person individually according to what he or she can grasp.[28] The whole idea is further elaborated, both in the treatise *De catechizandis rudibus*, written in 399 for the initiation of catechumens, and in later works.

Today, Augustine's grammar of experience is often analyzed under the rubric of "aesthetics". It is worth investigating whether an aesthetic experience could be considered to be a religious experience. In the works of Augustine, beauty occupies a prominent place (*"Pulchritudo tam antiqua et tam nova"*, *Conf.* 10,27).[29] The problem is that a human being, as a result of the Fall, can no longer perfectly and brightly observe this beauty. Once again, this does not mean that creation is bad and has to be rejected. To make this point clear Augustine, on almost one hundred occasions, uses a Pauline image (1 Cor 13:3 and 12)[30]: "At present we see in a mirror, darkly, but then face to face. Now, I know in part, but then, I will know even as also I am known." If Paul uses the image of a mirror, one has to keep in mind a mirror from the ancient times, i.e. a polished, metal plate which does not generate a clear reflection. Paul's imagery of mirrors aims at an act of distinction, an attempt to gather the meaning from the images and the shapes which one perceives in the mirror. The act of looking at vague and shadowy images in the mirror is, in the mind of the bishop of Hippo, a metaphor for the human condition after the Fall, when one no longer can look at God *facie ad faciem*, but *per speculum*. The mirror only allows a distorted and variable, material and temporal image of God. However, it is precisely because the image has those characteristics, that it is possible for fallen human beings to do

---

[28] Original CCSL 29 (1970) 195-196. Translation: Augustine, *De doctrina christiana*, ed. R.P.H. Green (Oxford: Clarendon, 1995) 177.

[29] Augustine defines this concept in several places: e.g. *Epistula* 18,2; *Epistula* 138, 1,5; *Confessiones*. 4,13,20.

[30] See James W. Wiles, *A Scripture Index to the Works of St. Augustine in English Translation* (Lanham, MD: University Press of America, 1995) 174; Wiles lists 91 references of Paul's text in Augustine's oeuvre. This metaphor (*Retractationes* 1,14,2), is one of Augustine's favorites, especially in *De trinitate*.

something with it.[31] This is especially applicable for the revelation of divine beauty in that sphere, which is able to reshape (*reformare*) the deformed (*deformis*) and ugly human being by inspiring his or her faith, hope and love.[32]

A human being is a mysterious combination of body and soul, and was once able to behold God directly. The Fall introduced death and destruction through a decay of the human will (*De genesi ad litteram* 11,30 and much later in *De civitate Dei* 14,13). This makes the *visio beatifica* impossible and one is relegated to a lesser place, characterized by a relative darkness, covered by a layer of clouds which prevents one from seeing the sun directly (the higher spiritual world). Again, however, the darkness is not complete, just like the reflection in the mirror. The *mens* (mind), in which the image of God resides, enables us to form opinions and turns our attention exclusively to God. The fact that we can be of the opinion that one beauty surpasses another, is proof of that we can remember and judge divine beauty as such (*Conf.* 7,17,23). The influence of platonism is not far off. Obviously, words, images, pictures and so forth are all examples of symbolic communications which help us to retrieve the image of God and help us to walk on the *via interior*, where

---

[31] Though the Fall is always an important theme for Augustine, it is only in his later works, especially *De genesi ad litteram* and *De civitate Dei* that he emphasizes that all humanity suffers from the consequences of the Fall which changed human nature. For a survey of the research on this topic, see R. Penaskovic, "The Fall of the Soul in Saint Augustine: A Quaestio Disputata," *Augustinian Studies* 17 (1986) 135-145.

[32] Again an allusion to 1 Cor 13. Harrison, *Beauty and Revelation*, 1-2. Harrison's point of view coincides largely with Karel Svoboda, *L'esthétique de saint Augustin et ses sources* (Brno: Filosofická Fakulta, 1933) but contrasts with Robert J. O'Connell, *Art and the Christian Intelligence in Saint Augustine* (Oxford: Blackwell, 1978). O'Connell takes issue with Svoboda's tendency to see an ever-increasing spiritualising in Augustine's thought and argues in favour of the opposite, an increasing 'incarnation'. O'Connell on the other hand is too radical when he states: "The adequacy of Augustine's aesthetic may be, accordingly, not an exclusive, but a specially sensitive, indicator of the adequacy of his entire philosophy" (p. 7). In my view, O'Connell's overemphasis on Augustine's Neo-platonism leads him to pay too little attention to the creative way in which Augustine deals with (neo-)platonism. Finally, he too generally asserts again a contrast between Augustine's aesthetic experience and his rationalism (p. 150). Often, the latter concept is unclear and problematic in Augustine. Four other important monographs which address Augustine's aesthetics are: E. Chapman, *St. Augustine's Philosophy of Beauty* (New York, NY, 1939); Josef M. Tscholl, *Gott und das Schöne beim hl. Augustinus* (Heverlee: Augustijns Historisch Instituut, 1967); Tina Manferdini, *L'estetica religiosa in S. Agostino* (Bologna: Zanichelli, 1969) and Johann Kreuzer, Pulchritudo: *vom Erkennen Gottes bei Augustin: Bemerkungen zu den Büchern IX, X und XI der* Confessiones (München: Fink, 1995). Also worth mentioning is the published doctoral dissertation of Anders Wikman, *Beiträge zur Ästhetik Augustins* (Jena: Thomas und Hubert Weida i. Thur, 1909).

we are illuminated.[33] Here, beauty plays a mediating but not a constitutive role. This is because eventually every object that embodies an intelligible truth is inadequate: it may resemble the truth, but it is not the truth itself.[34] The most important conclusion is that Beauty – in so far as related to God – may not be experienced for its own sake, but only insofar as it points towards God.

Because of the special nature of beauty, the soul occupies an important place in the process which defines the epistemological status of aesthetic experience. When, at the beginning of the *Soliloquia*, Reason asks Augustine what he wants to know, he answers: *"I desire the knowledge of God and the soul"* (*Soliloquia* 1,2,7 and 1,12,20). Knowing God and the soul is synonymous with knowing the Truth (cf. also *De ordine* 2,18,47) and all three of them are linked to beauty, because they refer to Beauty.[35] In a letter written in 387 AD to his youthful friend Nebridius, Augustine notes that we consist of body and soul, of which the soul is the better part. The body is only praised for its beauty, but the beauty of the body is inferior to the beauty of the soul and, therefore, the soul ought to be loved more than the body. Opposite are the senses and therefore the senses have to be resisted with the entire power of the mind, *mens* (*Epistula* 3,4).[36] Control of beauty over the soul and of reason over the senses and the body is the theme of *Contra academicos*, with the personifications of *Philosophia* (love for wisdom) and *Philocalia* (love for beauty). Both are close relatives, like two sisters, but when someone searches for beauty only in the sensitive sphere, rather than in wisdom, he/she is on a dangerous track (*Contra academicos* 2,3,7 and *Retractationes* 1,1,3). Beauty belongs to the domain of the incorporal, the relational and the spiritual and therefore, it belongs in its ideal shape to the *mens*, reason or soul (*De vera religione* 20,39 and 39,72-73). To know primary truth

---

[33] O'Connell, "Art and the Christian Intelligence," 102.

[34] Josef Lössl, "Religio, philosophia und pulchritudo: Ihr Zusammenhang nach Augustinus, De vera religione," *Vigiliae Christianae* 47 (1993) 363-373; Luis Rey Altuna, "Implicaciones éticas de la estética agustuniana," *Augustinus* 33 (1988) 297-305 and José Antonio Galindo, "Aspecto intellectual del arte," *Augustinus* 9 (1964) 37-48.

[35] On the link between beauty and wisdom see Josef Tscholl, "Augustins Beachtung der geistigen Schönheit," *Augustiniana* 16 (1966) 11-53, 21-25.

[36] This has to be nuanced. The soul is superior to the body, also because the soul takes the initiative concerning the corporal. It is not the body that perceives through the senses, but the soul which perceives in and through the body (*actio animae*). The soul is present at the body through *attentio*. Bodily objects produce effects on the body (*passiones*) which are positive or negative with respect to the soul, by which they demand respectively more or less attention from the soul. Humans call that experience 'perception' (*De musica* 6,5,9). The senses are nothing else but slaves of the soul (*De ordine* 2,2,6).

or beauty, humans have to turn inside themselves and leave the perceptible behind (*De vera religione* 20,39 and 39,72).[37]

In the *Conf.* Augustine has a clear statement with regard to arts and beauty. His system could be circumscribed as 'ascensional aesthetics', namely the way from physical to intelligible beauty, which exceeds the sensory and the temporal aspects of the sensible experience of beauty.[38] The spiritual interpretation of Christianity under the influence of the neo-Platonists and Ambrose leads him to the conclusion that all signs, depictions and symbols have to be considered as intermediaries and even have to be completely left behind in the unmediated contemplation of God.[39] If something like religious experience is possible, it must be mediated.

In this period, Augustine explicitly develops an argument from the existence of beauty for the existence of God. The sixth chapter of book 10 of the *Conf.* is considered by many authors as an aesthetic *locus theologicus*. The seemingly simple 'proof' runs as follows:

> My love for you, Lord, is not an uncertain feeling but a matter of conscious certainty. … But heaven and earth and everything in them on all sides tell me to love you. … But when I love you, what do I love? It is not physical beauty nor temporal glory nor the brightness of light dear to earthly eyes, nor the sweet melodies of all kinds of songs, nor the gentle odour of flowers and ointments and perfumes, nor manna or honey, nor limbs welcoming the embraces of the flesh; it is not these I love when I love my God. Yet there is a light I love, and a food, and a kind of embrace of my inner man, where my soul is floodlit by light which space cannot contain, where there is sound that time cannot seize, where there is a perfume which no breeze disperses, where there is a taste for food no amount of eating can lessen, and where there is a bond of union that no satiety can part. That is what I love when I love my God. And what is the object of my love? I asked the earth and it said: "It is not I." I asked all that is in it; they made the same confession. … I asked heaven, sun, moon, and stars; they said: "Nor are we the God whom you seek." And I said to all these things in my external environment: "Tell me of my God who you are not, tell me something about him." And with a great voice they cried out: "He made us." My question was the attention I gave to them, and their response was their beauty.Then I turned towards myself, and said to myself: "Who are you?" I replied: "A man." I see in myself a body and a soul, one external, the other internal. … What is inward, is superior. All physical evidence is reported to the mind which presides and judges of the responses of heaven and earth and all things in them, as they say "We are not God" and "He made us".

---

[37] Harrison, *Beauty and Revelation*, 12-15. Own translation of CCSL 32 (1962) 234.

[38] Luis Rey Altuna, "Augustín de Hipona: Un itinerario estético del orden universal a la trascendencia," *Augustinus* 29 (1984) 33-60.

[39] O'Connell, "Art and the Christian Intelligence," 94-99.

The inner man knows this – I, I the mind through the sense-perception of my body.[40]

Roland E. Ramirez is of the opinion that this proof for the existence of God cannot be reduced at all to a proof based on efficient causality (and consequently on sense experience) or, for that matter, on any causality of another kind. He has to face the objection whether nearly every proof for the existence of God based on beauty is not in a way based on causality, since it departs from the consequences (or given data) and arrives at the cause (or the source of those data). In those cases it does not really matter that the data upon which the proof is based are taken from the realm of existence, movement or beauty. In each instance, we are dealing with causal *a posteriori* proofs for the existence of God, and according to Ramirez, that is precisely what distinguishes the proof from beauty from all the others. All these proofs have causality in common in some sense, but it is not the thing that distinguishes them. Firstly, the qualitative starting point is clearly beauty, which means that this proof cannot be reduced to just another proof of causality. Secondly, there is a special relation between beauty and human existential experience; beauty is not an abstract concept like existence and movement and, therefore, it is more difficult to approach by a discursive logic.[41]

As mentioned above, all human knowledge about God is mediated: the aesthetical experience may prove to be an adequate medium, but how? Both things in heaven and on earth tell Augustine that he is supposed to love God and not God's created things.[42] He then asks himself who or what it is he loves if he loves God. He answers that it is certainly not physical beauty, nor temporary glory and sensory perceptions. Nevertheless, he loves a certain light, voice, and smell (in short: *sensus*) when he loves God. Although these are not things which can be grasped by the

---

[40] Original CCSL 27 (1981) 158-159. Translation: Saint Augustine, *Confessions*, ed. H. Chadwick (New York, NY: Oxford University Press, 1991) 183-184.

[41] Roland E. Ramirez, "Augustine's Proof for God's Existence from the Experience of Beauty: Confessions, X,6," *Augustinian Studies* 19 (1988) 121-130, 121-122. Ramirez does not take into account the fact that beauty in the ancient world has more to do with contemplation than with aesthetic experience. See E. De Bruyne, *Geschiedenis van de aesthetica. 3: De christelijke oudheid* (Antwerpen: Standaard, 1954).

[42] This is also true for artists: they are not allowed to create artefacts for the sake of human delectation. They should better strive for the transcendent, in order to realise why beautiful things can please (*vera rel.* 32,59,1). In that respect, Augustine breaks with ancient art theory, which conceived of delight (*iucundum*) as a goal of art (Hans-Jürgen Horn, "Lügt die Kunst: Ein kunsttheoretischer Gedankengang des Augustinus," *Jahrbuch für Antike und Christentum* 22 (1979) 50-60, 52). Horn states correctly: "Beauty, not delight, is the goal of art" (p. 54). The *pulchrum* should refer to God, the *Pulchrum*.

senses, they can be grasped by the inner man, where God's light, which cannot be grasped by anything else, flows into the soul. Here, Augustine does not follow discursively the standard procedure of moving from consequence to cause, he simply contemplates beauty. There is something in the object that catches Augustine's eye, which makes him desire the object. That thing is called 'beauty'. But these objects are not able to explain their own beauty and, therefore, they force Augustine to look for the one who gave them this beauty. Thus, this is mainly a proof from contemplative experience.[43]

If the world exists in God and if every moment is completely dependent on Him, the question remains for Augustine why the contemplation of the world does not directly lead to God as does the contemplation of oneself (the *via interior*). Probably, the answer is linked to the fact that the contemplation of the world does not lead immediately to God, but refracts thought towards its own beauty. On the Christian road, the temptation to love creation is often an obstacle for the love for God. In the tenth book of the *Conf.* Augustine describes how he became addicted to earthly pleasures via the abuse of the five senses (*Conf.* 10,27,38*ss.*).[44] The five senses must help us to go the inward way, and from that point on, the way upward can start.

4. The Object of Experience

It is clear that Augustine's epistemologal views were slowly evolving in this early period: he developed a new language, through his theological debate, reading and ongoing contemplation of the Scriptures. We should not be surprised that the object of Augustine's religious experience also slightly evolved. When he writes *Doctr.* Augustine simultaneously defines three elements from the Bible and the creed as *res*: God, Christ and the Church (the Holy Spirit). If one desires experiential knowledge of this transcendent reality, a purgation of the spirit is an absolute necessity. God is experienced by loving God. The ultimate reference is God alone, because everything is associated with God and because only God can be the object of delight (*Doctr.* 1,35,39). In this early period (but also in his later work), God is seen as a *summus modus* (ultimate mode), an unchanging and unchangeable transcendence (*De beata vita* 4).[45]

---

[43] Ramirez, "Augustine's Proof," 123-125.

[44] Gerard Verbeke, "Connaissance de soi et connaissance de Dieu chez saint Augustin," *Augustiniana* 3 (1953) 495-515, 502.

[45] Drecoll, *Die Entstehung der Gnadenlehre Augustins*, 27-49.

In spite of some differences in emphasis, many interpreters agree that Augustine, in a novel way, characterized human existence as being willingly and freely exposed to God's grace.[46] Such a characterization is a break with the cosmocentric ideas of the classical period. According to Augustine, the human person is the focal point for a true understanding of reality. Körner uses the terminology of Augustine: the me-you relation of the *homo interior* with the *Deus interior intimo meo* will be the foundation of his universalistic philosophical and theological thinking.[47] Because his hermeneutics was based on his experience of human individuality, Augustine can reread St. Paul and 'discover' in him a language of internalization, which reflects his own existential experiences.[48] Augustine is aware of his human inability to know and to do good without divine aid, without mediation of Christ, and therefore he experiences the need for divine grace, i.e. the most obvious characteristic of his religious experience.[49]

As Augustine is increasingly influenced by the Scriptures, his own existential experiences are expressed in another language.[50] True freedom refers to the immutable good, and is described as *feliciter vivere*, but since the fall, human beings have lost the capacity not to sin and to be eternally happy.[51] When a human, who is wholly self-centred, is placed in front of the personal God, he experiences two contradictory acts of the will. The central theme of the *Conf.* is precisely the Pauline idea (Gal 5:17 and

---

[46] These examples come from Gisbert Greshake, *Gnade als konkrete Freiheit: Eine Untersuchung zur Gnadenlehre des Pelagius* (Mainz: Grunewald, 1972) 238 n. 32; Ernst Benz, *Marius Victorinus und die Entwicklung der abendländischen Willensmetaphysik*, Forschungen zur Kirchen- und Geistesgeschichte, 1 (Stuttgart: Kohlhammer, 1932) 383ss.; Rudolph Berlinger, *Augustins dialogische Metaphysik* (Frankfurt: Klostermann, 1962) 12ss.; Mary T. Clark, *Augustine, Philosopher of Freedom: A Study in Comparative Philosophy* (New York, NY, Tournai, Rome, and Paris: Desclee, 1958) 78ss.; Ernst Troeltsch, *Augustin, die christliche Antike und das Mittelalter: Im Anschluß an die Schrift* (Aalen: Scientia, ²1963) 77ss.

[47] Franz Körner, *Vom Sein und Sollen des Menschen: Die existentialontologischen Grundlagen der Ethik in augustinischer Sicht*, Études augustiniennes: série Antiquité, 16 (Paris: Études augustiniennes, 1963) 30.

[48] Greshake, *Gnade als konkrete Freiheit*, 238-239. This is entirely in accordance with the ancient ethical tradition, particularly that of Stoicism. No act is a moral act, unless the agent himself willed it. Internalization is wanting to do something for oneself and not because one is obliged. See Troels Engberg-Pedersen, *Paul and the Stoics* (Edinburgh: T. & T. Clark, 2000) 212-216.

[49] Harrison, "Augustine and Religious Experience," 100.

[50] A normal process for an intellectual Christian in those days: Detlef Illmer, "Totum namque in sola experientia usuque consistit: Eine Studie zur monastischen Erziehung und Sprache," *Mönchtum und Gesellschaft im Frühmittelalter*, ed. Friedrich Prinz, Wege der Forschung, 312 (Darmstadt: Wissenschaftliche Buchgesellschaft, 1976) 430-455.

[51] Mathijs Lamberigts, "Augustine's View of Liberty Revisited," *St. Augustine Papers* 3 (2002) 1-11, 2.

Rom 7) that the dividing line between freedom and lack of freedom is not experienced between the other and oneself, but within oneself, a process which results in self alienation (*Conf.* 8,10,22):

> For me, when I, at last, deliberated upon serving the Lord, my God, as I had long purposed, it was I who willed, I who did not will, it was I myself. And I was neither totally willing, nor totally not willing. Therefore, I was at strife with myself, and dissociated from myself. This dissociation was in me against my will, though, it did not indicate the natural presence of a strange mind [= against Manicheism], but the punishment of my own.[52]

In the same way as Paul, Augustine experienced love as the essence of grace. To become free, it is not sufficient that the merciful God concretely enters history and breaks down the barriers that obstruct human freedom. God's gift of grace after the Fall has to enter into the dissociated human being to renew him or her fundamentally. In other words, grace moves from the cosmic order of creation to the relation between God and human beings, where God gives grace to them in a direct and gratuitious way, because nobody can claim that he or she deserves grace. As a consequence, freedom does not mean that everybody can live his or her life the way he or she wishes, but rather a state of reality which presumes a change of the heart (*Sermo* 74,4: *"Muta cor et mutabitur opus."*).[53] As Mathijs Lamberigts summarizes: "Augustine's concept of freedom clearly does not speak of a theoretical, natural capability but is a theological, spiritual freedom, a being attracted by a loving God. God realises that we will become what we must be (happy) by doing what we must do (in love): *oboedire Deo cum amore*. Then, and only then, are we truly free. Such freedom has to do with affection. Such a concept of freedom *cum amore* is still worthy of being a subject of reflection."[54]

As argued above, language and experience are integral parts of the human condition, even if one occasionally experiences a dichotomy between the two, namely, there where one cannot express at all what one experiences. In the Pelagian controversy, Augustine occasionally betrayed the discord between experienced reality and the theoretical formulation of it. Sometimes, Pelagius inspires Augustine to express himself more accurately concerning his experience of grace.[55] In the pre-Pelagian period,

---

[52] Own translation CCSL 27 (1981) 127. Gisbert Greshake, "Gnade als konkrete Freiheit," 239. More examples: *Confessiones* 6,11,19ss. en 8,5,10.

[53] Greshake, *Gnade als konkrete Freiheit*, 239-240.

[54] Lamberigts, "Augustine's View of Liberty Revisited," 8.

[55] *De natura et gratia* 39,46: "Our author [Augustine means Pelagius, but he never attacks Pelagius by name in this treatise] concludes this passage with an obviously important idea, when he says: 'Let us then believe what we read, and let us believe that it is

logically in his comments on the letters to the Romans and the Galatians and in *Ad simplicianum,* Augustine claims that the human lack of freedom shows itself in the inner struggle between wanting and doing. The sinful person knows that he or she acts badly, but he or she does not want to act badly. To sin is an act of the will: the sinner agrees with sin although he or she recognizes that he or she breaks the law. In that division, it calls for liberating grace (*Ad simplicianum* 1,1,9 and 1,1,12; almost a *verbatim* use of Rom 6-7).[56]

In the *Conf.,* the Pauline vocation is emphasized. Throughout his life, Augustine consistently experienced God's grace, which is clearly put forward throughout his confessions.[57] This concept is related to Augustine's former idea of admonition. Both concepts are biblical, but, whereas the admonition to reform oneself in order to know oneself is rather didactic, the vocation is more effective in the sense that it originates from God and effectively changes the will. God is able to both call and to move one inwardly and to do so in such a way, that one obeys (*Ad Simplicianum* 1,2,12*ss.* and *De spiritu et littera* 34,60).[58]

God's call is experienced as the good direction of the will. That change of perspective in the doctrine of divine grace yields Augustine two advantages. Firstly, he has an argument against the Pelagians, because in a sinful person there can never be a totally good willing of the good will. The good will of the sinner has to be attributed to grace. If one insists that this is not true, one makes the process of grace dependent on human beings. Secondly, Augustine is convinced that he can demonstrate that Pelagius' idea of grace does not heal man, but rather inwardly tears him apart between knowing what is good (namely to love) and doing the right thing. In other words, it confirms the inner dissociation we discussed above. Real grace has to solve this dichotomy. Human freedom is then experienced as *libertas*.[59] This way of thinking represents the ancient hierar-

---

wrong to add what we do not read, and let it suffice to have said this on all topics.' On the contrary, I say that we ought not to believe everything we read, because of the apostle's words, *Read everything; hold onto what is good* (1 Thes 5:21), and I also say that it is not wrong to add something that we have experienced, even if we may not have read it" (Aurelius Augustinus and Roland J. Teske, *Answer to the Pelagians: The Punishment and Forgiveness of Sins and the Baptism of Little Ones; The Spirit and the Letter; Nature and Grace; The Perfection of Human Righteousness; The Deeds of Pelagius; The Grace of Christ and Original Sin*, The works of saint Augustine: A translation for the 21st century, I/23 (New York, NY: New City Press, 1997) 248. Original PL 44 (1845) col. 269).

[56] Greshake, *Gnade als konkrete Freiheit*, 241-242.

[57] Ulrich Duchrow, *Sprachverständnis und biblisches Hören bei Augustin*, Hermeneutische Untersuchungen zur Theologie, 5 (Tübingen: Mohr Siebeck, 1965) 186-195.

[58] Greshake, *Gnade als konkrete Freiheit*, 242.

[59] Greshake, *Gnade als konkrete Freiheit*, 244.

chical model of harmony: lower authorities take advantage of obeying higher authorities.

It is striking that the object of experience is not the subjective impression of an autonomously (i.e. by autonomous human subjects) constructed image of God, but a reconstruction of that image of God which is heteronomously (i.e. apart from personal, human intentions) supplied by Scripture and tradition. In Augustine the important thing is the radical experience of incapacity and lack of freedom, generated by sin, which can be saved only by God's loving mercifulness. In his later works this point is constantly emphasized. In the meantime it becomes clear that in the study of the theme of religious experience in Augustine the broadest issues of his theology are connected to each other: sin, grace, love, salvation.

5. The Experience of God at Ostia: Is Augustine a Mystic?

Because a mystical experience is generally considered to be at the top of all possible forms of religious experiences, we cannot avoid asking the question whether Augustine was a mystic. As will be made clear below, everything depends on the definition of mysticism. There are two events in the life of Augustine which point to something usually called a mystical experience: the well-known garden scene in Milan (*Conf.* 8,12,29) and the conversation with his mother in Ostia just before her death (*Conf.* 9,10,24-26).[60]

The ninth book of the *Confessiones* can be divided into two parts. The first part describes the birthpangs of a new birth.[61] Augustine thanks God because He has liberated him from temporal and earthly bonds and he gives up his public function as a rhetorician. He decides to be baptized in Milan by Ambrose, from whom he had formerly requested some biblical literature. The second part opens with the departure from Milan to the port city of Ostia. Though his reasons for immediately discussing his mother are not quite clear, it may be, because he is going to proceed to recount her death. Augustine tells about Monnica's youth, her matrimonial faithfulness (constantly tried by her adulterous husband), the difficult relation she had with her mother-in-law, and her constant prayers and

---

[60] On other ascensional passages: Andrew Louth, *The Origins of the Christian Mystical Tradition: From Plato to Denys* (Oxford: Clarendon, 1983) 132-158.

[61] This terminology comes from Dieter Hattrup, "Die Mystik von Cassiciacum und Ostia," *Die Confessiones des Augustins von Hippo: Einführung und Interpretationen zu den dreizehn Büchern,* ed. Norbert Fischer, Maria Bettetini, and Cornelius Mayer, Forschungen zur Europäischen Geistesgeschichte, 1 (Freiburg: Herder, 1998) 389-488, 437.

concern for the conversion of both her husband and her son. According to Augustine's testimony, Monnica's spiritual growth paralleled that of Augustine, culminating in the Ostia experience.[62]

In *Conf.* 9,10,23 the conversation with his mother starts in Ostia, where, according to Augustine, both rest for a few days to regain strength for the sea-journey from Rome to Africa. He is standing alone with her at a window which overlooks a patio. The mystical experience which both undergo is not a vision in the traditional sense, nor is it an 'audition' (as O'Donnell advocates).[63] The voices they hear do not come from elsewhere but from each other. As they speak, both experience something transcendent. The decisive passage runs as follows:

> [24] The conversation led us towards the conclusion that the pleasure of the bodily senses, however delightful in the radiant light of this physical world, is seen by comparison with the life of eternity to be not even worth considering (Rom 8). Our minds were lifted up by an ardent affection towards eternal being itself. Step by step we climbed beyond all corporeal objects and the heaven itself, where sun, moon, and stars shed light on the earth. We ascended even further by internal reflection and dialogue and wonder at your works, and we entered into our own minds. We moved up beyond them as to attain to the region of inexhaustible abundance where you feed Israel eternally with truth for food. There life is the wisdom by which all creatures come into being, both things which were and which will be. But wisdom itself is not brought into being but is as it was and always will be. Furthermore, in this wisdom there is no past and future, but only being, since it is eternal. For to exist in the past or in the future is no property of the eternal. And while we talked and panted after it, we touched it in some small degree by a moment of total concentration of the heart. And we sighed and left behind us 'the first fruits of the Spirit' (Rom 8:23) bound to that higher world, as we returned to the noise of our human speech where a sentence has both a beginning and an ending. But what is to be compared with your word, Lord of our lives? It dwells in you without growing old and gives renewal to all things. [25] Therefore, we said: If to anyone the tumult of the flesh has fallen silent, if the images of earth, water, and air are quiescent, if the heavens themselves are shut out and the very soul itself is making no sound and is surpassing itself by no longer thinking about itself, if all dreams and visions in the imagination are excluded, if all language and every sign and everything transitory is silent – for if anyone could hear them, this is what all of them would be saying: "We did not make ourselves, we were made by him who abides for eternity" (Ps 79:3-5) – if after this

---

[62] We have to keep in mind that she is not specifically mentioned as having had a mystical experience.

[63] James J. O'Donnell, *Augustine. Confessions. III: Commentary on Books 8-13. Indexes* (Oxford: Clarendon, ²2000) 128. O'Donnell's comments seem to be related to the fact that in the second half of this account the lower levels of reality are described as falling silent until the voice of the wisdom is heard within.

declaration they were to keep silence, having directed our ears to him that made them, then he alone would speak not through them but through himself. We would hear his word, not through the tongue of the flesh, nor through the voice of an angel, nor through the sound of thunder, nor through the obscurity of a symbolic utterance. Him who in these things we love we would hear in person without their mediation. That is how it was when at that moment we extended our reach and in a flash of mental energy attained the eternal wisdom which abides beyond all things. If only it could last, and other visions of a vastly inferior kind could be withdrawn! Then, this alone could ravish and absorb and enfold in inward joys the person granted the vision. So too eternal life is of the quality of that moment of understanding after which we sighed. Is not this the meaning of 'enter into the joy of your Lord' (Mt 25:21)? And when is that to be? Surely it is when 'we all rise again, but are not all changed' (1 Cor 15:51). [26] I said something like this, even if not in just this way and with exactly these words. Yet, Lord, you know that on that day when we had this conversation, and this world with all its delights became worthless to us as we talked on, my mother said: "My son, as for myself, I now find no pleasure in this life. What I have still to do here and why I am here, I do not know. My hope in this world is already fulfilled. The one reason why I wanted to stay longer in this life was my desire to see you a Catholic Christian before I die."[64]

Earlier, Augustine mentioned an ascending movement. Nothing material is worth comparing with the magnificence of the next life. By borrowing cosmological terms – terms which Paul also uses in 2 Cor 12:2-4[64a] – Augustine describes how he and his mother – by constantly speaking more interiorly – rose higher and higher through the various heavens, described in *De animae quantitate* 33,70-76. He climbs so high that he transcends reason and reaches a place of inexhaustible abundance. This time, where there is no past and no future is a place where there is only being. Together, Augustine and his mother, at least momentarily touch the truth through a moment of total concentration of the heart.[65]

Near the middle of the text the contents of the conversation, which is essentially an affirmation of God's heteronomy, is related. Things can only testify that they have not made themselves. Afterwards they become silent, directing their ears to their Creator. If one constantly should hear one's Creator, one would already have crossed over into the everlasting

[64] Original CCSL 27(1981)147-148. Translation: Chadwick, *Confessions*, 171-172.

[64a] "I knew a man in Christ above fourteen years ago, (whether in the body, I cannot tell; or whether out of the body, I cannot tell: God knoweth;) such an one caught up to the third heaven. And I knew such a man (whether in the body, or out of the body, I cannot tell: God knoweth). How that he was caught up into paradise, and heard unspeakable words, which it is not lawful for a man to utter."

[65] O'Donnell, *Augustine. Confessions*, III, 127-129. O'Donnell is forced to admit that we will never know exactly what happened at Ostia: "Experience does not come with neatly printed labels."

life. O'Donnell: "If we should ascend to the silence where the Word of God speaks unmediated, and if we stayed there, rather than falling back to these shores – well, that would be heaven."[66]

In the next section Augustine admits that he does not remember exactly which particular words were spoken, but that it certainly was something similar to what he wrote in the *Confessions*. He repeats that while they where talking to each other, the pleasures of this world became worthless. His mother tells him that she has reached everything she wanted and that she is prepared to die. The conversation is the completion of one which they had started in Milan. Interestingly, it is immediately after this special scene that Augustine inserts the death and the funeral of his mother.[67]

The question whether Augustine is a mystic or not is reflected in a discussion that vacillates between the two extremes which attempt to answer the question of whether or not Augustine is a mystic.[68] At one extreme there is Harnack's clear "yes": "His [Augustine's] spirit dwells in the devout and the mystics of the Middle Ages, no less in Saint Bernard than in Thomas à Kempis. He inspires the Church reformers of the Middle Ages, the reformers of the Carolingian era, as well as Wycliff, Hus, Wesel and Wessel."[69] This interpretation is reaffirmed by Paul Henry: "Augustine is a born mystic."[70] Ephraem Hendrikx is an important opponent of Henry's theory: "In the closed system of Augustinian metaphysics, there is no room for mystical knowledge in the proper sense about God."[71] In other words, Hendrickx believes that mystical knowledge is metaphysically impossible for Augustine: "And everything we know, we know it through reason" (*De animae quantitate, 57*).[72]

---

[66] O'Donnell, *Augustine. Confessions*, III, 133.

[67] General commentary on this passage: Courcelle, *Recherches sur les confessions*, 223. Pierre Courcelle does not immediately answer the question whether the experience of Ostia is an intellectual or a mystical experience. Courcelle describes what happens at Ostia and connects the experience with the event at Milan: "A Ostie comme à Milan, l'ascension est intérieure; l'esprit se dresse; les phantasmes se dérobent; la réflexion parvient jusqu'à l'intelligence humaine, et la dépasse pour atteindre le divin." The only difference with Milan is the dwindling significance of Plotinus.

[68] Dieter Hattrup has provided us with an excellent *status quaestionis* for the 'Ostia-research': Hattrup, "Die Mystik von Cassiciacum und Ostia," 426.

[69] Adolf Harnack, "Augustins Konfessionen," *Reden und Aufsätze I*, ed. A. Harnack (Giessen: Töpelmann, ²1906) 49-79, 53.

[70] Paul Henry, *La vision d'Ostie: Sa place dans la vie et l'œuvre de saint Augustin* (Paris: Vrin, 1938) 88.

[71] Ephraem Hendrikx, *Augustinus' Verhältnis zur Mystik: Eine patristische Untersuchung* (Darmstadt: Wissenschaftliche Buchgesellschaft, 1936) 346.

[72] The examples and the discussion, see Dieter Hattrup, "Die Mystik von Cassiciacum und Ostia," 414-418.

The following argument prevents many writers from labelling Augustine a mystic: Augustine would not accept the requisite passivity of a true mystic, since for him it is always about knowledge of God, obtained by self application and all forms of radical experience of unity are conspicuous by their absence.

Tarsicius van Bavel grounds his definition of mysticism in the description of Paul Mommaers in *Wat is mystiek?*: "A mystic is someone who experiences in an overwhelming way a presence which surpasses him and which is more real than all the things one generally understands as being real."[73] Van Bavel attempts to find in the work of Augustine the two central terms from this definition, namely passivity and incomprehensibility. He locates the passivity in the stress Augustine places on the role of grace. He finds the incomprehensibility and the unpronounceability of God in places where Augustine emphasizes God's transcendence. This latter element compels some authors too hastily to label Augustine an apophatic theologian.[74]

It seems to depend upon one's definition of mysticism whether or not one calls Augustine a mystic. More interesting is the epistemological question of whether it produces deeper knowledge of God. The special event at Ostia must epistemologically be regarded more as an end point, rather than a point of departure. In the context of the description of the religious experience, along with the narrative setting of the event in Ostia, it seems that this 'mystical experience' is the reward of a spiritual way (the inner ascending way), rather than the starting point of new theological insights. The experience does not immediately generate new knowledge of God. It does, however, generate a deeper religious and existential

---

[73] Paul Mommaers, *Wat is mystiek?*, Spiritualiteit, 12 (Nijmegen: B. Gottmer and Brugge: Emmaüs, 1977) 25 (translation my own). Quoted in Tarsicius Van Bavel, "Augustinus en mystieke ervaring," *Mystiek: Augustinus en Hadewijch,* Augustinusdag 1999 (Heverlee: Augustijns Historisch Instituut, 2000) 21-38, 23. Mommaers offers two other features (the other, ultimate reality announces itself in the ordinary and the elevation of one's own personality), whereof Van Bavel finds traces in Augustine's theology. The same position is defended by Martijn Schrama in *Dictionnaire de la mystique*, ed. Peter Dinzelbacher, Petits dictionnaires bleus (Turnhout: Brepols, 1993) 79. Augustine received the gift of mysticism in the shape of the supreme fruit of love, offering itself to both God and men.

[74] Like Van Bavel, Matthias Smalbrugge is also nuanced, but this time concerning calling Augustine an apophatic theologian. For Augustine, apophatic theology means to show precisely of what consists our ignorance when we talk about God and further more on, to oppose this little bit of knowledge to the pretentions of those who claim they can penetrate in the divine mystery (e.g. the Arian Christians). Matthias A. Smalbrugge, "L'emploi de la théologie apophatique chez Augustin: Une question à l'historiographie," *Revue de théologie et de philosophie* 120 (1988) 263-274, 266.

understanding of our being human, of our capacities and limitations, and of our dependence upon mediaton. In the epistemological field, a mystical experience is a possibility at the end of a journey, rather than a point from which to begin a religious pilgrimage. Augustine's religious experiences in Milan and Ostia surely have influenced his will and his knowledge, but in an existential way, rather than in an epistemological one. The experience existentially confirms what he believes, but delivers no new intellectual insights in the mystery of who God is. More important than a mystic experience (understood as an intense and overwhelming sensory experience), is experiential knowledge of God, as elaborated in his mystagogical teachings. The style and content of his work hint at intense religious experiences in the sense of experiential knowledge, hence the close bond between knowledge and love in his theology. It can be understood as an interplay between reason and emotion, far from the dualism that arose in the modern period.

We investigated Augustine's mysticism because mysticism is today considered to be the ultimate variant of religious experience. We argued that it depends upon one's definition of mysticism whether or not Augustine could be called a mystic. Our answer is that Augustine had mystical experiences, but that he did not lead a mystical life. Augustine can have mystical experiences without being a mystic. In the light of what we said about the concept of religious experience in Augustine's works, our considerations can throw new light on the experiences at Milan and Ostia. Rather than being descriptions of mystical experiences, these stories can be considered to be literary devices, pointing towards Augustine's hermeneutics. He explains his experiences in the language of Paul. So, to consider Augustine as a dyed-in-the-wool mystic is to read him through a medieval lens.

6. Conclusions

There is always a danger involved in approaching an ancient author with a contemporary problem, in this case the question of religious experience. Augustine did not recognize the problem of religious experience as we do now, especially with its connotations of emotionality and subjectivity. Nevertheless, knowing what the concept of religious experience might have meant to Augustine, is a valuable contribution to our contemporary understanding of the concept.

Some features immediately catch the eye. Augustine consistently rejects subjective experience as a means to epistemological advancement concerning God's being, as is frequently the case with many contemporary religious movements. Nowadays, personal experience often becomes the defining aspect for an individual's relationship with God and the primary avenue for furthering our knowledge about God. For Augustine, only tradition and Scripture can provide us with genuine knowledge of God. After Augustine gained a thorough familiarity with the Scriptures, he describes his personal experiences in biblical terms. The best example of this are his *Confessiones*, his 'book of experience', with its emphasis on his being a sinful creature in profound need of redemption. The created world and personal, existential experiences can be very useful as we journey to God, but they are not foundational for our knowledge of God. They almost literally testify to the existence of God (based on Rom 1:21) and in that sense, they help us on our life-long pilgrimage to God.

In Augustine, the emphasis is on knowledge, or should we say experiential knowledge, since, in order to better understand the Scriptures and tradition, a Christian should existentially 'experience' Truth. However, this truth must always be mediated! As mentioned above, existential experiences, like the whole of creation, are important as *signa* with a referring character. Every *signum* refers to a *res*, which in its turn serves as *signum* for another *res*. In a nutshell, this fact is the difference between Augustine and modern thinkers, like e.g. William James. A second difference with James, is that, for Augustine, religious experience involves the totality of the human being: body, soul, and mind. On the other hand, James primarily sees religious experience as an individual, physical, phenomenon.

Thus, for Augustine, experience equals experiential knowledge. Religious doctrine must not only be understood, but it must also be experienced. Reason must penetrate the heart; only then, can the mysteries of faith be experienced as a genuine link to the ultimate reality. Augustine's thought is therefore a watershed. He diverges from the ancient systems which emphasize the primacy of the cosmos and he focuses on anthropology, i.e. the religious experience of God as a means of insight into the mysteries of faith. It is through this understanding of religious experience as experiential knowledge of God that he so profoundly influences the next thirteen centuries. It is only when modern thinkers introduced epistemological dualism, that Augustine's finely nuanced theological system was brought into question.

THE EXPERIENCE OF GOD
AQUINAS ON THE IDENTITY AND DIFFERENCE OF DIVINE AND HUMAN KNOWLEDGE

There is in the works of St. Thomas Aquinas no formal discussion of religious experience as such. In this sense our attempt to address it here already begins in difficulty. And yet, on the contrary, the fact that St. Thomas could get by quite adequately without identifying and enquiring into experience – religious or otherwise – as a specific category should indicate to us that we are, in making this enquiry into Aquinas, also bringing before us something about *ourselves*, something intimately connected with the way *we* think. In this sense Aquinas puts us into question, and forces us to confront why we bring the question of religious experience before ourselves as a topic at all. This paper is to some extent an attempt to provide an answer to that question.

We have become accustomed to understanding the work of St. Thomas – especially in the Catholic tradition – as normative. This is especially true in the wake of the restoration of the place of his work and the many schools of Neo-Thomism that have arisen since Pope Leo XIII's encyclical letter of 1879 calling for a renewed study of Aquinas, *Æterne Patris*.[1] In reality both in his own time and even now what Aquinas was doing was something quite remarkable, in attempting to synthesise Mediæval scientific learning – the tradition of neo-Platonism and the recovery of the texts of Aristotle together with their Jewish and Islamic commentators – with the Christian religion. This was an undertaking fraught with quarrels and heated debate. Only very shortly after his death much of the speculative enquiry of the Mediæval Schools was reined in by the issuing in 1277 of the 'Condemnations' of the Bishop of Paris, Étienne Tempier. These condemned so-called 'Latin Averroeism', or more loosely put, an over-dependence on pagan and infidel sources and wisdom in Christian centres of learning.[2] Aquinas was in the thick of these debates,

---

[1] Leo XIII, "Apostolic Letter *Æterni Patris*," *Acta Sanctæ Sedis* 12 (1879) 97-115.
[2] For the full text of these, together with a French translation, see David Piché and Claude Lafleur, *La condamnation parisienne de 1277: Texte latin, traduction, introduction et commentaire* (Paris: Vrin, 1999).

and far more loved in them in the faculties of arts than amongst the theologians, many of whom were suspicious and mistrustful of his teaching. And yet St. Thomas's is without doubt one of the most outstanding contributions to Mediæval thought, and for that alone, notwithstanding the sheer power of his work to speak to us in our faith even now, deserves serious attention.

The title of this paper contains an ambiguity: 'the experience of God' can refer, either to the experience that can be had of God (the objective genitive) or to the experience that God has (the subjective genitive). The ambiguity, however, is neither accidental, nor without its own importance in our considerations, for in this ambiguity the whole of our problematic with regard to the question of the meaning of experience resides.

Our topic is experience, and it seems that what 'experience' is need have no further investigation. Experience is, on the one hand, that which happens to us and so that which we genuinely know – and on the other hand (scientifically) that which we can verify as true, above all through its repeatability. If we know insofar as we *experience*, then the experience we have of God – religious experience – must, at least in some sense be like any other experience. We must be able to verify this experience and at the same time we must be able to reproduce this experience. Even here, however, an ambiguity appears, for 'religious experience' can mean an experience of a religious kind (we have yet to decide what this is more precisely, but an experience of God ought surely to count as at least a good candidate), but it also can mean familiarity, a knowing-your-way-around with regard to God. It has the twin resonance that the Greeks denoted on the one hand with the word αἴσθησις, that which belongs to the senses, and on the other hand, ἐπιστήμη, know-how, in the sense of knowing-your-way-around, knowledge gained through an accumulated store of trial and error.

The word 'experience' derives from the Latin verb *experior* and is related to the Greek περάω, I pass through, from which also the word πόρος, a passage or shallow ford between two river-banks derives. To pass through in this way has an ancient connection with truth, that is, a getting through to the truth by undertaking a work or enquiry, a wrestling at to get across – hence an ἀπόρια, something to whose truth we cannot yet find a way through. However, *experior* has another odd feature, belonging to that class of verbs in Latin which are deponent. Typically we say these are verbs with an active meaning but which are conjugated in the passive voice, but this is really not correct. They retain their passive resonance. Thus the passive infinitive *experiri* really means, to be passed

through, to be made a trial of, therefore it indicates *that which is tested.*
An *experimentum* is the means of bringing something to light through testing and trying it, hence its connection with know-how, with knowing your
way around and with Greek ἐπιστήμη, with that knowledge which Latin
calls *scientia* and we know as 'scientific': *experientia* are the things
brought to light by trial and by testing. It appears that what we experience
in the sense of what we know by sensation is thus that kind of knowing
that we personally 'put to the test by our being passed through' and are
ourselves 'passed through' with regard to some event or occurrence. In
experience we do not therefore address something, rather we are addressed
by it, we are oriented toward it such that it orders us to what it is.

It is the very *repeatability* of religious experience, something which
occurs to me a lot, something with which I am very familiar, which indicates not some sensible knowledge as such, so much as know-how, a
being-familiar-with in the sense of knowing my way about with regard
to something. For quite different reasons however, we now take for
granted and at the same time that the repeatability of experience is for
anyone. To cut a long story short, we see here the way in which the
repeatable becomes tied to *method.* If I follow the 'method' of the experiment, I will simply repeat the 'experience' and gain the results. Thus
inherent to the modern understanding of 'knowing your way around' is
that this knowing is *systematisable*, not simply reproducible, but, given
the right conditions, reproducible for *anyone*, and in the same way.

'Experience' – whether religious, or of God, or of any kind, suggests
experience of the experienceable, of what it is possible for me verifiably,
and so truthfully to know. In the modern, scientific sense, only that which
is at least potentially experienceable for me, that which is repeatable for
me, can be in this sense be 'true'. Thus a uniform, general, sense of 'me',
of who 'I' am is already given in every question concerning experience.
There can be no classes of experience which you can have which I cannot at least *potentially* have. If you prove by experiment that there is a
new quark in sub-atomic physics, I must at least potentially (with the
right equipment) be able to reproduce the proof: if you can see a colour
I have not yet seen, I must at least potentially be able to see it unless I
am colour-blind. However this aspect of repeatability conceals the way
in which experience also has a tendency to confer aptitude. When I begin
to use a chisel or hammer I am most likely to be clumsy – I may even
cut myself or flatten my thumb. Over time however, as I become dex-
terous with the use of hammers and chisels their use becomes familiar and
easy and my aptitude and skill grows.

Aristotle (and Aquinas, for that matter) held no different view with regard say, to the practices of what we now call the virtues. The repeated exposure of the self to specific practices, as much of the soul as of the hands or the body in general confers skill and aptitude with regard to what is at hand. Experience as a knowing-my-way-around therefore also has, or can have, a moral consequence as well as a technical outcome. For Aquinas the saints, habituated to prayer and to the practices and ways of the love of God, therefore are not just ones who 'know their way around' with regard to what is to be known of God, but are also by that very habituation more attuned to, more familiar with, the experience of God. The Greeks resolved this ambiguity in the character of aptitude by having two terms for 'habit'. The first kind of habit, a ἕξις, is therefore a disposition, a predisposition to be good at something; the second, συνήθειαν, however, denotes a habit that is learnt or acquired by habituation and custom. Συνήθειαν literally means 'to become accustomed to by being together with' – where it is presupposed that what is indicated is a length of time. Both are required in certain circumstances – if I have no prior aptitude for work with my hands, then I should never lift a chisel: if I have that aptitude, however, I may after time and the acquisition of familiarity learn how to carve a garland of oak-leaves around the head of a figure on a wood panel. The former ἕξις is perfected by the latter συνήθειαν. Aquinas introduces a third condition for experience, however, – prior even to my disposition or habituation, I must be granted the invitation to the Christian life by God. Without God's infused gift of grace, I will have no disposition toward holiness; even if a created intellect is given to be in heaven, he says, it does not know God perfectly, but only as it receives a greater or lesser light of glory – that is, only as much as God chooses to give it a greater or lesser light.[3]

Aquinas does not, therefore, think that all religious experience – insofar as that is what we are already speaking of – is as equally and methodically repeatable for one person as for another. In fact he precisely does not think this because first, experience is had of God only insofar as God grants grace for this experience to occur, and second, insofar as the one granted grace co-operates with the grace that is granted. Grace here, however, is not some invisible infusion of some prior but unseen quantity – rather it takes concrete forms, of, for instance, openness to the word of

---

[3] Aquinas, *Summa theologiæ*, Ia, Q. 12, art. 7, resp: "Nullus autem intellectus creatum potest Deum infinite cognoscere. Instantum enim intellectus creatus divinam essentiam perfectius vel minus perfecte cognoscit, inquantum maiori vel minori lumine gloriæ perfunditur."

God, of enjoyment of and openness to the sacraments, of the practices of
Christian living, the 'virtues' as it were, and so forth. Moreover the very
inequality at issue is itself a source of grace: the life of Christ and lives
of the saints wherein this grace is poured out in fullest and fuller measure is itself converting and draws the as yet unsanctified soul to thirst to
be the same manifestation of the redemptive activity of God.

This is, however, a more active sense of experience: of getting-to-
know-my-way-around in virtue of the acquisition of excellences of Christian practices – the practice of the virtues, life in the Church and so forth.
It is constructed on the basis of sensate experience, but it is a taking of
sensate experience in hand purposively for the sake of something else, for
the sake of perfecting the intellect. We tend now to conceive of experience only as that which happens to us – what the Greeks knew as πάθος
– which does depend on αἴσθησις, on sensation, but as that through
which the senses are passed. This passive sense is the one which, in consideration of questions especially concerning religious experience, has
come to predominate, but, although taken for granted by St. Thomas, is
in fact only the basis for an orientation of a consequent way of life.

What our own modern concept of experience in its very repeatability
equally for all who seek it conceals is that we have become accustomed
to the idea that experience of God, 'religious experience' as such is simply another category of either *sensible* or at the same time *verifiable*
experience which is explicitly concerned with the average and everyday
experience of things that we now take for granted. There is a further com-
plication. The (pagan) ancients presupposed almost without thinking that
the divine is something toward which we stand out (ἐκστάσις), toward
which we strive through the sensible, through αἴσθησις, through the
senses by means of the operation of νοῦς (or what is translated as *intellectus* and 'intellect'). The intellect is fulfilled in this standing-out, its
completion or perfection lies ahead of us, in the future. With the Christian preoccupation to demonstrate and assert that God is both *creator et
causa omnium* and that God is personal, the relationship to God undergoes a radical transformation. God is that one who already knows everything we know in advance of us having this knowledge. In this sense God
knows 'from within' (as knowing-already) what it is we will come to
know 'from without' (will come to know in the future). St. Thomas
resolves the difficulties this presents with regard to human freedom by
means of God's and our asymmetrical and, most importantly, asynchro-
nous relationship to creation. God experiences the whole of time as a single, open, free act, and he knows it directly by means of the intellect

alone – God has no body. We, on the other hand, experience time in its progression and through the body, hence through the senses.

With Descartes' conception of the structure of the human person, of the *subject* however, our knowledge of God comes also to be constituted 'from within'. Religious experience as we now understand it takes on a transformed character, as an aspect, not of that experience as derived through the senses from the world, but of human psychology. There appears to be no sensate experience 'of' God in the manners I have just described, only some kind of direct or immediate knowledge, the kind that Aquinas believes is the content of intellection, which for Descartes must be as certain as that knowledge which the *ego sum*, the *cogito*, has of itself. It is this transformation which even brings the question of religious experience before us as a separate and *differentiated* topic when compared to other forms or manners of experience. After Descartes and moreover, after the radical scepticism of Hume, God is no longer the concern of sensate experience, because sensate experience is dubious (as indeed it is for Aquinas, but now dubiety becomes the determining issue with regard to what anything is at all). Descartes, however, believes that knowledge of God and God's existence cannot in any way be allowed to be subject to dubiety but "the existence of God is required to be at the minimum in the same degree of certainty in which the truths of mathematics have so far been".[4]

Thus God is no longer *primarily* encountered through the sacraments and liturgically, through the hearing and digestion of scripture, through being manifest in the lives of the saints and in the person of Christ, but these are adjunct (if they are relevant at all) to the direct, intellectual, *intuition* of God which these things then must be set out to confirm. We so much take this view for granted that it therefore seems self-evident to us that wherever we look in the Christian tradition – or even outside it – we may demand that something like 'religious experience' is a genuine category of the psyche which may legitimately be enquired into. In this sense we read our own way of thinking about the world and the understanding of experience which we take for granted back into a world and a view of experience which did not think like this. Philosophically and hermeneutically we must always take into account and be aware that in considering questions like the question we are considering now, this is what we are doing.

---

[4] René Descartes, *Meditationes de prima philosophia*, ed. Charles Adam and Paul Tannery, vol. VII (Paris: Vrin, 1996) Meditation V, 65f: "In eodem ad minimum certitudinis gradu esse deberet apud me Dei existentia, in quo fuerunt hactenus Mathematicæ veritates."

It should come as a surprise, therefore, that St. Thomas Aquinas explicitly rejects the view that experience of God can be in any way like this.
Early on in the *Summa contra gentiles*, Aquinas raises the question of the
means by which it is possible for divine truth to become manifest.[5] By
manifest we may understand what is intended in the modern sense of experienceable, and from which experience we may then go on to understand
certain things through the work of the mind (*ratio*, reckoning). Aquinas
asserts that this manifestation of truth is twofold: on the one hand, the
truth that God is triune exceeds the ability of human reason to discover
unaided; but on the other, that God *is*, or that God is *one*, these things can
be reached by means of a natural reckoning. These latter truths about God
have, Aquinas argues, been shown by the philosophers – by which he
means the pagans, or at the very best, the non-Christian Arabs with whom
he was in dialogue. Aquinas asserts that "the human intellect is not able
to attain a comprehension of the divine substance through its natural
power".[6] He illustrates this by way of a detour, indicating that it is not
even a matter of varying degrees of comprehension or capacity or skill in
the practise of wisdom that is at stake (experience in the second sense we
have already identified). Unlike every other form of intellect (human,
angelic, etc.) the divine intellect is adequate to its substance, and understands perfectly what it is, and knows what all of its intelligibles are.[7] By
intelligibles Aquinas simply means, that which is able to be known about
something; by adequate is meant 'equal to' or transparent. In this sense
the divine substance is self-transparent. Here Aquinas is only reiterating
his frequent assertion that only God can know fully or comprehend God's
self. Thus he says: "Since everything is knowable inasmuch as it is actual,
God, who is pure act without any admixture of potentiality, in himself is
most excellently knowable. But what is supremely knowable in itself, may
not be knowable to some other (*alicui*) intellect, on account of the excess
of what is knowable [i.e. contained in it] over above that intellect."[8]

---

[5] Aquinas, *Summa contra gentiles*, I, Ch. 3: "Quis modus sit possibilis divinae veritatis manifestandae."
[6] Aquinas, *Summa contra gentiles*, I, Ch. 3, N. 4: "Nam ad substantiam [Dei] capien-
dam intellectus humanus naturali virtute pertingere non potest."
[7] Aquinas, *Summa contra gentiles*, I, Ch. 3, N. 5: "Ipse enim intellectus divinus sua
capacitate substantiam suam adaequat, et ideo perfecte de se intelligit quid est, et omnia
cognoscit quae de ipso intelligibilia sunt."
[8] Cf. Aquinas, *Summa theologiæ*, Ia, Q. 12, art. 1, resp: "Cum unumquodque sit
cognoscibile secundum quod est in actu, Deus, qui est actus purus absque omni permix-
tione potentiæ, quantum in se est, maxime cognoscibilis est. Sed quod est maxime
cognoscibile in se, alicui intellectui cognoscibile non est, propter excessum intelligibilis
supra intellectum."

Aquinas is indicating that God's self-transparency to God is of an entirely different order to the knowledge I might have of something other than me. The reference to excess here is simply to reinforce the point – it is not critical to Aquinas' assertion, but exemplifies and makes more understandable the problem, because it takes as its exemplary subject the unique substance that God is. Substance here simply means separate and actual being.[9] What is at issue is this: how I can have access to what is knowable about a substance has precisely a limitation in knowledge, especially where what it is I seek experience or knowledge of is different in kind from me. This is in contrast to comparing my capacity to know something about myself in virtue of my capacity to interrogate myself about what it is I seek knowledge of. We are talking here of two different kinds of experience – experience from without, as in that which is observable and testable for me, the very *experimental* experience that we today take for granted as providing us with an access to knowledge of what things are, and self-transparency, the ability to know based on self-interrogability.[10] Indeed in the *Summa contra gentiles* Aquinas reinforces this point. The limitation on knowledge of the divine substance that we experience with regard to God has an analogue in our knowledge *naturaliter* of everyday things. Here Aquinas says: "The same thing manifestly appears from the defect that is experienced in our everyday knowledge of things. We are ignorant of many properties of sensible things, and it is not possible for us perfectly to enter into the reckoning of those properties we apprehend by sense. All the more therefore, does human reckoning not suffice to investigate all the intelligibilities of that most excellent substance (i.e. God)."[11] Thus God as the exemplary substance reveals a quality that concerns experience and knowledge of substances in general.

---

[9] Care must be exercised here, however: strictly speaking, for Aquinas (as indeed should be the case for us) God is not 'a' being, though there is such a thing for Aquinas as the divine substance. In every other case, however, to speak of the substance that a thing is means to speak of the manifestness of an essence.

[10] This distinction is worked out dialectically by Aristotle in the *Nicomachæan Ethics*, especially in book six from his investigation of τέχνη, which we can translate as know-how, and φρόνησις, best perhaps translated as deliberation. Thus Aristotle gives ἐπιστήμη a dialectical and 'scientific' meaning in relation to τέχνη, as that kind of knowing which has do with the ordering and stabilising of know-how, and σοφία becomes highest deliberation, deliberation of the ever-same in contrast to deliberation over what is moveable and changeable – φρόνησις.

[11] Aquinas, *Summa contra gentiles*, I, Ch. 3, N. 5: "Adhuc idem manifeste apparet ex defectu quem in rebus cognoscendis quotidie experimur. Rerum enim sensibilium plurimas proprietates ignoramus, earumque proprietatum quas sensu apprehendimus rationes perfecte in pluribus invenire non possumus. Multo igitur amplius illius excellentissimae substantiae omnia intelligibilia humana ratio investigare non sufficit."

If is well-understood that Aquinas holds that only God truly knows God in God's essence we could still misunderstand what is indicated here unless we recall that we do not apprehend by means of sense, not only the most excellent substance, God, but *any* substance, except through its accidents (i.e its manner and circumstances of appearing), and so *a posteriori*. We do not, in other words, have direct (or essential) knowledge of any substances at all, only by means of accidents. Only God knows essences (i.e what makes substances what they are, in and of themselves) directly.[12] This is because, for Aquinas, only the intellect knows substances. Now God is nothing other than intellect – but the created intellect's knowledge of substances in this life is derived from the accidents under which substances appear and their modes of appearing – which indicate and make available to us through the work of the intellect their 'substantial form'. This indicating and making available is always for us provisional, incomplete, and dubious (though St. Thomas does not over-stress this). It is therefore difficult and requires work, the work of the intellect, to perfect. It is, nevertheless, the best in this life that we have. Moreover this indicating and making available occurs through the senses.

What Aquinas argues is that there is something in the very character of experiential knowing, knowing of the order both of knowing-your-way-around and familiarity-with and at the same time knowing *of* through having a sensation, that from the very outset excludes us from a perfect knowledge of the divine substance. The whole burden of this argument turns on the word *alicui* in the earlier quotation I took from the *Summa theologiæ*, which here means 'some other'. It is our very seperatedness from things which are different to us which indicates to us the difficulty that Aquinas says is pre-eminently evident with regard to the difference between us and God. This however, although it is most easily understood (from the perspective of the Mediæval mind) in relation to God (because of God's manifest intellectual excellence over and above the creature) in fact is grounded in an ordinary, everyday defect in the order of all sensual knowledge. Even the things of sense, whose properties we can investigate, do not thereby in that investigation become entirely or perfectly transparent to us through our investigations. Even where we have a knowledge of the properties of things, it remains always imperfect. There are always properties, or in Aquinas's language, essences

---

[12] For a full discussion of this, see Philip L. Reynolds, "Properties, Causality and Epistemological Optimism in Thomas Aquinas," *Recherches de théologie et philosophie médiévales/Forschungen zur Theologie und Philosophie des Mittelalters*, 67, no. 2 (Leuven: Peeters, 2001) esp. 283-295.

and forms, the understanding of which remain unknown to us, or only imperfectly known to us.

It becomes immediately clear that what is at issue here, even for St. Thomas, let alone for us, is the character of knowledge that is possible through what we now call – but even then was evidently also – experiential knowledge. Thus the distinction that many have attempted to draw in the orders of knowing between the 'speculative' knowledge of the Mediæval and Ancient worlds and the experiential, verifiable and experimental knowledge, on which an understanding of our own modern universe supposedly depends, was well known – to Aquinas at least – and is from the outset (i.e *a priori*) for him inadequate as a way to know the divine substance.

The distinction Aquinas relies upon relates to the self-knowability of God to God and at the same time to the separatedness implicit in sensate human knowing. It is not possible for us within the space available to us to answer why it is that only God has perfect self-knowledge, and that human self-knowledge would not, strictly speaking, equate for Aquinas to the same self-transparency available to God. Nor is it possible to investigate how it is God's *singularity* which guarantees this self-transparency, and how this relates to God's particular relation to time and eternity and to the absence in God of any potentiality, so that the knowledge God has is strictly speaking undetermined with regard to time. These questions, which are in the first instance questions in philosophy, are not now our prime concern. We are here examining a question which is theological, and having demonstrated the initial range of the question as it appears in Aquinas, and our relation to that appearance (which has already turned out to be rather different to what we might have expected), to ask what are the *theological* consequences of Aquinas's understanding of experience.

In order to carry this out, it is necessary for me to ask you to understand one thing in advance, which I intend to demonstrate in the course of this discussion, but which we already need to be aware of. Although in the course of developing his understanding of human knowing, Aquinas borrows heavily from philosophical understanding of what it is for human beings to know, nevertheless this is, even when it most appears not to be, a strictly theological understanding of human knowledge. Aquinas's development of what he finds in the philosophical tradition – from which, by the way, he borrows at times quite eclectically – from Aristotle, from Plato and Neoplatonism, as much as from the Mediæval and especially Arab commentators on the ancient texts – depends above all on two things, one of which appears to be derived from human reckoning *naturaliter*, but both in fact derive from Christian revelation. The first is that God is the first cause of all things: the second is, as Aquinas says, "thus we hold by faith the ultimate purpose of the human to be the vision of God".[13] Any philosophical conception of human knowing, of human experience as such, must always be consonant with scripture and with the things God has ordained and revealed, and not the other way round. In the first case, scripture asserts that "in the beginning God created the heavens and the earth";[14] in the second, "we know that when he shall appear we shall be like to him: for we shall see him as he is".[15]

Aquinas goes further than this, however, for he argues that "beneficially, therefore, did the divine mercy provide that even that which reason is able to investigate, might be taught and so held by faith, that all might easily be sharers in divine knowledge and that without uncertainty or error".[16] To be sharers in divine knowledge is something given in faith, which can even include those things which otherwise could be known by human reckoning. Reason cannot attain to certain kinds of knowledge, but faith can. Thus *faith* and not human reckoning is the primary basis for – what exactly? The Latin says "divinæ cognitionis", which the standard English (Pegis) translation renders "knowledge of God".[17] This however is ambiguous, or rather, it attempts too much to settle the ambiguity of *divinæ cognitionis*, since *divinæ* here does not mean 'of God', because it is feminine. It must therefore be adjectival of the knowledge – *cognitio* – which is the feminine noun it is agreeing with. What sort of divine knowledge are we here speaking of? Is it knowledge *about* God – ἐπιστήμη, the objective genitive – or the (purely intellectual) knowledge that God has – the subjective genitive?

If it is the latter, the knowledge God has, it cannot arise from 'sensation' – Aquinas above all is adamant, as I have already indicated, that God has no body, God cannot 'feel' or 'sense' in this way. God's self-transparency to God is not of a sensuous order. The knowledge at issue here

---

[13] Aquinas, *Summa theologiæ*, Sup. Q. 92, art. 1, resp: "Sicut secundum fidem ponimus finem ultimum humanæ vitæ esse visionem Dei."

[14] Gn 1:1: "In Principio creavit Deus cælum et terram."

[15] 1 Jn 3:2: "Quoniam cum apparuerit similes ei erimus quoniam videbimus eum sicuti est."

[16] Aquinas, *Summa contra gentiles*, I Ch. 4, N. 6: "Salubriter ergo divina providit clementia ut ea etiam quae ratio investigare potest, fide tenenda praeciperet: ut sic omnes de facili possent divinae cognitionis participes esse et absque dubitatione et errore."

[17] Cf. Aquinas, *Saint Thomas Aquinas: Summa Contra Gentiles*, trans. A. C. Pegis, vol. I (Notre Dame: University of Notre Dame Press, 1955) 68.

is already of a very strange character. The knowledge to which Aquinas refers appears not to fall under the category of ἐπιστήμη, of knowing-your-way-about in the sense of knowledge gained by trial and error, precisely because it excludes trial-and-error in its being had – it is *without* uncertainty or error. Knowledge gained through trial and error, as I said earlier would be *scientia*, and relates precisely to that which is discovered and perfected through the senses. The knowledge that Aquinas says here is divine cannot, however, be *scientia* and must be *cognitio*. Now *cognitio* can include that knowledge which I have by sense, but it is always personal to someone. It is not general, abstract know-how, ἐπιστήμη, scientific knowledge, but rather knowledge pertaining to some *one*. Hence we speak of cognition when we refer to that knowledge we have personally rather that scientific knowledge, knowledge which anyone in general can have.

Thus the knowledge that is had by faith is more a kind of *cognitio*, being in itself without doubt or error. It can be confirmed by *scientia*, by general know-how, but not the other way round (this is in exact contradistinction to what we would now take for granted, that insofar as we are to trust what is given in faith and by scripture, we can only do so insofar as this knowledge is consonant with and confirmed by scientific or sensate knowledge). Thus for Aquinas human reckoning, *scientia*, whose limitations for him we have indicated, is *second* in the order of knowledge to that knowledge, *cognitio*, which is given primarily in faith. We still have not quite settled the question of whether this divine knowledge is about God, or the knowledge that God has.

In his definition of truth, Aquinas is quite explicit about what makes the true 'true'. True knowledge for you or me is the adequation of thing and intellect,[18] but this is because what becomes true for me, the way my intellect is conformed to the truth of something is so because it is *already* productively true in that manner because intended to be so by its author, who is God. Thus Aquinas stresses that "natural things from which our intellect gets its knowledge [*scientia*] measure our intellect, as is said in Book X of [Aristotle's] *Metaphysics*: but these things are themselves measured by the divine intellect, in which are all created things, just as

---

[18] Aquinas, *Quæstiones disputatæ: de veritate*, Q. 1, art. 1, resp: "Veritas est adaequatio rei et intellectus." This is also how St. Thomas defines truth in the *Commentary on the Sentences*, where he speaks of the "relatio adaeqautionis, in qua consistit ratio veritatis" (*In I Sent*. Disp. 19, art. 5, resp.; cf. Disp. 40, art. 3 resp. and *In IV Sent*. Disp. 46, Q. 1, resp.) and in the *Summa contra gentiles* (Book 1, Ch. 59, no. 2) as well as the *Summa theologiæ* (Ia, Q. 16, art. 1, resp.).

all works of art find their origin in the intellect of the artificer".[19] Although Aquinas cites Aristotle's *Metaphysics* in support of his argument, in fact we can see here at work already the way in which Aquinas consistently reworks the ancient authors to reflect a Christian understanding. The reference in the *Metaphysics* has nothing to do with the origin of things in the divine intellect – indeed, Aquinas subtly reverses the very point that Aristotle is making there. Aristotle notes that although it seems that knowledge (ἐπιστήμη) is a measure which measures the things that are knowable (ἐπιστήτα), in fact it is the other way about, because knowledge is measured by (μετρεῖται) the knowable.[20] However, Aquinas here says the opposite: because God intends what is to be knowable to be knowable, as such and in the manner of its being, by a prior act of creation (because God is the author of the heavens and the earth), God's knowledge precisely *does* measure what is knowable, and thereby makes it true, in advance of our being measured by it. God has direct intellection and *cognitio* of that of which we really only have *scientia*, and so indirect intellection. Our intellects come into the truth only insofar as, by means of their perfecting work on what they know, they uncover in things what God first intended for those things. We discover by the work of the intellect the essence of the substances we come across, by means of their accidents – but God already knows in advance what the essences of things are, because God intended those essences in the first place, he created them to be as they are. (This means that the *adæquatio* formula of truth is more a matter arising out of faith, though it is not a matter *of* faith, than it is a philosophical definition – it depends for its effectiveness upon a Christian worldview, which only receives external confirmation by human reckoning *naturaliter*.)

Our *productive* knowledge is therefore only analogous to God's in the most extraordinary way, in that it is only directly analogous in the natural order to the knowledge the divine intellect has when we too are making or creating something. Thus Aquinas distinguishes between the human and the divine intellects in the following way: "The divine intellect, therefore, measures, and is not measured; a natural thing both measures and

---

[19] Aquinas, *Quæstiones disputatæ: de veritate*, Q. 1, art. 2, resp: "... quod res naturales, ex quibus intellectus noster scientiam accipit, mensurant intellectum nostru, ut dicitur X *Metaphysicis*: sed sunt mensuratæ ab intellectu divino, in quo sunt omnia creata, sicut omnia artificiata in intellectu artificis."

[20] Cf. Aristotle, *Metaphysics*, 1057 a 9-13: δόξειε μὲν γὰρ ἂν μέτρον ἡ ἐπιστήμη εἶναι, τὸ δὲ ἐπιστητὸν τὸ μετρούμενον, συμβαίνει δὲ ἐπιστήμην μὲν πᾶσαν ἐπιστητὸν εἶναι, τὸ δὲ ἐπιστητὸν μὴ πᾶν ἐπιστήμην, ὅτι τρόπον τινὰ ἡ ἐπιστήμη μετρεῖται τῷ ἐπιστητῷ.

is measured; but our intellect is measured, and measures only artifacts, not natural things."[21] It is only in this sense that Aquinas agrees with Aristotle, with regard to the created intellect. With regard to the uncreated intellect, God's, St. Thomas says the opposite of what Aristotle says. The primary way in which we know something to be true is when our intellect is passively conformed, through sensate experience and our intellection of it, to what is productively intended to be true by God. Only analogously, when we make something, do we (productively) decide *in advance* what it is that we will make, and whatever it is we produce is made in accordance with this 'in advance'. We are in the same relation to it as God is with regard to being the *causa et creator omnium*. When, however, we come across something which already exists, especially in the natural order, we can only by what we now call 'experience' and through the senses work out what was intended by its creator or producer *for* and *in* its making or production.

I want to move beyond how it is that St. Thomas's understanding of what we would now call experience is governed by the productive intention of God as first cause, and indeed how this discloses how a fundamental understanding both of truth and of 'essence' comes to predominate in Western thought, and indeed still does so, to indicate how it is that St. Thomas resolves the question of experience as a purely theological question, unrelated, strictly speaking, to the ancient enquiry into essence (οὐσία),[22] and distinct from any modern empirical or psychological account of experience which we might recognise.

In the *Supplement* to the *Summa theologiæ* (which is really an edited collection of bits and pieces left over from the fact that the *Summa* was unfinished at his death) St. Thomas and his editor note that "certain theologians held that the human intellect is never able to arrive at the vision of God essentially".[23] This occurs in the context of a discussion of what it means to see the essence of God. The question arises, as we have already noted, specifically because of the scriptural description of what it means to be present to God – 'we shall be like him for we shall see him

---

[21] Aquinas, *Quæstiones disputatæ: de veritate*, Q. 1, art. 2, resp: "Sic ergo intellectus divinus est mensurans non mesuratus; res autem naturalis, mensurans et mensurata; sed intellectus noster est menusuratus, non mensurans quidem res naturales, sed artificiales tantum."

[22] Cf. Aquinas, *De ente et essentia*, Cp. 2, N. 3: "Usia enim apud Græcos idem est quod essentia apud nos."

[23] Aquinas, *Summa theologiæ*, Sup., Q. 92, art. 1, resp: "Et [...] quidam theologi posuerunt quod intellectus humanus nunquam potest ad hoc pervenire ut Deum per essentiam videat."

as he really is'. The question therefore arises after a discussion of the meaning of death, of purgatory, the last judgement, and indeed of all the last things. Only the justified, those beckoned into heaven by God, will have the beatific vision. However, Aquinas does not hold the opinion that the human intellect can never arrive at the vision of God through his essence, or essentially, but rather the opposite. Now note that this question arises specifically in consequence of what it means to 'see' God. Surely, however, we see with the eyes, not the intellect? Except that Aquinas is always careful to bring before us that it is the intellect which really 'sees', and in a sense more truly than that seeing which is undertaken with the sight of the eyes. Intellective knowing, *cognitio*, is, for Aquinas at least, primarily a 'seeing', and of a kind that directly 'sees' truth. Elsewhere in the *Summa theologiæ* he argues "the eye is double: certainly, it is of the body, properly speaking; and it is of the intellect, as we might say, by similitude".[24] What Aquinas refers to here is the eye of faith, which, in being granted the beatific vision after death, is rewarded with confirmation of its faithfulness – it will 'see' directly what once it only saw in pious expectation.[25] Aquinas deduces this by appeal again to Aristotle, saying that "substance, therefore inasmuch as it is in this manner, is not visible to the bodily eye, neither does it underlie particular senses, neither the imagination, but alone [it underlies] the intellect, whose object is that which is, as is said in Chapter Three of the *De anima*".[26]

Salvation therefore precisely means the creature knowing God in God's essence. Does this not contradict Aquinas's often-made assertion that we can never know God in God's essence, the assertion that exemplified Aquinas's view that we cannot *by experience* know any essences directly at all? What this discloses, however, is that we are not saved, or rather, we do not experience the beatific vision, by virtue of experience, or as *an* experience, or as experience in general. Rather we are granted a direct conformity to the divine intellect, whereby the created intellect is directly united to God. However, Aquinas says: "This operation by which the human mind is conjoined to God does not, therefore, depend on the

---

[24] Aquinas, *Summa theologiæ*, IIIa, Q. 76, art. 7, resp: "Duplex est oculis: scilicet corporalis, proprie dictus: et intellectualis, qui per similitudinem dicitur."

[25] Once again, the warrant for this is strictly scriptural. Cf. 1 Cor 13:12: "For now we see through a glass, darkly; but then face to face: now I know in part; but then shall I know even as also I am known."

[26] Aquinas, *Summa theologiæ*, IIIa, Q. 76, art. 7, resp: "Substantia autem, inquantum huiusmodi, non est visibilis oculo corporali, neque subiacet alicui sensui, neque imaginationi, sed soli intellectui, cuius obiectum est quod quid est, ut dicitur in III *de Anima*."

senses."[27] Divine union is in no sense in consequence of some kind of summit of experience, but is rather by the graceful gift of God. Aquinas protects the difference between creator and creature by asserting that this union does not mean that the created mind in any sense 'comprehends' – that is, exceeds or is co-equal to the divine intellect, but rather, that this conjoinment is in virtue of the capacity of the creature to receive it and in virtue of the degree to which God chooses to flood the created mind with the light of glory, which is God himself.[28]

How, therefore, is the category of experience into which we are enquiring configured to this extraordinary understanding of *direct* intellection, of knowledge as such? First, we should be clear that although experience is a way into knowledge in terms of this earthly life, it is not a way into knowledge in virtue of our embodiment, although we require a body to have it. It would be easy to misunderstand the description of divine union which St. Thomas presents here as in fact destructive of embodiment (and so claim that Aquinas is some kind of a dualist), particularly as we, with our post-Cartesian understandings of the structure of the human being, the subject, are most apt to understand it in consequence of the psychology which after Descartes we take for granted.[29] Thus we could find ourselves drawn towards the view that the human intellect after this act of union is simply consumed with and by its union with God – it has no need of embodiment, and so experience as such ceases. A. N. Williams, in her study of Aquinas's understanding of deification and salvation, correctly notes that "Thomas's anthropology does not suggest one structure of human experience and existence in this life and a different structure in the next, and he definitely rules out any possibility of viewing sanctification in this life (which comes about through growth in the virtues, especially charity) as distinct and separate from salvific consummation in the next".[30] We will enter heaven and dwell there embodied.

---

[27] Aquinas, *Summa theologiæ*, Ia IIæ, Q. 3, art. 3, resp: "Non autem tunc operatio qua mens humana Deo coniungetur, a sensu dependebit."

[28] See note 3 above.

[29] And yet, although it is not the main subject of this paper, we can see immediately that the division upon which Aquinas rests, of knowledge before and after death, is parallelled by Descartes with the knowledge of the 'inner' and 'outer' of the structure of the *cogito*, the subjectivity of the subject. The direct intellection of God which St. Thomas accords to the redeemed soul is accorded by Descartes to the (unredeemed) subject in virtue of the method of doubt.

[30] A.N. Williams, *The Ground of Union: Deification in Aquinas and Palamas* (Cambridge: Cambridge University Press, 1999) 39.

Aquinas argues that after divine union, the human being will enjoy perfect bliss. Therefore "in perfect bliss the whole man is perfected, in the inferior part by an overflowing from the superior [part]. It is the other way about in the imperfect bliss of this present life, we advance from the perfection of the inferior part to the perfection of the superior".[31] The 'inferior' part is simply that which is lower in the cosmos, the sensing body: the superior that which is concerned with what is higher – the intellect. What this means is that in the present life, all sensate experience is properly ordered to the perfection of the intellect (indeed, this could be read even apart from an understanding of salvation). It is through working on and working out the experiences of the senses that the intellect by a dialectical process comes to a knowledge of substances. Because, however, Aquinas is first and foremost a theologian and really never a philosopher, these processes have as their end the task of disclosing and perfecting us in the ways of the most excellent substance, namely God. After divine union, however, experience no longer has this purpose: from now on whatever experience we can conceive of having is in consequence of our already-having-been-conjoined to God: thus our senses will operate in virtue of, and from out of, this conjoinment – they do not lead us closer to perfection (by which is meant salvation), but rather operate in virtue of our having been saved.

We discover, therefore, that Aquinas resolves the questions which we raise under the heading of religious experience by transforming our own experience from the objective genitive – knowledge that can be had of God – to the subjective genitive. Our knowledge will become one with the knowledge God has, to the degree that he chooses to flood our intellects with it. Our knowledge will be a genuine *divinæ cognitionis*, divine knowledge. This is in virtue of a Christianisation of the philosophy with which Aquinas became familiar and with which he worked, but above all it is in virtue of his need to reconcile scientific and dialectical understandings of the cosmos or world with scripture. The meaning of our experience will be transformed, ultimately, because we are to be made Deiform – we will be like him, for we shall see him as he really is.[32]

---

[31] Aquinas, *Summa theologiæ*, Ia IIæ, Q. 3, art. 3, resp: "In perfecta beatitudine perficitur totus homo, sed in inferiori parte per redundantiam a superiori. In beatitudine autem imperfecta præsentis vitæ, e converso a perfectione inferioris partis proceditur ad perfectionem superioris."

[32] Cf. Aquinas, *Summa theologiæ*, Ia, Q. 12, art. 5, resp.

EXPERIENCE AND KNOWLEDGE OF GOD
THROUGH IGNATIAN 'DISCERNMENT OF SPIRITS'

STIJN VAN DEN BOSSCHE

> *I was convinced that first, tentatively, during my ill-*
> *ness in Loyola and then, decisively, during my time*
> *as a hermit in Manresa I had a direct encounter with*
> *God. This was the experience I longed to communi-*
> *cate to others.*[1]

> *The theologian Martin Olave said that he had*
> *learned more in meditating the "Principle and*
> *Foundation" than in all of his theological studies.*[2]

This chapter will consist of two main parts. In the first part, we will enquire how in an Ignatian perspective one *knows* God in discernment. How, in arriving at these experiences, can we be sure that they reveal God to us? How can we order our experiences so that we find the ones 'of God'? The focus then, will be on the experience of the subject discerning. In the second part we will ask the question whether one knows *God* in this same discernment: whether and how that which is discerned in these particular 'experiences of God' offers us any real knowledge *of God*. The focus here will be on the knowledge of God as the 'object' (a bad term, as will appear) to be reached.

A methodological remark is in order before we begin. My contribution suffers from both a lack and an overabundance of resources. As concerns the lack, only very little has been done in the four hundred years of history of the Spiritual Exercises about the precise theology in them. Ignatius, who was not a theologian himself, at least not in the scholarly sense, does not explicitly treat of this theology. The Spiritual Exercises were subsequently treated more as a pedagogical instrument for spiritual

---

[1] Karl Rahner, "Ignatius of Loyola Speaks to a Modern Jesuit," K. Rahner and P. Imhof, *Ignatius of Loyola* (Londen: Collins, 1979) 11.

[2] Sylvie Robert, *Une autre connaissance de Dieu: Le discernement chez Ignace de Loyola*, Cogitatio Fidei, 204 (Paris: Éditions du Cerf, 1997) 267; the translations of all citations are mine. This 'principle and foundation' (Spiritual Exercises no. 23) can be considered as an overture and in a way a synthesis of the whole Spiritual Exercises.

growth than as a source for theology. That is probably very right, and is their first and most important intention. But at a time in which any possibility of knowledge of God is questioned, the question of how the Exercises do what they do – namely tell the retreatant God's will for his or her life – becomes more important. Karl Rahner is perhaps the first to have dealt with this question – even if he refers to the attempt already made in Erich Przywara's famous *Deus semper maior* – in an article that starts as follows: "It does not seem unfair to the achievements of the great commentators on the Spiritual Exercises of St. Ignatius of Loyola to say that an account of the actual theology of the Exercises is something we still lack, at least on the scale we cannot but wish to have today."[3] So there is a lack in resources, and an introductory overview article presenting the Ignatian experience and knowledge of God will not fill this lack.

Yet what I have to say also suffers from an overabundance of resources. For in 1997 the French religious sister and theologian Sylvie Robert published an impressive monograph in which she deals with Rahner's question in a way so detailed and exhaustive that the reader really does not feel that anything can be added to this in-depth investigation.[4] So my intention will be to follow, to a large extent, Robert's project in order to introduce to an English speaking audience what are, in my opinion, some of her major findings on the theological epistemology as implied in Ignatius's experience of God.

1. Experience of God through Discernment

a. Discernment Rooted in Ignatius's Personal Life-experience of Consolation and Desolation

At the base of the whole of Ignatian spirituality lies the biographical experience of Ignatius. It is well known that Ignatius was a Basque noble man, trained for a career somewhere between the diplomatic and the military. In battle he was severely wounded in his knee, and he went through a long period of convalescence. Lying on his bed he read everything at hand – mostly religious literature. When he was not reading, he indulged himself

---

[3] Karl Rahner, "The Logic of Concrete Individual Knowledge in Ignatius of Loyola," *The Dynamic Element in the Church*, Quaestiones Disputatae, 12 (Freiburg: Herder and Montreal: Palm Publishers, 1964) 84.

[4] Robert, *Une autre connaissance*, 604ff.

in fancies, sometimes about worldly matters – most of all about a lady of higher nobility to whom he wants to pay court – but sometimes about more spiritual matters, like how it would be to live in the manner of St. Francis or St. Dominic. After a while, something started to attract his attention, a central experience that he describes in his reminiscences as follows:

> Still, there was this difference: that when he was thinking about that worldly stuff he would take much delight, but when he left it aside after getting tired, he would find himself dry and discontented. But when about going to Jerusalem barefoot, and about not eating except herbs, and about doing all the other rigours he was seeing the saints had done, not only used he to be consoled while in such thoughts, but he would remain content and happy even after having left them aside. But he wasn't investigating this, nor stopping to ponder this difference, until one time when his eyes were opened a little, and he began to marvel at this difference in kind and to reflect on it, picking it up from experience that from some thoughts he would be left sad and from others happy, and little by little coming to know the difference in kind of spirits that were stirring: the one from the devil, and the other from God.[5]

Father Luis Gonçalves da Câmara, who wrote these reminiscences as Ignatius narrated them to him, notes between brackets: "This was the first reflection he made on the things of God; and later, when he produced the Exercises, it was from here that he began to attain clarity regarding the matter of the difference in kinds of spirits."[6] Indeed: the double series in the Spiritual Exercises of 'Rules by which to perceive and understand to some extent the various movements produced in the soul',[7] that are at the base of the Ignatian 'discernment of spirits', are an elaboration of this basic experience of the different movements of 'consolation' and 'desolation'. In the third rule, Ignatius calls consolation that experience "when any interior movement is produced in the soul that leads her to become inflamed with the love of her Creator and Lord, and when, as a consequence, there is no created thing on the face of the earth that we can love in itself, but we love it only in the Creator of all things." Desolation is "everything contrary to what is in Rule 3".[8]

---

[5] Reminiscences 8; see Saint Ignatius of Loyola, *Personal Writings*, translated with introductions and notes by J. A. Munitiz and P. Endean (London: Penguin Books, 1996) 15.

[6] Reminiscences 8.

[7] Sp. Ex. 313-336; see Saint Ignatius of Loyola, *Personal Writings*, 348-353. This translation uses 'movement' to translate the Spanish 'moción', whereas Robert prefers in french 'motion' on 'mouvement'. We will follow her and use 'motion', unless we quote the *Personal Writings*.

[8] Sp. Ex. 316 and 317.

b. *Motions Caused by Spirits: The Encounter with Personal, Non-human, yet Created Otherness*

We cannot present a full account of what these motions of consolation and desolation in the soul are about precisely, as Robert does extensively. We will instead focus immediately on clarifying how these motions through discernment offer an experience of God, without, however, bringing God into experience.

The first thing that needs to be said is that these motions have the character of events.[9] They come and leave, they produce themselves, and we experience them in a passive way, without being able to foresee them or say anything about them in advance. They arrive and disappear in time. And they move us, towards consolation or desolation. The important thing is that as events they confront us with a form of otherness: "Affected, modified one could even say, by motions that have the force and the autonomy of events, man finds himself in fact confronted to an otherness."[10] Or otherwise, Ignatius speaks about three kinds of thoughts in me: one that is mine, one of the good spirit and one of the evil spirit.

Indeed, the motions are not described as something merely psychological, even if that is a dimension of them. But they are 'received' from elsewhere, they clearly have an "author".[11] And this author is the 'good angel', or the 'bad angel' or 'enemy', says Ignatius, so one of two 'spirits': this is precisely what needs to be discerned.[12] On the one hand the otherness of the motion as an event is fortified by naming it a 'spirit', because as a spirit it has a personal character. But the otherness of the motion is also doubled, because it is not to something resembling himself to which the human being relates, but to something of a different kind, 'non-human': a spirit.[13] Casting our gaze then across Ignatius's late-medieval way of expression, the important matter to note here is the figure of a personal, non-human otherness affecting the human being in the motions that it experiences.

---

[9] Robert, *Une autre connaissance,* 69ff.

[10] Robert, *Une autre connaissance,* 76.

[11] Robert, *Une autre connaissance,* 88.

[12] We leave out of consideration the special and rather exceptional case of 'consolation without preceding cause' (Sp. Ex. 330), only mentioning that according to Robert (p. 259-260, 266, etc.) this special case does not make God enter into experience any more than the other kinds of consolation. Karl Rahner grants much more importance to this consolation, which he makes the criterion for each and every consolation, but in the end sees also a continuity between both types. More specifically, 'cause' does not mean here a 'second cause', he says, but the expression 'without preceding cause' refers to the purity of the consolation. See Rahner, "The Logic of Concrete Individual Knowledge," 129-170.

These spirits organize a complex of contrasts, which can be brought back to 'the good' and 'the bad' (in a vital rather than a moral sense) affecting, challenging, seducing the human being's mind. Yet here an important difference between Luther and Ignatius becomes manifest in the way the human being is sensitive to these forces that are exercised on him or her.[14] For Luther in his *De servo arbitrio*, the struggle is immediately between God and Satan, not between spirits or angels. Hence the human being has no free will to choose a master between the two: he is, says Luther, like a horse between two riders who struggle among each other about who will seize the horse that will then have to obey one of them. Ignatius constructs a quite different picture, of an encounter of the human spirit with two *created* othernesses or spirits. These spirits stand at the 'border' of the human being's mind. The good spirit tries to defend the human being, the bad attempts to invade where this human being is weak. The human being's own mobile, indeed unstable spirit – the instance that 'links' the soul to the body[15] – can become accomplice to the good or the bad spirit, which is why discernment becomes necessary for those who want to live with God. Finally, the good spirit is within the human being, and the bad spirit always comes from without, trying to invade the human being. We can speak thus of an interior otherness, the spirit coming from God, the good angel (not the Holy Spirit though, who is God), and an exterior otherness, the bad angel or the enemy, who both affect the human being's spirit. In any case, the spirits are not God, even if they are a real otherness to the subject. But how do they mediate God then?

c. *Experiencing God by Restoring the Creational Relation of all Things, and especially the Human*

The operation of discernment is to let oneself be guided by real consolation, the motion that has as its author the good angel or the spirit from God.[16] Yet consolation as motion is not an end in itself. It is rather a tool

---

[13] Robert, *Une autre connaissance*, 93.

[14] Robert, *Une autre connaissance*, 99.

[15] Robert, *Une autre connaissance*, 104-107.

[16] This does not mean that desolation is useless, but the good use of it will lead to consolation. We must not forget either that consolation is not the same as 'a good feeling', just as desolation is not 'a bad feeling'. Desolation is what separates me from God and consolation is what leads me to God, and in this sense consolation is "*le cap à tenir*", the cape to keep (Robert, *Une autre connaissance*, 149).

with which to arrive at a deeper level: the human being's relation to the
"Creator and Lord" who lets himself be known in consolation. Consolation – the motion coming from the spirit 'originally inside' the human
being – indeed lets one retrieve his or her creational condition. More
specifically, consolation is of a theological order.[17] Ignatius gives the
name of consolation in the end "to every increase of hope, faith and
charity, to all interior happiness that calls and attracts a person towards
heavenly things and to the soul's salvation, leaving the soul quiet and at
peace in her Creator and Lord."[18] So the restoration of creational relationship is at stake in the end, in consolation – whereas desolation corresponds to separation of the Creator and Lord, and the good use of it
leads back to the creational relationship again. In short: "What will result
from this operation of discernment if it leads in this way to receiving consolation, the light of creation, so as to guide oneself on it? A 'putting in
order'."[19] Consolation is the motion by which we meet creation as creation again, where we recover the original order of creation, where we
start loving things again not for themselves (as idols), but as created by
God. This will appear to be (indirectly) experience of God: to recover the
relationship with God such as we had in paradise, when things were originally 'in order'. Most importantly, consolation retrieves the human being
itself in his or her paradisal status: as facing the Other, encountering God.

We have reached now the 'principle and foundation' of the Spiritual
Exercises, as this is called by Ignatius himself in the short opening statement of the Exercises. The experience of God to which discernment leads
in Ignatian pedagogy is Ignatius' experience of the creational status of
everything and especially of the human being, because to be created
means to be 'of God':

> The human person is **created** to praise, reverence and serve God our Lord,
> and by so doing to save his or her soul. The other things on the face of the
> earth are **created** for human beings in order to help them pursue the end for
> which they are **created**. It follows from this that one must use other **cre-
> ated** things in so far as they help towards one's end, and free oneself from
> them in so far as they are obstacles to one's end. To do this we need to
> make ourselves indifferent to all **created** things, provided the matter is sub-
> ject to our free choice and there is no prohibition. Thus as far as we are con-
> cerned, we should not want health more than illness, wealth more than
> poverty, fame more than disgrace, a long life more than a short one, and

[17] In the sense of the theological virtues. The French has the word *théologal*; see
Robert, *Une autre connaissance*, 154ff.
[18] Sp. Ex. 316.
[19] Robert, *Une autre connaissance*, 158.

similarly for all the rest, but we should desire and choose only what helps us more towards the end for which we are **created**.[20]

2. Knowledge of God through the Experience of Discernment

a. Ignatius and his Philosophical-Theological Context

We can now move to the second question: if the experience of consolation is the experience of the creational status that is to be 'of God', how is this *experience* of God an experience *of God*? How does this experience offer knowledge of God?[21] Robert works here throughout her study with a double distinction. The first is the distinction between *unio* and

---

[20] Sp. Ex. 23, with the title 'principle and foundation', and preceded only by a number of 'annotations'. See Saint Ignatius of Loyola, *Personal Writings*, 289; my italics. We may remind ourselves that the present tense 'created' means something quite different from the past perfect 'has been created', and this in modern English as much as in medieval Spanish. The founding biographical event for this description of the human being as 'being created' is in what is known as Ignatius's illumination at the river Cardoner: "Once he was going in his devotion to a church, which was a little more than a mile from Manresa (I think it is called St. Paul's), and the way goes along by the river. Going along thus in his devotions, he sat down for a little with his face towards the river, which was running deep below. And as he was seated there, the eyes of his understanding began to be opened: not that he saw some vision, but understanding and knowing many things, spiritual things just as much as matters of faith and learning, and this with an enlightenment so strong that all things seemed new to him. One cannot set out the particular things he understood then, though they were many: only that he received a great clarity in his understanding, such that in the whole course of his life, right up to the sixty-two years he has completed, he does not think, gathering together all the helps he has had from God and all the things he has come to know (even if he joins them all into one), that he has ever attained so much as on that single occasion. *And this left him with the understanding enlightened in so great a way that it seemed to him as if he were a different person, and he had another mind, different from that which he had before*" (Reminiscences 30; see Saint Ignatius of Loyola, *Personal Writings*, 26-27). On all this, see more extensively and with further bibliography S. Van den Bossche, *De Godservaring bij Ignatius van Loyola: Een studie in pastoraal-theologisch perspectief over het Grondbeginsel en Grondslag uit de Geestelijke Oefeningen* (Leuven: unpublished licenciate dissertation, 1990). About the Cardoner experience as knowledge of God, see Robert, *Une autre connaissance*, 268-273.

[21] Robert deals with this *difficile question* in no less than five chapters and over 300 pp, through which we shall now have to find our way. Chapter V, entitled 'Ignace devant la difficile question de la connaissance de Dieu' introduces us into the questions at stake. We will give more close attention to chapter VI, where the central key of Ignatian theology is offered: 'Des motions à Dieu'. Chapter VII 'Entre union et notion' describes further how this knowledge is situated between the two classical ways of union with God and notion of God. Chapter VIII on 'Dieu connu comme créateur' will lead us back to creation once more. Chapter IX – 'Connaître Dieu sans le penser?' answers, also in a more contemporary perspective, to the possible objection mentioned in its title.

notio, or between uniting us with God subjectively in the way of spirituality, and acquiring knowledge of God as objectively as possible in the way of theology. It is probably once more the transition from the (neo-) platonic paradigm – in which the experience as sign brings God present as the Signified because God already offered this experience – to the Aristotelian paradigm – in which a question opens up about how the experience as sign refers to (hence mediates) the Signified that is God – that forced union and notion to grow apart as ways to encounter God. However, if we continue to explore what is at stake here, which is the question of the notion of God, another distinction within this question appears that can be roughly paraphrased as between the real and the nominal. The Sixteenth century is an age where Thomistic realism about the knowledge of God, weakened first by Scotism and then especially by Nominalism, seems no longer culturally plausible. The question of whether and how God can be known can no longer obtain an answer within theology. The answer is sought again in the field of spirituality – but with more attention to spirituality's theological relevance. This is where the theological genius of the Spiritual Exercises has to be discovered. Robert concludes her clear account of the theological situation in which Ignatius finds himself as follows: "Would the success of the Spiritual Exercises not be linked to this originality: in a theological context where one weighs the question of knowledge of God, and where this question cannot be solved along the trails that were previously efficacious, discernment, master piece of the Ignatian libretto, instead of fleeing the question or looking to resolve it with the help of the ancient theological solutions, accepts the shift towards spirituality as demanded by the age, but while making the discoverable spirituality's genuinely theological dimension, which is its fertility in the matter of the knowledge of God?"[22]

b. From the Motions to God Himself: Encountering God as the One Differentiated from History

Discerning consolation and desolation has to do with sensing interiorly the way in which motions affect the person. Ignatian discernment is a way of refining interior sensing, so as to discern what God wants from the human being. But how can we say 'God' here? Because in discerning we know, more than God's will, God himself, by distinguishing God in

---

[22] Robert, *Une autre connaissance*, 316.

God's very otherness. The whole operation of discernment consists in discovering, through the coming and going of different motions in the discontinuity of time, another dimension, *a temporal continuum*: "The whole work consists in discovering oneself to be carried by a more fundamental continuity, that can be perceived in the first place thanks to the attention that one gives to the global orientation of the soul. But, for Ignatius as for his age, this continuum is not a simple component of time."[23] Indeed, for Ignatius, observing events in time goes together with the recurrent incitation to retrieve, strengthen or maintain the fundamental orientation of the human being on God as the Other of time. In this way one finds one's way back across, thanks to the changes within time, to God as the One who is not subject to those changes, because he is the Other. "The point is, for man, that the ability to use discernment is the means to accord himself to this founding otherness and corresponds to the capacity he possesses to do this."[24] To become human is thus to accept and obey freely those motions that come from God, in which one can have access to oneself. So a double freedom is at stake here: the human being is free to decide between the motions, but his or her freedom will arrive only if he or she puts himself or herself on the wave-length of the Other in his founding freedom. "Discernment thus discovers this Other in the heart of nascent liberty of man."[25]

In short, discernment confronts me with the Other who makes me be myself. This confrontation becomes knowledge, in so far as a *differentiation* occurs. Discernment effects a triple differentiation: between the spirits or the enemy and God on the level of spirits, between the gift and the Giver on the level of the created things, and between the human being and God on the level of the human subject. In this differentiation itself, God is known as the One who makes me live, who gives what is given, and most importantly: who is not me.

Yet this is an indirect way of knowing. First, because it cannot be aimed at in a straightforward way, discernment does not aim at knowing God, but at knowing God's will. Only when the human being has found God's will, will he or she through this, have encountered the God who wills. Second, because God does not become an object to be known, God is known through who and what He is not: the spirits, the gifts, myself. As such God is never localised. God is not to be located in consolation

[23] Robert, *Une autre connaissance*, 316.
[24] Robert, *Une autre connaissance*, 316.
[25] Robert, *Une autre connaissance*, 333.

or in desolation: "One would more rightly have to say then: a consolation produced itself, a desolation produced itself; God was neither in the consolation nor in the desolation; but within and through the game of this movement He lets himself be known. To grant place to God by discernment, is not to localise Him to the risk of describing Him, it is on the contrary to forbid oneself to assign to Him a place."[26]

Finally, does this indirect knowledge of God provide a personal knowledge of God, does it lead to an encounter? Playing with words in French, Robert wonders whether the Spiritual Exercises orient to *un sujet à naître*, a subject to be born, rather than to *un Dieu à connaître*, a God to be known.[27] And indeed, the subject doing the Exercises and this subject's salvation are the prime concerns of Ignatius. It is precisely while getting into a deeper relationship with himself that the subject knows God as the One who makes him know himself. Knowledge of God becomes here radically subjective, even beyond revelation: "We touch there on the originality of a knowledge that cannot be reduced to the one that God gives of himself in revelation: it is in the individuality of the subject that God lets himself be known."[28] There is thus a concomitancy of the two operations: the advent of the subject and the knowledge of God. This is the original and capital place that Ignatius grants to the subject in knowing God. For Ignatius it is the subject who meets the radical Otherness or the 'Object' to which he is subject. Both go together here, or put another way: "Nothing to do hence with the debates between subjectivism and objectivism. The link between becoming a subject and knowing God is infinitely more fundamental."[29]

Indeed, the knowledge or 'cognition' (*connaissance*) of God does not undergo any changes throughout the Exercises, so as to become a new cognition, but rather becomes a personalised 'recognition' (*reconnaissance*).

---

[26] Robert, *Une autre connaissance*, 343. Robert adds an interesting note with regard to Rahner's 'The Logic of Concrete Individual Knowledge': "Probably it is on this point that we move away the furthest from the rahnerian reading of the rules of discernment. The knowledge of God in the way of discernment is in our sensing more fundamental than Rahner lets hear. God does not content himself with speaking in consolation, he lets himself be known in the game of alternations; and man opens up to such a knowledge in discerning."

[27] Robert, *Une autre connaissance*, 358.

[28] Robert, *Une autre connaissance*, 360. Robert refers to Rahner who even talks about a private revelation ("The Logic of Concrete Individual Knowledge," 89). Indeed, also in his *Ignatius of Loyola Speaks to a Modern Jesuit* Rahner makes Ignatius remind what he said in his Reminiscences: "Were you really never shocked that I said in my report of my pilgrimage that my mystical experiences had given me such certainty of faith that it would remain unshaken even if there were no Holy Scripture?" (*Ignatius of Loyola*, 12).

[29] Robert, *Une autre connaissance*, 363.

The general affirmation of God or cognition becomes a personal finding of whom God wants to be for me, of how He creates me, or a recognition of this same God in my life. And in this way this general cognition becomes personal encounter with a Present. Robert refers here to the place of the face-to-face in Ignatian prayer, in the *colloquium* or dialogue that Ignatius suggests at the end of meditation or contemplation.[30] Neither the biblical text, nor the motions (spirits), nor even the spiritual guide accompanying nor the Church, but God himself as the Creator of his creature, is in the end the vis-à-vis of the praying subject. This is confirmed in the famous '*ad amorem*', the contemplation for attaining love, that concludes the process of the Spiritual Exercises, and where the 'Principle and Foundation' is mirrored. Its first preamble asks the retreatant: "The composition, which here is to see how I am before God Our Lord, and before the angels and the saints who intercede for me."[31] The Exercises do not lead to knowing any-thing in the end, but to bringing God to be present so that I may live my personal relation to Him. Robert concludes: "Through the attention to the motions that produce themselves in the human being, and from the handling of these thanks to discernment, it is indeed God himself who gives himself to be known. Would this form of knowledge of which regulation supplies the means – knowledge of a presence, with the help of an operation of intelligence – not show a new trail compared to the classic trails of knowledge of God?"[32]

c. God Known as Creator

We have reached the Ignatian knowledge of God – *that* God is known, but have to further ask – *how* God is known, as we did in the first part of this chapter, where we focused on Ignatius's experience of God. There we retrieved this experience in Ignatius's biography (1,a), then explored what he experienced (1,b), and finally indicated how consolation and desolation through which God is experienced meant in fact the restoration of the creational relationship that makes us to be 'of God' (1,c). In the second part, on Ignatian knowledge of God, we follow a similar path. We first outlined this knowledge of God against its contemporary spiritual, philosophical and theological background (2,a). Subsequently, we

[30] Robert, *Une autre connaissance*, 369-370.
[31] Sp. Ex. 232. We use as elsewhere the Penguin translation. Compare for different versions of the text Robert, *Une autre connaissance*, 370.
[32] Robert, *Une autre connaissance*, 373.

explored how the motions make us know God himself, up to the person-alisation of this knowledge in a Present encountered (2,b). Our final step must now be to understand theologically how God is known as the radi-cally Other by the subject, or how the human as creature meets God as his Creator in discernment.[33]

It is indeed creation, or the creational act, that appears to be Ignatius's privileged source of knowledge of God in discernment, as we noticed earlier, rather than revelation or even incarnation. The ongoing nomina-tion of God as Creator in the 'Principle and Foundation' as Valso in the rules for discernment is not a coincidence: "To speak of God as creator, is to name God as the One from whom everything proceeds, specifying furthermore the precise interpretation that we give to the verb 'to pro-ceed': in terms of creation and not of emanation. One could say thus that the God Creator is the theological version of the [philosophical] Princi-ple and supplies with a religious representation that which, for the philosopher, is a concept."[34] Robert elaborates this in three aspects.[35] God as Principle first gives us being, and makes us exist continuously. So also each and every growth or 'increase' in all that is (created), is included in the act of the 'Creator' (le 'Créateur' nous fait 'croître' aussi). Secondly, God is the One who unifies the diversity, and orders it into a 'world' in which the human being can live: when everything is ordered according to the Principle, the world is 'in order'. So to discern will be to order one's life according to the Creator. And thirdly, because everything pro-ceeds from Him, God the Creator is unique and sovereign. Therefore, Ignatius privileges the double nomination 'Creator and Lord'. We cannot occupy God's place or confuse Him with anything else or fill in his Name. Again, this is exactly what is going on in the operation of discernment.

How then can we know what can never be reached, this Principle as Principle, this Creator as Creator? The creational theology of the Exer-cises appears now to be that God as Principle is never defined or known as an object, but that knowledge of God is reached through leaving the place of the Principle to God. Robert refers here as an example to the role of Christ in the Exercises: "Christ 'who is visible' (no. 47), comes to rejoin the human being there, where the relation of creation has been

---

[33] We skip then Robert's chapters on how Ignatius renewed in his own time ('Entre union et notion') and is relevant for our time ('Connaître Dieu sans le penser?'), to stick to the chapter in between, on the Ignatian knowledge of God itself: 'Dieu connu comme créateur'.

[34] Robert, Une autre connaissance, 429.

[35] Robert, Une autre connaissance, 431-433, relying here mainly on the thinking of Stanislas Breton.

wounded, but he does not save by manifesting God as Creator, by unveiling the Principle. He does it by putting the human being back on the trail
of the correct relation of the principiated to the Principle."[36] And this is
also what is going on in discernment: it allows for a discovery of God,
not in an objective way, but as the Principle 'to be found in all things'.
This is where we discover God as 'Creator and Lord'.

But how does Ignatius further construe the encounter with the radically Other? How does he construe the difference between the human
being and God in the encounter? Ignatius does not, as do several of his
contemporaries, opt for the path of negative theology, with its figure of
the paradox and the encounter in ecstasy – the negative vocabulary about
God does not occur in the Exercises. Nor does he explore analogy, nor
does he, like Luther, underline the modification of language when terms
pass on from philosophy into theology. Ignatius opts for the *struggle* with
the enemy who darkens our gaze and hinders us from seeing the creational condition of everything, as the moment of (negative) difference.
The struggle is not with otherness (like in paradox), but with bad otherness, the enemy. "The struggle, consequently, introduces no paradoxical
dimension at all in the relation between God and man. On the contrary,
it makes clear that the difficulty is of an other order, caused not by the
difference between God and man, but by the one who confuses this difference."[37] According to Robert, Ignatius's God is not the *Deus abscon-
ditus*, not the One present as absent. For Ignatius there is only struggle,
no paradox in the difference between God and the human being. Paradox
always risks living with regret. Struggle refers to the human being's time
and world, and to his or her forces. It is there, in the area of the human
being, that for Ignatius God is known as Creator, and Ignatius thereby
pronounces an utterly positive judgment about the human condition. And
this is mirrored in the Exercises. The first of the four weeks that the Exercises take is the moment when the difference between God and *sinful*
creation has to be meditated in several ways as negative. But in the *ad
amorem*, at the end of the four weeks, when the retreatant has gone the
way of Christ's life, death and resurrection, the difference has turned into

---

[36] Robert, *Une autre connaissance*, 435.

[37] Robert, *Une autre connaissance*, 445. Indeed, in paradise – or before sin – creation
was the perfect icon of the invisible God, so there was in a way dif-ference without difference, di-stance without distance. It is strange that Robert does not refer to the figure of
the icon on these pages, for that would make very clear the difference between the dis-
figured icon that lost its paradisal beauty (of which the eminent example is marriage), and
the perfect icon Jesus Christ, but who is still the (visible) icon of the *invisible* God
(Col 1:15).

a thoroughly positive experience: "Discernment, that blooms here, makes of difference the place where God is known as giver."[38] Difference is understood here, not in the realm of concurrence (which is the sinful mis-understanding of it), nor in the realm of the disproportionate (as in the paradox), but in the realm of dialogue: it makes it possible to say "You" to the Creator, in a radically positive way that makes the paradox super-fluous as a means to protect difference.

Of this dialogue between Creator and creature, the beautiful prayer in the *ad amorem* gives witness, which is certainly the best known part of the Spiritual Exercises:

> Take, Lord, and receive all my liberty, my memory, my understanding, and my entire will, all that I have and possess. You gave it all to me; to you Lord I give it all back. All is yours, dispose of it entirely according to your will. Give me the grace to love you, for that is enough for me.[39]

---

[38] Robert, *Une autre connaissance*, 461.
[39] Sp. Ex. 234; see Saint Ignatius of Loyola, *Personal Writings*, 329.

ON THE RELATIVE UNIMPORTANCE OF RELIGIOUS EXPERIENCE IN THE EARLY SCHLEIERMACHER

JORIS GELDHOF

1. Schleiermacher's Place in the History of Theology

On several occasions, the Catholic theologian Hans Küng has indicated the important place in the history of Christian thought that Friedrich Schleiermacher holds. "A new period in Church history did not begin with Schleiermacher, as was said in a communication to the students after his death, but it did come to theological maturity in him. Here the theological paradigm shift from the Reformation to modernity virtually takes on bodily form."[1] In Schleiermacher, Küng further argues, we meet a fully modern man, who integrated the merits of modern philosophy, affirmed historical criticism and lived a life that was steeped in a fascination for modern literature, art, and social life. He was a member of the circle of the early Berlin romantics, including Friedrich Schlegel and Henriette Herz, who became his intimate friends.[2] He never regarded his Protestant Christian convictions as contradicting the realizations of modernity. This does not mean, however, that he did not face serious difficulties in trying to harmonize religion and the modern mindset. In his famous early work *On Religion: Speeches to its Cultured Despisers*,[3] first published in 1799, he was aware of the fact that most intellectuals of his age were no longer familiar with the beliefs of traditional Christianity. And if they were, they nevertheless felt uncomfortable with the social form religion had taken and the nature of the prevailing Christian apologetic. Religion in general and Christianity in particular had become weary. The dominant and repressive power of the Church in the domain of personal life, the appeal to incomprehensible propositions and immoral stories in order to defend its truth claims and the unclear relationship

---

[1] Hans Küng, *Great Christian Thinkers* (London: SCM Press, 1994) 161.

[2] For all biographical data I refer to Kurt Nowak, *Schleiermacher: Leben, Werk, Wirkung* (Göttingen: Vandenhoeck und Ruprecht, 2001).

[3] We will exclusively make use of the 2002 reprint of the second edition of Crouter's excellent English translation: Friedrich D.E. Schleiermacher, *On Religion: Speeches to its Cultured Despisers*, trans. and ed. Richard Crouter, Cambridge Texts in the History of Philosophy (Cambridge: Cambridge University Press, 1996).

between ecclesiastical and secular authorities gnawed at the plausibility of Christianity.

This was the context in which Schleiermacher emerged, a man who saw "it as his almost prophetic mission, his divine calling, to bring religion to bear in a completely new way, for to him as a critical thinker religion, despite all his personal objections to particular doctrines, [was] anything but a 'neglected subject'; it [was] virtually the content and guiding light of his life. He [wanted] to introduce it both to those contemporaries who [had] completely succumbed to the earthly and sensual and to those who speculate[d] and moralize[d] over empty ideas."[4] Indeed, *On Religion* seeks to locate the essence of religion elsewhere, to move beyond either pure immanence or materiality, beyond dry metaphysical speculation about the supernatural or ethical systems and common moral behavior.

In Küng's eyes, the question of the essence of religion is at the heart of Schleiermacher's emergence as the paradigmatic representative of modern theology. According to Schleiermacher, the specific nature of religion is an intuition of the universe, one which resists both theoretical and practical systematization. In taking this position, Schleiermacher accomplished the (Kantian) Copernican turn to subjectivity within theology. Schleiermacher sought a stable basis for Christian faith, one uncontaminated by an excess of either rationality or morality. He found it in the purity of man's specific relation with his surroundings. In all this, the Kantian terminology must have attracted attention.

The philosophical influence of Immanuel Kant on Schleiermacher's thought is indeed enormous, something which is noted in almost every general introduction to Schleiermacher. It is a fact that, before the publication of *On Religion*, he critically commented on Kant's moral philosophy.[5] During his whole life, however, the heritage and impact of Kant's epistemology continued to operate, preventing him from falling back into traditional theistic thinking. Reflecting on this connection between a famous philosopher and an important theologian, Küng makes a remarkable but not entirely surprising claim regarding Schleiermacher's influence on nineteenth and twentieth century theology: "There is no denying that no theologian was to give such a boost to the history, phenomenology, and psychology of religion which was to develop so strongly: no

---

[4] Hans Küng, *Christianity: Its Essence and History* (London: SCM Press, 1995) 696-697.

[5] Hans-Olof Kvist, "Kants praktische Philosophie in den Jugendmanuskripten Schleiermachers: Einige kritisch-grundsätzliche Gesichtspunkte zur Kant-Rezeption des jungen Schleiermachers," *200 Jahre Reden über die Religion: Akten des 1. Internationalen Kongresses der Schleiermacher-Gesellschaft (Halle, 14.-17. März 1999)*, ed. Ulrich Barth and Claus-Dieter Osthövener (Berlin and New York, NY: Walter de Gruyter, 2000) 383-396.

theologian worked it out intellectually to such a degree as Schleiermacher. If there is still so much talk of *experience* in religious studies and theology this is essentially because of Schleiermacher."[6]

Yet another theologian from a different denominational background has arrived at almost the same judgment: George A. Lindbeck. In his 1984 book, *The Nature of Doctrine*, he considers Schleiermacher as the founder or forefather of the "experiential expressivist" approach to religion. In contrast to what Lindbeck describes as 'propositionalism' and his own 'cultural-linguistic' approach, the current of thought attributed to Schleiermacher emphasizes the experience-orientated dimension of religion. According to Lindbeck, this approach regards doctrines as mere non-discursive symbols expressing inner religious feelings. It has no interest in the rational content of religion, it is not useful in ecumenical discourse and it cannot deal with the variability and the plurality of religion, because it stubbornly holds to its conviction that there exists something like a universal religious experience. According to Lindbeck, religion "need not be described as something universal arising from within the depths of individuals and diversely and inadequately objectified in particular faiths".[7] Therefore, "it seems implausible to claim that religions are diverse objectifications of the same basic experience".[8]

It is interesting to note that Lindbeck too refers to Kant in the context of his description of the philosophical origins of experiential expressivism.[9] Historically, he argues, this approach is a rather recent phenomenon, for, in theology, it is reducible to Schleiermacher, who did not start reflecting in a vacuum. He understood the signs of his time and integrated contemporary cultural, philosophical and literary tendencies in his thought. In Lindbeck's view, the "experiential tradition" goes behind Schleiermacher to Kant, the enlightened thinker who developed a fundamental critique on the traditional proofs for God's existence in his *Critique of Pure Reason*. Kant definitively rejected the classical propositionalist theories, which took the reality of supernatural claims for granted. Moreover, he accomplished the 'Copernican' turn to subjectivity by radicalizing the centrality of the human subject, a notion which had been present in western philosophy since Descartes. Within the framework of his transcendental philosophy, Kant understood that reality should be sub-

---

[6] Küng, *Christianity*, 703; *Great Christian Thinkers*, 170.
[7] George A. Lindbeck, *The Nature of Doctrine: Religion and Theology in a Postliberal Age* (Philadelphia, PA: The Westminster Press, 1984) 40.
[8] Lindbeck, *The Nature of Doctrine*, 41.
[9] Lindbeck, *The Nature of Doctrine*, 20-21.

jected to the cognitive structures of human reason, like the accused to his judge, and not the other way round. By doing this, Kant created the possibility for human beings to take their place at the center of the universe, even in those systems which are less reason-orientated. And this is exactly what happens in Schleiermacher's theology.

It seems probable that both Küng's and Lindbeck's judgments about the meaning of Schleiermacher's thought are influenced by Karl Barth. Küng's doctoral dissertation was devoted to Barth's theology of justification, and he makes no attempt to hide his personal affiliation with his fellow Swiss theologian.[10] Lindbeck's manifest Protestantism is also often associated with Barthian influences.[11] Like Barth, Lindbeck resists subjectivism in theological reflection.[12] Barth developed his own theology in direct confrontation with Schleiermacher's and, by extension, with the whole tradition of liberal theology in the nineteenth and twentieth centuries that began with him. According to Barth, the starting point and deepest motivation for theology has nothing to do with human achievements, efforts or interests (thus Barth's reproach to liberal theology). Theology must begin with the Word of God as revelation and with its witnesses in scripture. Theology should not be corrupted by philosophy and hence by too much analysis of human experience, for ultimately this makes God's free will and revelation dependent upon outer – and ultimately irrelevant – factors.

All significant features of Küng's and Lindbeck's presentations of Schleiermacher's thought can be observed in Barth's treatment of the 'church father of the nineteenth century', as he elaborated this in his *Protestant Theology in the Nineteenth Century*. Firstly, there is respect for the undeniably important role of Schleiermacher in the history not only of theology, but of western Christianity as well. It is clear for Barth that we possibly still do not have overcome his dominant influence. Barth recognized in Schleiermacher "our man of destiny", the greatness of whom "possibly consists in the indissoluble unity of his timeless individual power on the one hand, and on the other of the temporal, historical conditions into which he was placed".[13] Secondly, Barth acknowledges

---

[10] See e.g. Küng, *Great Christian Thinkers*, 193 and 206.

[11] See e.g. David Tracy, "Lindbeck's New Program for Theology: A Reflection," *The Thomist* 49 (1985) 465: "As his frequent references to Barth … make clear, Lindbeck's substantive theological position is a methodologically sophisticated version of Barthian confessionalism. The hands may be the hands of Wittgenstein and Geertz but the voice is the voice of Karl Barth."

[12] Lindbeck, *The Nature of Doctrine*, 24 and 135.

[13] Karl Barth, *Protestant Theology in the Nineteenth Century: Its Background and History* (London: SCM Press, ²1972) 426.

that Schleiermacher was and wanted to be a modern man in all aspects of life. This means not only that he had an enormous interest in what was going on in society and culture, but also that he tried to affirm cultural development. Consequently Barth evaluates his theology as pure 'cultural theology', thereby suggesting that Schleiermacher's theological activities were rather peripheral to the whole of his philosophical and literary interests. Thirdly, Barth discerns in Schleiermacher's intellectual heritage a strong anti-dogmatism and anti-intellectualism. For Schleiermacher did not construct his theology on a solid basis of unshakable rational convictions and propositions. As an epigone of the romantics, who had been formed by the community of the Moravian Brethren, he centered his thought around the bipolar tension of 'experience' and 'history'. Therefore, Schleiermacher's attention for individual feelings, affections and emotions comes as no surprise.

Barth interprets all of these elements in a negative fashion. He holds Schleiermacher responsible for several pernicious (and even deplorable) shifts in theological reflection. According to Barth, these included the turn from theocentrism to anthropocentrism, and the replacement of 'Gospel', 'Word of God' and 'Christ' by 'religion' and 'piety' – all of which amounted to a betrayal of the spirit of the Reformation. The dependence of theology on the analysis of human consciousness ultimately results in the abandonment of the necessary condition for all theology, because "there was in fact no need for the Copernican conception of the universe to acquire the significance of a command that theology should in future be anthropocentric theology".[14]

2. Schleiermacher as Alleged Experientialist

Is the widely-held view that Schleiermacher's theology is purely subjectivist and experientialist really justified? Is Schleiermacher really the initiator of a restricted focus on human conscience in theology? Does he undermine traditional conceptions of the core of Christianity by rendering theological reflection more person-orientated? Does his experientialism mean that he overlooks other constitutive elements of religion? Is religious experience, in his view, an affair of the individual, and therefore suspicious, dangerous or threatening? Is religious experience really as important for him as Küng, Lindbeck, and Barth suggest?

[14] Barth, *Protestant Theology*, 459.

In order to be able to answer this cluster of questions, it is first necessary to develop a workable definition of religious experience. We recall
that our conversation partners Küng, Lindbeck, and Barth emphasize both
the individual and the universal dimensions of such experience. They
regard it as something which happens to individual persons in all times,
cultures and contexts, something which displays few variations with
respect to content, and something which is difficult to communicate with
others. In this sense, their view is in continuity with a generally accepted
view on experience, which "is easily thought of as a stream of private
events, known only to their possessor, and bearing at best problematic
relationships to any other events, such as happenings in an external world
or similar streams in other possessors. The stream makes up the conscious life of the possessor."[15] Such a view might easily lead one to
regard experience as an immediate source of knowledge of reality, albeit
one which is impervious to external testing. It is, however, clear that
experience could not be what it is without a dynamic interplay with interpretation. And it is the element of interpretation which opens up the possibility of both communication and critique. "*All* experience, on this view,
involves interpretation, and it is thus senseless to suppose any unvar-
nished, direct acquaintance with the given. But since it would be equally
senseless to suppose an interpretation with nothing to interpret, it is com-
monly admitted that an 'epistemic' given must nonetheless be present in
experience, though impossible to view independently, since this would
ipso facto be to construe it in some fashion under the auspices of
thought."[16] It will be an important task for us to examine how Schleiermacher thinks about this tension between experience and interpretation.

Up until now, we have only thematized the more general category of
'experience'. We have not yet said anything about its qualification as
'religious'. This is because we take the view that religious experience is
nothing special, in the sense of alien to experience as such.[17] It, too, concerns the way in which human beings learn something about the external
world. In our contribution, therefore, we shall not take into account the
empiricist theory of the sciences, which has narrowed the conception of
'experience' to simple sense perception and which regards this as the
basis for all rationally-justified knowledge (thereby leaving no room for

[15] *The Oxford Dictionary of Philosophy*, ed. Simon Blackburn (Oxford and New York,
NY: Oxford University Press, 1994) 130.

[16] *The Encyclopedia of Philosophy*, ed. Paul Edwards, vol. II (New York, NY and London: MacMillan, 1967) 157.

[17] We will not pay any attention to this opinion, although it has been defended by some
thinkers.

specifically 'religious' experience). Nevertheless, religious experience does go beyond the ordinary understanding of experience as "familiarity with some matter of practical concern, based on repeated past acquaintance or performance".[18]

In this regard, it is worth recalling the thought of Antoon Vergote, who draws our attention to the fact that 'religious experience' is a fairly recent concept in the history of ideas. "The term 'religious experience' is an inheritance from the theories dating from the beginning of the twentieth century; theories which sought to explain the origins of religion and to justify their truth and value as founded in an original and emotional form of knowledge."[19] This does however not "mean that the background reality could not have existed at a time in which it had not yet been given a name".[20] Indeed, in Schleiermacher's texts, the term 'experience' (*Erfahrung*) is not a common one, especially not in connection with the term 'religious'. In *On Religion* it is mentioned only a few times and might, therefore, be described as a rather marginal term. Moreover, it occurs in contexts where the most fundamental issues concerning religion are not at stake.[21]

However, this terminological clarification alone does not establish the relative unimportance of 'religious experience' in the early Schleiermacher. The notion does play an unmistakable role in his description of the essence of religion as an intuition of the universe. It is our task to look at this conception more closely. Before we do that, however, we will attempt to complete our quest for an adequate definition of religious experience. Our guide here will be Vergote, and we will use his insights to clarify our reading of Schleiermacher.

Vergote undeniably affirms the subjective character of religious experience: "Religious experience ... refers to immediate impressions, but

---

[18] *The Encyclopedia of Philosophy*, 2:156.

[19] Antoon Vergote, *Religion, Belief and Unbelief: A Psychological Study* (Leuven, Amsterdam, and Atlanta, GA: Leuven University Press and Rodopi, 1997) 134.

[20] Vergote, *Religion, Belief and Unbelief*, 135.

[21] *Erfahrung* (experience) appears exactly six times in the first edition of *On Religion*: three times in the plural form and three times in singular; one time in the first speech (p. 8/14), three times in the second (p. 33/58 and p. 42/76), one time in the fourth (p. 98/176) and one time in the fifth (p. 165/294). It is never qualified by *religiöse* (religious) and seems to refer to a set of inner states of mind. Schleiermacher is using the word very spontaneously, so that one might be sure about the common evidence the term had for his audience. We refer to the handsome German edition of Hans-Joachim Rothert: Friedrich D.E. Schleiermacher, *Über die Religion: Reden an die Gebildeten unter ihren Verächtern*, Philosophische Bibliothek, 255 (Hamburg: Felix Meiner, 1970), but in order to be able to look up these passages easily in the *Kritische Gesamtausgabe* we have added the original pagination.

the descriptions witnesses give are so diverse that we may well wonder if they have anything at all in common. The commonality, the immediacy of the impressions, however, clearly points to the central role of the subject in his or her subjectivity. The experience occurs in private intimacy. Moreover, the language in which it is expressed demonstrates that it is brought about in or through the emotions."[22] Corresponding with this subjective core, Vergote distinguishes five modalities of religious experience – some of which will appear to be relevant in our discussion about Schleiermacher's conception. Vergote does not limit himself to the mystical-affective experiences, visions and private revelations, which are mostly thought of as representative of religious experience. He also stresses the intuitive, stable and habitual character of religious experience, its radically changing but enduring force in personal life after an unexpected discovery, and its cognitive operationality in the sense of "a retrospective and synthetic understanding of the intimate and specific identity of an object, a practice or a person".[23] Of course, not all modalities can occur at the same time. They are five possibilities by which religious experience is expressed. According to Vergote, Schleiermacher's understanding of religious experience is not dominated by "ecstatic experiences", but rather by "the general human emotion which, it was believed, inspired all religion".[24] In what follows, we shall inquire whether and to what extent Vergote's assertion is accurate.

Before we turn to Schleiermacher, however, we must further delimit our inquiry. Clearly, it is beyond the scope of this paper to provide a comprehensive discussion of Schleiermacher's entire oeuvre. We shall therefore limit ourselves to *On Religion: Speeches to its Cultured Despisers* (1799), which is generally considered to be Schleiermacher's main early work. It represents the first time that he dealt with religion and Christianity so compactly, so originally and so systematically,[25] that we may feel broadening our conclusions regarding the five speeches to the 'early' Schleiermacher as such. Moreover, according to Barth, there is a definite continuity of the early Schleiermacher and the later one. The general theological intuitions that he first formulated in *On Religion* are found again in the famous description of the essence of religion in the introduction of his mature

---

[22] Vergote, *Religion, Belief and Unbelief*, 127.

[23] Vergote, *Religion, Belief and Unbelief*, 132.

[24] Vergote, *Religion, Belief and Unbelief*, 142. Schleiermacher appears in Vergote's text in his discussion of Rudolph Otto's theory of religious experience.

[25] By this characterization we try to do justice to the literary form of *On Religion* as speeches. It will further become clear that, in our interpretation, the rhetorical element is extremely important.

dogmatic work *The Christian Faith* of 1821/22. There he offers his short-
est definition of religion, namely, "the feeling of utter dependence".[26]
It seems reasonable, therefore, to accept the parameters we have suggested.
Nevertheless, we shall not seek to extend our conclusions to the whole
work. Instead, we shall attempt to find indications that religious experience is not as important as it is often thought to be. In our view, religious
experience in the early Schleiermacher must be related to several contexts, which require that we take a more nuanced view of the importance
which is all too often attributed to it by, among others, Küng, Barth, and
Lindbeck. The following paragraphs are therefore to be read as contextu-
alizations of the notion of religious experience as it occurs in *On Religion*.

3. Religious Experience in a Determinate Historical Context

First of all, it should be made clear that in *On Religion* religious experience is not conceived of as a certain universally occurring phenomenon
detached from any historical setting or context. Schleiermacher is strongly
aware of the indispensability, inevitability and necessity of a background
against which every single religious experience takes place. Therefore, it
is unfair to suggest that it forms a stable basis upon which a religious tradition rests as its one and only legitimate foundation – as Lindbeck is
apparently doing.[27] Religious experiences always refer to determinate sit-
uations, which can be approached from a variety of angles, i.e., socio-
logical, juridical, philosophical, linguistic, psychological, and historical.
In this sense, one could argue that Schleiermacher's thought comes surprisingly close to Lindbeck's allegedly original cultural-linguistic
approach to religion. Lindbeck's approach is an attempt to recognize the
external influences on religion. He emphasizes the surrounding elements
to such a degree that he sometimes seems to forget the active dimension
of becoming familiar with a religious tradition. In any case, the question
of where religion is – ideally – to be found, is answered by Schleiermacher in a very Lindbeckian way: "Guard yourself against both; you will

---

[26] Barth, *Protestant Theology*, 449. For the more elaborated standpoint of Barth concerning the continuity of Schleiermacher's early and later work, I refer to the text of the
lectures that he gave in 1923-24: Karl Barth, *Die Theologie Schleiermachers: Vorlesung
Göttingen Wintersemester 1923-24*, ed. Dietrich Ritschl, Karl Barth Gesamtausgabe II, 5
(Zürich: Theologischer Verlag, 1978) especially 435-463.
[27] Lindbeck, *The Nature of Doctrine*, 39-41.

find the spirit of a religion, not among rigid systematizers or superficial indifferentists, but among those who live in it as their element and move ever further in it without nurturing the illusion that they are able to embrace it completely."[28] Religion and religious experiences are understood most adequately from within, and that means in relation to a certain historical context.

Moreover, Schleiermacher himself is by the way very explicit in his view of the relation between religion and history. In the second speech of *On Religion* he unambiguously states: "History, in the most proper sense, is the highest object of religion. It begins and ends with religion – for in religion's eyes prophecy is also history, and the two are not to be distinguished from one another – and at all times all true history has first had a religious purpose and proceeded from religious ideas. In its realm, therefore, lies also the highest and most sublime intuitions of religion."[29] One of the reasons why Schleiermacher is emphasizing this point so conspicuously is to be found with his distinction between history and nature. He regards all kinds of so-called natural religion with suspicion. Religion is not to be found in matter outside us, but it is rooted in an incomparably unique moment in the history of humankind or in the individual history of one's personal life. Religion and religious life always refer to that mysterious moment of coming into contact with a special dimension of the universe – or with the divine, as Schleiermacher expressed it later.[30] The distrust of a natural (or philosophical) religion is also an indicator of the fact that Schleiermacher was already thinking beyond an Enlightenment point of view. Against the fascination of many enlightened thinkers with a naturally obtained religion, he claims that every religion necessarily starts with a positive fact: "The essence of natural religion actually consists wholly in the negation of everything positive and characteristic in religion and in the most violent polemic against it. Thus natural religion is also the worthy product of an age whose hobbyhorse was a lamentable generality and an empty sobriety, which, more than everything else, works against true cultivation in all things. There are two things that

---

[28] Schleiermacher, *On Religion*, 113.

[29] Schleiermacher, *On Religion*, 42.

[30] In the later editions of Schleiermacher, *On Religion* (1806, 1821 and 1831) a tendency can be discerned to use by preference 'God' and 'the divine' instead of 'the universe'. Cf. Meckenstock's introduction to the volume of the *Kritische Gesamtausgabe* of Schleiermacher's work, in which these versions are published: Friedrich D.E. Schleiermacher, *Über die Religion* (2.-) 4. Auflage, ed. Günter Meckenstock, KGA I, 12 (Berlin and New York, NY: Walter de Gruyter, 1995). This will not be the only terminological change that we mention.

they especially hate: They do not want to begin with anything extraordinary or incomprehensible, and whatever they might be and do is in no way supposed to smack of a school. … So their bristling against the positive and voluntary is simultaneously a bristling against everything definite and real. If a specific religion is not supposed to begin with a fact, it cannot begin at all; for there must be a basis, and it can only be a subjective one for why something is brought forth and placed in the center; and if a religion is not supposed to be a specific one, then it is not religion at all, but merely loose, unrelated material."[31]

Another reason why Schleiermacher stresses the role of history in the area of religion is the fact that an historical vision warrants the essential vitality of a religion. Religion is a developing, flexible and dynamic reality moving through history in the fashion of a vehicle moving on a trip through the most variegated landscapes. Religion is normally able to adapt itself to all possible circumstances. Moreover, when it does not make any effort to accommodate itself, it becomes a rigid system that in the long term is to be doomed to die.[32] According to him, "religious people are thoroughly historical".[33] 'People' here refers to living human beings, people like you and me, not a mere abstraction. Schleiermacher describes in almost psychological terms the all-too-human tendency to refer to important past events in one's personal life, especially when religion is concerned. This attention for the concrete, so to speak, is the only guarantee for vitality and flexibility in religion. When religion is alien to people's life, it loses its relevance and its meaning. For this reason, Schleiermacher felt very strongly that religion should be freed from fixed structures and from general – and therefore repressive – enactments. This was a view which he shared with his audience of cultured despisers of religion.

Schleiermacher's attention to the historically concrete is probably best reflected in the way in which he depicted his own age. The simple fact that he preferred to write speeches, not letters or treatises, can be interpreted as supporting the claim that every standpoint in the history of humankind

---

[31] Schleiermacher, *On Religion*, 110.

[32] Schleiermacher strongly dislikes 'systems', which becomes clear when he rejects the possibility of systematizing different original intuitions of the universe in the second speech: "A system of intuitions? Can you imagine anything stranger? Do views, especially views of the infinite, allow themselves to be brought into a system?" (*On Religion*, 26). Of course, these rhetorical questions have to be answered negatively. In the first speech, too, he expresses his disapproval of systems: "In all these systems you despise, you have accordingly not found religion and cannot find it because it is not there" (*On Religion*, 13). In the fifth speech he mentions "the principle of building systems and sects that is so completely opposed to the spirit of religion" (*On Religion*, 101).

[33] Schleiermacher, *On Religion*, 112.

is irreducible and unique. It was not his aim to write about eternal or ever-lasting truths; he wanted to communicate his ideas concerning religion to a specific type of addressee. Therefore, one cannot speak meaningfully about *On Religion* without taking into account its literary form.

Already at the beginning of the speeches, Schleiermacher is looking for his own position in confrontation with his audience. He describes how he was introduced to religious affairs and how he became familiar with the theme. He is convinced that his audience is the right one with which to exchange ideas: "If I am so permeated by religion that I must finally speak and bear witness to it,[34] to whom shall I turn with this matter other than to you? Where else would there be listeners for my speech? It is not blind partiality for my native soil or for my companions in disposition and language that makes me speak thus, but the deep conviction that you are the only ones capable, and thus also worthy, of having the sense for holy and divine things aroused in you."[35] So he seems willing to do two things. On the one hand, he tries to understand and to situate the arguments against religion as social and spiritual phenomenon which were current among the intellectuals of his age. On the other hand, he seeks to persuade them of the meaningfulness of religion in general, and of Christianity in particular. Indeed, although the text does not contain much specifically theological or Christian vocabulary, it is Schleiermacher's wish to lead the cultured despisers, "as it were, to the God who has become flesh".[36]

At different moments in the course of the five speeches, Schleiermacher portrays the age in which he lived. His attitude towards it is twofold: on the one hand, he accepts most of its contemporary cultural and philo-sophical presuppositions; on the other hand, he shows himself to be crit-ical of its attitude towards religion, especially when religion is interfered with by domains foreign to it. The independence of religion seems to be his key issue, so that his plea for the original autonomy of a plurality of irreducible and authentic intuitions of the universe is completely in line with this major concern. Schleiermacher explicitly contends that he does

---

[34] In Schleiermacher's *On Religion*, the idea is developed that, once one has had an original intuition of the universe, it is impossible to deny it. So to bear witness to one's own religion is not as noncommittal as it seems to be here. It makes one take the floor, because an unexpectedly strong willingness to speak publicly and to let people know what one has experienced, is working in the soul. Elsewhere, Schleiermacher states: "That I speak does not originate from a rational decision or from hope or fear, nor does it happen in accord with some final purpose or for some arbitrary or accidental reason. It is the inner, irresistible necessity of my nature; it is a divine calling; it is that which determines my place in the universe and makes me the being I am" (*On Religion*, 5).

[35] Schleiermacher, *On Religion*, 9.

[36] Schleiermacher, *On Religion*, 96.

not want to look down on the mentality of his age;[37] otherwise his contemporaries would not give him their earnest attention. He does take the arguments of his audience against religion seriously,[38] strongly believing "that our age is no less propitious for religion than any other".[39] Thus one can hardly say that Schleiermacher was a cultural pessimist. This does not mean, however, that he is reluctant to make telling critical remarks. So, for instance, he objects to widespread superstition in the society of his day: "I grant there is more support in this society for understanding or belief and for action and observance of customs than for intuition and feeling and that, therefore, however enlightened its doctrine may be, this society always verges on superstition and clings to some kind of mythology; but you will admit that it is so much the more removed from true religion."[40]

What does Schleiermacher's tendency to connect religion and history tell us about religious experience? His speeches make clear that such experience is undeniably embedded in a determinate historical context, without which it makes no sense at all. Consequently, it is wrong to assume that Schleiermacher postulated something like a clearly discernible, culture-independent and universal religious experience, which might be described, in vague terms, as contact with (dimensions of) transcendence.

4. Religious Experience and Religious Community

In the previous section, we pointed out that the historical context is a necessary constituent of religious experience. Let us now turn our attention

---

[37] Schleiermacher, *On Religion*, 19: "Do not, therefore, be indignant and explain it as disdain for the present if, for the sake of clarity, I frequently lead you back to those more childlike times where, in a less perfected state, everything was still distinct and individual. If I begin at once with that theme, and in some way or other meticulously come back to it, this is to warn you emphatically about the confusion of religion with things that sometimes look similar to it and with which you will everywhere find it mixed."

[38] Schleiermacher even encourages his audience to further develop its critique: "Look there, the goal of your present highest endeavors is at the same time the resurrection of religion! It is your efforts that must bring about this event, and I celebrate you as the rescuers and guardians of religion, even though unintentionally so. Do not retreat from your posts and your works until you have unlocked the innermost element of knowledge and, in priestly humility, opened the sanctuary of true science where, to everyone who enters and even to the sons of religion, everything is replaced that superficial knowledge and arrogant boasting caused them to lose" (*On Religion*, 70). And in the last sentence of the third speech, Schleiermacher mentions the "imperishability" of their merit (*On Religion*, 71). Of course, these are excellent passages with which to demonstrate Schleiermacher's rhetorical skills.

[39] Schleiermacher, *On Religion*, 66.

[40] Schleiermacher, *On Religion*, 82.

to the (necessary) link between such experience and the religious community. All too often, the latter aspect has been neglected and misunderstood. Although certain currents within liberal theology seem to overemphasize the individual character of religious experience, this is not Schleiermacher's view. Hans Küng rightly observes that: "If religion is no longer understood as mere private religion but in communal terms, this again is largely due to Schleiermacher."[41] Indeed, for Schleiermacher, every religious experience is embedded in a particular community. As we will argue, the simple fact of being affected by the universe, i.e. of having an original religious experience, implies that one participates in a community. The nature of this very specific community might be problematic, confusing or simply reprehensible, because Schleiermacher hardly gives satisfying information about it. But it cannot be denied that Schleiermacher defended the importance of a religious community in the bosom of which every religious experience occurs.

This conclusion is not immediately evident, however. We shall have to establish it by a particular line of argument. In the 1799 edition of *On Religion* Schleiermacher does not thematize the social environment of those who are affected by the universe as explicitly as one might have wished.[42] We should namely not be misled by his assertions concerning the religious community that is constituted by those who have already had a religious experience. These people participate in a particular community, which, as we indicated, might be problematic or reprehensible. But what of those people who do share in the life of any community? These people are ordinary women and men, living in a particular culture, in a determinate society, at a specific time and in a specific place. They can actively participate in the religious life of a determinate tradition, but this is not essential, since everybody can be affected by the universe and thereby have a religious experience: "A person is born with the religious capacity as with every other, and if only his sense is not forcibly suppressed, if only that communion between a person and the universe – these are admittedly the poles of religion – is not blocked and barricaded, then religion would have to develop unerringly in each person according to his own individual manner."[43] Religion is something essentially free

---

[41] Küng, *Great Christian Thinkers*, 170; *Christianity*, 703.

[42] We are not suggesting that he did so in later editions, but we are reminded of the fact that he later on significantly changed the fourth speech, which is our most important source concerning this issue.

[43] Schleiermacher, *On Religion*, 59. Again, in this quotation, we can discern Schleiermacher's criticism towards the spirit and mentality of his time. But this is not what we are wanting to indicate here.

for Schleiermacher, something that never can be forced, without losing its authenticity and its meaning. It communicates itself by means of a totally free spirit that cannot be manipulated. Of course, this implies that authentic religion will probably not occur in everyone's life, because all too often religion is contaminated by factors such as moral or philosophical considerations, power and social institutions.[44] Nevertheless, with a view to our argument, we may assume that Schleiermacher certainly took account of the social surroundings of people who are about to have a religious experience in the near future. He was aware of the specificity of every (social) context in which people live – as we argued above – and he excluded nobody from the possibility of being originally affected by the universe. Hence, everyone who experiences the universe in an original way is part of a determinate community, without which he or she would never have had that particular (kind of) experience.

Another consideration supports our line of reasoning. We now take as our starting point those people who have recently had a religious experience. Schleiermacher describes the fundamentally anthropological fact that people want to communicate their experiences. He seems to suggest that one not only feels an urge to tell people about the strange reality by which one has been affected, but that this original experience contains in itself an irresistible urge to be expressed. To discern the beginnings of one's own religious life is by no means an easy task. It is an inherent consequence of the experience itself, the grounds of which remain hidden in the mystery of the encounter with the divine. At the beginning of the fourth speech, he writes: "Once there is religion, it must necessarily also be social. That not only lies in human nature, but also is preeminently in the nature of religion. You must admit that it is highly unnatural for a person to want to lock up in himself what he has created and worked out."[45] Schleiermacher even adds something like an anthropological law, in that "the more passionately something moves him [i.e. a person], and the more intimately it penetrates his being, the stronger is the urge also to glimpse its power outside himself in others, in order to prove to himself that he has encountered nothing other than what is human".[46]

So we discover religion to be necessarily social, although personal religious experiences seem to belong to the strictly individual realm. This

---

[44] Throughout the whole work, but most conspicuously in the second speech, Schleiermacher attempts to clearly distinguish religion from metaphysics and ethics. And above all in the fourth speech, he shows his disdain for the state's involvement in religious affairs.

[45] Schleiermacher, *On Religion*, 73.

[46] Schleiermacher, *On Religion*, 73.

could indicate a contradiction, but do we find plausible arguments sustaining the suspicion that Schleiermacher is negligent or inconsistent? Let us, therefore, have a look at Schleiermacher's further reflections on the religious community formed by those who once experienced the immediate affectivity of the divine. In order to attain a proper view of this issue, it is necessary to introduce the distinction that Schleiermacher makes concerning the 'true church' and the 'mass church'. The true church is constituted by those individuals who have already had an experience of intuiting the universe. Apparently, these women and men know automatically what the communal consequences of their experience are. They become members of "a band of brothers", "a choir of friends" or "an academy of priests"[47] for whom religion is the highest good and the centre of their lives. They do not need to be introduced to any aspect of religion, because they intimately know what it means to live from it, in it and for it. They are steeped in a deep sense of the universe and they are much more the communicators of (their) religion than those to whom religion's secrets and mysteries need to be communicated. It would appear that their solidarity, based as it is on mutual understanding, makes them absolutely tolerant towards one another. Laws, rules or imperatives are completely foreign to them, because they have interiorized something more profound than the most meaningful moral obligation can ever express.

It comes as no surprise that the mass churches are far removed from this ideal. Schleiermacher says: "I presented you a society of those who have become conscious of their religion and for whom the religious view of life has become one of the dominant ones. Since I hope to have convinced you that such people must have some cultivation and much strength and that, therefore, there can always be only very few of them, you must certainly not seek their union where many hundreds are assembled in great temples and where their song already shocks your ear from afar; you certainly know that people of this type do not stand so closely to one another."[48] Schleiermacher unmistakably expresses his disdain for mass churches, but he is aware of some anthropological standards too. According to him, human reality is such that structures, organizations and unambiguous agreements are essential. People need to be guided and educated; differences between teachers and pupils, leaders and followers

---

[47] Schleiermacher, *On Religion*, 94. Through the course of his speeches, Schleiermacher uses other terms for this kind of community too. Just like it is the case with these ones, they mostly evoke a rather closed group of 'haves', the secrets of which cannot be shared with the 'have nots'.

[48] Schleiermacher, *On Religion*, 78.

are therefore necessary. All these relations are bound to finitude, and hence marked by shortcomings. No human organization will ever be free from corruption, and the Church is no exception. She is certainly not the only human association in which instruction does not play any role.[49]

The distinction between the true Church and the mass churches is essential to the correct understanding of Schleiermacher's thought. The true religion is something exclusively for the happy few,[50] although Schleiermacher clearly asserts that this religious elite, as it were, does not coincide with an intellectual or a moral one.[51] His fascination for this particular elitism probably sprouts from the general Romantic fascination for genius or the virtuoso.[52] He knows, however, that it is not realistic to expect everyone to have religious experience in the very specific sense which he accords to this notion. When he is describing the community of those who participate in the true Church, he has an ideal in mind, the characteristics of which originate from beyond real society and culture. On the other hand, when he is depicting real states of affairs in the church, he is working with conceptual standards, which are taken from contemporary critics and from Enlightenment thought. Indeed, Schleiermacher shares many points of critique with the cultured despisers of religion whom he is addressing.[53] Nevertheless, the individual who has such a religious experience cannot be compared to the individual without it, certainly not as far as their belonging to the church is concerned. This means that Schleiermacher must employ two different discourses: an ideal, philosophical one and an ordinary, real and phenomenal one. One needs to be very attentive to this double-layered approach when one reads *On Religion*. One thing is certain, however: Schleiermacher does not conceive of religious experience as detached from religious community.

---

[49] Schleiermacher, *On Religion*, 81: "Or shall religion be the sole human affair in which there are no institutions for the benefit of pupils and novices?" Of course, this rhetorical question must be answered negatively.

[50] See e.g. Schleiermacher, *On Religion*, 84: "The true Church would quietly have separated out again in order to enjoy the more intimate and higher fellowship of which the others were not capable."

[51] Schleiermacher, *On Religion*, 66: "The extent and truth of intuition depend on the sharpness and breadth of one's sense, and the wisest person without sensibility is no nearer to religion than the most foolish who has a proper view."

[52] Throughout the text Schleiermacher regularly uses expressions like "religious virtuosos" or "heroes of religion".

[53] The most important and remarkable of these points is undoubtedly the requirement of the separation between church and state. In the 1799 and 1806 editions of *On Religion*, his critique on the intermingling of both (which is mostly a contamination by the state) is incredibly sharp.

5. Religious Experience and Objective Realities

In this section we will attempt to refute the bias against Schleiermacher's concept of religious experience as a purely subjective affectedness by relating it to a third field of interest, a cluster of what we call 'objective realities'. These elements are not at all forgotten in *On Religion*. Our concern here is to identify them and to place them into a proper perspective, in order to do justice to Schleiermacher's intentions. It is simply not conceivable that he appealed exclusively to the personal emotions of his well-educated audience. It is our conviction that he would not have been heard (and that he would certainly not have had to reedit his text more than once), if he had dealt with religion only in sentimental terms. His discourse is filled with arguments; it is the fruit of a thoroughgoing reflection, not of an upwelling of emotions.[54] In what follows, we attend to his view on dogmas and on holy books. But we will begin with an important consideration of Schleiermacher himself regarding the interplay of subject and object in the constitution of the essence of religion.

Louis Dupré rightly observes that "whatever one may think of the appropriateness of the term 'feeling' to describe the religious experience, Schleiermacher certainly intends something other than pure subjectivity".[55] And he continues: "A closer analysis of the religious experience, as described by Schleiermacher, will show that although feeling has a subjective connotation, strictly speaking, it is not more subjective than objective, since it belongs to a stage of consciousness in which subject and object are still basically identical."[56] Schleiermacher himself maintains

---

[54] This can be demonstrated by biographical data. Schleiermacher wrote the five speeches as an answer to a challege of some of his best friends. In November 1797, at the occasion of a surprise birthday party for him, Henriette Herz, Friedrich Schlegel and some others urged him to write a book. First Schleiermacher demurred, but he effectively began writing when he was asked in 1799 by his ecclesiastical superiors to replace the court preacher in Potsdam. There he found the necessary quiet atmosphere to structure his thoughts. Schleiermacher's progress is well documented thanks to the many letters he wrote to his friends in Berlin. See Nowak, *Schleiermacher*, 88ff.

[55] Louis Dupré, *A Dubious Heritage: Studies in the Philosophy of Religion after Kant* (New York, NY, Ramsey, MN, and Toronto: Paulist Press, 1977) 10. Dupré's contribution about Schleiermacher in this book studies his conception of "religion as feeling". This focus on 'feeling' should not surprise us, since Dupré is referring to an English translation of the third edition of *On Religion* (i.e. the one that appeared in the same year as *The Christian Faith* (1821), in the introduction of which the famous expression "the feeling of absolute dependence" occurs). We mentioned earlier that Schleiermacher somewhat changed the terminology in his later publications. One of these changes is the preference for 'feeling' (*Gefühl*) above the combination of feeling with 'intuition' (*Anschauung*). He took the view that 'intuition' smacked too strongly of rationalist and transcendental philosophy. It is indeed a fact that Schelling, for example, used 'intellectual intuition' (*intellektuelle Anschauung*) in a specific sense in his philosophy of identity.

that the essence of religion is "neither thinking nor acting, but intuition and feeling".[57] It "is the sensibility and taste for the infinite".[58] We further learn that every intuition of the universe is radically unique and pure, and that it is impossible to capture it in any systematization (see above). Moreover, "every intuition is, by its very nature, connected with a feeling".[59] They are even so closely united, that Schleiermacher, paraphrasing a well known quotation from Kant's *Critique of Pure Reason*, declares: "Intuition without feeling is nothing and can have neither the proper origin nor the proper force; feeling without intuition is also nothing; both are therefore something only when and because they are originally one and unseparated."[60] It is only a (usurping) act of reflection upon this primary experience that is able to distinguish between intuition and feeling, for – as Dupré indicated – these two are originally but one. It has no sense to utter this as if it were two different spheres of reality that must be combined or reconciled. But from the very moment one speaks about it in a philosophical or theological language that tries to do right to it, one has to integrate both the subjective and the objective: "Like Kant, Fichte, and Schelling, Schleiermacher is looking for the *absolute*, not for a sentimental experience."[61]

Once we acknowledge this, we can extend or apply this insight to other thoughts of Schleiermacher concerning 'objective realities' in the area of religion, i.e. realities that exceed the abilities and capacities of the subject. Let us begin with religious doctrines. He thematizes these explicitly towards the end of the second speech. He does so in view of his conviction that doctrines are unavoidable. Subsequent to the original moment in which (one's) religion is born, one is obliged to speak about one's experience. Schleiermacher defends the legitimacy of religious doctrines, but – again – he is thinking and speaking then from a realistic and phenomenal point of view, and not from his ideal perspective where the subject experiences a kind of union with the divine (the universe). When the latter is the case, all doctrines lose their significance; all possible rationalization is subsumed, as it were, in the holy atmosphere into which one is

---

[56] Dupré, *A Dubious Heritage*, 11. The extent to which idealist philosophers (Schelling, Fichte, Hegel) thematized an original unity of the subjective and the objective and the way in which they related this unity to consciousness shows once again that Schleiermacher was a child of his time.

[57] Schleiermacher, *On Religion*, 22.

[58] Schleiermacher, *On Religion*, 23.

[59] Schleiermacher, *On Religion*, 29.

[60] Schleiermacher, *On Religion*, 31. It is significant that Schleiermacher replaced precisely the term "concepts" in Kant's dictum by "feelings". Dupré is quoting this passage too (*A Dubious Heritage*, 15).

[61] Dupré, *A Dubious Heritage*, 22.

lifted up. This means that "some [dogmas and propositions] are merely abstract expressions of religious intuitions, and others are free reflections upon original achievements of the religious sense, the results of a comparison of the religious with the common view".[62] According to Schleiermacher, "miracles, inspirations, revelations, feelings of the supernatural[63] – one can have much religion without coming into contact with any of these concepts. But persons who reflect comparatively about their religion inevitably find concepts in their path and cannot possibly get around them. In this sense, all these concepts surely do belong to the realm of religion, indeed, belong unconditionally, without one being permitted to define the least thing about the limits of their application."[64] It is, therefore, not his intention to dismiss these. His concern is rather to put them in the proper perspective.

With a view to holy books Schleiermacher seems to defend a different position. In fact, he does not seem to have any trust in books as reliable mediators of the divine: "Of all that I praise and feel as its [i.e. of religion] work there stands precious little in holy books."[65] In this, he clearly reflects Enlightenment critique on the bible. However, there is more at stake here. His rejection of books as objective realities in religious affairs is not reducible to a kind of mistrust in objective realities as such. The deepest source of his hostility to (holy) books is his admiration, indeed his absolute preference for, the spoken word.

In a sense, Schleiermacher took Plato's famous witticism in the *Phaedrus* very seriously. There the Greek philosopher describes the impotence of the written word if it is not orally supported by the one who originated it.[66] For Schleiermacher, the word that is simply written is something fixed, definitive or even dead, whereas the spoken word possesses vitality: "You are right to despise the paltry imitators who derive their religion wholly from someone else or cling to a dead document by which they swear and from which they draw proof. Every holy writing is merely

---

[62] Schleiermacher, *On Religion*, 48.

[63] This translation might be confusing, because the German text does not mention *Gefühle* but *Empfindungen*.

[64] Schleiermacher, *On Religion*, 48.

[65] Schleiermacher, *On Religion*, 9. Cf. p. 74: "Unlike other concepts and perceptions, religious communication is not be sought in books."

[66] Plato, *Phaedrus*, 275 d-e. It is known that Schleiermacher was very well acquainted with Plato's dialogues. He is pre-eminent among the German translators of them, and began translating them from 1799. The *Phaedrus* was one of the first texts he treated. Cf. Nowak, *Schleiermacher*, 131-134. For a more systematic discussion of Schleiermacher's platonism, see Jan Rohls, "'Der Winckelmann der griechischen Philosophie' – Schleiermachers Platonismus im Kontext," *200 Jahre 'Reden über die Religion'*, 467-496.

a mausoleum of religion, a monument that a great spirit was there that no longer exists; for if it still lived and were active, why would it attach such great importance to the dead letter that can only be a weak reproduction of it? It is not the person who believes in a writing who has religion, but only the one who needs none and probably could make one for himself."[67] Therefore, according to Schleiermacher, "it is impossible to express and communicate religion other than verbally with all the effort and artistry of language, while willingly accepting the service of all skills that can assist fleeting and lively speech."[68]

Schleiermacher treats (holy) books distrustfully not because of any general view on the impossibility of objective realities in religion. The 'absolute' that he seeks and desires is both objective and subjective – in epistemological terms. But Schleiermacher's point lies beyond epistemology: he wants to defend a flexible, many-sided and dynamic process of religious intuitions.[69] This process is hindered by any unshakable medium, and hence by the written word, because these fix the spontaneous flux of lively religion. This insight is reflected in Schleiermacher's decision to write speeches instead of a treatise on his theme. *On Religion* is an excellent example of how the form and content of a text are intertwined. Accordingly, one does not interpret *On Religion* rightly if one does not take into account its rhetorical form. This means, of course, that the objective element, which is certainly present in the text (as we have established), must be sought through the rhetorical phrasing.

---

[67] Schleiermacher, *On Religion*, 50. Cf. p. 121: "The holy writings have become Scripture by their own power, but they prohibit no other book from also being or becoming Scripture, and whatever had been written with equal power they would gladly have associated with themselves."

[68] Schleiermacher, *On Religion*, 74. This basic conviction has by the way remarkable consequences for Schleiermacher's ecclesiology and for his view on the role of the priest. See *On Religion*, 90: "According to the basic principles of the Church, the mission of a priest in the world is a private affair; ... let there be an assembly before him and not a congregation; let him be a speaker for all who will hear, but not a shepherd for a particular flock."

[69] This plural form is of great importance, since Schleiermacher spoke explicitly about "religions" in the fifth speech, whereas he had already defined the "essence of religion" in the second speech. In the interpretation history of *On Religion* the alleged difference between the second and the fifth speech was a key issue. Nowadays one is convinced of the inner necessity of both a more speculative or philosophical and a more phenomenological or historical approach of religion within the framework of the whole text. For some background concerning this discussion, see e.g. Paul Seifert, *Die Theologie des jungen Schleiermacher* [sic], Beiträge zur Förderung christlicher Theologie, 49 (Gütersloh: Gütersloher Verlagshaus Gerd Mohn, 1960) 181-187; Jacobus W.A. Laurent, *Friedrich Schleiermacher, een denker in twee dimensies: De soteriologie in de 'Reden über die Religion' en in 'Der Christliche Glaube'* (Kampen: Kok, 1997) 103-110.

6. Concluding Remarks

After our threefold contextualization of religious experience according
to the early Schleiermacher, the question that remains is how we are to
understand and define what it is. Since we seem to have made the problem more difficult by seeing the matter from the point of view of different relationships, we shall attempt to synthesize our reflections and to
offer a conclusion.

Our major concern has been to illuminate the necessity of relating
Schleiermacher's conception of religious experience to domains of theological reflection that apparently threaten its purity. We defended the position that, in Schleiermacher's view, religious experience is not an isolated
phenomenon serving as the only legitimate source of religion, to the exclu-
sion of others. We also defended the view that the authentic unity of intuition and feeling of the universe must not be regarded as a merely individual, subjective and hence dangerously arbitrary reality. Instead, it must
be interpreted in an integral and comprehensive fashion. We tried to find
evidence for the assertion that factors such as historical context, ecclesiastical embedding and doctrines are included in Schleiermacher's idea of
religious experience. In Schleiermacher's own words: "Just as no human
being can come into existence as an individual without simultaneously,
through the same act, also coming into a world, into a definite order of
things, and being placed among individual objects, so also a religious
person cannot attain his individuality without, through the same act, also
dwelling in a determinate form of religion."[70] So it is wrong to suppose
that all three aforementioned aspects are not harmoniously connected with
each other, or that irreconcilable contradictions can be found in the text
of *On Religion*. In our view, there are no logical inconsistencies in this
work. On the contrary, it is best seen as a complex and tensile whole that
aims to formulate one basic intuition regarding the essence of religion.

According to Schleiermacher, religion cannot be 'understood' except
from within, from the very core of which so many women and men speak
of as the centre and the meaning of their lives. Every other attempt to
grasp religion, be it philosophically, morally or from the point of view of
the state (recall Schleiermacher's examples of the antipodes to religion),
does not do justice to its originality. Religion deserves its rightful place,
whether in the human soul or in the life of society. In this respect,
Schleiermacher is indeed rightly regarded as a modern thinker. He accomplished Kant's task by dissociating religion not only from theoretical

---

[70] Schleiermacher, *On Religion*, 108.

reason, but from reason as such.[71] It is clear that Schleiermacher no longer wished to house religion under the roof of practical reason either. Only in this way, he believed, could the freedom of religion be guaranteed. Schleiermacher takes account of all five modalities of religious experience proposed by Vergote. Both the sudden and the permanent characteristics are represented, and mystical experiences no less than private revelations can be neatly fitted into his framework. Although Schleiermacher emphasizes the uniqueness of the simple moment of a person's intuition of the universe, he also included the enduring aspects in personal life which flow from this original experience. In his view, religious experiences exert a continuous influence on one's life, and this with respect to the past as well as the future.[72] An original intuition of the universe deeply penetrates all aspects of one's life. It is as if one repainted the room in which one lives in a totally different colour. Moreover, the distinction between experience and interpretation is inappropriate and inaccurate from Schleiermacher's point of view, since the indissoluble correlation of these two is presupposed in his thought.[73] The givenness of a religious experience is never seen as an absolute fact, but it is brought into relation with a situation, a community and 'objective realities' – as we have demonstrated.

What, then, might we conclude? We can certainly deny that Schleiermacher gives as much importance to the peculiar kind of religious experience which Küng, Lindbeck and Barth contend is discernible in his work. In *On Religion*, we do not encounter religious experience as a separate source of religion next to revelation, tradition or the Church. We have argued that all these realities are involved in Schleiermacher's conception of what it means to intuit and feel the divine. Obviously, this does not mean that we, today's theologians, have no problems in relation to Schleiermacher's idea of religious experience. Among the issues that surface are the unclear referent of the experienced, its somewhat esoteric

---

[71] Cf. Dupré, *A Dubious Heritage*, 10: "Kant had banned religion from the realm of speculative reason but, as a strange inconsistency, preserved it as a necessary complement of practical reason. Schleiermacher completes Kant's critique by banning it from the sphere of reason altogether."

[72] Schleiermacher, *On Religion*, 106: "That is to say, this moment is simultaneously a definite point in his life, a link in the series of spiritual activities that are wholly characteristic for him, an occurence that, like every other, stands in a particular relationship with a before, a now, and an afterward."

[73] One should not forget that one of Schleiermacher's philosophical merits (next to – but in close connection with – his theological realizations) is that he stands at the origin of hermeneutics. This is a relevant consideration, even if hermeneutics had not yet appeared in Schleiermacher's thought as an explicit point of interest at the time he wrote the speeches.

character, and the fascination for immediate contact with the divine. Of course, it is beyond the scope of our contribution to solve these problems. Our concern has been to defend the profound significance Schleiermacher attributes to religious experience in the concrete life of an individual, against the prejudicial view that his thought were merely subjectivist, experientialist or sentimentalist. One does not do justice to the early Schleiermacher if one tries to deduce a fixed interpretation of religious experience in order to reject it as restricted. The clearest lesson to be learned from both the literary form and the import of the five speeches is the following: that is impossible to develop a universally valid and qualitatively determinate conception of religious experience![74]

[74] I would like to express sincere thanks to my promotor, Prof. T. Merrigan, who corrected earlier English versions of this text, and made numerous suggestions to improve it.

MAKING RELIGION SAFE FOR DEMOCRACY: WILLIAM JAMES AND THE MONOTONY OF RELIGIOUS EXPERIENCE

FREDERICK CHRISTIAN BAUERSCHMIDT

1. Situating William James and *The Varieties of Religious Experience*

William James's 1900-1902 Gifford Lectures, given at the University of Edinburgh and published as *The Varieties of Religious Experience*, are one of the great works of modern religious studies. They are beautifully and engagingly written, crammed with the brilliant insights of a truly creative thinker, and highly sympathetic to their subject matter. They are also, I will eventually suggest, entirely wrong in their approach to religious experience and ultimately pernicious in their effect. But before we get to this critique, I wish to briefly sketch their context and try to account for their enduring appeal.

a. The Context of The Varieties of Religious Experience

The Gifford Lectures were established by Lord Adam Gifford in his will as a series of lectures, given at the ancient Scottish universities of Edinburgh, Aberdeen, Saint Andrews and Glasgow, to "promote and diffuse the study of Natural Theology in the widest sense of the term – in other words, the knowledge of God". Since the first lectures given in 1888, the Gifford Lectures have constituted a veritable who's-who of modern theology, philosophy and religious studies, including series of lectures by Henri Bergson, James Frazer, Alfred North Whitehead, Étienne Gilson, Albert Schweitzer, Reinhold Niebuhr, Rudolf Bultmann, Karl Barth, Paul Tillich, Niels Bohr, Iris Murdoch, Paul Ricoeur, Alasdair MacIntyre, Stanley Hauerwas, and David Tracy. Being asked to deliver a series of Gifford Lectures is, in the world of religion, analogous to winning a Nobel prize. Indeed, so important have the Gifford Lectures become that in recent years many Gifford lecturers feels compelled to spend much of his or her lectures in talking about past Gifford Lectures.[1]

---

[1] For a general account of the Gifford Lectures, see Stanley L. Jaki, *Lord Gifford and His Lectures: A Centenary Retrospect* (Macon, GA: Mercer University Press, 1987). For

While the Giffords had not yet achieved this status in 1900 when James began his lectures, he still took time to note that his invitation to give the lectures was something of a sign that American thought had "arrived", or that its arrival was at least on the horizon. Having spent his life learning from Europeans, *he* was now asked to teach *them*. As he says at the beginning of his first lecture, "the current ... has begun to run from west to east" (21).[2] He also expresses the hope that, as British and American thinkers begin to mutually influence one another, "the peculiar philosophic temperament, as well as the peculiar political temperament, that goes with our English speech may more and more pervade and influence the world" (21-22). We will have occasion to return to this peculiar pair of temperaments.

It is also worth noting how James connected with the idea behind the Gifford Lectures. William James (1842-1910) was a physician (his first academic position was teaching anatomy and physiology at Harvard Medical School), a pioneer in the field of psychology (the opening lecture in the *Varieties* is entitled "Religion and Neurology"), and one of the founders, along with C. S. Pierce, of the pragmatist school of philosophy. Of all these things that he was, you will note that he was not, nor did he claim to be, a theologian. He begins at the outset noting that his will be a *psychological* inquiry into religion; in other words, it will be scientific. It will not be "natural theology" in the sense of beginning from principles available to unaided human reason and proceeding to argue for God's existence, but in the sense of treating religion as a "natural" phenomenon to be subjected to scientific inquiry. It is no accident that when James published *The Varieties of Religious Experience* he subtitled them, "a study in human nature". His focus is on the human experience of God, not on God. He hoped that virtually all of what he says about the psychology of religious experience will be as (but not more) acceptable to the atheist as to the theist. In taking this approach, James saw himself as contributing to the formation of a "Science of Religion" (331).

It is important to note, however, what sort of "psychologist" James was. In his day "psychology" was quite a different discipline than it is today. Though James himself contributed greatly to developing the experimental

a critical account of the ideology underlying the Giffords, see Alasdair MacIntyre's own Gifford Lectures, published as *Three Rival Versions of Moral Inquiry: Encyclopaedia, Genealogy, and Tradition* (Notre Dame, IN: University of Notre Dame Press, 1991).

[2] All citations are from *The Varieties of Religious Experience: A Study in Human Nature* (New York, NY: New American Library, 1958). Subsequent citations will be in the body of the text.

– and therefore "scientific" – character of psychology, it was for James still primarily a science of the soul. Rather than our modern management of mental illness through pharmaceuticals or psychotherapy, James' psychology was a deep reflection on what it meant to be human, to know and act as a human, to think and experience as a human. So today he is remembered more as a philosopher than as a psychologist (though some might argue that he was a better psychologist than a philosopher).

It is also important to note what sort of philosopher James was. "Pragmatism" is a philosophical approach that James himself traces to Charles Sanders Peirce (1839-1914), but it was James who was its first great advocate (Peirce published little, and what he published was not nearly as readable as James's writings).[3] Because James took up Peirce's notion of pragmatism and put it to his own uses, in the end producing something quite different from Peirce himself, we can turn directly, and briefly, to James himself in order to understand what *he* meant by pragmatism.[4]

In a 1907 series of lectures, later published as *Pragmatism*, James offers an account of what he means by "the pragmatic method":

> The pragmatic method is primarily a method of settling metaphysical disputes that might otherwise be interminable. Is the world one or many? – fated or free? – material or spiritual? – here are notions either of which may or may not hold good of the world; and disputes over such notions are unending. The pragmatic method in such cases is to try to interpret each notion by tracing its respective practical consequences. What difference would it practically make to any one if this notion rather than that notion were true? If no practical difference whatever can be traced, then the alternatives mean practically the same thing, and all dispute is idle. Whenever a dispute is serious, we ought to be able to show some practical difference that must follow from one side or the other's being right.[5]

In other words, the meaning of a concept is the practical difference that it makes: a difference that makes no difference, *is* no difference. As James puts it in *The Varieties of Religious Experience*, "beliefs, in short, are rules for action" (339). So, for example, when confronted with a term like "substance", the pragmatic philosopher will ask not whether or not such a thing as a "substance" exists, but rather how the concept "substance"

---

[3] See James, *Varieties*, 338-39. The essay by Peirce that James points to is: "How to Make Our Ideas Clear," *Popular Science Monthly* 12 (January 1878) 286-302.

[4] For one account of the differences between Peirce and James, see Christopher Hookway, "Logical Principles and Philosophical Attitudes: Peirce's Response to James's Pragmatism," *The Cambridge Companion to William James*, ed. Ruth Anna Putnam, Cambridge Companions to Philosophers (Cambridge: Cambridge University Press, 1997) 145-165.

[5] William James, *Pragmatism* (Buffalo, NY: Prometheus Books, 1991) 23.

functions. What real difference does it make if we hold (following, say, Berkeley) that the qualities of the thing adhere in each other rather than (following, say, Aristotle) in something called a "substance"? James's answer is that it makes *no* difference whatsoever.[6]

James's "pragmatic method" is important for his treatment of religious experience. What he attempts to do in *The Varieties of Religious Experience* is to ask "what practical difference do religious experiences make?". As he rather crassly puts it, what is the "cash value" of such experiences (338)? Again and again in dealing with religious experiences and beliefs, James asks, what difference do these experiences and beliefs make? What actions do they engender? Are these actions commendable of condemnable? Such question, he believes, can be answered scientifically by a sympathetic but external scientific gaze. Once again, the natural theology of which Lord Gifford spoke becomes what James calls "the Science of Religion", a science that might "eventually command as general a public adhesion as is commanded by a physical science" (347).

I think that, in attempting to contextualize *The Varieties of Religious Experience*, we should see it as part of a shift from the natural theology over which Lord Gifford somewhat naively enthused, to the science of religion that James saw as the future of "public" discourse about religion. As such, *The Varieties of Religious Experience* are of crucial interest to us today because we still live in a world in which the science of religion (or, as we call it today, religious studies) is the dominant public discourse for speaking of religion. Part of the reason why *The Varieties of Religious Experience* has remained an appealing and vital work for a century now, is because it operates within the paradigm of religious studies, a paradigm that still functions in the academic world today.

b. *The Appeal of* The Varieties of Religious Experience

But the appeal of *The Varieties of Religious Experience* goes beyond the familiar paradigm within which it operates. James was a scientist and a philosopher, but more than this, he was a great man of letters, as anyone who has read *The Varieties of Religious Experience* can attest. As much as his novelist brother Henry, William James is a master-stylist who tosses off memorable lines with aplomb, as when he notes that the lamentations of Nietzsche and Schopenhauer "remind one, half the time,

---

[6] See James, *Pragmatism*, 39-41. The one exception James makes is what he no doubt considers the curious case of the scholastic doctrine of transubstantiation. In this case, the idea of substance *does* affect what we do: i.e. how we treat the Eucharistic elements.

of the sick shriekings of two dying rats" (47). No doubt part of the success of *The Varieties of Religious Experience* is due to the sheer pleasure they bring to the reader. It probably does not hurt that the sizzle of James's prose is accentuated by its contrast with the long and often tedious first-hand accounts of religious experiences with which *The Varieties of Religious Experience* are filled. After reading several pages of Henry Alline's account of his religious conversion, one returns with relief to James's way with a turn of phrase.

Another aspect of their appeal is that the beauty of the language is often at the service of greatness of insight. James is often faulted for a certain fuzziness in his thinking, for inconsistency and self-contradiction. To take but one well-known example, James never seemed entirely clear on what he meant by "truth". In some places (the places neo-pragmatists like Richard Rorty like) James seems to identify truth with "what works" in practice, what you can convince others of. In other places, perhaps reflecting the influence of Peirce, he adopts a more "realist" stance. In a footnote in the final lecture in *The Varieties of Religious Experience* he notes, "The word 'truth' is here taken to mean something additional to bare value for life, although the natural propensity of man is to believe that whatever has great value for life is thereby certified as true" (384). We see here some of what drives philosophers crazy about James. What is this "something additional" to which he appeals? Why can he not distinguish more clearly between "truth" as a property of statements and "truth" as utility?

Yet part of James's greatness as a thinker lies precisely in this fuzziness, this unresolved plurality. It reflects the unresolved plurality that is the human person. As the philosopher Owen Flanagan puts it: "The attraction of James the philosopher is that he is to me the best example I know of *a person doing philosophy*; there is no hiding the person behind the work, no way of discussing the work without the person, no way to make believe that there is a way of doing philosophy that is not personal."[7] It is this refusal to be anything less than personal that makes James so insightful.

Perhaps the most appealing thing about the *Varieties*, at least for religious readers, is the great sympathy with which James approaches the topic of "religious experience". In a way analogous to Max Weber's *Protestant Ethic and the Spirit of Capitalism*, but located in the realm of psychology rather than sociology, James wants to give a non-reductive

---

[7] Owen Flanagan, "Consciousness as a Pragmatist Views It," *The Cambridge Companion to William James*, 47.

account of religion by showing that there is something called "religious experience" that is not reducible to something else. And, again like Weber, he wants to argue that religious beliefs and experiences make an actual, empirical *difference* in the world and that therefore, according to James's pragmatic definition of truth, we can speak of those beliefs and experiences as "true". James is convinced that even if one accounts for religious experience psychologically – or biologically, or sociologically – one has in no sense "disproved" them, because for a pragmatist like James, origins are only half, indeed, somewhat less than half, of the story. As he says, adapting the words of Christ, "by their fruits ye shall know them, not by their roots" (34). Though frank about his own difficulties with traditional Christianity, James is not dismissive of traditional beliefs when looked at from the perspective of their pragmatic effects. As Carol Zaleski has put it: "Never at home in the Christianity of his ancestors, James nonetheless manages in *The Varieties of Religious Experience* to keep the door open for orthodoxy, for supernaturalism, for moral conviction, and for the kinds of religious engagement that make a real difference in the public square."[8]

James offers us, therefore, what appears to be a defense of religious experience, well written and filled with insight. I want to suggest, however, that the allure of *The Varieties of Religious Experience* is one that we ought to resist. To make this case, I want to first explore what James means by "religion" and "experience", and then try to show why he conceives of religious experience in the way he does. Then, in good pragmatist fashion, I will try to sketch some of the consequences of such a conception of religious experience, which I hope will be a convincing argument to resist its enticements.

2. "Religious Experience" According to James

a. James on "Religion"

William James was one of the first people to use "religious experience" as a technical category.[9] James has rather interesting and original ideas about the nature of "experience", which I will come to in a moment, but

---

[8] Carol Zaleski, "William James, *The Varieties of Religious Experience*," *First Things* 101 (2000) 61.

[9] See John E. Smith, "William James's Account of Mysticism: A Critical Appraisal," *Mysticism and Religious Traditions*, ed. Steven T. Katz (Oxford: Oxford University Press, 1983) 277, n. 3.

first I would like to focus on the term: "religion". What exactly do we mean when we describe an experience as "religious"? How are religious experiences different from other experiences? Is an experience designated as "religious" because of the object of the experience (e.g. a religious experience is an experience of God), or because of some subjective quality of the experience itself (e.g. a religious experience is one that unifies one's worldview), or does the designation "religious" depend on both subject and object? James was aware of these sorts of questions and the deeper issues that give rise to them. So, in his second lecture, he offered a "circumscription of the topic". In this, he attempted to spell out what *he* means, at least in the Gifford Lectures, by "religious experience".

He says, quite wisely, that "the word 'religion' cannot stand for any single principle or essence, but is rather a collective name" (39). Abstract definitions of religion are not only unlikely to be helpful, but they may be positively misleading. Therefore, James says, his "lectures must be limited to a fraction of the subject" (40). James then goes on to note that there is "one great partition which divides the religious field"; on one side of this partition lies "institutional" religion, and on the other "personal" religion (40-41). Institutional religion is a matter of structures and rituals and creeds, which perhaps an anthropologist or sociologist or even a theologian might well treat, whereas what he calls "personal religion pure and simple" is a matter of "inner dispositions" (41), which makes it the obvious choice for James the psychologist.

But James's choice is guided by more than his own particular area of expertise. In opting for the personal over the institutional he believes himself to be getting closer to the heart of religious experience. Though it is obviously not the whole of religion, James believes it is "more fundamental" than institutional religion. At the very beginning of his first lecture James speaks somewhat disdainfully of the "ordinary religious believer ... [whose] religion has been made for him by others, communicated to him by tradition, determined to fixed form by imitation, and retained by habit" (24). In his second lecture he writes:

> Churches, when once established, live at second-hand upon tradition; but the founders of every church owed their power originally to the fact of their direct personal communion with the divine. Not only the superhuman founders, the Christ, the Buddha, Mahomet, but all the originators of Christian sects have been in this case; – so personal religion should still seem the primordial thing, even to those who continue to esteem it incomplete (42).

Returning to this topic in a later lecture, James notes that those who live first-hand upon experience gather followers to themselves, and that these followers build structures and institutions, and then "the spirit of politics and the lust of dogmatic rule are … apt to enter and to contaminate the originally innocent thing" (262). But this loss of innocence – what Weber called the "routinization of charisma" – is an alienation from religion in its primordial, personal form.[10] So James's circumscription of his topic is not simply a practical delimiting of his field, but rather a narrowing that in fact allows us to discern religion more clearly.

But what is it that we find in this pure and simple personal religion? James writes: "Religion … shall mean for us the feelings, acts, and experiences of individual men in their solitude, so far as they apprehend themselves to stand in relation to whatever they may consider the divine" (42). This description is borne out by the many examples James presents during the course of his twenty lectures.

First, his concern is almost exclusively with the emotional and volitional side of religion, rather than the intellectual. The various theologies and doctrines that provided the vocabularies with which his examples speak are described by James as "over-beliefs, buildings-out performed by the intellect into directions of which feeling originally supplied the hint" (330). James acknowledges that over-beliefs can be interesting and important, particularly to the person who holds them (388), but they are very much outside his core definition of religion. This can be seen by looking at how, in trying to give some order to his description of religious experience, James focuses not on differences of belief, but on differences of mood and action. Thus he distinguishes between the once-born soul's religion of healthy mindedness and the twice-born soul's – the "sick soul's" – religion of redemption (Lectures 4-7). He looks at the event of conversion (Lectures 9-10), the activity of saintliness (Lectures 11-15), and the experience of mysticism (Lectures 16-17), but is totally uninterested in the theology of conversion, sanctity, or mystical union. Even when the examples he gives speak scriptural or doctrinal language, James almost never comments on that language, but rather treats it as the clothing in which (perhaps for the sake of modesty?) feeling must be dressed.

Second, as we have already seen, religion is essentially a private and individual matter. James seems to gravitate toward examples, such as George Fox or Leo Tolstoy, who were alienated from both the religious

---

[10] The one place where "ecclesiastical" religion seems to touch some primordial religious impulse is in the realm of the aesthetic (349-350). James's remarks on this topic, brief though they are, are typically insightful. However, I would venture to say that he could not take the aesthetic very seriously as a religious category, for to do so would call his "great partition" between the personal and the institutional into question.

and secular cultures of their days. Religion, particularly in the extreme case of the religious genius, is a lonely matter:

> The religious experience which we are studying is that which lives itself out within the private breast. First-hand individual experience of this kind has always appeared as a heretical sort of innovation to those who witnessed its birth. Naked comes it into the world and lonely; and it has always, for a time at least, driven him who had it into the wilderness, often into the literal wilderness out of doors, where the Buddha, Jesus, Mohammed, St. Francis, George Fox, and so many others had to go (262).

This isolation is of a piece with James's emphasis on religion as mood and action. Because religion is essentially non-rational, and therefore prior to thought and language, it cannot be communicated to others without loss, without becoming "second-hand". And, in the case of the religious genius, when the individual's powerful religious experience is forced into the ossified vocabulary of prior orthodoxies, it cannot help but take the form of heterodoxy.

Third, while various experiences may involve the mood and action of individuals, it is essential to *religious* experience that it has to do with the individual's experience of whatever he or she may consider divine. The formulation in James's definition – they *apprehend* themselves to stand in relation to whatever they may *consider* divine – is important. In speaking of the *object* of religious experience, James exhibits great circumspection. As the mentioning together of Buddha, Jesus and Mohammed above indicates, James is very aware of the issue of religious pluralism, and he is also aware that not all religions share the Christian or Jewish or Islamic understanding of God. Buddhism might be the most obvious case, but James also includes Emersonian Transcendentalism as an essentially "religious" standpoint. In light of such examples, James says, "we must interpret the term 'divine' very broadly, as denoting any object that is god*like*, whether it be a concrete deity or not" (44). Yet he is not really satisfied with such vagueness, so he further specifies that godlike objects "overarch and envelope, and from them there is no escape": they have to do with one's "total reaction upon life" (45). Even more specifically, one's attitude toward a godlike object must be "serious", but not "grumbling" (47). Note that what makes an object godlike has nothing to do with its intrinsic properties, such as eternity or omnipotence. Indeed, James has some uncharacteristically unkind words for those who speculate about divine attributes, saying that they offer a "metaphysical monster ... to our worship" (340). What makes an object godlike is our stance toward it; how we apprehend ourselves in relation to it.

James is not afraid to draw certain logical conclusions from this view. For "us Christians" it is natural to "call this higher part of the universe by the name of God" (339),[11] but James realizes that from a pragmatic point of view all one need possess is "the belief that beyond each man and in a fashion continuous with him there exists a larger power which is friendly to him and to his ideals" (396). All we need of our gods is that they be more powerful than we are, just powerful enough to draw us forward, beyond ourselves. He frankly acknowledges that this "larger power" could simply be "a larger and more godlike self" and notes that if this were the case we would have a radical religious pluralism, indeed, a sort of polytheism, with each person possessing his or her own god. James does not shy away from such a conclusion, since it follows clearly from the emotional and individualist understanding with which he begins.

Yet what is particularly striking is that for all his celebration of pluralism and diversity, James ends up having a fairly low opinion of the religious particularities that constitute pluralism. They are "over-beliefs", and while James says that "the most interesting and valuable thing about a man are usually his over-beliefs" (388), he does not himself, as I have noted, show much interest in them. He is like a number of other nineteenth century intellectuals (the young Schleiermacher comes to mind) who are very interested in Religion, but not very interested in any particular religion.[12] Despite the title of his Gifford Lectures, there is not a lot of variety in religious experience as James presents it. It is true that he offers us the testimonies of Catholics and Calvinists, Buddhists and Baptists, Methodists and Muslims, and that these testimonies are themselves rich in the highly particular language of highly particular communal traditions, but what he draws from these testimonies, in the end, amounts to a fairly interchangeable set of moods and emotions that he calls "personal religion pure and simple" (41).

---

[11] The fact that James thinks of "God" as part of the universe indicates the elasticity of the category "us Christians" for him.

[12] There is some evidence that James had some familiarity with Schleiermacher's work, but none that Schleiermacher exerted any great influence on him. It seems more likely that the similarities between them are a result of similar cultural milieus (though separated by an ocean and nearly 100 years) and intellectual influences. For some brief comments on the Schleiermacher-James connection, see Stanley Hauerwas, *With the Grain of the Universe: The Church's Witness and Natural Theology* (London: SCM Press, 2002) 62, n. 60.

b. James on "Experience"

I will deal more briefly with James's account of "experience", not because what he says about experience is less interesting and important than what he says about religion, but because what he says on the topic is so interesting and rich that I am not even tempted to give anything like a comprehensive account. I will simply mention three points.

First, James thinks of experience in terms of consciousness. In his *Principles of Psychology* (1890), he describes experience as the "impress" of something "foreign" upon us.[13] To have an experience is to be affected by something external to us, something that changes our mind or brain so that our consciousness is (to borrow a scholastic term) conformed to it. More specifically, in experience our consciousness is not simply determined by an external agent, but we are *aware* of that agent as determining. This distinguishes experience from other, non-experiential determinations of consciousness. I may be depressed because of a chemical imbalance in my brain, but I do not *experience* that chemical imbalance because it does not itself enter into my consciousness. However when I see a tree because of the "impress" of the tree upon my senses, I do, in fact, experience the tree. So James normally restricts "experience" to those modifications of consciousness that enter through "the front door, the door of the five senses".[14]

Second, James's understanding of "consciousness" is highly nuanced. In particular, he opposes any reification of consciousness, any notion that consciousness is a "thing". In *The Principles of Psychology* he writes: "No one ever had a simple sensation by itself. Consciousness, from our natal day, is of a teeming multiplicity of objects and relations, and what we call simple sensations are results of discriminative attention, pushed often to a very high degree."[15] Though he describes his view as "empiricism" – indeed as "radical empiricism" – his is not the empiricism of John Locke, with its discrete ideas jostling around in the mind. Rather, for James, consciousness is a "stream" or a "flow"[16] from which distinct objects of experience are, as it were, carved out. This, of course, is reminiscent of Kant's transcendental idealism, but with this difference: for James the tools with which we carve out the objects of our experience are

---

[13] William James, *The Principles of Psychology*, vol. II (New York, NY: Henry Holt, 1890) 619.
[14] James, *Principles*, 2:628.
[15] James, *Principles*, 1:224.
[16] James, *Principles*, 1:239.

not universal categories of reason, but rather are the accumulated "habits", both of the individual and of the human race.[17] Yet these objects of experience are still not the discrete "ideas" of Locke and Hume, rather they are "waves" or "fields" of consciousness, which, "contain sensations of our bodies and of the objects around us, memories of past experiences and thoughts of distant things, feelings of satisfaction and dissatisfaction, desires and aversions, and other emotional conditions, together with determinations of the will, in every variety of permutation and combination".[18] What James particularly emphasizes is the way in which fields of consciousness have fuzzy, ill-defined boundaries, so that shifts between one field of consciousness and another are often gradual, even unnoticed.

These brief indications should be enough to show the nuance with which James approaches "experience" and "consciousness". In particular, I hope they show that, for James, "experience" is always shaped by a variety of forces: our embodied existence, our education (and therefore the traditions in which we have been educated), the language we speak, our goals and aspirations and moods and what we had for lunch. The list could go on indefinitely. We know the world not because it is successfully mediated to us by sense impressions or ideas, but because we are *in* the world that we know, acting and reacting.[19]

Third, James's account of experience seems to take a sharp turn when we come to *The Varieties of Religious Experience*. Here, experience is not shaped by the multitude of forces that normally shape our experiences; rather, religious experiences seems oddly isolated from the normal sorts of forces that operate within a field of experience.[20] Indeed, in *The Varieties of Religious Experience* James's account of "experience" becomes at times almost solipsistic. This has already been indicated by

[17] On the similarities and differences between James and Kant, see Thomas Carlson, "James and the Kantian Tradition," *The Cambridge Companion to William James*, 363-383. According to Carlson, on the issue of experience, the chief difference between James and Kant was that "the influence of Darwin had shifted James's attention from an abstract and universal Reason to the concrete reasoning individual in the natural order" (371).

[18] William James, *Talks to Teachers on Psychology and to Students on Some of Life's Ideals* [1899] (New York, NY: Dover Publications, 2001) 28. For James's discussion of "fields of consciousness", see James, *Varieties*, 186-189.

[19] As Hillary Putnam says, James "was the first modern philosopher successfully to reject the idea that our impressions are located in a private mental theatre (and thus constitute an interface between ourselves and 'the external world')" ("James's Theory of Truth," *The Cambridge Companion to William James*, 181-182).

[20] The separation of religious experience from everyday experience is a major element in Nicholas Lash's critique of James in *Easter in Ordinary: Reflections on Human Experience and the Knowledge of God* (London: SCM Press, 1988).

his emphasis on "personal religion", but it becomes particularly evident in his discussion of mystical states of consciousness, which he calls the "root and centre" of all "personal religious experience" (292).

James lists four characteristics of mystical states of consciousness, four characteristics that have achieved almost canonical status in the English-speaking world of the philosophy of religion. These are:

1. *Ineffability:* mystical experience "defies expression, no adequate report of it can be given in words" (292-293).
2. *Noetic quality:* mystical states of consciousness *seem*, to those who have them, to be "states of insight into depths of truth unplumbed by the discursive intellect" and they "carry with them a curious sense of authority for after-time" (293).
3. *Transiency:* mystical states are of brief duration (usually half an hour, at most an hour or two).
4. *Passivity:* as James puts it, "the mystic feels as if his own will were in abeyance" (293).

Let me make a few brief remarks about these characteristics, designed to draw out how this account of mystical experience diverges from James's account of everyday experience. Keeping in mind James's preferred metaphor of "fields of consciousness", we ought to note the way in which James, with amazing and uncharacteristic consistency, refers to "*states* of consciousness" when speaking of mystical experience. Without making too much of the metaphors of "field" and "state", one does get the distinct impression that mystical states have tightly policed borders. No one enters or leaves a mystical state casually and unknowingly: the guards are there and you had better have your papers in order. This is a territory where the language is different (ineffability) and information is doled out (noetic quality). It is so distinct from our ordinary field of consciousness that we cannot stay there long (transiency), and the actions that shape our normal consciousness must be left at the boarder (passivity).

Defenders of James might claim that it is a mistake to take what James says about mystical states as applying to *all* religious experience.[21] However, it is clear that James's account of religious experience culminates in his account of mystical states of consciousness. Or as he puts it: "Such states of consciousness ought to form the vital chapter from which the other chapters get their light" (292). This would seem to imply that the earlier discussions of religious experience ought to be read in light of his discussion of mystical experience. So what we see in James's treatment

---

[21] See, for example, Smith, "William James's Account of Mysticism," 248-249.

of mysticism is simply an intensification of what he has presented regarding religious experience already. Though he begins his lectures by saying: "Things are more or less divine, states of mind are more or less religious, reactions are more or less total, but the boundaries are always misty, and it is everywhere a question of amount and degree" (47-48), by the time we are finished with the lecture on mysticism, the boundaries between the religious and the everyday are clearly marked.

c. The Politics of "Religious Experience"

Why does James's account of religious experience not have the embodied, communal, linguistic character that his account of everyday experience does? Is it simply the case that religious experience just *is* drastically different from ordinary experience, a fact that James is faithfully recording? Or, might we ask what interests are served by segregating religious experience from other sorts of experience? In the rest of this essay I will argue that James's account of "religious experience" is determinatively shaped by his commitment to the American form of democracy. More specifically, it seeks to segregate religious experience from ordinary experience in order to create a pluralistic public space.

It is striking how the category of "religion" is transformed in the modern era. In the ancient and medieval worlds, *religio* referred to public acts of piety that served to "re-bind" (*re-ligere*) the members of the body politic. This meaning was still operative in Thomas Aquinas's discussion of the natural virtue of religion, which he treated as a part of justice.[21a] Religion was, by its very definition, a public matter, indeed, a political matter. It was analogous to Americans saying the pledge of allegiance or French people singing the *Marseilles*. Of course, it was at the same time more than that. Aquinas put it: "It denotes properly a relation to God." It is by their common worship of God or the gods that the members of a body politic are bound into one. And, as Augustine argued in *The City of God*, the character of the god you worship determines the character of your political community.

All of this begins to change, of course, in the modern era. Exactly how this changes has been a matter of some dispute in recent years.[22] The way

---

[21a] Thomas Aquinas, *Summa theologiae* 2a 2ae, Q. 21, art. 1.

[22] For what follows, both the "standard account" and the "revisionist account", see William Cavanaugh, *Eucharistie et mondialisation: La liturgie comme acte politique* (Genève: Éditions Ad Solem, 2001) esp. 33-58.

in which the story has traditionally been told is that with the break up of Christendom in the sixteenth century and the Wars of Religion in the sixteenth and seventeenth centuries, the modern secular state arose as a response to religious violence. Religion had not only failed to serve as the ligaments binding together the body politic, but actually had become the source of violence and disunity. Thus religion had to be relegated to the private sphere, while the public sphere would be religiously neutral. This movement toward the privatization of religion culminates in the United States of America, with its separation of Church and State and its religious pluralism.[23]

This is what we might call the "standard account" of religion and the modern state. In recent years a "revisionist" account has been offered that rejects the view of State as "saviour" from religious violence. This revisionist account points out, first, that from an historical point of view, the chronology is wrong. Well before Luther, to say nothing of Phillip II, thinkers like John Wycliff and Marsilius of Padua had argued that only the secular powers had a right to the use of coercive force. Also, the era of violence that evolved into the so-called 'Wars of Religion' was not initially motivated by religion at all. Charles V and Phillip II were far more interested in the fortunes of the Habsburg Empire than they were in the beliefs of their subjects, and when one actually looks at the combatants in the various conflicts it is difficult to assign confessional allegiance based to who was fighting whom.

In this revisionist account, the point is not simply that rulers were cynically using the religious enthusiasms of their subjects to manipulate them. If this were the case, then the liberal state would still be the "saviour" of society from religious violence, only in this case religion becomes simply the dangerous weapon that must be taken away from those who would use it for their own purposes. Rather, the claim is that the violence of the sixteenth and seventeenth centuries were the "birthpangs" of the modern state, and part of that birth was the replacing of the Church by the State as the bearer of those bonds by which the body politic was united. By the end of the sixteenth century, as John Figgis argues, "for many minds the

---

[23] Judith Shklar's version of this story is as follows: "Liberalism ... was born out of the cruelties of the religious civil wars, which forever rendered the claims of Christian charity a rebuke to all religious institutions and parties. If the faith was to survive at all, it would do so privately. The alternative then set, and still before us, is not one between classical virtue and liberal self-indulgence, but between cruel military and moral repression and violence, and a self-restraining tolerance that fences in the powerful to protect the freedom and safety of every citizen" (Judith Shklar, *Ordinary Vices* [Cambridge, MA: Harvard University Press, 1984] 5, quoted in Cavanaugh, *Eucharistie et mondialisation*, 34).

religion of the State has replaced the religion of the Church, or, to be more correct, that religion is becoming individual while the civil power is recognised as having the paramount claims of an organized society upon the allegiance of its members."[24] The liberal State actually fulfills one of the goals of the warring princes of the fifteenth and sixteenth centuries: religion becomes a private matter, leaving the public realm free to be managed by the State. As Alexis de Tocqueville wrote: "If it be of the highest importance to man, as an individual, that his religion should be true, it is not so to society. Society has no future life to hope for or to fear; and provided the citizens profess a religion, the particular tenets of that religion are of little importance to its interests."[25]

What does this debate over the interpretation of the Wars of Religion have to do with William James? For one thing it helps us understand how James's individualist, privatized account of religion is part of his commitment to democracy. Religion must be contained within its own individual, private sphere in order to insure the secular neutrality of the democratic public space. James's strongly individualist account of religion, and his near-solipsistic account of religious experience, are ways of effecting such a containment.

While James is not known primarily as a political writer, his strong commitment to democracy manifests itself in a number of his works. It was perhaps only a bit of run-away rhetoric when he told one audience: "Democracy is a kind of religion."[26] But even when speaking more soberly, he does seem to think that the advent of democracy has fundamentally shifted our way of thinking, not least about matters of religion. So, in *The Varieties of Religious Experience*, after recounting some of the "absurd and puerile" things Saint Gertrude reports Christ saying to her, James goes on to say:

> What with science, idealism, and democracy, our own imagination has grown to need a God of an entirely different temperament from that Being interested exclusively in dealing out personal favors, with whom our ancestors were so contented. Smitten as we are with the vision of social righteousness, a God indifferent to everything but adulation, and full of partiality for his individual favorites, lacks an essential element of largeness; and even the best professional sainthood of former centuries, pent in as it is to such a conception, seems to us curiously shallow and unedifying (269).

[24] John Neville Figgis, *From Gerson to Grotius, 1414-1625* (New York, NY: Harper Torchbook, 1960) 124, quoted in Cavanaugh, *Eucharistie et mondialisation*, 49-50.

[25] Alexis de Tocqueville, *Democracy in America* [1835/1840], vol. I (New York, NY: Alfred A. Knopf, 1972) 303.

[26] William James, "The Social Value of the College-Bred" [1907], *The Moral Equivalent of War and Other Essays*, ed. John Roth (New York, NY: Harper Torchbooks, 1971) 21.

In a later series of lectures, he states: "The vaster vistas which scientific evolutionism has opened, and the rising tide of social democratic ideals, have changed the type of our imagination, and the older monarchial theism is obsolete or obsolescent."[27]

Such remarks not only show that, in James's estimation, growing democratic consciousness undermines traditional Christian claims, they also make clear the low esteem in which James held traditional Christianity. In his own recent Gifford Lectures, Stanley Hauerwas has charged that "what is wrong with Christianity for James was not that it failed to be pragmatic but that it failed to be democratic."[28] In other words, Christianity is a threat to democracy. But why is this the case? Perhaps some light is shed by the kind of god (or "superhuman consciousness") James proposed to replace "older monarchial theism". In his 1909 Hibbert Lectures at Oxford University, James concluded by proposing that we "be frankly pluralistic and assume that the superhuman consciousness, however vast it may be, has itself an external environment, and consequently is finite".[29] Human beings should embrace a god, or what James called in the *Varieties* the "more", that "is finite, either in power or in knowledge, or in both at once".[30] Such a finite god is entirely able to fulfill the requirements for an object of religious experience laid out in *The Varieties of Religious Experience* and, in James's eyes, is infinitely preferable to the old God of Christianity.

The problem with traditional Christianity is that it insists on a God who is both infinite and other, indeed, a God who is not contained in any genus at all. As James puts it, such a God has a connection to us that "appears as unilateral and not reciprocal ... our relation, in short, is not a strictly social relation".[31] Of course what James means by "social" is in fact "democratic" (the only serious option for society). What is so offensive about traditional Christian notions of God is that such a God cannot be a fellow citizen with us of our pluralistic universe. Such a God is under no obligation to try to persuade us to his point of view, to engage in the give and take of democratic discourse, to compromise his own will in order to achieve social peace, or to run the risk of common suffering that all other citizens of the universe share. Rather, he is the one who commands and

---

[27] William James, *A Pluralistic Universe* [1909] (Lincoln, NE: University of Nebraska Press, 1996) 30.

[28] Hauerwas, *With the Grain of the Universe*, 85.

[29] James, *A Pluralistic Universe*, 310-311.

[30] James, *A Pluralistic Universe*, 311.

[31] James, *A Pluralistic Universe*, 26-27.

it is done. Such a God, unleashed in the public realm, undermines the pragmatic, pluralistic democracy that James so valued.[32]

It would, of course, be undemocratic to eliminate Christianity, given democratic commitments to freedom of religion. But it *can* be contained, trivialized, made into the metaphysical equivalent of a hobby, and thereby disarmed. James writes in *The Varieties of Religious Experience* that "over-beliefs in various directions are absolutely indispensable, and ... we should treat them with tenderness and tolerance so long as they are not intolerant themselves" (388). But what does it mean to be "tolerant"? Is it sufficient for the transubstantiationist Catholic to refrain from cleaving the skull of his consubstantiationist Lutheran neighbor? There are hints in James's writings that he is asking for more, that anything short of a purely individualist and pragmatic version of religious belief fails the test. In particular, religious belief must give up any claim to any sort of public authority, any authority that extends beyond the range of the individual's private life. Richard Rorty, in his characteristic fashion, makes the same point more bluntly, noting that a pragmatist can be a theist, but:

> Pragmatist theists ... do have to get along without personal immortality, providential intervention, the efficacy of the sacraments, the virgin birth, the risen Christ, the covenant with Abraham, the authority of the Koran, and a lot of other things which many theists are loathe to do without. Or, if they want them, they will have to interpret them "symbolically" ... for they must prevent them from providing premises for practical reasoning ... Demythologizing amounts to saying that, whatever theism is good for, it is not a device for predicting or controlling our environment.[33]

In other words, religious belief is fine, so long as it is treated as something the truth of which is trivial for determining public behavior. One may believe in the resurrection of Christ, so long as one believes it purely as a matter of personal opinion and does not let it shape one's political life, which ought to be governed by the principles of pragmatic compromise. Maybe this is what James meant at the outset of his lectures when he spoke of "the peculiar philosophic temperament, as well as the

---

[32] We should not underestimate the way in which Jamesian pragmatism has affected contemporary theology. For a critique of Catherine LaCugna's *God with Us* for its pragmatist interpretation of the Trinity, see Matthew Levering, "Beyond the Jamesean Impasse in Trinitarian Theology," *The Thomist* 66 (2002) 395-420. It is interesting to note that what LaCugna finds unacceptable in Thomas Aquinas's theology is exactly what James finds objectionable: the idea that God does not have a "real" relation to creatures.

[33] Richard Rorty, "Religious Faith, Intellectual Responsibility, and Romance," *The Cambridge Companion to William James*, 92.

peculiar political temperament, that goes with our English speech", the temperaments that he hoped would "more and more pervade and influence the world".[34]

Perhaps we ought to take James's remark that "democracy is a kind of religion" a bit more seriously. If we accept the "revisionist" account of the Wars of Religion and the rise of the State, we ought to entertain the possibility that James's segregation of the Christian God in the private realm of "religious experience" is simply the continuation of the campaign waged by the absolutist monarchs of the sixteenth and seventeenth centuries, in which the State replaced the Church as the true *religio* of the body politic. Certainly his relentless individualism and his effective dismissal of "ecclesiasticism" and "over-beliefs" point in such a direction. And if the democratic and pragmatic temperament of the English-speaking peoples does in fact come to pervade the world, what place does this leave for a Christianity that refuses to be a species of "pure personal religion", but rather claims to be the body of Christ, a visible and historical sign of God's redemption of the world? What place does this leave for the pilgrim city, whose belief in the risen Christ marks it out as a distinctive people in the midst of the nations? Because it prompts such questions, much is to be learned from *The Varieties of Religious Experience*, though what is learned may not be what James wanted to teach.

---

[34] James, *Varieties*, 41.

NEWMAN AND RELIGIOUS EXPERIENCE

TERRENCE MERRIGAN

1. Introduction

In 1967, a book appeared with the title *The Rediscovery of Newman*. The book contained the fruits of the first Oxford Newman Symposium, held in March 1966, just three months after the Second Vatican Council had ended. The participants in the conference were united in the conviction that the council marked the first step in "the vindication of all the main theological, religious, and cultural positions" developed by John Henry Newman.[1] One speaker, Bernard Dupuy, drew a parallel between the council's historic recognition of the place of 'experience' in Christian life (*Dei Verbum*, §8) and Newman's attention to this theme. "Newman," he said, "reminds theologians that belief, to be living, must always be linked with personal experience."[2]

In 1974, in an article entitled "Revolution in Catholic Theology", Bernard Lonergan identified one of the major sources of this revolution as the "dethronement of speculative intellect or of pure reason", and its replacement by a way of knowing that is based on observation, discovery and experimentation. The process of dethronement, Lonergan observes, "has been a general trend in modern philosophy", and he goes on to point up certain paradigmatic moments in that process:

> Empirical science led to empiricist philosophy. Empiricist philosophy awoke Kant from his dogmatic slumbers. The German absolute idealists, Fichte, Schelling, Hegel, attempted to restore speculative reason to her throne, but their success was limited. Kierkegaard took his stand on faith, Schopenhauer wrote on the world as will and representation, Newman

[1] John Coulson and A.M. Allchin, "Introduction," *The Rediscovery of Newman: An Oxford Symposium*, ed. John Coulson and A.M. Allchin (London: Sheed and Ward and SPCK, 1967) xi. The authors are quoting Bishop Butler's assessment of the significance of the Second Vatican Council for Newman's work, but they claim that Butler's remarks "might as fittingly stand for the united judgment" of the 1966 symposium. Butler's comments are contained in his contribution to the volume that was the fruit of the symposium. See B.C. Butler, "Newman and the Second Vatican Council," *The Rediscovery of Newman*, 245. These texts are also mentioned by Nicholas Lash in his article, "Tides and Twilight: Newman Since Vatican II," *Newman after a Hundred Years*, ed. Ian Ker and A.G. Hill (Oxford: Clarendon, 1990) 447-464.

[2] Bernard Dupuy, "Newman's Influence in France," *The Rediscovery of Newman*, 173.

toasted conscience, Dilthey wanted a *Lebensphilosophie*, Blondel wanted a philosophy of action, Ricoeur is busy with a philosophy of will, and in the same direction tend the pragmatists, the personalists, the existentialists.[3]

Reflecting on this passage, Nicholas Lash comments that the names of Heidegger and Wittgenstein "should surely be added".[4] This is undoubtedly the case, but what interests us now is Lonergan's claim that Newman belongs at home in the list of those thinkers who have advanced the cause of experientially-based insight.

The same point had already been made by another Jesuit scholar, Erich Przywara, in 1923. He endeavored to highlight the complementarity between the inductive, historical approach characteristic of Newman's theological method and the more logical and deductive method of traditional Catholic thought. In fact, Przywara viewed Newman's whole theological-philosophical program as the 'obverse', as it were, of Scholastic reflection, i.e. as the subjective 'counterpart', so to speak, of the objective, metaphysical system developed in classical Catholic thought. Przywara went on to make the striking claim that, in the contemporary setting, what was required for a comprehensive Catholic intellectual life was a synthesis of the historical and metaphysical approaches, epitomized respectively by Newman and St. Thomas.[5]

All these authors applaud Newman's attention to experience and we see no reason not to applaud with them. But it was not always thus! Both during his life as a Catholic, and in the period leading up to Vatican II, Newman paid a heavy price for his empirical bent. His contemporaries, trained as they were in neo-Scholasticism, could not comprehend his theological method and more or less left him to his own devices. Then, shortly after his death, Newman was claimed by the so-called Modernists who drew explicitly on his work to justify their appeal to religious experience. Newman's first biographer agonized about whether Newman had been – retrospectively and implicitly – condemned along with the 'Modernists'. Even though it has since become clear that Newman's views were not those of the Modernists, Gabriel Daly, an authority on both, could still claim that they were united in "their emphasis on experience, especially moral

---

[3] Bernard Lonergan, *A Second Collection: Papers by Bernard J.F. Lonergan*, ed. W.F.J. Ryan and B.J. Tyrrell (London: Longman, Darton, and Todd, 1974) 234. See also p. 235: "The modern scientist does perform logical operations: he formulates, defines, infers. But he also observes, discovers, experiments."

[4] Lash, "Tides and Twilight: Newman Since Vatican II," 458 n. 40.

[5] Erich Przywara, *Gottgeheimnis der Welt: Drei Vortrage über die geistige Krisis der Gegenwart* (Munich: Theatiner Verlag, 1923) 173.

experience, and on the crucial role played by the imagination in the apprehension and interpretation of experience".[6]

I shall return to the question of the relationship between Newman and the Modernists. For the moment, however, these few references suffice as an indication of Newman's significance for the theme under consideration, namely, religious experience. They also provide some clues about Newman's contribution to the theme, namely: his turn to the subject, the distinctly ethical dimension of his approach and the significance he attaches to the imagination. In what follows, we shall touch on all these themes. We shall begin, however, with the heart of Newman's thought on religious experience, namely his understanding of conscience.

2. Newman on Conscience

In his *Philosophical Notebook* (a collection of reflections and jottings which was only published in 1970), Newman ponders Descartes' celebrated 'Cogito, ergo sum'. He writes as follows: "Though it is not easy to give a list of those primary conditions of the mind which are involved in the fact of existence, yet it is obvious to name some of them. I include among them, not only memory, sensation, reasoning, but also conscience."[7] So Newman can write that it is as legitimate to say 'Sentio ergo sum', or 'Conscientiam habeo, ergo sum', as it is to say 'Cogito ergo sum'. In all these formulations, however, the linking 'ergo' is the product of a 'post-factum' analysis of what is originally "one complex act of intuition", in which the 'apprehension' and the 'judgment' are simultaneous.[8]

According to Newman, conscience is characterized by two indivisible, but not indistinguishable, dimensions which he described as a 'moral sense' and a 'sense of duty'. As a 'moral sense', conscience is manifest in the awareness that "there is a right and a wrong", which is not, of course, the same as knowing, in a particular instance, what is right or wrong. As a 'sense of duty', conscience is manifest as a "keen sense of obligation and

---

[6] Gabriel Daly, "Newman, Divine Revelation, and the Catholic Modernists," *Newman and the Word*, ed. Terrence Merrigan and Ian Ker, Louvain Theological and Pastoral Monographs, 27 (Leuven: Peeters and Grand Rapids, MI: W.B. Eerdmans, 2000) 66. See also p. 50.

[7] John Henry Newman, *The Philosophical Notebook of John Henry Newman,* ed. Edward Sillem, 2 vols. (Leuven: Nauwelaerts, 1969-1970). See 2:43. See also 2:31-33.

[8] Newman, *Philosophical Notebook,* 2:71; see also 2:33, 43, 45, 63, 83.

responsibility", namely, to do good and avoid evil.[9] Newman speaks of
these two dimensions, respectively, as "a rule of right conduct", and "a
sanction of right conduct".[10] It is peculiar to conscience that it "has an intimate bearing on our affections and emotions". Indeed in Newman's view
conscience "is always emotional". Hence he sometimes speaks quite simply of "the feeling of conscience" to describe its operation. Newman
describes this feeling as "a certain keen sensibility, pleasant or painful –
self-approval and hope, or compunction and fear" which follows upon the
performance of certain actions. For Newman, the feelings generated by
conscience – or, more accurately, by our behavior – are possessed of profound theological significance. As he expresses it:

> Inanimate things cannot stir our affections; these are correlative persons.
> If, as is the case, we feel responsibility, are ashamed, are frightened, at trans-
> gressing the voice of conscience, this implies that there is One to whom we
> are responsible, before whom we are ashamed, whose claims upon us we
> fear. If, on doing wrong, we feel the same tearful, broken-hearted sorrow
> which overwhelms us on hurting a mother; if, on doing right, we enjoy the
> same sunny serenity of mind, the same soothing, satisfactory delight which
> follows on our receiving praise from a father, we certainly have within us
> the image of some person, to whom our love and veneration look, in whose
> smile we find our happiness, for whom we yearn, towards whom we direct
> our pleadings, in whose anger we are troubled and waste away. These feel-
> ings in us are such as require for their exciting cause an intelligent being;
> we are not affectionate towards a stone, nor do we feel shame before a horse
> or a dog; we have no remorse or compunction on breaking mere human
> law: yet, so it is, conscience excites all these painful emotions, confusion,
> foreboding, self-condemnation; and on the other hand it sheds upon us a
> deep peace, a sense of security, a resignation, and a hope, which there is no
> sensible, no earthly object to elicit. 'The wicked flees when no one pur-
> sueth' [Proverbs 28:1]; then why does he flee? Who is it that he sees in soli-
> tude, in darkness, in the hidden chambers of his heart? If the cause of these
> emotions does not belong to this visible world, the Object to which his per-
> ception is directed must be Supernatural and Divine.[11]

For Newman, then, religion or at least religious consciousness is a profoundly ethical affair. It is born out of the inevitable requirement – the
necessity – to act. One might say, then, that the soul's encounter with God
in conscience is as much a question of volition as of sentiment – i.e. the
emotions attendant on the performance of particular deeds – though it is,

---

[9] John Henry Newman, *An Essay in Aid of a Grammar of Assent*, ed. Ian Ker (Oxford:
Clarendon, 1985) 74; see also p. 105. All references to the *Grammar of Assent* will be to
the Ker edition. See also Newman's *Philosophical Notebook*, 2:49.

[10] Newman, *Grammar of Assent*, 74.

[11] Newman, *Grammar of Assent*, 76.

of course, the presence of these emotions which implies "a living object, towards which [conscience] is directed".[12] Walgrave says as much when he writes that while the apprehension of God by conscience is "spontaneous", it remains a free act which "supposes" a serious moral commitment, a willingness to obey the moral imperative, and a fundamental choice for generosity.[13] The relationship between the soul and God which attention to conscience makes possible is not therefore merely a matter of present religious experience – it is, above all, (to use another of Walgrave's formulations) an "absolute religious goal".[14] And for Newman, this goal is only realizable in and through a sustained moral commitment made incarnate in the mundane routine of every day. As he explains:

> Whether [the image of the Divine within us] grows brighter and stronger, or, on the other hand, is dimmed, distorted, or obliterated, depends on each of us individually ... Men transgress their sense of duty, and gradually lose their sentiments of shame and fear, the natural supplements of transgression, which ... are the witnesses of the Unseen Judge.[15]

For Newman, then, in the experience of conscience the subject apprehends not only itself, but itself as subject in relation to God. In other words 'Conscientiam habeo, ergo sum' is also – and more or less simultaneously – 'Conscientaim habeo, ergo Deus est'.[16] This conviction explains Newman's oft-cited remark that, for him, there were "two and two only absolute and luminously self-evident beings, myself and my Creator".[17] It accounts, too, for his declaration that: "If I am asked why I believe in God, I answer that it is because I believe in myself, for I feel it impossible to believe in my own existence (and of that fact I am quite sure) without believing also in the existence of Him, who lives as a Personal, All-seeing, All-judging Being in my conscience."[18]

[12] Newman, *Grammar of Assent*, 109.

[13] J.H. Walgrave, "La prevue de l'existence de Dieu par la conscience morale en l'experience de valeurs," *L'existence de Dieu*, Cahiers de l'actualité religieuse, 16 (Paris: Casterman, 1961) 117.

[14] J.H. Walgrave, *Newman vandaag*, Periodieke uitgave van het Geert Groote Genootschap, 698 (Marienburg and 's Hertogenbosch, 1957) 25.

[15] Newman, *Grammar of Assent*, 116. See also John Henry Newman, *Fifteen Sermons Preached Before the University of Oxford between A.D. 1826 and 1843* (Notre Dame, IN: University of Notre Dame Press, 1997) 80-81.

[16] Newman, *Philosophical Notebook*, 2:59: "[As] our consciousness [of thought] is a reflex act implying existence (I think, therefore, I am), so this sensation of conscience is the recognition of our obligation the notion of an external being obliging, I say this, not from any abstract argument for the force of the terms (e.g. 'a law implies a lawgiver') but the peculiarity of that feeling to which I give the name of Conscience."

[17] John Henry Newman, *Apologia pro vita sua*, ed. Ian Ker (Harmondsworth: Penguin, 1994) 25.

[18] Newman, *Apologia*, 182.

Newman acknowledged that his claim on behalf of conscience, namely that "it has a legitimate place among our mental acts", or "that we have by nature a conscience", constituted an unproved "assumption", a "first principle", the rejection of which made further discussion meaningless.[19] He makes no apology for this. In his *Lectures on the Present Position of Catholics in England* (1851) he declared that to think at all one must be possessed of at least some "opinions which are held without proof", and these are rightly called "first principles":

> If you trace back your reasons for holding an opinion, you must stop some-where; the process cannot go on forever; you must come at last to some-thing you cannot prove, else life would be spent in inquiring and reasoning, our minds would be ever tossing to and fro, and there would be nothing to guide us. No man alive, but has some First Principles or other.[20]

Of course, for Newman the 'inevitability' of first principles does not divest the individual of responsibility in regard to them. It is basic to New-man's philosophical outlook that humanity is "emphatically self-made", and charged with the task of "completing his inchoate and rudimental nature, and of developing his own perfection out of the living elements with which his mind began to be".[21] Where conscience is concerned, the implications of this principle are staggering. Not only is it one's "sacred duty" to acknowledge conscience's legitimate place among those "living elements" with which the mind begins (in accordance with "the law of our being"), the failure to do this prejudices, if it does not entirely pervert, the elaboration of a whole body of derivative principles. For Newman then, the task of thinking soundly is, from the outset, a moral, as well as a prac-tical imperative, one to be fulfilled most 'conscientiously' in fidelity to our being.[22]

---

[19] Newman, *Grammar of Assent*, 105, 60.

[20] John Henry Newman, *The Present Position of Catholics in* England (London: Long-mans, Green, and Co., 1903) 279.

[21] Newman, *Grammar of Assent*, 349.

[22] Newman, *Present Position of Catholics*, 279: "From what I have said, it is plain that First Principles may be false or true; indeed, this is my very point, as you will presently see. Certainly they are not necessarily true; and again, certainly there are ways of unlearn-ing them when they are false: moreover, as regards moral and religious First Principles which are false, of course a Catholic considers that no one holds them except by some fault of his own." These words date from 1851. By the time Newman came to write the *Gram-mar of Assent* (1870), he expressed himself much more cautiously regarding the problem of defectiveness in first principles, and recognized the possibility of inculpable error. See *Grammar of Assent*, 241, 249, 259. The 'decisiveness' of Newman's position in the 1851 lectures must be viewed in the light of the apologetic character of the lectures, and his status as a convert, that is to say, his concern not to seem to call into doubt traditional thinking.

3. Newman on Religion

For Newman, the apprehension of God in the phenomena of conscience is not the product of a rational analysis of our experience (though such an analysis might well, in his view, issue in a proof of God's existence). It is instead an immediate, "existential" (Walgrave)[23] awareness – an instinct or intuition[24] – that we stand before One who is to us as a father, One in whose presence we feel a "tenderness almost tearful on going wrong, and a grateful cheerfulness when we go right".[25]

There is no suggestion here of private revelation or of some sort of mystical encounter with God. God is present as the source of the phenomenon, and the person – most obviously the child – who has been secured from influences hostile to religion or moral behavior, spontaneously apprehends Him in the sanction (and its attendant emotions) which accompanies his decisions.[26] Hence, conscience is described as the "voice" of God, or more accurately as the "echo" of God's voice in us.[27]

As we have seen, Newman holds that the experience of conscience impresses on the mind a "picture" or "image" of God:

> These feelings in us are such as require for their exciting cause an intelligent being … If the cause of these emotions does not belong to this visible world, the Object to which his perception is directed must be Supernatural and Divine; and thus the phenomena of Conscience, as a dictate, avail *to impress the imagination* with the picture of a Supreme Governor, a Judge, holy, just, powerful, all-seeing, retributive.[28]

It is precisely in view of its role in generating an 'image' of God in the minds of men and women that Newman describes conscience as the "creative principle of religion". Religion here – or 'natural religion' as Newman preferred to call it – is that living relationship between the

---

[23] J.H. Walgrave, "Conscience de Soi et conscience de Dieu: Notes sur le 'Cahier philosophique' de Newman," *Thomist* 71 (1971) 377.

[24] Newman, *Grammar of Assent*, 46-47, 71-73. For a discussion of 'instinct' and 'intuition' in Newman, see Father Zeno, *Our Way to Certitude* (Leiden: E.J. Brill, 1957) 95-97.

[25] John Henry Newman, *Parochial and Plain Sermons*, 8 vols. (London: Rivingtons, 1868) 2:61.

[26] Newman, *Grammar of Assent*, 73-75. The sanction is "conveyed in the feelings which attend onright or wrong conduct" (74).

[27] Newman, *Grammar of Assent*, 74-78.

[28] Newman, *Grammar of Assent*, 76 (emphasis ours). For an extensive discussion of the nature and function of the imagination in Newman's work, see Terrence Merrigan, *Clear Heads and Holy Hearts: The Religious and Theological Ideal of John Henry Newman*, Louvain Theological and Pastoral Monographs, 7 (Leuven: Peeters and Grand Rapids, MI: W.B. Eerdmans, 1991) 48-81, 177-178, 186-192; "The Image of the Word: John Henry Newman and John Hick on the Place of Christ in Christianity," *Newman and the Word*, 1-47.

believer and a personal God which comes to expression in stories and myths (narrative), rituals and devotions (spirituality), and codes of conduct (ethics). It was this view of things that allowed Newman, in 1833, to affirm "the divinity of traditionary religion" or the "dispensation of paganism" (Clement of Alexandria). "All knowledge of religion," he wrote, "is from [God], and not only that which the Bible has transmitted to us. There never was a time when God had not spoken to man, and told him to a certain extent his duty."[29]

Newman's discussion of 'natural religion' mixes historical and what we would now call phenomenological analysis. As history, Newman's presentation is certainly not up to contemporary standards. The heart of his reflections, however, is not the history of religions, but the growth of religious consciousness. And on this point, Newman displays a remarkable sensitivity to the insights of modern psychology. He is, for example, well aware that the development of an 'image' of God is heavily dependent on all sorts of 'external' factors and circumstances:

> How far this initial religious knowledge comes from without, and how far from within, how much is natural, how much implies a special divine aid which is above nature, we have no means of determining ... Whether its elements, latent in the mind, would ever be elicited without extrinsic help is very doubtful.[30]

Newman insists that the "image" of God must be expanded, deepened and completed "by means of education, social intercourse, experience, and literature".[31] At least initially, and this remains the case if one's education and religious practice do not contribute to a "filling out" of one's emergent image of God, the individual experiences Him primarily as "Lawgiver" and "Judge".

However, while conscience reveals God primarily as a lawgiver, it also reveals Him as One who wills our happiness and has ordered creation accordingly. From the outset then, the individual looks to the divine lawgiver as to a benevolent ruler, who has one's best interests at heart.[32]

---

[29] John Henry Newman, *The Arians of the Fourth Century* (London: Longmans, Green, and Co., 1921) 79, 81. See Wilfrid Ward, *Last Lectures* (London: Longmans, Green, and Co., 1918) 38-39, 41.

[30] Newman, *Grammar of Assent*, 79.

[31] Newman, *Grammar of Assent*, 80.

[32] Newman, *Grammar of Assent*, 78. See also Terrence Merrigan, "'One Momentous Doctrine which enters into my Reasoning': The Unitive Function of Newman's Doctrine of Providence," *Downside Review* 108 (1990) 254-281. Note that on p. 59 of the *Grammar of Assent* Newman places the "thought" of "Divine Goodness" before the thought of "future reward", or "eternal life" as objects of real assent. See our discussion of this point in

Walgrave gives expression to this when he observes that, unlike Max
Scheler or Albert Schweitzer and others, Newman does not reduce the
experience of conscience to that of 'bad conscience'. Instead, he views it
as a dialectical relationship between 'good' and 'bad'.[33] This tensile experience issues in two major characteristics of 'natural religion', namely,
prayer and hope, with the former serving as the vehicle par excellence for
the expression of the latter.[34] The hope of which Newman speaks is perhaps best described as an irrepressible existential longing or perhaps even
anticipation that the One who calls us to perfection will come to our aid:

> One of the most important effects of Natural Religion on the mind, in prepa-
> ration for Revealed, is the anticipation which it creates, that a Revelation
> will be given. That earnest desire of it, which religious minds cherish, leads
> the way to the expectation of it. Those who know nothing of the wounds
> of the soul, are not led to deal with the question, or to consider its circum-
> stances; but when our attention is roused, then the more steadily we dwell
> upon it, the more probable does it seem that a revelation has been or will
> be given to us. This presentiment is founded on our sense, on the one hand,
> of the infinite goodness of God, and, on the other, of our own extreme mis-
> ery and need – two doctrines which are the primary constituents of Natural
> Religion.[35]

So it is that the expectation of a revelation, that is to say, of some initiative on the part of the divine, emerges, for Newman, as an 'integral part
of Natural Religion'.[36] The naturally religious person is, as it were, "on
the lookout" for God. It is at this point that the specificity of the Jewish-
Christian tradition comes most sharply into focus.

4. Newman on the Christian Religion

Not surprisingly perhaps, Newman was convinced that only the Jewish-
Christian tradition could satisfy the religious hunger engendered by the
experience of conscience.[37] The key to Christianity's appeal in this regard

Terrence Merrigan, "'Numquam minus solus quam cum solus': Newman's First Conversion – Its Significance for His Life and Thought," *Downside Review* 103 (1985) 99-116,
106-107.

[33] J.H. Walgrave, "Newman's leer over het geweten," *Selected Writings – Thematische
Geschriften*, ed. G. De Schrijver and J.J. Kelly (Leuven: Peeters, 1982) 195.

[34] Newman, *Grammar of Assent*, 258-260.

[35] Newman, *Grammar of Assent*, 272. See also his *Discourses to Mixed Congregations*
(London: Burns, Oates, and Co., 1886) 277-279.

[36] Newman, *Grammar of Assent*, 260-261.

[37] On a number of occasions throughout his life, Newman reflected on the inability of
'natural religion' to relieve the 'disquiet', as it were, generated in the hearts of its

is its radical 'historicity'. It is this feature of Christian teaching which, for · Newman, constitutes its appeal to the beleaguered practitioner of natural religion:

> Revelation meets us with simple and distinct *facts* and *actions*, not with painful inductions from existing phenomena, not with generalized laws or metaphysical conjectures, but with *Jesus and the Resurrection* ... The life of Christ brings together and concentrates truths concerning the chief good and the laws of our being, which wander idle and forlorn over the surface of the moral world, and often appear to diverge from each other.[38]

In the Incarnation of Christ, above all, "the revealed doctrine ... takes its true shape, and receives an historical reality; and the Almighty is introduced into His own world at a certain time and in a definite way", namely, "in the form and history of man".[39] For Newman, Christ is the perfect realization of the sacramental principle – in Him, God is visibly and tangibly active in history. "Surely His very presence was a Sacrament," writes Newman. In Him, "God has made history to be doctrine."[40] The Incarnation is an unparalleled 'theological-historical' fact, that is to say, an historical event charged with theological significance.

Christianity, for Newman, is not the mere perfection of man's natural religious instincts, though it does involve the perfection of all the authentic elements of natural religion. It is the introduction into history of something hitherto unknown; it is a revelation of God that would be unthinkable were it not already realized in the person of Jesus, and

adherents. These included conscience's lack of a sanction, beyond itself, for its elevated claims about the Moral Governor and Judge. These are therefore prey to societal pressures and to the individual's own inclination to abandon the moral ideal as impracticable. In an early University sermon, (and it would seem, again in the *Grammar of Assent*), Newman maintains that it is, above all, the obscurity of the object of one's religious instincts and aspirations, that is, the dearth of information about God's 'personality', which saps one's moral resolve and raises the specter of the futility of the moral and religious enterprise. Elsewhere, it is the sense of one's culpability and one's inadequacy to the moral task which exposes natural religion's inherent insufficiency. In all three cases, Newman proposes that the only adequate complement to the essentially incomplete natural religion of man is 'revealed' religion, which is to say, "the doctrine taught in the Mosaic and Christian dispensation, and contained in the Holy Scriptures", which does not supplant, but builds on, nature's authentic teaching. (See Newman, *The Arians of the Fourth Century*, 79; *Grammar of Assent*, 313; for a complete discussion of Newman's analysis of the deficiencies of natural religion, including the sources in his work where each position is elaborated, see Merrigan, "One Momentous Doctrine which enters into my Reasoning," 265-266.)

[38] Newman, *Discourses to Mixed Congregations,* 347; *Fifteen Sermons Preached Before the University of Oxford*, 27 (emphasis Newman).

[39] Newman, *Discourses to Mixed Congregations,* 347; *Parochial and Plain Sermons*, 2:155, 32, 39; 3:156.

[40] Newman, *Parochial and Plain Sermons*, 2:62, 227; 3:114-115.

"represented in the Church by means of certain sacramental 'extensions of the Incarnation'".[41] According to Newman, Christianity has provided us with a fuller vision of the divine person than conscience ever could. Great though our (potential) knowledge of God may be under natural religion, Newman reflects, it is but "twilight" in comparison to "the fullness and exactness" of "our mental image of the Divine Personality and Attributes" furnished by "the light of Christianity". Newman actually speaks of an "addition" to our image of God, and maintains that it is "one main purpose" of revealed religion to "give us a clear and sufficient object for our faith". Indeed, "the Gospels ... contain a manifestation of the Divine Nature, so special, as to make it appear from the contrast as if nothing were known of God, when they are unknown."[42]

Christianity is a "revelatio revelata":

> a definite message from God to man conveyed distinctly by His chosen instruments, and to be received as such a message; and therefore to be positively acknowledged, embraced, and maintained as true, on the ground of its being divine, *not as true on intrinsic grounds*, not as probably true, or partially true, but as absolutely certain knowledge ... because it comes from Him who can neither deceive nor be deceived.[43]

Christian faith is not simply the recognition of the suitability of certain doctrines to the human condition; nor does it emerge naturally out of the experience of conscience. It is instead a response to God's unprecedented action in history in Jesus Christ.[44] In making this claim, Newman puts paid to the suggestion that he defended the sort of immanentism so characteristic of Modernism. This does not mean, however, that he did not speak in a manner which was *also* open to a Modernist reading. So, for example, speaking of the Christian appropriation of the Christ-event, Newman observes that "the original instrument" of conversion and the "principle of fellowship" among the first Christians was the "Thought or Image of Christ". Moreover, he argues, this "central Image" continues to serve as the "vivifying idea both of the Christian body and of individuals in it". The image of Christ is the principle of Christian fraternity, and the source and soul of Christian "moral life". It "both creates faith, and then rewards it".[45] The whole life of the Church can be conceived as

---

[41] E.R. Fairweather, "Introduction," *The Oxford Movement*, ed. J. Dillenberger *et al.*, Library of Protestant Thought (New York, NY: Oxford University Press, 1964) 11.

[42] Newman, *Grammar of Assent*, 81 (emphasis ours).

[43] Newman, *Grammar of Assent*, 249-250 (emphasis ours).

[44] John Henry Newman, *Essays Critical and Historical*, 2 vols. (London: Basil Pickering, 1871) 1:39.

[45] Newman, *Grammar of Assent*, 298-299.

the endeavor to promote and perpetuate this image. Indeed, the Church's narrative, ritual and doctrinal traditions can be regarded as – ideally – the objectification of this image in history. So Newman can write that, in time, "what was at first an impression on the Imagination" became "a system or creed in the Reason".[46]

There is, however, an important difference between Newman and the Modernists. The latter effectively disassociated *faith* (which is founded on religious experience) from *belief* (i.e. the historically determined articulation of that experience). For Newman, on the other hand, *faith* (which is founded on the testimony to Christ) and *belief* (which is the Church's articulation of her experience of Christ) "are to each other as implicit to explicit, inarticulate to articulate, and pre-conceptual to conceptual. They modulate into each other, therefore, and may be said to share a common grammar".[46a] In view of this fact, as John Coulson points out, Newman "does not press the distinction between assents to the primary forms of religious faith (expressed in metaphor, symbol, and story), and to the beliefs and doctrines derived from them".[47]

This explains why in the *Grammar of Assent* Newman argues that a religious truth-claim (such as, 'The Son is God') can be held "either as a theological truth, or as a religious fact or reality". In the first instance, "the proposition is apprehended for the purposes of proof, analysis, comparison and the like intellectual exercises". That is to say, it is regarded "as the expression of a notion". In the second instance, the proposition is apprehended "for the purposes of devotion." In this case, it is "the image of a reality".[48]

According to Newman, religion "lives and thrives in the contemplation" of images. It is this which provides the believer with "motives for devotion and faithful obedience". Precisely because it is "an image living within us", precisely because it occupies "a place in the imagination and the heart", a dogmatic proposition, such as the claim that 'the Son is God', is able to "work a revolution in the mind", to inflame the heart, and to shape our conduct.[49]

---

[46] Newman, *Fifteen Sermons Preached Before the University of Oxford*, 329. This edition contains en axcellent introduction to the sermons by Mary Katherine Tillman. See especially *xxxvi-*xliii (the asterisks distinguish Tillman's introduction from Newman's Preface).

[46a] John Coulson, *Religion and Imagination: 'In aid of a Grammar of Assent'* (Oxford: Clarendon Press, 1981) 51.

[47] Coulson, *Religion and Imagination*, 51.

[48] Newman, *Grammar of Assent*, 82.

[49] Newman, *Grammar of Assent*, 94, 86.

This is not – and need not – be the case where the same proposition is looked upon as the expression of a notion and subjected to critical scrutiny. Indeed, Newman observes that the application of the intellect to religious issues may well issue in a diminishment of lively faith. "In the religious world," he observes, "no one seems to look for any great devotion or fervor in controversialists, ... theologians, and the like, it being taken for granted, rightly or wrongly, that such men are too intellectual to be spiritual, and are more occupied with the truth of doctrine than with its reality."[50]

That being said, however, Newman's religious and theological ideal was a tensile or polar unity between both activities – "religion using theology, and theology using religion".[51] Newman insisted that, to be effective, the theologian must engage in what he called a "theology of the religious imagination",[52] that is to say, a theology which unites a concern for the notional elaboration of faith with a profound respect for, and immersion in, its fundamental symbols and images. This recalls the remark by Dupuy with which I opened this presentation, namely, that Newman serves as a reminder "that belief, to be living, must always be linked with personal experience".[52a]

5. Conclusion

On the basis of our discussion up until now, I think the following conclusions are fairly evident.

First, it is clear that Newman sees the relationship between God and the human person in very experiential terms, and that it is, therefore, legitimate to regard him as a representative of the turn to the subject and the turn to experience in theology. Moreover, as far as Roman Catholic theology is concerned, he is one of the first modern thinkers in whom this turn is so visible.

Second, in Newman's case, the category of 'religious experience' is certainly not out of place in regard to his discussion of conscience, if by 'religious experience' we mean – to use the words of Gerald O'Collins

[50] Newman, *Grammar of Assent*, 141.

[51] John Henry Newman, *The Via Media of the Anglican Church*, 2 vols. (Longmans, Green, and Co., 1899) 1:xlvii. See Terrence Merrigan, "Newman's Experience of God: An Interpretive Model," *Bijdragen* 48 (1987) 444-464; "Newman on the Practice of Theology," *Louvain Studies* 14 (1989) 260-284.

[52] Newman, *Grammar of Assent*, 80.

[52a] Dupuy, "Newman's Influence in France," 173.

– experience that allows us to "consciously experience the depth and ultimacy in life"[53] that Christians identify as God.

Third, for Newman, religious experience is irreducibly 'ethical' in character. That is to say, it is inextricably bound up with the choices men and women make regarding their conduct in the world.

Fourth, for Newman, religious experience is 'universal' in character, which is to say that it is a real possibility *for* all men and women. Indeed, it seems fair to say that, for Newman, religious experience is an integral dimension of human existence – which is, of course, not to say that it is always 'exploited' (so to speak) *by* all men and women. In any case, it is certainly not the exclusive preserve of a 'religious' elite.

Fifth, for Newman there is such a thing as properly Christian religious experience, namely, the experience which is shaped by reference to Jesus Christ.

Sixth, properly Christian religious experience is only possible within the Christian Church whose task it is to mediate the presence of Christ to its members.

Seventh, religious experience, whether universal or properly Christian, involves the 'whole' person, which is to say that it calls into play our affections, our intellect and our will.

Eighth, for Newman, the imagination is essential to this process. It is the medium by which the religious object is able to be appropriated as an object of affection and reflection, and to act as a stimulus for the will.[54]

---

[53] Gerald O'Collins, *Fundamental Theology* (Mahwah, NJ: Paulist, 1981) 51.

[54] See Terrence Merrigan, "Imagination and Religious Commitment in the Pluralist Theology of Religions," *Religious Imagination and the Pluralist Theology of Religions*, ed. T. Merrigan and D. Robinson, a special issue of *Louvain Studies* 27 (2002) 197-217, 208-217.

EXISTENTIAL PARTICIPATION: RELIGIOUS EXPERIENCE IN TILLICH'S METHOD OF CORRELATION

ANNEKATRIEN DEPOORTER

1. Introduction

Contemporary culture seems to be awash with religious experience. Whenever one searches the Internet, one discovers all kinds of web sites providing information (whether useful or not) about the religious experiences to be had. They tantalisingly offer to introduce one to the many varieties of religious experience, to specialise in the psychology of religious experience or even simply to enjoy the religious experience in one's life. There is even a 'Religious Experience' salsa sauce, whose divine taste is guaranteed to take one to heaven.[1] Alas, these web sites fail to shed light on the delicate matter of actually defining the concept of religious experience. What do we mean by religious experience? How do we conceive of its importance and role in contemporary belief? Moreover, does religious experience play an active role in theology? What is its significance for theology today? Is religious experience fundamental to theological method or is it being over-emphasised?

Friedrich Schleiermacher is often credited with being the first to emphasise the crucial importance of religious experience to theology. In the late eighteenth and early nineteenth century, he advanced a new understanding of religion, namely religion as a 'feeling of absolute dependence'. In his view, religion is neither theoretical knowledge nor a moral activity. Schleiermacher interprets religion as *feeling* (*das Gefühl*), indicating that it concerns the impact of the universe upon us in the depths of our being, rather than subjective emotion. He states that there is an immediate awareness of that which is beyond subject and object, of the essence of everything within us.[2] This awareness constitutes the core of religion. Schleiermacher wished to trace the lost religious dimension of culture, for he was convinced that there were fundamental points of agreement between the religious dimension and the deepest intentions of the

---

[1] See http://www.thewrath.com

[2] Paul Tillich, *Perspectives on 19th and 20th Century Protestant Theology*, ed. Carl. E. Braaten (London: SCM Press, 1967) 96.

human spirit. In that sense, Schleiermacher considered religious experience a central concept. These ideas have been hugely influencial in theology, both in the nineteenth and twentieth centuries.

Paul Tillich used Schleiermacher's thoughts and applied them to the consciousness of his own time. He attempted to formulate an appropriate answer to the dilemma that entered theology under Schleiermacher: was it possible for there to be an alliance between Christianity and culture where both partners maintained their independence and if so, how? Searching for that new alliance, he developed a specific theological method – the 'method of correlation'. In this method, religious experience plays a significant role.

This chapter will focus first on Tillich's understanding of religious experience. I will investigate how he defines and describes this phenomenon. For this, I will refer to his *Systematic Theology*,[3] where Tillich fully elaborates on his method of correlation. In addition to this main work, I will also discuss an article in which Tillich wrote on the problem of theological method,[4] a paper in which he devotes some attention to the function of religious experience in the work of the theologian.

Second, I will investigate how religious experience functions in his method of correlation. Does Tillich invoke religious experience to connect religion and culture? How significant a role does experience really play in his method? What are, in his view, the possibilities and the difficulties when religious experience is considered to be a central concept in theology?

In conclusion, I will look at the actual impact of religious experience in Tillich's method of correlation, his understanding of the role of the theologian, and his view of the connection between religion and culture. These discussions are still of great importance for current theology even though the context has completely changed since. I will endeavour to make a connection between Tillich's ideas on religious experience and the current theological situation.

---

[3] Paul Tillich, *Systematic Theology* (Chicago, IL: University of Chicago Press, 1951 [vol. I], 1957 [vol. II], 1963 [vol. III].

[4] Paul Tillich, "The Problem of Theological Method," *Four Existentialist Theologians: A Reader from the Works of Jacques Maritain, Nicolas Berdiaev, Martin Buber, and Paul Tillich*, ed. Will Herberg (Westport, CT: Greenwood, 1975) 238-255.

2. Tillich's Definition of Religious Experience

a. Apologetic Theology

For Tillich, theology is essentially an answering theology. It has to give answer to the needs of the specific time in which we are living, without renouncing the eternal truth of the Christian message. It is an exercise in maintaining balance between two poles: the contemporary situation and Christian truth. "Theology moves back and forth between two poles, the eternal truth of its foundation and the temporal situation in which the eternal truth must be received. Not many theological systems have been able to balance these two demands perfectly."[5] With his 'apologetic theology' Tillich intends to link the Christian message with the needs of his generation. He seeks to direct theology away from focusing so much on eternal truth that it no longer contains a message relevant to the contemporary situation in which Christians live. On the other hand, he does not want to sacrifice elements of the truth to the situation either.[6] An apologetic theology avoids both pitfalls. It formulates answers to questions which arise from the human situation, by employing the means provided by the contemporary situation itself. The situation to which theology responds is the "totality of man's creative self-interpretation in a particular period".[7] Tillich's *Systematic Theology* is intended to present such an answering theology.

Because he is trying to balance the Christian message and the human situation, Tillich situates himself on a fine line – 'on the boundary' as he would call it – between supra-naturalism and naturalism, between kerygmatic theology and liberal theology. These two methods have their own ways of relating Christian faith to a person's spiritual existence, but both fail to bring the message and the human existence together in balance. Either they overemphasize the unchanging character of the message, or they make the message totally subordinate to the human situation. The supranaturalistic method takes the Christian message to be the sum of revealed truths which have fallen into the human situation "like strange bodies from a strange world".[8] The creative receiving role of human beings is totally denied in this view. The message becomes a living message only

---

[5] Tillich, *Systematic Theology*, 1:3.
[6] Tillich, *Systematic Theology*, 1:3.
[7] Tillich, *Systematic Theology*, 1:4.
[8] Tillich, *Systematic Theology*, 1:64.

when human beings receive it and interpret it in such a way that it becomes of value to their lives, so that the message can give answers to the questions that lie in human existence. That is why Tillich has worked out the role of the theologian as a receiver and an interpreter of the message for the people of his time. The naturalistic method, on the other hand, derives the Christian message from a person's natural state.[10] Tillich terms it a 'humanistic' method, which explains the Christian message as a creation of man's self-realisation. For Tillich this is not an option because the human situation only provides the questions to which theology gives an answer. In his view it is incorrect to place questions and answers on the same level: "Revelation is spoken to man, not by man to himself."[11]

The role of human creativity is important for Tillich, but not so important that it can either replace the Christian message spoken to man or make it disappear. Tillich endeavours to preserve the role of human creativity and interpretation without running the risk of overemphasising them. Experience, religious or otherwise, plays a constitutive role in the development of his answering theology. It is clear that his apologetic theology attributes a creative role to human beings in receiving and interpreting the Christian message. Tillich's vision of theology as an answering theology has influenced his view on the role and meaning of experience.

b. Religious Experience in an Augustinian-Franciscan Tradition

It is nothing short of ambitious to attempt to define the meaning of religious experience in Tillich's thought since Tillich is not so clear about the concept himself. He uses the word in various ways and in different contexts. Several definitions can be found in his works to explain what religious experience could possibly mean. I will focus mainly on Tillich's view of (religious) experience as a constitutive element for his theological method. To that end I will restrict myself to the first volume of *Systematic Theology*, as well as to an article which Tillich wrote on the problem of theological method. My aim is not intended to exhaust the different definitions of religous experience Tillich provides, but rather to investigate the manner in which experience functions in his theological method.

[10] Tillich, *Systematic Theology*, 1:64.
[11] Tillich, *Systematic Theology*, 1:64.

Tillich notes that the question of experience has been a central question whenever the nature and method of theology are under discussion. He argues that the theologians of the early Franciscan school were well aware of what is today called an 'existential' relation to truth. In their opinion, theology was practical knowledge, based on a participation of the knowing subject in the spiritual realities.[12] Tillich's interpretation pursues the same course. He notes that the endeavours of the Franciscan 'experiential' theologians are rooted in "the mystical-Augustinian principle of the immediate awareness of 'being-itself', which is, at the same time, 'truth-itself' (*esse ipsum – verum ipsum*)".[13] In his opinion the Augustinian-Franciscan tradition never lost its foothold and ultimately found a classical theological expression in Schleiermacher's theological method.

c. Tillich's Perception of Schleiermacher's Idea of Religious Experience

On more than one occasion, Tillich points out that Schleiermacher has been misread and unfairly treated in respect of his definition of religious experience.[13a] In his apologetic theology, Schleiermacher finds the possibility of creating a new understanding of religion. He terms the experience of identity, between the human being and God, 'feeling'. As I said earlier, Schleiermacher defines religion as a feeling of 'absolute dependence'. Because of the use of this term he has been criticized by many psychologists and theologians who consider the concept too psychological.[14] Although Tillich argues that Schleiermacher had no intention of speaking about religion as a psychological function, he recognises that Schleiermacher should have avoided using the psychological concept of 'feeling'. In Tillich's view Schleiermacher failed to defend himself against this criticism. However, Tillich argues that this is a misconception of Schleier-

---

[12] Tillich, *Systematic Theology*, 1:40.

[13] Tillich, *Systematic Theology*, 1:41.

[13a] In his lectures on the history of protestant theology, he mentions in particular Hegel's misunderstanding of Schleiermacher's theory. In Tillich's view this had to do with the fact that Hegel and Schleiermacher were both pupils of Schelling and did not like each other. According to Tillich Hegel interpreted Schleiermacher's words according to the worst possible meaning of what Schleiermacher had said and therefore treated him unfairly. Tillich considers this as regrettable because Hegel should have understood the meaning of the principle of identity that Schleiermacher, following Schelling, wanted to express (Tillich, *Perspectives*, 96-97). In the *Systematic Theology*, Tillich refers to the successors of Schleiermacher who also misunderstood him (Tillich, *Systematic Theology*, 1:15). A few pages further down he repeats that a psychological interpretation of Schleiermacher's definition of religion is mistaken and unfair (Tillich, *Systematic Theology*, 1:41).

[14] Tillich, *Perspectives*, 96.

macher's intentions: his 'feeling of absolute dependence' is not a subjective oceanic feeling as Freud stated it. It is Tillich's opinion that Schleiermacher's idea of religion defines religious experience as "the presence of something unconditional beyond the knowing and acting of which we are aware".[15] Tillich acknowledges the emotional element but notes that there is an emotional side to everything when a whole person is involved. Yet this emotional element does not define the character of religion as a whole. If it were only feeling it would be just detached aesthetic pleasure and nothing more. In Schleiermacher's opinion however, the 'feeling of absolute dependence' transforms the whole existence of the person who experiences it.[16] This element will come to be of great importance to Tillich's own perception of religious experience, together with Schleiermacher's conviction that God is present at every moment of our secular life.

Schleiermacher's thought exerted a huge influence on Tillich's own search for a contemporary interpretation of religious experience. Tillich states that no present-day theologian should avoid discussing Schleiermacher's experiential method, whether in agreement or disagreement. According to Tillich, it is unfair to disagree with Schleiermacher only on the basis of the misconception that his famous definition of religion can be seen only from a psychological view, for the 'feeling of absolute dependence' means "the immediate awareness of something unconditional in the sense of the Augustinian-Franciscan tradition".[17] In this tradition 'feeling' refers not to a psychological function but to the awareness of that which transcends intellect and will, subject and object. For Tillich, the 'feeling of absolute dependence' comes very close to what is called in his system "ultimate concern about the ground and meaning of our being".[18] With this, we come to Tillich's own concept of religion and religious experience.

d. Religious Experience as Encounter with Reality

Religion, for Tillich, is essentially 'the experience of the unconditional', as he states it in his earliest works.[18a] Later on he describes religion as an

---

[15] Tillich, *Perspectives*, 99.
[16] Tillich, *Perspectives*, 105.
[17] Tillich, *Systematic Theology*, 1:41.
[18] Tillich, *Systematic Theology*, 1:42.
[18a] For example in Tillich, "Über die Idee einer Theologie der Kultur" [1919], Tillich, *Gesammelte Werke IX* (Stuttgart: Evangelisches Verlagswerk, 1967) 13-31.

ultimate concern. Every person has an ultimate concern, something that concerns her more than anything else. For religious people this ultimate concern is God. In his *Systematic Theology*, Tillich links his earlier thought on the unconditional to his later concept of ultimate concern. Influenced by existentialist philosophy, with which he had become acquainted after the First World War, he points out the existential character of religion and religious experience. *Ultimate concern* is, for Tillich, the abstract translation of the great commandment: "The Lord, our God, the Lord is one; and you shall love the Lord your God with all your heart, and with all your soul, and with all your mind, and with all your strength" (Mk 12:29). The religious concern is ultimate and excludes all other concerns from ultimate significance. That is why Tillich terms the *ultimate concern* unconditional, independent of any conditions of character, desire, or circumstance. He uses the word 'concern' to emphasize its existential character. Tillich avoids speaking of *the* ultimate, for fear of the danger of arguing about it in detached objectivity. That which is ultimate gives itself only to the attitude of ultimate concern demanding the surrender of our subjectivity.[19] When we then ask what the content of our ultimate concern is, the answer, states Tillich, cannot be a special object, not even God. Our ultimate concern is, in his view, that which determines our being and non-being. By 'being' Tillich means "the whole of human reality, the structure, the meaning and the aim of existence".[20] It becomes clear that the existentialist influence on Tillich's thought is expressed in his definition of religion and religious experience.

In his essay on the problem of theological method Tillich makes a distinction between what most people call 'experience' but what he wishes to term 'encounter' on the one hand, and 'theoretically interpreted encounter' – which he then designates 'experience' – on the other. Whereas most theologians use the term 'experience', Tillich desires to rescue it from losing its specific meaning. He defines the pre-theoretical relation to reality as an encounter with reality. The presupposition of his theology (and, in his opinion, of all theology) is that there is a special encounter with reality or, to put it differently, that there is a special manner in which reality imposes itself on us. This special encounter with reality is called 'religious'. In his paper Tillich states that "having a religious encounter with reality" means "being ultimately concerned about reality".[21]

---

[19] Tillich, *Systematic Theology*, 1:12.
[20] Tillich, *Systematic Theology*, 1:14.
[21] Tillich, "The problem of theological method," 240.

The reason why Tillich avoids the word 'experience' by replacing it with 'encounter' lies partly in the way in which the *Erlangen* school in Germany developed Schleiermacher's idea of religious experience. Tillich states that for the *Erlangen* school religious experience can mean all sorts of things. The word is even used so extensively that it borders on the problematic. For Tillich, the word 'experience' has become meaningless. For this reason he introduces the word 'encounter', which is taken from Buber's concept of the I-Thou encounter.[22] It is striking that Tillich mentions here that he *tried* to introduce the word 'encounter'. He is not convinced that he has really managed to do so. It is true that he himself did not succeed in using the word 'encounter' consistently. The difference that he introduces between a pre-theoretical and an interpreted encounter with reality does not seem to be borne out, even in his own writings. In his *Systematic Theology* for example, Tillich uses 'experience' instead of 'encounter'. Another striking element is that in his lectures for students he refers to Buber's I-Thou encounter, which involves a *personal* encounter with God. This contradicts to his stress on encounter as the existential encounter with reality. Most times Tillich does not focus on personal encounter with God. His view of religious experience is much wider than that, namely experience as a mediating principle between human beings and reality. In his lectures, however, we find several references to a personal God when Tillich speaks about religious experience as encounter, for instance when he states that he is convinced that every period of human history uses different images to express the encounter between the infinite within ourselves and the infinite in the whole universe. That 'encounter' is possible at every time and in every context means (for Tillich) that God is present at every moment and that we have to consider every moment of our secular life as filled with the divine presence, "not pushing the presence into a Sunday service and otherwise forgetting it".[23] Here too Tillich abandons his original statement that religious experience is encounter with the whole of reality, so that he focuses on a personal relation with God in daily life. The existentialist influences on Tillich's thought do not prevent him from speaking about God in personal terms. On the other hand, it is clear that a distinction needs to be drawn between Tillich's speaking about encounter with reality on a broad scale, and his view of encounter with God in a narrow sense. Later on I shall connect this with his broad and narrow view of

---

[22] Tillich, *Perspectives*, 211.
[23] Tillich, *Perspectives*, 101.

religion as a whole. In any event, Tillich speaks far more easily about the personal relation with God in his lectures to students than in his method-ological articles and his *Systematic Theology*. This can be explained by the fact that Tillich felt compelled to talk about God in the lectures he gave as a professor in theology, whereas in his methodological articles he could stick to the philosophical approach he applied in his earlier work, namely his *theology of culture*. Or possibly his view of religious experi-ence as an encounter with a personal God was a phenomenon that arose only during his years in America.[24]

e. Encounter with Reality through Existential Participation

As I have already said, an Augustinian concept of religious experience influenced Tillich's interpretation of experience. In his view this Augus-tinian concept has a very existential character: it was understood as "immediate awareness of being-itself".[24a] Tillich is very much in favour of the inward and immediate dimension of this definition, but in the intro-duction of *Systematic Theology* he makes clear that this awareness is only possible when there is an existential participation in the sources of the-ology (Bible, Church history, history of religion and culture). Religious experience has a specific role in theology, it functions as the medium through which the sources are received. I will return to this later. Tillich states that the sources are "sources only for one who participates in them, that is, through experience".[25] In order to avoid being misunderstood, Tillich carefully explains what he means by experience as a medium for theology. For an understanding of Tillich's theological method, the ques-tion of experience is a central point of discussion where everything depends upon the sense in which the term 'experience' is used.[26] Although Tillich obviously intends to clarify the use and meaning of religious experience in the *Systematic Theology*, the question remains whether he

---

[24] In 1933 the Nazis forced Tillich to leave Germany because of his critique of national socialism. His emigration not only demanded of him an adaptation to a different language and culture, but also to another vision and practice of religion. In America he became engaged in the religious life of the Church, whereas in Germany he was engaged in a more distant way, interested in the religious life of people in a broad sense. For an extensive biography of Paul Tillich, see Marion Pauck and Wilhelm Pauck, *Paul Tillich: His Life and Thought. Volume I: Life* (London: Collins, 1977).

[24a] Tillich, *Systematic Theology*, 1:41.
[25] Tillich, *Systematic Theology*, 1:40.
[26] Tillich, *Systematic Theology*, 1:40, 42.

actually succeeded in doing so. A survey of the different meanings of experience will make clear which interpretation Tillich prefers.

In his introduction to his *Systematic Theology*, Tillich distinguishes three basic uses of the word 'experience' in present theological thought, namely the ontological, the scientific, and the mystical sense.[27] The ontological sense is a consequence of philosophical positivism as developed by James and Dewey. Its basic presupposition is that we can only speak meaningfully of the reality that is positively given, and this is only given in experience. In this view, experience is identical with empirical reality. Tillich states that when this is applied to theology it makes experience the source of theology. It also implies that "nothing can appear in the theological system which transcends the whole of experience".[27a] This excludes a divine being in the traditional sense from theology and it shows that "the religious objects are not objects among others, but that they are expressions of a quality or dimension of our general experience".[27b] Tillich points out that the empirical theologians who use this ontological concept of experience do not derive their theology from this experience but from their participation in a concrete religious reality. In Tillich's view they seek to discover the corresponding elements within the whole of experience. This means that there is an immediate participation in religious reality, preceding any theological analysis of reality as a whole. This idea of participation is very useful for Tillich in view of his own idea of existential participation. That is why he states that empirical theology of this type has made a definite contribution to systematic theology.

Tillich describes a second understanding of experience as the scientific definition of experience, namely as the experimentally tested experience of science. In his view, the application of this method of scientific experience to theology is doomed to fail for two reasons. First, the object of theology (for Tillich, the 'ultimate concern and its concrete expressions') is not an object within the whole of scientific experience. It cannot be discovered by conclusions derived from observation. As Tillich says: "It can be found only in acts of surrender and participation."[27c] Second, Tillich points out that it cannot be tested with scientific methods of verification because these methods require the testing subject to be outside the test situation. Here Tillich elaborates his central idea, namely that being a theologian means to participate in reality, to *experience* reality:

---

[27] I will follow Tillich's explanation as it is described in *Systematic Theology*, 1:42-45.
[27a] Tillich, *Systematic Theology*, 1:43.
[27b] Tillich, *Systematic Theology*, 1:43.
[27c] Tillich, *Systematic Theology*, 1:44.

"The object of theology can be verified only by a participation in which the testing theologian risks himself in the ultimate sense of 'to be or not to be'. This test is never finished, not even in a complete life of experience."[28] Tillich also makes clear, however, that although experience is an important element in the method of theology, it can be a mediating principle only: "In no case can scientific experience as such produce a foundation and source of systematic theology."[28a]

The real problem, therefore, is the third concept of experience, namely the mystical. It is in fact presupposed by the other two concepts of experience. "Without an experience of participation neither the whole of experience nor articulated experience would reveal anything about our ultimate concern."[28b] But exactly what does experience by participation reveal? After giving a survey of possible answers to this question, Tillich concludes that considering experience as the medium through which the objective sources are received, excludes two extreme positions, namely the idea that 'open experience' is the source of systematic theology on the one hand and, on the other, the assertion that experience is in no sense a theological source. For Tillich experience is important for theology, but not in a sense that it can add some new material to the other sources. Theology is based on the unique event of Jesus Christ, which is the criterion of every religious experience as such: "This event is given to experience and not derived from it."[28c] Here we come to the core of Tillich's thought about the role of religious experience in theological method, which I will elaborate further in the second part of this article.

The theologian is, in Tillich's view, the one who receives the sources through the medium of experience. Therefore, it is important that the theologian participates in an existential way in the whole of existence. Although the theologian has received the revelatory answers to the questions that mankind asks itself, she must participate in its situation as if she had never received the answer. "He must participate in man's finitude, which is also his own, and in its anxiety as though he had never received the revelatory answer of 'eternity'. He must participate in man's estrangement, which is also his own, and show the anxiety of guilt as though he had never received the revelatory answer of 'forgiveness'."[29] Tillich makes it very clear that the theologian can only interpret the sources

---

[28] Tillich, *Systematic Theology*, 1:44.
[28a] Tillich, *Systematic Theology*, 1:44.
[28b] Tillich, *Systematic Theology*, 1:45.
[28c] Tillich, *Systematic Theology*, 1:46.
[29] Tillich, *Systematic Theology*, 2:16-17.

through experience, through participation in the sources and in human existence. This is why Tillich describes the basic attitude of the theologian as 'existential commitment'. By this a theologian is connected to the whole of existence that gives seriousness to his theological statements.[30] From the preceding, Tillich gives the impression that experience plays an important role in the work of a systematic theologian. I will now investigate how he makes it concrete in his method of correlation and explore whether experience really plays a significant role in it.

3. The Role of Experience in the Method of Correlation

a. The Method of Correlation as Part of an Apologetic Theology

Tillich's method of correlation is meant to indicate the relation between the existential questions asked by human persons and the theological answers given. This method has an apologetic character: it seeks to make clear that the Christian message provides a significant answer to general human questions. On the other hand, the method also demonstrates that the answers are influenced by the questions. The correlation between the situation in which people live and the Christian message is a relation of mutual-influence-in-independence. In general we can state that Tillich wishes to overcome two – and in his opinion, dangerous – extremes. On the one hand, he wants to avoid overemphasising the message vis-à-vis the culture; on the other, he does not wish to adjust the message to the culture in an uncritical way. Since Tillich uses the term 'correlation' to indicate several kinds of relations, it is not possible to speak of any *one* method of correlation. He uses the term to describe the relation between human questions and theological answers, between culture and religion, and finally between philosophy and theology.

The method of correlation functions in an apologetic theology not merely to make apparent the relation between message and context, but also as a good method for showing that the Christian answer is valuable to those who situate themselves outside Christian belief. Apologetic theology can prove that elements from different kinds of religions and cultures all lead to the Christian answer in the end: "It is the task of apologetic theology to prove that the Christian claim also has validity from the point of view of those outside the theological circle. Apologetic theology

---

[30] Tillich, *Systematic Theology*, 1:23.

must show that trends which are immanent in all religions and cultures move toward the Christian answer."[31] To questions that are raised in any culture or religious context, the Christian answer can appeal as both significant and acceptable. This is what Tillich wishes to attest with his apologetic theology and his method of correlation in particular.

b. The Role of the Philosopher and the Theologian

When the theologian makes an analysis of the human situation she is actually doing the work of a philosopher while still being a theologian. This means that she does not make the analysis free from engagement. She does it in such a manner that the Christian message and symbols become clear and meaningful. For this reason her analysis differs from that of the philosopher's: "In the light of this message he may make an analysis of existence which is more penetrating than that of most philosophers. ... He cannot help seeing human existence and existence generally in such a way that the Christian symbols appear meaningful and understandable to him."[32] While philosophy is concerned with the structure of reality, theology focuses more on the meaning of reality for us. Tillich identifies three main differences between the philosopher and the theologian. First of all, the philosopher tries to maintain objectivity whereas the theologian realises that she herself is part of the reality that she is investigating. Therefore the theologian sees her work as an engagement: she is involved in an existential way.[33] Secondly, the source for the philosopher is the universal *logos* that can be found in all aspects of reality. The theologian, on the other hand, seeks her knowledge not in the universal *logos* but in the *Logos* who "became flesh".[34] Thirdly, philosophers dwell upon the cosmological structure of philosophical assertions, but theologians try to reveal the soteriological character of their statements. Theology relates life's structures to the creative ground of being, the divine Spirit.[35] Although Tillich clearly underlines the differences between the philosopher and the theologian, he also stresses that there is one aspect in common, namely that they are both located within the reality they seek to describe and therefore cannot avoid doing theology. Like anyone else,

[31] Tillich, *Systematic Theology*, 1:15.
[32] Tillich, *Systematic Theology*, 1:63.
[33] Tillich, *Systematic Theology*, 1:22-23.
[34] Tillich, *Systematic Theology*, 1:23.
[35] Tillich, *Systematic Theology*, 1:24.

the theologian and the philosopher are both influenced by the power of an *ultimate concern*, whether they be aware of it, or not. This brings Tillich to say that: "Every creative philosopher is a hidden theologian ... in the degree to which his existential situation and his ultimate concern shape his philosophical vision."[36]

c. The Method of Systematic Theology

It is important to briefly explain how Tillich describes the theological method employed in his *Systematic Theology* because it demonstrates what place he reserves for religious experience in his theological system. Tillich emphasises that any reflection upon a method is derived from the cognitive work that has already been done. It is only after following a theological method that you are able to give a definition of that method and not the other way around. Thus the description of his theological method in *Systematic Theology* has to be seen as the articulation of a manner of working which he practised since his early years. Before clarifying the method of correlation, Tillich first raises some important issues, namely the question of (1) the sources, (2) the medium and (3) the norm of theology.

(1) For Tillich the Bible is not theology's only source. The 'word of God' must be seen as something much wider than merely the Bible: "If the 'Word of God' or the 'act of revelation' is called the source of systematic theology, it must be emphasized that the 'word of God' is not limited to the words of a book and that the act of revelation is not the 'inspiring' of a 'book of revelation', even if the book is the document of the final 'Word of God', the fulfilment and criterion of all revelations. The biblical message embraces more (and less) than the biblical books. Systematic theology, therefore, has additional sources beyond the Bible."[37]

For Tillich, the other sources are Church, cultural and religious history.[38] It remains his conviction that a common ground can also be found outside the theological circle in all cultures and religions. In Tillich's view, the activities of the Spirit can be found in each culture or religion. By making the statement that culture is a source for theology, Tillich paves the way for his method of correlation. Once a theologian views

---

[36] Tillich, *Systematic Theology*, 1:25.
[37] Tillich, *Systematic Theology*, 1:35.
[38] Tillich, *Systematic Theology*, 1:35-40.

culture as a source he can begin to map the existential questions arising out of that culture in order to give theological answers to them at a later stage. Tillich is convinced that the various cultural expressions such as philosophy, a political system, an artistic style, or ethical and social principles, manifest an ultimate concern and are, as such, a source for theology. This idea is not new in Tillich's thought. He had already suggested it in his earlier work *Theologie der Kultur*.[39] In his opinion, a theology of culture makes for a valuable source to practise theology within an apologetic project. It provides the theologian with the ability to ask existential questions which then function as the foundation for formulating theological answers.

(2) The sources of theology can only function as such if they are received in the right manner. Only one who participates in the sources, by means of experience, can use the sources for a theological purpose. The religious experience of the theologian is a central element in Tillich's perception of theology, because this experience is the medium through which the sources are received and handed down. Although Tillich thinks of experience as a major category, he describes it as being very passive: "Experience receives and does not produce. Its productive power is restricted to the transformation of what is given to it. But this transformation is not intended. The act of reception intends to receive and only to receive."[40] Restricting the influence of the theologian's experience, Tillich intends to steer clear of two extreme positions: the influence of the medium, the theologian's religious experience, should not be so minimal that it results in theology only repeating the sources without transforming them; on the other end, it should not be so major that new elements are being produced, instead of realizing a transformation.[41] Thus experience is not an independent authority that can produce the content of revelation. It is the medium through which the message is handed down. In each new situation a transformation of the message is possible only when the content of the message is not endangered. The theologian is occupied in reformulating the message in any new context, but her experience cannot be the foundation of a new religious doctrine.

(3) The sources of theology as well as their mediation through experience are bound to a specific criterion. The necessity of such a criterion,

---

[39] Cf. Paul Tillich, "Über die Idee einer Theologie der Kultur," *Gesammelte Werke IX* (Stuttgart: Evangelisches Verlagswerk, 1967) 13- 31; Paul Tillich, *Die Religiöse Lage der Gegenwart* (Berlin: Ullstein, 1926).

[40] Tillich, *Systematic Theology*, 1:45.

[41] Tillich, *Systematic Theology*, 1:45.

in Tillich's view, becomes evident when one considers the variety of the potential materials. The incorporation of sources and medium can only lead to a theological system if they are guided by a criterion, if there is a norm to test them.[42] Tillich states that already in the early periods of Church history the need for such a norm was felt. In each context this norm changes under the influence of the encounter of Church and context, so the norm differs for every generation of Christians. Tillich adds that this happens in a rather unconscious manner.[43] He seeks to formulate an adequate norm for contemporary theology within his own context. The human situation of his day was frequently described in literature, art, philosophy, and politics, as well as in the psychology of the unconscious, in terms of conflict, self-destruction, meaninglessness and despair. Because of this Tillich speaks of a new theological insight in the demonic-tragical structures of the individual and of social life. He holds that from this specific situation a specific answer, fitting the spirit of the time, should be found: "The question arising out of this experience is not, as in the Reformation, the question of a merciful God and the forgiveness of sins; nor is it, as in the early Greek Church, the question of finitude, of death and error; nor is it the question of the personal religious life or of the Christianisation of culture and society. It is the question of a reality in which the self-estrangement of our existence is overcome, a reality of reconciliation and reunion, of creativity, meaning and hope."[44] This reality is called the 'New Being' by Tillich. He understands the Christian message as a message of the New Being, an answer to the human situation of his time and of all times.[45] Once again, the apologetic character of his project is evident. He indicates firstly that there is an intrinsic bond between situation and message and secondly that the Christian faith is also meaningful for non-believers because the Christian message is also the answer to any human question.

The term 'New Being', however, does not sufficiently clarify what is really at stake. In Tillich's view, systematic theology has to state that the New Being manifests itself in Jesus the Christ. He who is Christ brings us the new *aeon*, the new reality. With 'Jesus Christ as the New Being' Tillich links hands with the ancient Christian confession of faith that Jesus is the Christ. Thus this ancient confession changes across the times yet always finds its adequate expression at every point in time.

[42] Tillich, *Systematic Theology*, 1:47.
[43] Tillich, *Systematic Theology*, 1:48.
[44] Tillich, *Systematic Theology*, 1:49.
[45] Tillich, *Systematic Theology*, 1:49.

Nevertheless, there is a paradox for, on the one hand, the norm is the criterion that governs the interpretation of the sources but, on the other hand, the norm changes through the times, influenced by the experiences through which the sources are mediated. Tillich himself is fully aware of the paradox. He puts it as follows: "Collective as well as individual experiences are the mediums through which the message is received, coloured and interpreted. The norm grows within the medium of experience. But it is, at the same time, the criterion of any experience. The norm judges the medium in which it grows; it judges the weak, interrupted, distorted character of all religious experience, although it is only through this feeble medium that a norm can come to existence at all."[46]

This tension reveals the importance of the concrete historical situation in Tillich's thought. The mediation of the sources as well as the norm of theology is affected by the changes appearing in the context. The role of historical conditions cannot be minimalised to such an extent that the question of how people expressed the unchanging message in their own situation should be the only one left for theology to answer. Theology is not a historical discipline; it is "a constructive task".[47] This statement seems to contradict Tillich's stress that the role of the medium in theology is a non-creative one. It may be clear that Tillich himself is wrestling with the role of experience in theology. On the one hand he objects to overemphasising the role of experience, on the other hand he does not want to minimalise it. This tension is never dissolved in his work.

d. The Method of Correlation

In his *Systematic Theology*, Tillich's method of correlation is expressed in terms of a question-answer model: theology formulates the answers to the questions arising out of human existence. For Tillich, theology has always functioned according to the method of correlation, although he realizes that his own method has to be a product of his own time and that the changes in reality will lead to changes in the theological method. Still, he seems to accord his own theory some authority by stating that theology has always followed the method of correlation.

Tillich makes use of the word 'correlation' to describe the real dependence of things and incidents in a structured whole. In theology, correlation is the real dependence between a person's ultimate concern and what

---

[46] Tillich, *Systematic Theology*, 1:52.
[47] Tillich, *Systematic Theology*, 1:52.

that individual is ultimately concerned about.[48] In Tillich's view, correlation is about the relation between a human being and God, a relation that lies in religious experience. This does not mean that God becomes dependent on humanity, but that his self-manifestation is dependent on the way it is received by them. The relation between God and humanity changes throughout the different stages in the history of revelation, just as God and humanity do so themselves. For Tillich, the encounter between God and humanity is a correlation in the real sense of the word.[49] The bond between them is a bond of reciprocity and dependence in an independent way. To Tillich, this ontological correlation forms the basis for speaking of the logical (epistemological) correlation, namely the correlation between human questions and theological answers. An elaboration of the correlation method is based upon the idea of an epistemological correlation. The movement of this correlation can be described as follows: "Theology formulates the questions implied in human existence and theology formulates the answers implied in divine self-manifestation under the guidance of the questions implied in human existence."[50] The correlation ceases when questions and answers come together, but this can never occur at any one moment in history. The fact that humans ask themselves questions indicates the existential separation between human beings and the endlessness to which they belong in essence. Our existence is a question by virtue of its separation from the endless. This explains why crucial questions about existence were already being asked in humankind's early history, as analyses of mythological material show. Furthermore, little children ask existential questions already when they are very young. Being human means raising questions about one's own existence. At the same time, being human also implies receiving the answer to the questions and then asking more questions based upon the answers that have been obtained. Humankind is ruled by the dynamics of the asking and receiving of questions and answers.[51]

A systematic theology that applies the method of correlation has to make an analysis of the situation from which the questions arises, and by doing so, demonstrate that Christian symbols offer the answers to those questions. This means that the theologian has to look at existence in all its aspects (philosophy, poetry, drama, novels, psychology, sociology) in such a way that Christian symbols can appear understandable

[48] Tillich, *Systematic Theology*, 1:60.
[49] Tillich, *Systematic Theology*, 1:60-61.
[50] Tillich, *Systematic Theology*, 1:61.
[51] Tillich, *Systematic Theology*, 1:61-62.

and meaningful. The Christian message contains all the answers: the theologian only has to trace them through the medium of religious experience and under guidance of the norm.[52] For Tillich it is obvious that the Christian tradition is *the* answer to humanity's questions. It does not occur to him that for some people the Christian answer is only one possible answer among many others. He is convinced that the Christian answer is meaningful to every human being.

Although Tillich seems to make clear that there is an intrinsic bond between situation and message, his method of correlation deals with the dependence between two independent factors. Tillich stresses that in spite of their dependence, the two poles of the correlation are independent. In the introduction to the second part of his *Systematic Theology*, he explains what he means by this dependence-in-independence. He was obliged to do so since his obscure explanation in the first volume made his idea of correlation to susceptible to criticism. It was attacked from both sides: for either stressing the independence too much, or for making allowance for too much dependence. In once again explaining the interaction between the two poles, Tillich was therefore seeking to give answer to his critics. The supranaturalists were correct in saying that the revealed answer cannot be deduced from the existential question but, in the same breath, Tillich had to acknowledge that the statements of the naturalists were equally justified. The latter stated that the answer must be in relation to the human situation: a person cannot receive an answer to a question that was not asked.[53] His delicate balancing act aimed at overcoming both the supranaturalistic and naturalistic views, leads Tillich to a rather long-winded explanation on how the two poles are correlated: "Correlation means that while in some respects questions and answers are independent, they are dependent in other respects."[54] Yet, he does not go further into elaborating this. The tension that exists in the first part of the *Systematic Theology* is hardly resolved by this additional statement. Tillich finds himself in an awkward situation. He does not wish to say that the theological message is fully influenced by the context but, at the same time, he desires to state clearly that the theological message has always to connect itself to the context in which people live in order to be meaningful. Even though he is completely convinced by this, he does not always succeed in making his point clear.

[52] Tillich, *Systematic Theology*, 1:62, 64.
[53] Tillich, *Systematic Theology*, 2:14-15.
[54] Tillich, *Systematic Theology*, 2:15.

4. Evaluation and Discussions

Tillich's apologetic theology presents the Christian doctrine as a set of answers to general human questions. Theology is in a position to formulate satisfying answers to the questions that arise from human existence. In Tillich's theology, the Christian message appears to be the pre-eminent answer. He makes use of existentialism's analyses because they help him to reach his goal, namely proving the plausibility of Christian faith. The analysis of the human situation constitutes one of two central points in the theological circle (since it is in fact an ellipse having two focal points). The other central point consists of the theological answers that lie within Christian doctrine and have to be confronted with only one norm, namely the New Being in Jesus Christ. This norm – the event in Christ – cannot be derived from experience but is given to it. Keeping this norm in mind, the theologian has to inquire into the different sources by participating in human existence, and formulate the answers to the questions which arise. It is important to note in this respect that not only the Bible is a source for theology, but also Church history and the culture in which we live.

Up to this point, our summary of Tillich's correlation method shows it to be a straightforward matter: the theologian analyses the culture in which she lives (with a little help from the philosopher) and the sources of theology in order to formulate the answers that can be evaluated as good or bad theological answers, depending on their conformity with the norm.

However, the method is not that simple. There are two factors that determine the significance of the method depending on how they are interpreted, namely (a) the role of the religious experience of the theologian, and (b) how the dependence and the independence of the poles are understood. In addition, there are two other factors that make for discussion: (c) Tillich's own view of culture and (d) his universalistic presuppositions.

a. How Significant Is the Role of Experience in Tillich's Method of Correlation?

We have already mentioned that there is a certain tension in Tillich's text when it comes to the role of the theologian's experience. In seeking to avoid two extreme positions, Tillich does not succeed in steering a middle course. He seeks not to allocate too active and creative a role to the theologian because this might lead to too large a transformation of the

Christian message. Yet, on the other hand, he does not consider theology to be a mere repetition of an eternal and unchangeable message. Since Tillich is concerned about how the message can be comprehensible to modern people, the message needs at least to be 'translated' into a contemporary language. From such a point of view, the theologian actually *must* bring about a transformation. This transformation can be understood both narrowly and broadly. How the impact of that transformation is interpreted determines the evaluation of the role of religious experience in Tillich's method of correlation. When, firstly, the importance of the transformation is overestimated, the suggestion may arise that Tillich permits the theologian to adapt the theological message to the spirit of the times or, in the worst-case scenario, to sacrifice the Christian identity to a contemporary interpretation of faith. Secondly, when the impact of the transformation is minimised, Tillich may give the impression that the theologian only has the possibility to repeat the eternal message in a modern language, without changes in the interpretation of the message being possible. By providing an explanation without going into detail on the actual impact of the transformation, Tillich gives free rein to his interpreters to either limit or overemphasise the role of religious experience. In his search for a middle course, Tillich fails to strike a balance. Perhaps this is why his text falls victim to different interpretations.

b. The (In)dependence of the Question and the Answer

Tillich's view of the role of experience is not the only problem which may lead to different evaluations of his method of correlation. How he defines the (in)dependence of question and answer, namely as 'the dependence of two independent factors', is also rather unclear. Those exploring Tillich's method of correlation have at some point to deal with the actual implication and impact of this dependence of two independent factors.

The ontological correlation between God and the human – Tillich's point of departure to speak of the epistemological correlation – signifies that it is not only a matter of an independence of two poles (on the one hand human beings and their questions, on the other hand the theological answer that 'falls' into history from beyond and is spoken to human beings as a strange word), but also a dependence. There is a mutually dependent relation between God and humanity and therefore there also has to be an interdependence between the human question and the theological answer. Tillich states clearly that there is a dependence, but he does not explain how it should be imagined, nor in which way the dependence functions. This leaves room for various interpretations.

From the quarter of dialectical theology[55] we find the criticism that Tillich overemphasizes the human question, at the expense of the theological answer. In the spirit of Barth's thought, the dependence of question and answer is questionable and unacceptable. For Barth and his adherents the message is independent of the human situation. Thus the message has to be detached from the question, whether or not it is in agreement with the human situation or not, before it can be investigated. Contiguously, Barth considers that theology, whose only source is the Bible, is given the task to examine the message that God speaks to human beings and not the manner in which we ought to talk about God. In this view revelation is not dependent on the human question and should not be influenced by it.

There is also another possible problem when the influence of the question dominates, namely the risk that God is presented as the 'answer' to a human need and that theology thus becomes a pure anthropocentric theology. Tillich's theology may force the conclusion that God is an *ultimate concern* for humanity only because of the dependence that human beings experience before God since God possesses the power to threaten or to save life. The question arises whether Christian belief has only to do with feelings of dependence. Does a Christian only believe in God to save her life? Does Christian faith not also contain a belief in God for God's sake? One might even think that too much existentialist influence on theology poses a danger. When human existence and the questions that originate from it are overstressed, the faith in God for God's self is likely to be set aside and, as may be concluded, harms the holiness, majesty, and power of God.[56] From this point of view, Tillich's method of correlation risks losing its integrity on account of the apologetic character of theology.[57] Crucial aspects of Christian doctrine may be abandoned for the sake of

---

[55] In twentieth century religious thought, this term is almost exclusively used to indicate the theology of Karl Barth and his adherents who set themselves in a movement opposed to Protestant liberalism. Tillich confronts Barth's dialectical thought with his method of correlation to demonstrate that his own theology is truly dialectical. Cf. John P. Clayton, *The Concept of Correlation: Paul Tillich and the Possibility of a Mediating Theology* (Berlin and New York, NY: De Gruyter, 1980) 160, 164.

[56] George F. Thomas, "The Method and Structure of Tillich's Theology," *The Theology of Paul Tillich,* ed. Charles W. Keygley and Robert W. Bretall (New York, NY: Macmillan, 1952) 85-105, 89. In this article Thomas articulates his apprehension that Tillich's method of correlation gives in too much to an anthropocentric theology and thus advantages the human situation over against the Christian message.

[57] Thomas, "The Method and Structure of Tillich's Theology," 91.

an acceptable presentation of Christian faith in a modern time. But we must not forget that Tillich is himself aware of and preoccupied with this problem. After all, he does not wish to identify himself with liberal theology and dissociates himself from too large a turn to culture. In his theology, Tillich is always careful to consider the Christian message as the starting point for any theology. Although he tries to balance message and context in a rather roundabout way, his intention to preserve the message is prevalent.

This brings some scholars to the opposite opinion, namely that Tillich stresses the Christian message too much to the detriment of the human situation. An argument can also be made for the statement that the question-side is undervalued in Tillich's method of correlation. Tillich's view on the task of the theologian turns out to be, after a close reading, an over-rating of the position of the theologian, describing it as a rather dominant one compared to the position of the philosopher. Even when the theologian acts like a philosopher, namely in making an analysis of the human situation, she cannot lose her theological focus. As a theologian, she analyses the situation in the light of the message. Thus, simultaneous with the dominance of the theologian over the philosopher, a dominance of the message over the situation can be discerned in Tillich's system. His main concern is to formulate the message in an acceptable way for people living in a modern period. The dominance of the message in Tillich's system consists of the message being considered, implicitly, as theology's starting point for theology. Tillich has never openly expressed this presupposition, but he underscores the importance of the message in a concealed way. *Systematic Theology* only mentions two phases in the theological process, namely (1) the analysis of the human situation and (2) the theological answers the message provides.[58] Although Tillich mentions in the introduction that the situation will be analysed in light of the Christian message, this is not revealed in the application of his theological method. In *Systematic Theology*, he gives the impression that the analysis is made autonomously while in fact the analysis is made from a presumed angle. This makes Tillich's system a three-stage instead of a two-stage process, since his method of correlation presupposes the possibility of correlating message and situation, as well as presupposes that the situation be analysed within this particular perspective. In Tillich's method of correlation there is no such thing as

---

[58] Hans van Leeuwen, "Een theologie van het Nieuwe Zijn: Proeve van waardering van Paul Tillich's Systematische Theologie," *Bijdragen* 29 (1968) 2-23, 4-5.

an autonomous analysis of the situation. The overemphasis of the message may in this regard be interpreted as a weakening of the autonomy of the human situation. Thus Tillich's theology can be called a kerygmatic theology, as he himself has admitted. Or, as van Leeuwen points out: "Right has been done to the kerygma and it is rather in the sphere of the existential questions that a complaint should be lodged. ... Against to what it seems to be, I have the opinion that the danger in Tillich's thought doesn't lie in the fact that the answers are determined by the question but rather in the possibility that the questions are nothing more than the negatives of the answers."[59]

Van Leeuwen's comment indicates that the balance Tillich wanted to achieve between the independence and the dependence of the question and the answer in his method of correlation does not hold out. The autonomy of the message, as well as that of the answer, is doubtful. It once again shows that Tillich really wants to preserve a golden mean but fails. By starting with the Christian message and trying to make it understandable for modern people, it may look as if Tillich is giving priority to the human situation, but his stress on the position of the theologian (within the theological circle) and the minimal contribution of his experience (which is not a source but only a medium) leads us to the inevitable conclusion that Tillich really puts the Christian message first in his theological method.

It cannot be denied that with his idea of religious experience as existential participation, Tillich tries to take the human situation seriously, but some theologians reject this idea of participation. Nevertheless, they should bear in mind that this participation is already conceived from within a horizon of belief, namely the Christian faith, and that the influence of the human situation upon Christian answers in Tillich's system seems larger than it is in reality. It bears remembering too that the role of religious experience in Tillich's method should not be overestimated.

c. Tillich's View on Culture

Tillich uses the question-answer model, as described above, to offer insight into his method of correlation. But more is at stake in this method than just the relation between questions and answers. Tillich turns it into a statement on the relation between culture and religion. He cannot tolerate

---

[59] Van Leeuwen, "Een theologie van het Nieuwe Zijn," 8-9.

the separation between a faith that is not acceptable to culture and a culture that is not acceptable to faith.[60]

Tillich states that the theologian, while analysing the human situation, should employ materials made available by human beings' creative self-interpretation in all realms of culture. Philosophy contributes to this, but so also do poetry, drama, the novel, therapeutic psychology, and sociology. These materials should be correlated with the theological concepts derived from Christian faith.[61]

This means that the idea of religious experience as participation in human existence includes a participation in culture, for the human situation is humanity's creative self-interpretation in culture. But what is the meaning of culture for Tillich? Amazingly, he never gives a definition of this even though he uses the word quite often to describe different realities in various stages of his thought.

Two problems arise when we consider Tillich's concept of culture: firstly, his concept is rather elitist, and secondly, everyday reality is not included in his view of culture. Both problems have consequences for the idea of religious experience as participation in human existence, since it is not clear which existence Tillich has in mind and which realms of reality are excluded in his thought as spaces where religious experience may take place. Although Tillich was active during his life in religious socialism and denounced the middle-class capitalist bourgeois-society,[62] he was never really engaged with the alienation of the proletariat. He was mostly concerned with the alienation from Christianity that he noticed among so-called cultivated people. In his view, their alienation from historical Christianity determined the social situation of their time, and for him theology was challenged to react to this situation.[63] Thus, his theology was mainly directed to the cultivated people who thought that they did not need religion, rather than the proletariat whose situation was not really Tillich's concern. Nor did he occupy himself with the 'popular culture' or 'mass-culture' of his time. He makes an analysis of the situation by using philosophy, poetry, drama, novels, therapeutic psychology and sociology. But he remains selective about the sources that he chooses to interpret the human situation. If it really were his purpose to describe how most people situate themselves in a certain period of time, he should have turned to – quoting Clayton – "the mass media (radio, cinema and

---

[60] Tillich, *Systematic Theology*, 3:4-5.
[61] Tillich, *Systematic Theology*, 1:71.
[62] He did this for example in Tillich, *Die Religiöse Lage der Gegenwart*.
[63] Clayton, *The Concept of Correlation*, 127.

later on also television), the tabloid newspapers, the pulp magazines, the paperbacks which sell well at railway stations and airports. ... When Tillich describes the present cultural situation, he turns not to those sources I have just listed, but to those writers whose appeal is mainly to the intellectuals, to those painters whose works had little popular appeal, to the leading philosophers of the day and to those mythologies (such as psychoanalysis) which appeal again mainly to a relatively small and educated segment of society."[64] Tillich's statement that culture is to be designated as 'the *totality* of man's creative self-interpretation'[65] seems to be in contrast with his rather biased representation of the fields that he considers as constituting the culture of a certain period. His concept of culture is clearly aimed at a certain segment of culture, with a specific preference for the more philosophical aspects of culture. Philosophy, in his view, reveals the cultural feeling of a specific time even more than art and science.

Tillich's interpretation of culture is closely linked to his own way of life and interests. It is no coincidence that he stresses the importance of the arts and sciences, where his own personal interests lay. Moreover, he was deeply affected by art, and this formed the basis of his conviction that there is a relation between art and religion, science and religion, and ultimately, culture and religion. In his autobiography *Auf der Grenze* (On the Boundary) he mentions that the mosaics in Ravenna, the paintings on the ceilings of the Sistine Chapel and Rembrandt's self-portrait as an old man almost made him experience a revelation.[66] In particular, expressionism captured his attention because he saw in it an ally in the struggle against capitalist society.[67] But still, in his personal life Tillich was not only interested in art and philosophy. In the biography of Pauck and Pauck we read that Tillich was also interested in modern dance and several times invited a modern dance group to parties at his house so that his guests could join in the creative way of dancing.[68]

Tillich also enjoyed playing games and letting imagination into his life, as he explains in *Auf der Grenze*: "Imagination expresses itself, for example, by joy in the game. This joy has accompanied me my whole life, either in the actual game, or sports ... or party games, or in an insight into a game that accompanies moments of productivity and makes them into expressions of the most heavenly form of human freedom."[69]

[64] Clayton, *The Concept of Correlation*, 128-129.
[65] Tillich, *Systematic Theology*, 1:4.
[66] Paul Tillich, *Auf der Grenze* (Stuttgart: Evangelisches Verlagswerk, ²1965) 40.
[67] John H. Thomas, *Tillich* (London and New York, NY: Continuum, 2000) 9-10.
[68] Pauck, *Paul Tillich*, 105-106.
[69] Tillich, *Auf der Grenze*, 16. My translation.

It is remarkable that Tillich did not include these kinds of cultural expressions, to which he himself was attracted and relished practising. When he came to know the pleasure of modern dance, he wrote an essay about it, *Tanz und Religion*,[70] but in his method of correlation as described in *Systematic Theology* he does not integrate those findings nor his views on play, sport, party games and the role of imagination.

In some contemporary theological approaches, the attention to expressions of culture other than art and science is developing. Greater recognition is now given to the multitude and variety of the different aspects of culture. This means that some theological approaches also see the rather daily aspects of life as possible sources for theology, next to the cultural areas Tillich considered as sources for theology, such as art and philosophy. Culture then does not mean 'the creative expressions of a moment in arts and sciences' but rather 'the experienced and lived reality' with not just all its creative and lofty aspects but also its everyday components. In this way, 'forgotten' aspects such as imagination, fantasy, rituals, celebration, parties, movies, singing, dancing, eating and drinking are recognised as true witnesses of a certain culture. Starting with the ambiguity and complexity of daily life represents a real challenge to theology for it is clear that these aspects of culture are much more difficult to interpret owing to their ambiguous character. Contemporary theological approaches of culture are challenged by Asian, African, Afro-American, Latin American and feminist theologies. Within these theologies, life as a whole is celebrated in the midst of injustice, poverty and oppression, because life as a whole is conceived as source and starting point for theology. In so doing, these theologies intend to challenge 'academic theology' and/or expose it as being ideological by pointing to its western, white, masculine or elitist character.[71] The western concept of culture has evolved greatly under the influence of these theologies. Not only are more daily expressions of culture now considered as sources for theology, but also the complex character of reality is reflected in new conceptions of culture. Tillich's attempt to design a comprehensive theological view on the totality of culture, seen as a solid whole constituted by sciences, philosophy and art, seems to be impossible today. A modern master narrative about the culture as a whole has become problematic today because of the insight

---

[70] Paul Tillich, "Tanz und Religion," *Gesammelte Werke* XIII (Stuttgart: Evangelisches Verlagswerk, 1972) 559ff.

[71] Maaike A.C. De Haardt, "Spel van Verbeelding: Een theologie van omkering en alledaagsheid," *Over Spel: Theologie als drama en illusie*, ed. Herman Beck, Rein Nauta, and Paul Post (Leende: Damon, 2000) 23-46, 41-42.

that culture is much more complex than Tillich and other modern theologians have suggested. In a criticism on Tillich's concept of culture, Clayton expresses his problems with Tillich's modern concept as follows: "Perhaps it would be better if theologians, like anthropologists, learned to be content with a more piecemeal approach to cultural analysis, even if their aim where ultimately to describe the 'style' of a whole culture. Perhaps it would be better if the over-grand 'problem of religion and culture' were broken up into a number of smaller, more manageable issues, each of which would need to be addressed in its own terms."[72]

d. Tillich's Universalistic Presuppositions

It is not just Tillich's concept of culture which is in need of reconsidering in the contemporary context, but also his concept of religion is not always that clear and asks for adjustment. Although he speaks about the correlation between culture and religion, he uses the latter in different contexts of meaning. It is not clear which (meaning of) religion he intends to correlate with the human situation. He is wrestling with his apologetic intentions and, at the same time, his attachment to the theological circle and the statement that Jesus Christ is the norm for every theology. As a result he comes into conflict with his other conviction that every human being is religious once they have an ultimate concern. Both dimensions of religiosity may be found in his method of correlation.

On the one hand, Tillich considers religion to be a depth dimension that can be found in every aspect of mental and cultural life, both in the practical and theoretical spheres. In his early period, Tillich calls this 'the experience of the unconditional'; later on he describes religion as 'ultimate concern'. On the other hand, he uses the word 'religion' in a more restricted sense, namely to point out the religious sphere that exists side by side with other spheres in socio-cultural life. In this case he speaks of a religion, i.e. a *specific* religious tradition like Christianity.

In fact, Tillich needs the idea of a broader sense of religiosity to give shape to his method of correlation. After all, when he wants to correlate theological answers with human questions, he must presuppose that these questions ask for a religious answer, and that thus the questions are religious in nature. On both sides of the correlation there has to be a religious dimension in order for there to be a correlation to speak of.[73] By means

---

[72] Clayton, *The Concept of Correlation*, 152.
[73] Clayton, *The Concept of Correlation*, 114.

of the concept of ultimate concern Tillich makes this evident: every
human being has something about which she is more concerned than anything else – each human being has an ultimate concern and is engaged in
it. For someone who belongs to a religious tradition (*a religion*) this concern is God, for a non-religious person (not belonging to *a religion*) this
ultimate concern is something else.[74] But a human being can never, in
Tillich's view, be a-religious because there is always something that concerns her. Therefore, Tillich states that religion is not a sphere separate
from other spheres, but a dimension that penetrates all aspects of life and
plays a role in everything which human beings undertake.[75] Likewise, in
an apologetic manner, Tillich points out that religion is not alien to human
life and that every human being has a religious dimension. The method
of correlation is directed at relating the general religiosity (religion) of
human beings with the specific message of Christianity (*a religion*).
Tillich's ultimate vision is of a spiritual community wherein *a religion* is
no longer needed because the correct relation between culture and religion has been established. He expresses this opinion in Biblical terms:
"There is no temple in the fulfilled Kingdom of God."[76] For Tillich, no
concrete religion can be the ending point of history in an ultimate sense.[77]
Only the founding of Christian religion – namely what happened in Jesus
Christ – is fundamental, not the historical manifestation of Christianity
itself.[78]

Tillich creates confusion by using 'religion' to denote both the general
religiosity of human beings and the specific Christian tradition. It follows from this confusion that the reader almost spontaneously identifies
universal religiosity with the Christian religion, the latter being the particular expression of the former. In this way it is not only made acceptable that every human being is religious, but also that a religious person
is a Christian without knowing or acknowledging it. For Tillich there is
no gulf between being religious and a Christian. He does not see any
problems in speaking about universal religiosity and connecting it immediately with Christianity. This has consequences for his views on other
religions or the secular context.

Because Tillich identifies the universal religious feeling with the particular Christian religion and defines Christian theology as *the* theology,

---

[74] Clayton, *The Concept of Correlation*, 110.
[75] Clayton, *The Concept of Correlation*, 105.
[76] Tillich, *Systematic Theology*, 3:157.
[77] Tillich, *Systematic Theology*, 3:337.
[78] Tillich, *Systematic Theology*, 3:381.

he seems to present other religions as inferior or incomplete. His view on religions is that they all move toward the ideal religion, i.e. Christianity. It shows that he does not pay regard to the truth claims of other religions. This can be seen as problematic in the contemporary context of religious plurality. Although Tillich can never be held to speak negatively about other religions, it seems that he considers them as inferior to and as only having any value in relation to Christianity.

Some Tillich-specialists note that this changed when Tillich personally encountered some eastern religions on a trip to Japan. He is reported to have said that he would have to completely rewrite his *Systematic Theology* in light of these experiences.[79] There is not much information on this but we presume that the rewriting Tillich had in mind would certainly have influenced his theology of non-Christian religions. I consider it to be significant that under the influence of a personal experience with other religions Tillich questions his own theology. It means that he lets his personal experiences penetrate his theology. The way in which theologians relate to adherents of other religions certainly has some impact on how they practise contemporary theology. Personal contacts with people of another religion can cause one to question and adjust one's own theological system.

Not only in relation to other religions, but also in respect of his own secularised society does Tillich present Christianity as the only meaningful way to live. With his apologetic theology he seeks to convince people that Christianity provides *the* answers to the questions people ask themselves. For Tillich, his society is comprised of Christians and those who are not Christian anymore because the message failed to reach them in a contemporary language. Seeking new words for the old message will convince people to join Christianity again. Tillich supposes that people are implicitly Christian, even if they do not call themselves believers. He situates the 'latent church' among what he terms 'Christian humanism'. Those who are alienated from the organised Church and from the traditional symbols are still in his view part of the Church, because they embody the true Church more than the organised Church can do. Humanists or atheists can, in Tillich's opinion, be called Christians because they

---

[79] Pauck, *Paul Tillich*, 245. His Japanese trip inspired him to say that he would have to re-write his whole system in light of his new view on the Eastern World. Tillich was mostly interested in Shintoism and Buddhism. During his trip he visited their temples, participated in their rituals, acquainted himself with their theology and spoke to their spiritual leaders (259-260). Thomas on the other hand is not convinced by Tillich's so-called remark, because he does not notice any subsequent differences in Tillich's theology after his trip to Asia (cf. Thomas, *Tillich*, 24-25).

are also concerned with human experiences of limitation and the surrender to justice and love. They share the Christian faith and acknowledge Christian norms in an implicit way, and they have a keen awareness of (organised) Christianity's ideological abuse of power in Church and state.[80] Although they do not call themselves Christians, they are Christians in reality. And if the Christian message were expressed in an actualised way, these humanists would recognize themselves again in the Christian story of faith.

Tillich's opinion on other religions and his secularised society reveals his universalistic presuppositions. He does not acknowledge that his theology is influenced by his own position in Church and society. He seems to speak for every human and for every period in time. When he contemplates human life, culture, religion, belief, he never specifies which human beings, culture, religion or belief he is talking about. In a universalistic way he speaks about *the* human being, *the* culture, *the* religion, generalizing his own point of view to a general truth. His opinion about what a human is becomes a definition of being a human, his own religion becomes *the* religion as does his own culture become *the* culture. This is not without problems because some aspects of reality are overlooked in this way (as I illustrated in the discussion on his concept of culture). Starting from his own cultural and religious position, Tillich expands his view on culture and religion to all human beings. In theory this is not a problem for we all practise theology from within our own situation in life, church and society. This makes our theology closely associated with the context we live in. The problem resides in the fact that the influence of Tillich's own point of view is never admitted, discussed or questioned. When we investigate his theology today, it is obvious that Tillich tried to speak a theological language understandable for the people of his time and context. But the fact that he makes use of universal categories of culture, religion and human being makes it seem as if he is talking for anybody in any context. In today's theological reflection we are more aware of the particularity of our own theological discourse. To recognise this and to integrate this in our theological way of speaking means to respect the particularity of all speaking and leave an openness to let other standpoints challenge our theology. As Christian theologians we are starting from very particular Christian presuppositions. In a pluralist context it is only fair to make these premises clear when talking about culture, religion and human beings. Tillich cannot be blamed for not doing this because in his context the question of particularity was not raised in

---

[80] Tillich, *Auf der Grenze*, 40.

the same way as it is done today. But the fact that Tillich's general opinions were so deeply influenced by his own particular situation show that theology and biography are closely linked to each other. To take this seriously is a real challenge for theologians today.

5. Conclusion

Tillich obviously defines religious experience in a specific way, namely as existential participation. Although Tillich indicates that religious experience is an important factor in theological method, the actual role he attaches to it is rather minimal. He goes on to weaken the influence of religious experience by his description of the task and role of the theologian in his introduction to *Systematic Theology*, where he clearly states that the religious experience of the theologian only receives the message and does not produce it.

Therefore the risk that Tillich's idea of religious experience would give too much leeway for an adaptation to the modern world and would thereby threaten the message is not really an actual danger. Tillich clearly foresaw the possible points of criticism and gave in to these objections by limiting the role of religious experience in his system.

When reading Tillich in a postmodern context, several questions arise in relation to his view on culture and religion. When we look at his rather one-sided description of what constitutes the culture of a certain time, we can mention several aspects of life that are not included. From within a contemporary theological view we consider culture to be much broader and more complex than Tillich himself did. If culture is a source for theology, the question is pertinent which aspects of culture we consider to be relevant for theology.

Also when it comes to Tillich's definition of religion, the question can be raised "how we can take into account the changed reality in our theological view?" The confusion Tillich caused by mingling a broad and a narrow sense of religion without distinguishing the two should be clarified. It seems impossible in contemporary theology to identify a general feeling of religiosity with the confession of Christian belief. In the current pluralist situation we should show respect for our own traditions as well as for the other – or non-believer. This means that we consider Christian belief as a particular position instead of assuming that people who experience a religious feeling can be seen as Christians, even if they don't name themselves Christians.

Therefore I suggest that Tillich's idea of religious experience as existential participation is in need of reinterpretation. We should acknowledge the fact that Tillich was talking as a Christian to the people of his time. To do that today means to be aware of the differences there are between Tillich's context and ours. Using generalising concepts as Tillich did, seems impossible in the current situation. Still this doesn't mean that Tillich's view of religious experience has nothing valuable to say to us.

When situated within the particular context of the Christian belief, Tillich's question concerning the relation between – and the mutual dependence of – context and faith is indeed still highly pertinent. Tillich's concern to connect the message with the daily situation in which people live and to speak a theological language that people understand because it appeals to their own experiences, should remain the concern of the contemporary theologian. For this reason, it is worthwhile to inquire into Tillich's concept of religious experience and, by studying it, to discover that his ideas – when situated in a specific religious tradition and having fully taken account of the complexity of reality – still challenge us to be theologians who are deeply concerned about the connection between the message and the reality in which we live.

THEOLOGICAL METHODOLOGY, RELIGIOUS EXPERIENCE AND CHRISTIAN FAITH IN THE WRITINGS OF WOLFHART PANNENBERG

Marc Dumas[1]

Considering Pannenberg's impressive body of work,[2] how does one, in a few pages, account for this theologian's approach to religious experience, a seemingly simple idea, but complex in fact, given also that his thinking on religious experience, and his entire body of work in fact, rests upon remarkable insight into philosophical and theological traditions? What importance does Pannenberg give to religious experience and what is its relation to Christian belief? I shall examine a number of significant texts,[3] which I hope will afford an examination of a theme that will produce results, pertinent to our questioning. In order to identify and evaluate the status of religious experience in Wolfhart Pannenberg's body of work, it is relevant first to state what he meant by religious experience and how that experience fits into his thinking. A detour is in order, in order to give a methodological outline of his theological stance, which might seem to some superfluous, but which will permit a better grasp of Pannenberg's enterprise.

Given that Wolfhart Pannenberg studied under Karl Barth in Bâle, we can be forgiven for assuming that he would see religious experience in a

---

[1] Translation from French by Catherine Baril.

[2] W. Pannenberg was born in 1928 in the city of Stettin, now situated in Poland. He began his studies in theology in Berlin at the close of the Second World War. He also studied in Göttingen, Bâle and Heidelberg. It was in the latter university town that he obtained his doctorate in 1953 and his habilitation in 1955. He taught there up to 1958 and then accepted a position at the *Kirchliche Hochschule* in Wuppertal. He began teaching systematic theology in 1961 in Mayence and in 1967 in Munich.

[3] Of the material consulted, I cite the following: "Theologie als Wissenschaft von Gott," *Wissenschaftstheorie und Theologie* (Frankfurt/Main: Suhrkamp, 1973) 299-348. Following, in notes, WT [*Theology and the Philosophy of Science* (London: DLT, 1976) (WTe)]; "Eschatologie und Sinnerfahrung," *Die wirkliche Wirklichkeit Gottes*, ed. Kurt Krenn (Paderborn: Schöningh, 1974) 143-158 (ES); "Sinnerfahrung, Religion und Gottesfrage," *ThPh 59* (1984) 178-190 (SRG); *Systematische Theologie*, vol. I (Göttingen: Vandenhoeck und Ruprecht, 1988) (STI) [*Systematic Theology*, vol. I (Grand Rapids, MI: W.B. Eerdmans, 1991) (STIe)]; "Religiöse Erfahrung und christlicher Glaube," *Religiöse Erfahrung und theologische Reflexion*, ed. Armin Kreiner and Heinrich Döring (Paderborn: Bonifatius, 1993) 113-123 (RECG).

negative and harsh light. His defining text on revelation as history, *Offen-barung als Geschichte*,[4] for which he became known at the beginning of the 1960s, could well give this impression. Unexpectedly absent from that defining text, is the theme of religious experience.[5] Indeed, as Pannenberg reworked and developed the design of his theology and its key concepts over the years, he frequently tied such concepts to religious experience. How did this theme evolve? In what follows, as we proceed through the questionings of the theologian from Munich, his clarifications and discoveries, we intend to seperate religious experience within his theological synthesis. To begin with, we shall identify particular and original methodological elements. His reflections on theology should help us better understand his theological work. We will then present the concepts and roles of religious experience, and indicate their relation to Christian faith. We will conclude with a critical evaluation of his place in contemporary theology.

1. Theological Method or the Possibility of Theological Act in Modern Times, According to Pannenberg

The contributions of this prominent twentieth century Protestant theologian endeavour to go beyond the pit-falls into which nineteenth and twentieth century theology have fallen, that is to say theological positivism and subjectivism.[6] Pannenberg's thought moulds itself to the modern paradigm, but he refuses to draw the same conclusions as those who critique religion, those who opt for atheism and the opinion that religion is passé and illusory.[7] His thesis presented in *Offenbarung als Geschichte* is developed in remarkable ways over the course of his career: each new publication is a further step in following through on his innovative thinking, the thinking of a man open to dialogue with philosophy, the natural sciences and the humanities. Pannenberg remained true to his theological stance. He did not lose his precision, but fully explored the avenues of God's revelation in history. We consider more closely the main lines of this theology.

---

[4] Wolfhart Pannenberg, "Dogmatische Thesen zur Lehre von der Offenbarung," *Offenbarung als Geschichte*, (Götttingen: Vandenhoeck und Ruprecht, 1961) 91-114.
[5] He speaks of the experience of the Spirit in the writings of Saint John, as well of the experience of reality as history, but religious experience is not made explicit.
[6] Cf. WT, 301.
[7] Cf. WT, 301; 310-311.

a. Theology as Science of God

It is worth commenting on *Wissenschaftstheorie und Theologie*, a book published in German in 1973. This work came out at a time when the German university was in a process of reform and the book actively contributes to discussions of scientific theories that called into question theology as a university science. Its fifth chapter explores the idea of theology as science of God.[8] We examine in somewhat less detail his fascinating and instructive excursions into the history of philosophy and theology, we focus less on the modalities that give to theology a scientific character, and delve more into his desire to see theology take on the modern horizon, as 'science of God'. How is human experience, of the world, of self, a place for 'experiencing' God, experience that has an all-determining power over perceived reality?

Such are my preliminary remarks with respect to Pannenberg's thinking on religious experience. These remarks perhaps are also a reflection on what the plausible and credible conditions and possibilities are within modernity for active theological work. Pannenberg exposes his understanding of theology, its presuppositions, its differences vis-à-vis other positions he views as reductive, the paths to which such understanding leads, to justify pursuit of theological work at the university level. He integrates this thinking into his written discussions that emerges from his 1961 text, and states more clearly what theological action is, as it reaches toward new limits on the horizon of modernity. Is theology science? A science of God? What does that mean?

Pannenberg defines at the outset theology as the science of God and briefly revisits the validity of such an understanding throughout history. He notes that during the nineteenth century, an attempt to define theology in other ways, as 'science of Christianity', for example, had undesirable consequences. Theology became a mere historical discipline, limited by positivism, by decisionism, unable to aspire to any scientific status. Does defining theology within modernity as the science of God leave it open to the aporia of positivism? Is God then an outdated religious idea?

Pannenberg affirmed that if such was the case, expressions other than 'theology' or 'God' would be necessary, in order better to render the reality behind the words. The question of God was still an open issue, and therefore by understanding the object of theology as a problem, and not as a dogmatic issue, eliminated the problematic of positivism and

---

[8] The pages that follow analyse page 299 onward of WT.

questioned the narrowness of the views of reality as defined by non-theological sciences.

But is it not problematical for theology if God produces problems? Was it not risky to try solving the 'problem' via the non-theological sciences? Pannenberg felt we must avoid this temptation. But, by doing so, were we not once again led to consider God as a hypothesis, and if this is the case, is it not impossible to build a science whose object is hypothetical? Pannenberg's answer is to the point, since, as with the other sciences, it is possible to measure and validate a hypothesis merely by its implications, in this case, its implication for the world and for the individual: "In other words, the idea of God (which is by definition, the reality which determines everything), must be substantiated by the experienced reality of man and the world."[9] This demonstration of the idea of God through the experience of the reality of the world and self remains for Pannenberg still open, indeterminate, and the idea of God therefore remains a hypothesis. Theological knowledge continues to be hypothetical, because its reality is still not fixed, and also because our capacity to know continues to be limited by finitude. The idea of God, or the reality of God, is not an object 'among' other objects of knowledge. The reality of God is given 'through' objects of experiencing. Theological thought therefore gains indirect access to the reality of God. To think God as object in theology is to determine how the idea of God is problematic in our experience and how theological clarification risks losing its object. Theology then becomes something else, it becomes another discipline.

These first reflections on Pannenberg's understanding of theology as the science of God showed the hypothetical and indirect aspect of the idea of God: it is a given, or is 'co-given', within other objects of experience. Pannenberg's method labelled theological activity as a science, whose hypothetical object must be demonstrated through human experience. The *Sitz im Leben* of theological activity was the difficult and precarious situation of theology at the university level. It is within this context that Pannenberg considered the 'possibility of the conditions' of this science, whose invisible object is not found alongside other objects of human experiencing. It was to be supposed that God, or the reality of God, is 'co-given', is given within the other objects of experience. Theological thought gained indirect access to its object.[10]

---

[9] WTe, 300.

[10] He considers briefly the possibility of an immediate experience of God. We shall take this up again further on. For such an experience to be valid, it must be subject to other scientific conditions.

b. *Experience as Access to Reality*

Let us now speak of the role played by human experience of the world and of the self, and distinguish it from religious experience *per se*, which the next section will focus on. As a science, theology works at developing sharable knowledge, that is to say, that which pertains to inter-subjectivity, as Pannenberg puts it. Which is why the theologian pays attention to the indirect character of what is given in divine reality: the theologian seeks to find traces of divine mystery in things of the world and in living. Ostensibly, since God is the all-determining reality, any object of experience may serve as an indirect medium for God, since divine traces imprint themselves on experience. In this context, from the Christian perspective, this nominal definition of God is incomplete, but it allows one to suppose that all that is real can show traces of divine reality.

Pannenberg designates reality thus: it does not concern objects considered separately, but on the contrary, objects in their contextuality, in their mutual relations. This requirement of 'contextualisation'[11] in theology pulls it toward classical philosophy, which not only considers the particularities of that which is real, but also considers it in its totality. Philosophy is concerned with the real in and of itself. That such reality is solely given through human experience does not discount, however, the oneness of that which is real. For the philosopher, though the question of God is there for him to consider, it is often placed within parentheses. Theology addresses the question of the totality of reality, all the while considering the reality of God as an all-determining reality.

This link between God and the totality of reality is not self-evident, since in and of itself the idea of the totality of reality is problematic, and, considering the history of philosophy, has led to a multitude of answers throughout history. The connection between God and the totality of reality has been particularly disrupted within modernity. Modernity establishes humanity as the foundation on which the certainty of the knowledge of God rests. Though the modern anthropological stance borrows the idea of God, theologically speaking such 'anthropoligisation' of the idea of God does not suffice. This idea leads in theology to an interest in human religiousness, and to a view of theology as a positive science, no longer concerned with divine mystery in human experience. The 'anthropologisation' of the idea of God leads to God as projection, as illusion.

---

[11] The quotation marks are to show a difference in meaning from what is usually understood by this word. We do not refer to contextual theologies here. Rather, the author is evoking the relational aspect of reality objects, not the situated aspects of objects.

Pannenberg looks to get away from such a projection, beyond the modern aporia with respect to God and the totality of reality, a necessary part
of his scientific demonstration of the justification of theology. The anthropological shift of modernity is insufficient: the idea of God must also
have force in the experience of the world. "To this extent experience of
the world and the search for the power that ultimately determines it is,
even today, essential to any attempt to gain knowledge about the reality
of God."[12] The relation to God via the world is no longer a direct given:
in modernity, relating to God is possible only in man's self-understanding and in his relation to the world. In the experience of the world and
of self, Pannenberg asks how is the totality of finite reality 'given', and
how is it that 'donation' is related to the idea of God as an all-determining reality?

c. Pannenberg's Originality

To answer these questions, we need to present Pannenberg's understanding of the totality of reality. For many, totality of reality is enclosed in
itself. For Pannenberg, it is incomplete, turned towards the future, yet
undetermined: man and the world are still in a process of unfolding. The
open-ended aspect of reality imprinted by temporality and historicity
touches our existence and our experiencing of the world. How does Pannenberg imagine totality? Differently from the closed cosmos of the
Greeks, he sees the world as incomplete, as 'a going beyond' that which
exists in the present, as transcending our present reality. If individual experience develops its specificity only within a relating to the whole of meaning, it follows that the idea of the totality of reality is the necessary condition for all experience and the condition for the experience of an
individual given. And yet this totality of reality is not a given, it is always
to be determined. The totality of reality is anticipated as the totality of
meaning. Such a totality is the condition of possibility of experience. It is
the framework that makes experience possible. To anticipate totality is to
imagine, over and above the idea of a hypothesis, a subjective moment
which must either be confirmed or shaken up in the course of the unfolding of an experience. Experience therefore plays a determining role in
the structuring of the totality of reality. Experience serves as model that
tests unfolding reality, on its way to being transcendent totality.

---

[12] WTe, 309.

We are not yet talking about religious experience in the strict sense, but what has been said impacts in a real way on how God can be spoken about with respect to the human experience of reality: "The reality of God is always present only in subjective anticipations of the totality of reality, in models of the totality of meaning presupposed in all particular experience. These models, however, are historic, which means that they are subject to confirmation or refutation by subsequent experience."[13]

In the process of revelation the reality of God rests upon a hypothetical, subjective anticipation of human experiencing of meaning. Furthermore, the reality of God is conditioned by the historicity of unfolding experience: "The anticipative aspect of experiencing the totality of reality as the totality of meaning, makes comprehensible the historical aspect of self-proclaiming divine reality."[14] Pannenberg in fact restates biblical arguments, which links the historicity of the revelation of God with the totality of finite experience that encloses the reality of God. If the totality of *reality* is open ended, if it can only be anticipated using subjective models of *meaning*, it follows that individual experience of reality as totality must be subjective and historical. It follows that the reality of God can be grasped and experienced in the same way as the wholeness of reality, that is to say historically.

In addition to making evident the relationship between the *part* and the *whole* and in situating unfolding experience, Pannenberg also gives importance to the *moment of anticipation*, which not only is the foundation for historicity of God's revelation, but also what conditions it. The reality of God proclaims itself as reality experienced in history.

As early as 1961 Pannenberg already understood revelation not as the unveiling of truths about God, but as the self-revelation of God. This revealing of God, he said, was effected indirectly through God's acts in history. Pannenberg did not reduce revelation to a few specific events, that supposedly contained the self-revelation of God. On the contrary, reality in its entirety can be the occasion for divine revelation. And revelation is to be received in full at the end of time. It is in the final outcome of history that meaning is given. The eschatological perspective would seem be the place where the light of God gives meaning to reality. The story of Jesus of Nazareth, and in particular his resurrection, makes real the final outcome of time in advance, because the glory of God is in all.

If modern currents in the sociology or philosophy of religion regard religions as human expressions of reality as totality, that validate a social order

[13] WTe, 310.
[14] WT, 313.

or understanding of the meaning of reality, on the other hand, for Pannenberg the theologian, religions can mostly be the locus for defining the expression of the experience of the proclamation of God in the totality of reality. The main historical religions and individual religious experiences that are linked to organized religion play a role precisely of defining 'experience'. Sociality has great importance here, as individual experiences are given credibility and inter-subjective validity. Individual experience is connected to, is an integral part of, a whole. This means "that religions and their history are to be regarded as the locus of explicit perception of particular self-revelations of divine reality in human experience."[15]

If theology as the science of God peers into religious traditions with a view to informing itself about God's self-proclamation in religions, it does not fall back into the aporia of positivism as it processes the historical material of religion. In this sense, Pannenberg conceives of historical religions as the traces left over from the experiential process of the self-proclaiming of divine reality.

Before moving on to our section on religious experience, I would like to make a brief summary. Pannenberg's consideration of theology as the science of God, styled after fundamental theology,[16] allowed Pannenberg to situate his theological effort as he turned his attention toward the modern epistemological horizon. God, defined nominally as the all-determining reality, is experienced in conjunction with the reality of the self and of the world, particularly within the unfolding of history that anticipates reality as totality. Experience of the self and of the world permits the grasping as reality the world's network of meaning. Individual meaning can be inscribed in the network of the totality of meaning in a world that is unfolding since any manifestation of totality or partiality is mere anticipation of the totality that fully manifests meaning, God. The self-manifestations of God are anticipated during the unfolding of history. The historical character of religions awaken man to a consciousness of the historical experience of God's self-manifestation.

2. Religious Experiences in Pannenberg's Thought

In a short presentation of his work in 1981 that appeared in *Christian Century*, Wolfhart Pannenberg recalled an experience of enlightenment that occurred to him when he was a teenager:

---

[15] WTe, 313.

[16] Pannenberg is looking here to validate the conditions of possibility for theological action within modernity.

The single most important experience occurred in early January 1945, when I was 16 years old. On a lonely two-hour walk home from my piano lesson, seeing an otherwise ordinary sunset, I was suddenly flooded by light and absorbed in a sea of light which, although it did not extinguish the humble awareness of my finite existence, overflowed the barriers that normally separate us from the surrounding world. … I did not know at the time that January sixth was the day of Epiphany, nor did I realize that in that moment Jesus Christ had claimed my life as a witness to the transfiguration of this world in the illuminating power and judgment of his glory. But there began a period of craving to understand the meaning of life, and since philosophy did not seem to offer the ultimate answers to such a quest, I finally decided to probe the Christian Tradition more seriously than I had considered worthwhile before.[17]

Would this become the author's characteristic religious experience? We will discover further on how he treats such an experience. It is insufficient, he says, it is not enough, but it cannot be got around, pedagogically speaking. Let us first discuss direct religious experience, as opposed to indirect religious experience.

a. Direct Religious Experience

Though he is relatively sparse in his comments about direct religious experience, Pannenberg validates it. Such an experience usually results from "a direct awareness of divine reality, an 'encounter' with the reality of God".[18] It does happen, but must be validated on a case-by-case basis. It expresses how man is already and always connected to the ultimate mystery of his life, a mystery that surpasses all that exists. It happens, and, as Tillich was already saying in 1920s, it becomes pertinent when religious content is lost in the fog of existence. It happens, like a fundamental and unavoidable Giver of life, a Certainty that can be counted upon. It can be somewhat non-thematic, more or less articulated for the person experiencing it, or its religious nature can be very clear. It can be pertinent indeed when it leads to an understanding of self and of the world; in other words, when it has inter-subjective value. Direct religious experience is theologically meaningful when it takes on a collective quality, relational, and therefore religious, regardless of whether expressed in conventional religious language or not. Direct religious experience can happen, but must be considered with caution: it expresses with

---

[17] W. Pannenberg, "God's Presence in History," *The Christian Century* (March 1981) 261.
[18] WTe, 301.

more or less distinctness our fundamental relationship to the ultimate
mystery of life. And it plays no particular role in giving credibility to
*in*direct religious experience or in validating personal experiences of God.

b. Indirect Religious Experience

In 1973, wanting to give to theological utterances a hypothetical, multi-
layered structure, Pannenberg said that they were *"hypotheses about
hypotheses about hypotheses"*.[19] He distinguishes 'meaning experience'
from 'religious experience'. Meaning experience, like ordinary experience, implicitly anticipates totality of meaning. Religious experience is
explicit consciousness of the totality of the meaning of reality, thought
indirectly, it is consciousness of the divine foundation of that which is
real. Theological utterances in this context are hypotheses of truths or non-
truths regarding the imprint onto religious consciousness left by self-
proclamations of divine reality. We ponder the distinction between meaning experience and religious experience to better grasp the specific nature
of religious experience, because if *theological utterances* have to do with
religious experience, its historical character, then *religious experience* has
an essential role in *theological activity*. We feel we should speak as well
of the importance Pannenberg gave to two relationships, that between the
part and the *whole* (between *Bedeutung* and *Sinn*, between *Erlebnis* and
Erfahrung), and speak of the relationship between the *non-thematic* and
the *thematic* (between meaning and religion). Direct and indirect experiences have bearing on these relationships. Several texts of Pannenberg's
comment further on these relationships: a 1974 text, one in 1984, and
another in 1993. The authors he cites and the conceptual distinctions are
the same, and so we may affirm a certain continuity in this theme. Each
text gives a particular highlighting of one aspect or the other of these different relationships and it is worthwhile to take them up chronologically.[20]

The 1974 text, entitled *Eschatologie und Sinnerfahrung*, bridges the
fundamental structure of human experience and religious experience by
means of a reflection on eschatology and meaning experience. The author

---

[19] WTe, 333.

[20] Though considering his publications in chronological order does facilitate the illustration of the evolution in his thinking on this subject, since the evolutions are more of the
order of the epistemic and less so of the themes of religious experience (which have
nuanced differences, but for the most part are the same), we could just as well have taken
a systematic approach.

qualifies the meanings of hope for Christians and introduces the notion of *Wesenszukunft*, the essential future of mankind, insisting upon the importance of understanding essential future within the religious sphere. It is in this framework that he presents the categories of *Sinn* meaning-experience and *Bedeutung* meaning-experience. These two categories describe the formal structural moments of all human experience.[21] These moments are then associated with *Erlebnis* (particular experience) and *Erfahrung* (lived experience), and with two other words, 'part' and 'all', which have a structuring effect on the religious experience. *Erlebnisse* are associated with *Sinn*: it is in them that *Sinn* expresses meaning. If meaning (*Bedeutung*) is more readily attributed to that which is particular (that which is individual), albeit in context (not isolated), then meaning as *Sinn* has more to do with the *whole*, the totality or even with the 'particular-as-a-part' of the whole. Thus, particular happenings take on meaning as they relate to a life situation. Pannenberg refers at this point to Dilthey, for whom *Erlebnis* is a happening within the context of living that puts one in touch with one's self, with the entirety of one's life. But since our life is in progress, taking place within a historical unfolding, we live in continual anticipation for all our life. The *Erfahrungen* over the course of a lifetime interpret anew that anticipation, and such adjustments are able to change the meaning of previous *Erlebnisse*. Still with reference to Dilthey, Pannenberg concludes that it is only after the living of life that the meaning of *Erlebnisse* can truly be grasped. The future therefore takes on an important role with respect to the total meaning of life and with respect to the ultimate meaning of individual *Erlebnisse*. The whole of life is in historical forward march, and the experience of meaning assumes a 'historicality'. The essential future of the individual, inserted into the future of the rest of humanity, in the end gives meaning to life and meaning to moments in that life.[22]

The analysis of the structure of the meaning of experience and the analysis of its historical character lead the theologian to introduce the religious thematic, for does religion not have to do with the totality of meaning of life? Pannenberg turns to Schleiermacher, who is his author of choice when it comes to questions relating to religion and religious experience. For Schleiermacher, the totality of meaning is the universe, *das Universum*. Religious experience and religious conscience are the sites where the totality of meaning expresses itself thematically. This

---

[21] Cf. ES, 149.
[22] Cf. ES, 151.

totality presupposes things, actions, and events, a totality habitually implicit and not expressed. In his second discourse, *Reden*, Schleiermacher speaks of religion in terms of 'part' and 'whole': "That which is religion is to see each individual as a part of a whole, to see all that is limited as presentation of all that is unlimited."[23] He also speaks of religion using the concept of the Universe, which seems to correspond to Dilthey's concept of the totality of meaning. If Schleiermacher links meaning-experience and religious-experience, then totality of meaning, which was implicit, becomes explicit. Religion is the capacity to see in that which is finite and individual, that which is of the infinite and of the universe. What is religious reflex for Schleiermacher corresponds to totality of meaning for Pannenberg. Religion's particularity is to see the infinite in the finite and the particular. In day-to-day events we are concerned with the finite, not the infinite. Religious experience changes, reverses the poles of interest, because experience is received as the manifestation of the totality of meaning. Pannenberg was already correcting Schleiermacher here, who did not make a sufficient distinction between the totality of meaning and God, between totality and that which, as totality, allows him to exist. He further says: "In the case of religious experience, totality of meaning is usually indirectly thematic, whereas divinity, which establishes and guaranties such totality of meaning, is central in the considerations. ... That which we feel acting upon us is not the totality of meaning of the universe, but the oneness of divine reality, which of itself makes up the totality of meaning and makes meaning one."[24]

We restate the importance given to the moment of anticipation, for it is through human meaning-experience that the historicity of the self-proclamation of divine reality is realised. In other words, for Pannenberg it is in history, in the experience of the world and of mankind, that God's self-proclamation is completed. Historical religions serve as the thematic structure for the experiences of the self-proclamation of divine reality. Historical religions are able to discern in the hustle and bustle of unfolding history the anticipation of the totality of meaning that announces divine reality. Religious experiences are related to historical religions. Historical religions ensure inter-subjective pertinence of religious experiences. This correlation to tradition validates, or documents, the self-proclamation of God in history, but remains open to contemporary indirect

---

[23] Friedrich D.E. Schleiermacher, *Über die Religion* [1799] (Göttingen: Vandenhoeck und Ruprecht, 1967) 53. Quoted by Pannenberg (ES, 153).
[24] ES, 153.

experience, which is an anticipation of the totality of meaning of reality. Pannenberg affirms strongly that theology's object is indirect self-proclamation of God in experiences that anticipate the totality of meaning of reality, which the faith traditions of historical religions refer to.

We note as well the singular parallel between *Bedeutung* and *Sinn*, *Erlebnis* and *Erfahrung*. *Sinn* is the link with *totality*, just like *Erfahrung*. *Bedeutung* and *Erlebnis* are more related to the *individual*. This says something about Pannenberg's understanding of experience in theology, of its collective nature, indeed religious nature. The importance of the social aspect of religious experience must not be forgotten: a religious experience is valid insofar as it is articulated within a tradition or society. The distinction between totality and individual is the reason why individual *Erlebnis* is of less interest to the author until he 'converts' it, as it were, into *Erfahrung*, that is to say within an interpretative framework. To situate what is carried in *Erlebnis* within the domain of *Erfahrung* is to integrate, but also to test how unfolding history proceeds (or not) toward its full and complete eschatological fulfilment.

Should we not stress the relation between the 'totality/individual' distinction and the 'thematic/non-thematic' character of religious experience? As long as it is non-thematic, as with Schleiermacher, religious experience brings to awareness a dimension neglected by modern man. The 'thematisation' of religious experience will be what makes it Christian, for the believer does not simply encounter its mystery, the believer encounters a relational, personal God.

Pannenberg's writing of *Eschatology and Experience of Meaning*, his treatment of the theme of the future might seem like an effort to maintain a correlation between faith and the world.[25] More precisely, his understanding of 'meaning linkings' for an event, his integration of them into the totality of meaning, via experience, brings him to make two comments: one on the structure of meaning and one on the profound and mysterious reality that underscores that totality, which is revealed as history and events unfold. Here we see the author's need to speak of the universality of religious thematics, in his thoughts on experience of meaning. His next text concerns itself with this correlation as well, though through a different locus. In each text Pannenberg's global theological stance is a given, only his perspective varies: in 1974, he speaks of the future of man, in 1984, of the presence of God as the founding of meaning and not as a simple human projection. What purpose does religious

[25] ES, 146.

experience serve, if not to deposit God at the heart of humanity's meaning experience?

In 1984, Pannenberg turns his interest once more to the relationship
between the meaning of life and the question of God. His underlining
thought is to justify or to correct the idea that man can create the meaning of life. Is the meaning of life not present, an under-current, a given,
and have we not simply to perceive it, to notice it? For Pannenberg, questionings about the meaning of life lead at some point to considering religion, or the conception of God, as the total and unconditional source of
meaning. His demonstration arises from a discussion of the theory of language and he questions our capacity to invent meaning or our capacity
to receive a given meaning. Pannenberg avoids a theory of language that
would diminish the meaning of language: "Meaning is accessible through
language, but it is not a product of language."[26] This critical idea is
needed, he says, properly to explore the relationship between meaning
experience and religion: "Experienced meaning precedes man's understanding, and is not to be understood as a product of man as meaning
giver."[27] Pannenberg takes up again Dilthey's distinction between *Bedeutung* and *Sinn* to show that the answer to the question he poses needs
nuancing. Man indeed does produce meanings with words and sentences,
but man's use of language articulates realities that are already given.[28] On
this basis, Pannenberg sees meaning as accessible through language.

If he insists as much as he does on the 'meaning-givingness' of language, it is to thwart the idea that meaning could be a mere product of
man. Does man not serve rather as 'secretor' of meaning, as Cioran puts
it? Otherwise, religion would be no more than human projection. It is in
order to justify this position that he considers meaning structure in *Erlebnis*. With *Erlebnis*, while having a particular experience, one also experiences *all* of reality, an experience of the vague presence of something
transcendent and infinite. Here too, Schleiermacher is referred to in presenting religion as intuition of the Universe. In the 1973 and 1974 texts,
there is a validation of the distinctions between ordinary conscience and
religious conscience. The latter explicitly expresses the totality of meaning and therefore the divine reality, which is the foundation of the totality of meaning for the world. The historical dynamics of knowing and of
experience are also elaborated to justify his hypothesis. His conclusion
begins with the event of Jesus of Nazareth as the locus for the historical

---

[26] SRG, 181.
[27] SRG, 182.
[28] Cf. SRG, 180.

realisation of the end of time, because, in the Nazarene, creation and its history find eschatological fulfilment.

Next, Pannenberg published three volumes of his *Systematic Theology* (1988-1993).[29] He notes, in 1988, that the modern paradigm shift has led theology to give a much more important place to experience. In this way, the truth of faith becomes guaranteed by connecting it to subjective experience. In essence, giving renewed access to God via experience is a good idea. It parallels the fashion of the time, but, he adds, things are not so simple. Reducing experience to a pietistic happening for example, presents a grave problem for the idea of experience. One can, like Luther, *relate* faith to an experience, but experience does not *establish* faith. For Luther, it is the exact opposite: faith brings newness to consciousness and produces an interpretation, an experience.

It is therefore necessary to curb the modern philosophical reflex that attempts to establish religious experience as the starting point for the idea of God. In fact, God must be seen as the source of all religious experience: "The concept of God serves to interpret experience."[30] Religious experience must be situated in the context of an encounter with God. Experience implies an entire interpretative structure here: "Interpretation of the individual experience is referred to general characteristics which go beyond the detailed impression of the moment and are set in broader contexts of understanding. We can include this whole process of interpretation in the concept of experience."[31]

With that, we move toward our next section, since Pannenberg sees the Christian way of speaking about God as keeping us from usages of 'God' that are too functionalistic in the context of religious experience.[32] Simply resorting to religious experience to justify religious discourse on God is more or less useful. If religion and religious experience have any meaning, it is in order to find a reality that corresponds to the idea of God.

3. Christian Faith

Pannenberg's 1993 text is entitled *Religious Experience and Christian Faith*. Can this text serve to connect religious experience and Christian

---

[29] We have concentrated on passages from volume I. An examination of this theme throughout his entire comprehensive survey would be desirable.

[30] STIe, 66.

[31] STIe, 66-67.

[32] Cf. STI, 78. This corrective is a distinctive criterion of Christian faith. In this case, it makes a fundamental change with respect to a usage of God that is too vague or too general.

faith and better position the one with respect to the other? Is religious experience involved and does it compare with faith experience? After such a consideration, we might ask how Pannenberg sees faith in Christ with respect to religious experience? A clarification of such a juxtaposition will better reveal the continuity or the discontinuity of religious experience. Pannenberg acknowledges first of all the completely new situation of religion in modernity. Religion can no longer take advantage of a general recognition of the divine in the world: the presuppositions of religion can no longer be taken for granted, nor can it be taken for granted that divinity or even God is knowable as a reality distinct from all others. To counter the forgetting, the unawareness of God, do we not need an experience to make us aware of divine reality, seen as unfathomable mystery that carries and sustains our world and existence? Many today no longer understand God as mystery, to the point of it being necessary to help them grasp the religious, in order that they may follow when we speak of God. Schleiermacher understood this need well and spoke best how to make the people of his time receptive to religion. And Pannenberg once again calls upon Schleiermacher, for he is an important witness in his time for those limited by worldly things. But is this awakening to religious sensibility true religious experience, is it an encounter with divine reality, all together different from worldliness?

The idea of an encounter with a reality different from that of the world is formalized in the religious sciences. Even the story of Jacob at the Jabbok River tells of this religious experience in the Biblical text. Pannenberg explores Schleiermacher's critical view of religious experience, which inasmuch as it is not thematic, appears as a problematic religious experience. His analysis of Schleiermacher's body of work, which accounts for *The Christian Faith*, allows him to clarify and respond in the negative to our question. He refers in some instances to the encounter of an 'other-against', but only to relegate it to the shadows. How does one reconcile Schleiermacher's awakening with an encounter with consuming and gripping divine power, which declares its desire to be involved with man in a particular manner?

Pannenberg proposes another relationship between Schleiermacher's understanding of religious experience and religious experience seen as encounter with a divine reality different from finite reality. That relationship is effected through the non-thematic or the thematic, which is what distinguishes Schleiermacher's work from other Christian theologians that see the experience in the encounter of mysterious power, and through stories (such as Bible stories), which identify divine mystery. Pannenberg distinguishes between a divine power made known non-thematically (as in, for example, a natural religion), and an explicitly defined divine power (as, for example, in a historical religion). Thematisations produce historical religion where, for example in Christianity, divine mystery is gripping, is identified by Jesus with Father, Abba. Thematic revelation surpasses non-thematic manifestations in that it claims to be an encounter with a concrete otherness that manifests itself and has to do with man.

Pannenberg clarifies the conceptual ambiguity in Schleiermacher's different definitions of religion, outmoded in part in 1821, with the idea of mediator and the idea of saviour. Jesus Christ is mediator for mankind insofar as he reinforces in man the consciousness of God when such consciousness is suppressed by the world. He is saviour as well in this sense! He allows the believer to participate in the primordial force of his consciousness of God. Such a conception makes it possible to hold together the historical commencement of Christianity and its essential character, since the believer's Christian existence is to always be connected to the Saviour Jesus Christ, and to accede to the saving effects that emanate from him.[33]

Schleiermacher understands religious experience as the rousing of the infinite within the finite and this differs from concrete experience of God in the sense of an experience of divine reality different from finite reality. Is it possible to link the two conceptions? Pannenberg does so in the following way. The relationship is mutually profitable, because Schleiermacher's stance awakens us to an idea of God as genesis of the world that is different from the reality of the world. The gods of religions are very mysterious and it is their personal moment that distinguishes them from Schleiermacher's context of 'the universe'. Religious discourse has meaning only if one assumes a religious backdrop and a religious sensibility. That is what makes discourse today about God dramatic, the absence of knowledge of divine mystery as backdrop, a disposition for thematic religious experience.

Schleiermacher described the process of awakening to religious consciousness, but did not succeed in meshing that awakening with the thematic character of religion. Thematisation makes known divine mystery and carries it toward identification, never definitively. Jesus utters the word 'father' to speak that mystery that stresses unimaginable confidence in the Creator as much as it does personal intimacy with this mystery. Jesus as Christ constitutes for the faithful an intrinsic link with the Father

---

[33] Cf. RECG, 117-118.

and the personal face of God. Through their faith, Christians participate in Trinitarian life, which is actualised in the looking to the Son, actualised in the gifts of the Spirit, in the joy and freedom in being children of God. For Pannenberg, the Christian faith experience does not mean dissolution into impersonal mysticism, rather, Christian experience is the carrying out of our participation in the intimacy of the Son Jesus with his Father, mystery of the world.

Consequently, a distinction must be made between Schleiermacher's feeling of the Universe and the God of Christ. In both cases he is concerned with the experience of divine mystery as well as concerning himself with religion. The difference lies in the passage from the indirect to the direct aspect, the passage from the non-thematic to the thematic via *Erlebnis* toward *Erfahrung*, and lies in the prolepsis of the historical process that is the resurrection of Jesus of Nazareth, anticipation, from inside history, of the glory of God. There is continuity in the mystery of God and discontinuity in its identification in the Christian faith experience.

4. Conclusion

The question now is, how do we evaluate Pannenberg's thinking about religious experience? He does not give greater importance to possible direct experiences of God. He in fact prefers indirect experiences of God via the experiences the individual has of the self and of the world. Non-thematic religious experiences are possible, perhaps such as the one Pannenberg describes as having had as a teenager. Such experiences can awaken modern man's consciousness to a forgotten or profound dimension of reality, the mystery that carries and sustains the totality of reality. But such non-thematic experiences do not satisfy the author, for they do not altogether account for the reality of God that reaches out to man. The vagueness, the indistinctness of a religious experience calls out to human consciousness, granted, but that consciousness needs thematic religious experience.

In the modern world, religious experience seems to be the path of access to God and God's truth, since modernity praises experience and deems it as knowledge. But this view needs qualification, reversal even, for God is not found as a result of an experience: God is the originator of religious experience, its source. Otherwise we risk creating an illusion, otherwise we are merely producing man-made transcendent reality.

Thematic religious experience is what is to be found in historical religions. In them are deposited the '*already present*' divine revelation, the self-proclamation of God. Anticipating the reality of the end-time is inscribed in the actual historical process of the experiencing of reality. Fragmented history is that process of revelation. Religious experience makes this revelational historicity known.

Religious experience is therefore not simply *Erlebnis*. A possible understanding of the latter is allowable, because it falls within the interpretative horizon of *Erfahrung*. Here again, it is not a question of a meaning given by man: meaning is given *to* man, an unfolding collectiveness and individuality with eyes cast in the direction of the end-time. Pannenberg speaks of Christian faith as a participative experience of believers in Jesus Christ, who identify the mystery of God with Father. Christian faith is a religious experience related to a specific historical religion. But, despite integrating religious experience into the body of his theological production, questions remain. I gather those questions around elements that indicate well a gap between his theological production and theology's present state: problems posed by his epistemological paradigm and therefore his hermeneutics, his difficulty in responding to the situation of postmodernism.

As both theologian and man of faith, Pannenberg feels a responsibility and loyalty to render faith plausible for today. Pannenberg genuinely collaborated with the modern culture of his time. He responded to a secularized culture, still dealing with the effects of nineteenth century atheism. He proclaimed the presence of God via human experiencing of the self and the world. In a way, he sought to render faith in Jesus Christ intelligible for his world. To achieve that, he cast his net wide, in order to formulate the most distinct thought of how God comes out to meet us. Despite his deep analysis, does he succeed in getting past the aporia of modernity? Do current criticisms of the concepts of truth, universality, historicity, totality, reality, with which he worked without difficulty, not directly influence the pertinence and reception of his theological work?

Such questioning is perhaps abrupt, but of vital importance. Did his study of experience and of religious experience modify his theological activity? Do not Dilthey's hermeneutics and Schleiermacher's religious sensitivity entirely reinforce the modern stance of the theologian from Munich? How can the breakdown or the fragmentation of meaning, how can the radical linguistic turn, how can deconstruction thematics, or concrete individual, plural experience, indeed, how can these parameters not have an impact on a contemporary theological stance? New currents in theology risk upsetting Panneberg's paradigm. Some of his epistemological presuppositions must therefore be re-evaluated, if our thinking with this major contributor to twentieth century Protestant theology is to go forward.[34]

[34] E.g. Christoph Schwöbel, though a commentator favourable disposed to Pannenberg, nevertheless concludes his presentation leaving unanswered the question of Pannenberg's theological reception in the future. "Wolfhart Pannenberg," *The Modern Theologians*, vol. I, ed. David F. Ford (Oxford: Blackwell, 1989) 284ff.

EXPERIENCE ACCORDING TO EDWARD SCHILLEBEECKX: THE DRIVING FORCE OF FAITH AND THEOLOGY

LIEVEN BOEVE

1. Introduction

Edward Schillebeeckx[1] may well be considered an exemplar of a Catholic theologian living and working in the second half of the twentieth century, from his formation in Neo-Thomist philosophy and theology and evolving *via* the Second Vatican Council to become one of the exponents of late-modern theology.[2] In the late sixties, after having attempted to elaborate a theology of culture,[3] Schillebeeckx makes a hermeneutical turn,

[1] For an intellectual biography, see Erik Borgman, *Edward Schillebeeckx: Een theoloog in zijn geschiedenis. Deel 1: Een katholieke cultuurtheologie* (Baarn: Nelissen, 1999); ET: *Edward Schillebeeckx: A Theologian in His History. 1: A Catholic Theology of Culture 1914-1965* (Dulles, VA: Continuum, 2002). For Schillebeeckx's primary bibliography: Ted Schoof and Jan van de Westelaken, *Bibliography 1936-1996 of Edward Schillebeeckx o.p.* (Baarn: Nelissen, 1997).

[2] Born in 1914, in Antwerp in a Flemish Catholic family, Schillebeeckx entered the Order of Preachers (Dominicans) in 1934. In Ghent he was taught at the Dominican philosophical institute by Domien De Petter who attempted to bring into dialogue philosophical Thomism and Husserlian phenomenology. Schillebeeckx studied classic Neo-Thomist theology at the Dominican theological institute in Leuven and later studied in Paris at Le Saulchoir and the Sorbonne. In Paris he enjoyed contacts with the French Dominicans of the *nouvelle théologie* Yves Congar and Marie-Dominique Chenu. In 1951 Schillebeeckx concluded a doctorate in theology with a dissertation on the sacramentology of Thomas Aquinas. After some years as a professor in the Dominican Theologicum in Leuven, he left for the chair of dogmatic theology and the history of theology at the theological Faculty of the Catholic University of Nijmegen, the Netherlands. He served as an expert for the Dutch episcopacy at Vatican II, was one of the founders of the progressive international theological review *Concilium*, and had a major influence on the Pastoral Council in the Netherlands, including the publication of the *New Catechism*, which was one of its primary results. In the seventies he accomplished one of the major theological efforts in his career with the publication of the first two books of his Jesus-trilogy (the third part only appearing in 1989). In 1982 he became an emeritus professor. At present, he still writes and publishes, and we are awaiting his often-announced new *Sacramentology*. Three times the Congregation for the Defence of the Faith investigated the orthodoxy of Schillebeeckx, but his theology was never condemned: in 1968 there was a general investigation; in 1979 his Christology became the subject of scrutiny; and in 1984 he was targeted for his views on ministry.

[3] Until the late Sixties Schillebeeckx was in search of a new theology of culture in a context of secularisation. Important results of this endeavour were published in the first four volumes of his *Theologische peilingen* (Theological Soundings). One may consider

and exchanges a more neo-Thomist metaphysically-grounded theology for a theology rooted in history and language. It is at this point that the category of experience assumes a very important place in his theology, at the level of both theological method and content.

In the introduction of *Geloofsverstaan* (*The Understanding of Faith*),[4] Schillebeeckx defines *theological hermeneutics by describing its two major tasks*: (a) 'how to interpret the biblical message of God's Reign, and how to affirm such interpretation as a Christian interpretation?', and (b) 'how to account for such a Christian interpretation of reality to modern thinking, at least to the legitimate demands this thinking brings to the fore?'. It is from this hermeneutical perspective that his Christological trilogy, *Jezus het verhaal van een levende* (1974) (*Jesus: An Experiment in Christology*, 1979), *Gerechtigheid en liefde: Genade en bevrijding* (1977) (*Christ: The Christian Experience in the Modern World*, 1980) en *Mensen als verhaal van God* (1989) (*Church: The Human Story of God*, 1990) were conceived.[5]

Schillebeeckx's goal has been the construction of a plausible and relevant theology within a modern context proceeding from a critical dialogue with this context. The result has been a critical-hermeneutical, praxis-oriented theology that places Christians in the midst of an emancipatory and liberating struggle of humanity for a more just and humane society. In this respect, Schillebeeckx's theological position is very near the political theology of Johann Baptist Metz.[6] Both reject a theology that

Gaudium et spes as exemplary for this attempt on the ecclesial level. In relation to today's world Schillebeeckx intended to elaborate "a theological perspective on the historical form of human existence in its concrete involvement with the world and its religious meaning" (Borgman, *Edward Schillebeeckx*, 454). In line with *Gaudium et spes* – including the optimism of the Sixties – he envisaged a new partnership between Church and world. The Church is not an escape hatch of security and unchangeability, to flee from the insecurities and ambiguities of history and society, but has to link itself with the questions implicit in the contemporary sensibilities. Salvation is encountered in the daily living and working of human beings in the world in their relation with what is of the earth.

[4] Edward Schillebeeckx, *Geloofsverstaan: Interpretatie en kritiek,* Theologische peilingen, V (Bloemendaal: Nelissen, 1972); ET: *The Understanding of Faith: Interpretation and Criticism* (London and New York, NY: Sheed and Ward, 1974).

[5] Edward Schillebeeckx, *Jezus het verhaal van een levende* (Bloemendaal: Nelissen, 1974); ET: *Jesus: An Experiment in Christology* (New York, NY: Seabury Press and London: Collins, 1979). *Gerechtigheid en liefde: Genade en bevrijding* (Baarn: Nelissen, 1977); ET: *Christ: The Christian Experience in the Modern World* (London: SCM Press, 1980). *Mensen als verhaal van God* (Baarn: Nelissen, 1989); ET: *Church: The Human Story of God* (New York, NY: Crossroad and London: SCM Press, 1990).

[6] Which he at the same time appreciates very much and criticises, because for Schillebeeckx Metz is wrong in positing God as the subject of history, and not humanity (see his "Erfahrung und Glaube," *Christlicher Glaube in moderner Gesellschaft*, ed. Franz Böckle,

allows for an anti-modern, culture-inimical dogmatism or fundamental-ism, and thus opt for a theology that appreciates the gains of modernity and its dream of a more humane world. Both, therefore, enter into a crit-ical dialogue with modernity. Schillebeeckx, as much as Metz, protests against a theology that is oriented to a doctrinally pure set of eternal and deductive truths. They both search for a theology that is posited in the midst of a concrete praxis of faith, itself an expression of the ongoing Christian search for the meaning of the gospel for one's own time. And finally, against a theology that only focuses on the spiritual well-being of individual souls, they construct a theology which is (also) involved in the political and socio-economic realm and in the concrete histories of suf-fering and the resistance of humanity in need of and striving toward a just and liberated world. As already mentioned, it is in such a theological pro-ject that Schillebeeckx accentuates the crucial role of experience in faith and theology – to such a degree that some call Schillebeeckx's theology resolutely a theology of experience.[7]

In this contribution, I first want to consider how the turn to hermeneu-tics challenged Schillebeeckx to highlight the notion of experience (as well as correlation). Second, I will investigate his methodological views on experience, revelation, tradition development, and correlation as he developed them in his Jesus-trilogy. I will then conclude with a schematic presentation of Schillebeeckx's theological hermeneutics and some remarks and questions.

2. Hermeneutics Calls for Experience

In order to construct a theological hermeneutics of his own, in *Geloofs-verstaan* (*The Understanding of Faith*) Schillebeeckx enters into a dia-logue with philosophical hermeneutics (Heidegger, De Saussure, Ricoeur, Gadamer), with theological hermeneutics (Bultmann, Fuchs, Ebeling,

---

vol. 25 (Freiburg, Basel, and Wien: Herder, 1980) 73-116. For Johann Baptist Metz, see his most important monograph: *Glaube in Geschichte und Gesellschaft: Studien zu einer praktischen Fundamentaltheologie* (Mainz: Grünewald, 1977); and the collection: *Zum Begriff der neuen Politischen Theologie* (Mainz: Grünewald, 1997).

[7] Cf. the presentation of Schillebeeckx in Rosino Gibellini, *Panorama de la théologie du XXe siècle* (Paris: Éditions du Cerf, [2]1994) 371-398: 'Théologie et expérience' (theol-ogy as the understanding of the Christian experience). See also Marc Dumas' qualifica-tion of Schillebeeckx's project as 'une correlation d'expériences', later on corrected in 'une interrelation critique d'expériences' (cf. Marc Dumas, "Corrélation d'expériences?," *Laval théologique et philosophique* 60 (2004) (still to be published)).

Tillich, Pannenberg) and linguistic philosophy (Ramsey), and critical theory (Habermas). In this endeavour the category of experience arises, especially in the search for criteria of an authentic dogmatic and theological language, and thus for legitimate changes or shifts in theological doctrine and dogma. Next to the doxological criterion (the primary aim of theological language is to praise God for God's salvific involvement in human history and world), Schillebeeckx stresses the importance of the experiential context of our faith concepts. But, for the first time, other, basic concepts and theological strategies are presented in this volume: the importance of orthopraxis, negative dialectics (contrast-experience), and the criterion of correlation.

a. Theological Language and Experience

In one of the contributions of *Geloofsverstaan*, namely *Ervaringscontext en doxologische waarde van het gelovige spreken*, Schillebeeckx defines the *"relationship with lived experience as criterion for the meaning of theological interpretations"*.[8] He further elaborates this criterion under two aspects.

First, theology is in need of "a hermeneutics of experience before embarking on a system of hermeneutics of christian tradition, because it is not by any means certain that every real aspect of human experience will be expressed in the self-understanding of christian experience, which of course, forms an integral part of that experience".[9] That is the reason, according to Schillebeeckx, why one has to distinguish between, first, a dogmatic or theological faith understanding (which is always a linguistically expressed interpretation), and, second, the experience that is interpreted. One should thus hold the distinction between an experience-bound or experienced *interpretandum* and the linguistic interpretation models, *interpretaments*, in which this *interpretandum* is expressed.

Second, what "is said about Jesus in the church's interpretation of faith has therefore, if it is to be meaningful and intelligible to us – and this is the most important condition to be fulfilled if we are to give ourselves completely in faith – to have a real relationship with our ordinary everyday experience with our fellow-men in the world".[10] Indeed, the link with

---

[8] Schillebeeckx, *Geloofsverstaan*, 57-62; ET: "The Context and Value of Faith-Talk," *The Understanding of Faith*, 14-19, 14.

[9] Schillebeeckx, *The Understanding of Faith*, 16.

[10] Schillebeeckx, *The Understanding of Faith*, 16.

contemporary human experience is the only way to make the theological, interpretative language of the church meaningful and understandable.[11] Schillebeeckx even radicalises this point: "All theological interpretation must, as a reflection about religious talk, have a meaning that can be understood in and by the world. In other words, it must have ... a secular meaning."[12]

b. Orthopraxis, Critical Negativity, and Correlation

In order to develop these insights, Schillebeeckx not only investigates the structure and nature of language, but also some (other) theological criteria. It is in this context that he, next to the criterion of the proportional relation between 'interpretament' and 'interpretandum' and the role of the reception by the faith community in validating new interpretations, profiles the criterion of *orthopraxis*. Whoever has come to understand his own existence will be led to a renewal of this existence: there is a mutual, intrinsic relation between theory and praxis, between Christian orthodoxy and Christian orthopraxis. Orthodoxy is only 'orthos' in as much it is realised in concrete praxis.[13]

Another crucial element which will fundamentally determine Schillebeeckx's endeavour is the criterion of *correlation*,[14] which he conceives of as a correction of Paul Tillich's question-answer-correlation. For Schillebeeckx it is far from evident that out of the human quest for meaning arises the quest for the God of Christian faith. Schillebeeckx, likewise, wonders if this link could only be evident from the point of view of revelation. It seems that Tillich makes a category mistake and too hastily combines two different language games in linking a religious answer to a non-religious question. According to Schillebeeckx, theology is not concerned with a correlation of human questions and religious answers, but a correlation of answers. For a human question, only a human answer

---

[11] In summary: "The basic condition, then, for every interpretation of faith which is faithful to the gospel is the meaningfulness of that interpretation. In other words, it must reflect real experience. On the other hand, the experience of our everyday existence in the world must also give meaning and reality to our theological talk" (Schillebeeckx, *The Understanding of Faith*, 16-17).

[12] Schillebeeckx, *The Understanding of Faith*, 17; with a reference to Paul van Buren, *The Secular Meaning of the Gospel Based on an Analysis of Its Language* (London: SCM Press, 1963).

[13] Schillebeeckx, *The Understanding of Faith*, 67-69.

[14] Schillebeeckx, *The Understanding of Faith*, 78-101: "Correlation between Human Question and Christian Answer."

can be meaningful. It is the task of the theologian to bring about a correlation between what is humanly meaningful and what is meaningful in light of the Gospel. Only then, when God is not in principle needed for a meaningful life, does God cease to function as "a 'stop-gap', something to which you resort if you can find no other way out of your deepest problems".[15]

In discussing these human answers, Schillebeeckx points to negative and positive human experiences. Negative 'contrast-experiences' have to do with the experience of a threat to the *humanum*, and impulses to resist suffering. In this context Schillebeeckx mentions the *'critical negativity' or 'negative dialectic'* as the universally acknowledgeable pre-understanding of all (pluralistic) positive human projects of meaning. These negative experiences bear in themselves a positive potential that inspires the manifold struggles for a more humane world, for human integrity. This is "the context of human experience in which christian talk about God can be heard in a way which is both secularly meaningful and universally intelligible. There is indeed a convergence or correlation between what is affirmed in the gospel message as a promise, a demand and a criticism and what man experiences as emancipation in his resistance to the threat to the *humanum* that he is seeking".[16]

There are, however, also *positive partial experiences of meaning*, which, according to Schillebeeckx, implicitly call for ultimate meaning, that is, for fulfilment. Here a link with the Christian message may become apparent: "From the point of view of man's question about the authentic fulfilment of his life, about salvation, I see the only explicitly non-religious context within which it is meaningful to speak correlatively about God ... The ultimate fulfilment of man at the end of time, which all men are seeking but cannot formulate and can only partly realise, is the universal pre-understanding of the *humanum* that is promised to us in Christ."[17] Only when human beings already experience in their daily life 'signs and glimpses of transcendence' is it meaningful to talk about the Christian God.

---

[15] Schillebeeckx, *The Understanding of Faith*, 90.

[16] Schillebeeckx, *The Understanding of Faith*, 94.

[17] Schillebeeckx, *The Understanding of Faith*, 98. The text goes further: "Human reality, which can, despite everything, be meaningfully interpreted in secular terms and especially by realising meaning in praxis within a history of meaninglessness, receives from christianity meaning in abundance: the living God himself, who is ultimately the abundance to which all secular meaning is indebted for its own secular significance" (Schillebeeckx, *The Understanding of Faith*, 98-99).

Finally, in the last part of *Geloofsverstaan*, Schillebeeckx develops the importance and impact of Habermas's new critical theory on a modern hermeneutical theology, and accentuates the *practical-critical intention*, and thus the striving for orthopraxis of such theological hermeneutics, which therefore qualifies itself by its Christian-emancipative intention.

c. Provisional Conclusion

It is fair to say that in *Geloofsverstaan* all the preparatory work was completed for Schillebeeckx's theological project from the seventies until the present day. To conclude this section, I sum up some of the crucial elements:

– the introduction of the category of experience, the importance of the context of experience for a theological hermeneutics of dogmatic language, and the distinction between an experiential *interpretandum* and linguistic interpretation models (interpretaments);
– the need for a correlation of the Christian message to contemporary non-religious experiences to highlight the plausibility and relevance of theological language in the current modern context (1972), giving rise to new interpretations;
– the analysis of such non-religious experiences in terms of contrast-experiences of critical negativity, and of experiences of partial meaningfulness;
– and, finally, the crucial role of orthopraxis as the hallmark of an authentic practical-critical, emancipative Christian faith in search of the *humanum*: orthodoxy is a matter of orthopraxis; Christian salvation has to do with the realisation of human integrity.

It is from here that Schillebeeckx undertakes his Christological trilogy. Often he explicitly refers to the part experience plays in faith and faith reflection. Likewise, from time to time, in his methodological texts and paragraphs, he elaborates anew the role of experience in theological epistemology.

3. Experience as the Driving Force of Faith and Theology

I already mentioned that during his Jesus-research Schillebeeckx further elaborates his theological method, and a number of the crucial elements stemming from his earlier writings are taken up again and further developed in view of new elements and questions. A noteworthy, clear synthesis is offered in 1978, after having completed his second Jesus-book: *Tussentijds verhaal over twee Jezusboeken* (*Interim Report on the Books Jesus and Christ*).[18] In this rather short monograph Schillebeeckx presents – in dialogue with or reacting to some of his reviewers and critics – some clarifications on his method, very closely linked to the way in which he proceeded in his Jesus-research (especially to the first methodological part of *Christ*).

I take this booklet as the starting point for a more systematic analysis of the theological-epistemological role of experience in Schillebeeckx's theology. I also examine *Erfahrung und Glaube* and *Mensen als verhaal van God* (*Church*),[19] and when appropriate also his valedictory lecture as a professor in Nijmegen, titled *Theologisch geloofsverstaan anno 1983* (The Understanding of Faith in the year 1983), the title of which evidently refers to his first hermeneutical monograph.[20] To a large extent, the lecture itself has been integrated in the first part of *Mensen als verhaal van God*.

The word 'experience' is to be found throughout *Tussentijds verhaal* (*Interim Report*). It is the key term (a) not only to understand what inspired the *first Christians* to testify that Jesus was the risen Christ, but also to gain insight into the 'what' and 'how' of revelation and what is at stake in the two thousand year tradition of Christianity; (b) furthermore, for Schillebeeckx, the category of 'experience' is crucial in order to analyse the *current situation*; and (c) lastly, by 'correlating' both 'experiences' Schillebeeckx is able to develop how *Christians today* can live out their faith in a contextually credible and relevant manner. The ubiquitous presence of 'experience' in Schillebeeckx's theology thus has a double consequence: it teaches us something about his vision of what belief is, and the method in which this belief can still function.

For a clear understanding of this, it is important to make a preliminary note before starting our close reading of the *Interim Report*. Schillebeeckx distinguishes three elements in his analysis of what experience is: an *experiential* dimension (or let us better term this a 'lived' dimension), an *interpretative* dimension that acquires concrete form by the expression of

[18] Edward Schillebeeckx, *Tussentijds verhaal over twee Jezusboeken* (Bloemendaal: Nelissen, 1978); ET: *Interim Report on the Books Jesus and Christ* (London: SCM Press and New York, NY: Crossroad, 1980).

[19] For references, see resp. notes 5 and 6.

[20] Cf. Edward Schillebeeckx, *Theologisch geloofsverstaan anno 1983* (Baarn: Nelissen, 1993).

that experience into concrete images, concepts and narratives ('interpretaments'), and a *theoretical* dimension (a model) that forms the framework in which experience and interpretation occur and are contained. In his own words: "Thus, in what is called a religious experience, there is not only interpretation (understood as certain concepts and images), but moreover a theoretical model from which one synthesises divergent experiences."[21]

a. Christianity Began with an Experience – Revelation and Experience

For Schillebeeckx, Christianity began with an *experience*, an encounter with Jesus of Nazareth, which caused people to discover new meaning and direct their lives in a new direction. Through actual, liberating events people experienced God's closeness. A quick look at the two Jesus-books already published at the time of *Tussentijds verhaal* (*Interim Report*) clearly illustrates this point.

In his first Jesus-book Schillebeeckx refers to two basic experiences, elementary to understand Jesus's life, message and praxis, and the origin of the Christian faith community after his death. First Schillebeeckx refers to Jesus's abba-experience,[22] related to Jesus's 'unconventional' praxis of praying to his Father, to explain Jesus's self-understanding. This experience underlies and is the source of his message and praxis of the coming Reign of God, "which without this religious experience, or apart from it, lose the distinctive meaning and content actually conferred on them by Jesus".[23] Further, according to Schillebeeckx, the abba-experience points to the very characteristic specificity of Jesus with regard to his own context (which is not to say that in this basis the supra-historical significance of Jesus could be sustained). Second, Schillebeeckx refers to the Easter experience of the first disciples, as the experience of conversion, on the initiative of Jesus, to Jesus as the Christ – which is the experience of having found forgiveness, grace and salvation in Jesus, and of returning to the actual community with Jesus, now professed as the Christ, the coming Judge (Son of Man) or Risen Crucified.[24] It is on the basis of this experience, which is new – however not discontinuous with the experiences of the disciples with the pre-paschal Jesus – that the disciples gather

---

[21] Schillebeeckx, *Theologisch geloofsverstaan anno 1983*, 26 (my translation).
[22] Schillebeeckx, *Jesus*, 210-221.
[23] Schillebeeckx, *Jesus*, 266.
[24] Schillebeeckx, *Jesus*, 379-397.

again (on the historical initiative of Peter). It is also in this experience that
the reality of what in the pascha-christologies is called 'resurrection' and
later is received as the 'leading and canonical kerygma', is revealed.

In his second Jesus-book, Schillebeeckx focuses on the experience of
grace, that is, of having found salvation in Jesus from God (Dutch *van
Godswege*), in the variety of interpretaments to which the New Testament testifies. It is at this point that Schillebeeckx again makes a difference "between the interpretation brought by the *Christian experience*
itself (and this includes historical and social conditioning, though the
experience of Jesus as the Christ or as decisive and final salvation can also
include universal human experiences), and what I might call the subsequent culturally conditioned thematization and theoretical development of
these Christian interpretative experiences".[25]

In the *Interim Report* Schillebeeckx further reflects on these religious
experiences in terms of revelation. Because revelation, for Schillebeeckx,
always has to do with experience. In *Erfahrung und Glaube* and *Church*,
he will become even more explicit about 'revelational experiences'.[26]
However, even though there can be no revelation without experience,
revelation is not equivalent to human experience, and yet it can only be
discerned "in and through human experiences".[27] The confession of the
first Christians that Jesus is the Christ is then not only *their* articulation
of an experience but, first and foremost, evidence of something *that has
overtaken them* and has made or taught them to look at Jesus in another
light.[28] The faith experience that Jesus is the Christ is thus not a purely

---

[25] Schillebeeckx, *Christ*, 634.

[26] In *Erfahrung und Glaube,* there is a long section about the false dilemma between
'Glaube aus dem Hören' en 'Glaube aufgrund von Erfahrung' – a false dilemma because
faith never starts from an unmediated hearing, but can only be realised and mediated
through personal experience – cf. p. 81: "Erst wenn die lebendige Geschichte einer bes-
timmten religiösen Tradition erzählt und lebendig in Praxis umgesetzt ist, können heutige
Menschen aus und in und mit ihren heutigen menschlichen Erfahrungen christliche
Erfahrungen machen, das heißt sich mit dieser Geschichte identifizieren oder sich von ihr
distanzieren [reference is made here to some other works, including some of his own]. In
dieser Geschichte können sie in und mit ihren menschlichen Erfahrungen in der Welt
zugleich sich selbst entdecken." The Christian tradition is therefore the history of Christian faith experiences: human experiences that, by their embodiment in the Christian histories and narratives about experiences of God, become experienced as Christian experiences. See further also *Church*, 22ff.

[27] Revelation occurs "through a long process of events, experiences and interpretations". For this and following quotes see: *Interim Report*, 11.

[28] "But when Christians claim that Jesus is God's decisive revelation, they understand
this in a twofold way, both objectively and subjectively. On the one hand, there are people (Christians) who affirm, 'this is the way we see him'." It is because of their liberating encounters and experiences of salvation with Jesus before his death, and in the events

subjective human intuition, sensation or feeling and, thereby a product of human interpretation, rather, it contains a cognitive claim (an 'objectivity') that unravels itself together with the experience. Truly this revelatory initiative of God can only become expressed through a person's answer in faith (for instance, in confessing Christ). Nonetheless, it cannot be reduced to this, even if paradoxically enough it is only in and through this human answer in faith that revelation becomes visible to us. Put differently: there can be no experience without interpretation.

Schillebeeckx unfolds this 'objectivity' of the experience by distinguishing between 'experiential elements' and 'interpretative elements' within the '(revelatory) experience' itself. Already present *within the experience itself* are intrinsic interpretative aspects that can be distinguished from other interpretative elements that originate from the situation in which the experience takes place. Here Schillebeeckx mentions love as an example. Those who are caught up in the experience of love know that their experience is about love.[29] The experience of love thus speaks for itself: it has a transparency of its own. This does not mean that *interpretative elements* (interpretaments) from elsewhere – for instance, from literature or popular culture – do not really matter. On the contrary, on the one hand, they give expression to the inexhaustible richness of this experience of love and, at the same time in doing so, demonstrate that it cannot be contained in words – both being the catalyst to the continually renewing search for forms of expression. On the other hand, they thoroughly colour the experience of love as a whole and describe how actual love is experienced. The interpretation thus does not come from above but rather, as the self-expression of the experience, is deeply interwoven in the actual experience.[30] Schillebeeckx designates expressions that are primarily an articulation of this 'original' interpreted experiential dimension of the experience as 'first-order' expressions. Expressions

surrounding his death, that people began to think of him in this manner. "On the other hand, in accordance with this self-same understanding on the part of the disciples, this affirmation also carries the implication, 'We must see him like this, because this is the way he is'." From their experience of liberation and salvation the disciples mean to answer the question: "Who is he that he can act thus?" with the following conclusion: Jesus is the definitive revelation of God. Expressed more technically: "Soteriology is the way to christology" (Schillebeeckx, *Interim Report*, 11-12).

[29] "Thus this interpretative identification is an intrinsic element of the experience of love" (Schillebeeckx, *Interim Report*, 13).

[30] "Real love is fed by the experience of love and its own particular ongoing self-expression ... However, this growing self-expression makes it possible to deepen the original experience; it opens up the experience and makes it more explicit" (Schillebeeckx, *Interim Report*, 13-14).

that schematise this experience further, from out of a 'further, advanced, reflexive, interpretative experience', are 'second-order' expressions.

Applied to the experience of the first Christians, such first-order expressions as 'Jesus is the Christ', or 'He lives', refer to the common *fundamental basic experience* of 'having experienced salvation in and through Jesus'. It is this basic experience that received an interpreted expression in the New Testament writings in various ways and in relation to the Old Testament and the contemporary context. The fundamental basic experience *is not disconnected from* the New Testament *interpretations* (second-order expressions) – it can, in fact, not be disconnected from it. However, it does not coincide with these interpretations because this basic experience is already contained within pre-existing interpretative frameworks from the outset – frameworks that are already influenced by underlying theories and models. There simply cannot be an 'unmediated experience'.

Nonetheless, Christian belief is all about this basic experience, certainly and especially if we ask ourselves what this Christian belief can still mean for us today. Schillebeeckx's primary concern is that the adherence to interpretaments handed down to us by tradition will end up restricting precisely that open access to this basic experience. For, just as the New Testament gave testimony to that basic experience in various ways depending on the situation, so too did the 'living tradition' as a history of consecutive contextually-coloured interpretations of *that same shared basic experience* because, through the combined action of experience and interpretation, tradition is both the condition of possibility for, and the result of, participating in the same fundamental experience of 'finding grace in Jesus'. When an appeal to tradition does not make this possible, then only traditionalism and dogmatism devoid of experience remain. The only legitimate development of tradition should be that which makes it possible for Christians today to also have access to that faith experience.

From this perspective Schillebeeckx further develops Gadamer's tradition hermeneutics and arrives at his well-known scheme of the *identity between the proportions between faith expression and the historical context in the course of history*.[31] The dialectics between (new) experiences (in new contexts) and (old) interpretations (stemming from older contexts) fosters a continuous process of tradition development, in which ruptures do not threaten the continuity of tradition, but may be urged precisely to guarantee this continuity. The relationship between Jesus's

---

[31] See Schillebeeckx, *Church*, 40-45.

message and his historical context is fundamentally similar to the relation between the New Testament message and the historical context that gave it form. Despite the difference between both expressions there is identity and continuity – 'proportional similarity'. This identity of meaning continues to persist through the subsequent proportions between faith expression and context in the patristic, medieval and modern times. But Schillebeeckx's real message is that this relation will also once again acquire form today. It is here again that the category of 'experience' occupies a prominent place in his thought.

b. Our Modern World of Experience

Schillebeeckx states: "What once was experience can only be handed down in renewed experiences, at least as living tradition."[32] To this a connection must be made with *our modern world of experience* which, according to Schillebeeckx, is fundamentally associated with, on the one hand "our ineradicable expectation of a future in which men can live, and on the other hand the utter horror" regarding the suffering and senseless injustice that threatens the future of the overwhelming majority of people.[33] Modern hope for a better society is after all thwarted by utilitarian and individualistic understandings of 'freedom'. Increasing wealth and power runs parallel to an instrumentalisation of the human person and society at the expense of ecology and human well-being. However, the ethical resistance that places both of these under critique and, in particular, the suffering that they generate, betrays a *'new sense of ethical values'* in terms of solidarity that, according to Schillebeeckx, 'are Biblical' at their core. Furthermore, against the background of suffering, disintegration and uprootedness, the religious question, which is a question of healing, restoration, salvation, and human integrity, becomes a question of being a human being, regardless of whether one is religious or not. "The question of salvation is not just religious or theological; in our time it has become universal and even explicitly is now the great driving force of all human history."[34]

At other places Schillebeeckx develops this new sense of ethical values and the experiences involved in the question of salvation as the question of the whole of humanity, often in relation to the notion of *contrast-experience*.

---

[32] Schillebeeckx, *Interim Report*, 50.
[33] Schillebeeckx, *Interim Report*, 55.
[34] Schillebeeckx, *Interim Report*, 58.

He does this again, for example, in his so-called 'theological testament', published in Dutch in 1994, on the occasion of his 80th birthday. The 'radical contrast-experience' is an experience that is foundational, accessible to all people, pre-religious and even pre-reflexive, "a basic experience which is common to all human beings, and which, as such, is ... pre-religious, accessible to all human beings".[35] Such contrast-experience intrinsically bears within itself both a negative and a positive element. *Negatively*, it is the experience of indignity that arises in human beings when perceiving the factual world with its histories of suffering and injustice, oppression and misfortune. It calls for an irresistible veto against the inhumanity in our history; a 'No' to suffering. Schillebeeckx adds: "Moreover, this experience possesses a greater evidence and certainty than all what philosophy and human sciences may bring in as verifiable knowledge."[36] Positively, it invokes an open 'Yes' that is at the very basis of all kinds of resistance and that reveals evil and injustice as evil and injustice to us. This positive side reveals an unspecified openness to a new and more humane situation, which can justifiably claim our unconditional yes. It gives raise to a positive expectation that a better world is possible. It is the ground for human *belief* in the humaneness of humanity, and for hope that suffering and injustice do not have the last word in this history, which is marked by ambiguity: "Without this hope the factual available indignity is as lived experience non-existent, intrinsically impossible, meaningless and without humane content. The human indignity itself is without at least a latent positive yearning for humaneness essentially absurd."[37] Therefore this 'open yes' is more radical than negative contrast experiences, which in fact presuppose it. This 'open yes' is also nurtured, affirmed and supported by fragmentary experiences of happiness, meaning, fulfilment, etc., for both believers and unbelievers. Religions, then, are the offspring of pairing negative experiences and positive salutary conceptions and expectations. Most often they do not theorise about suffering and the way in which it can be solved, but offer ways to deal with it, in a praxis of liberation. This is also true for Christianity.[38] Because "asking what *Christian identity* is about is not to be separated from asking what *human integrity* is about. Moreover, this quest for identity cannot be solved in à merely theoretical way. It essentially implies a

[35] Edward Schillebeeckx, *Theologisch testament: Notarieel nog niet verleden* (Baarn: Nelissen, 1994) 128. The translation of this citation and the following is mine.

[36] Schillebeeckx, *Theologisch testament*, 128.

[37] Schillebeeckx, *Theologisch testament*, 130.

[38] Cf. Schillebeeckx, *Theologisch testament*, 131-132.

quest for a Christian, specific praxis of a both mystical or theological and ethical-practical nature, extending itself to the domain of ecology and of the social and political life. To speak of God only receives its proper meaning and 'productive' weight in the framework of the *praxis of the Reign of God.*"[39]

c. Towards a Critical Correlation between the Christian Tradition and the Modern Situation

It is to this modern context of experience that the Christian faith has to relate. It thus makes necessary a *'critical correlation' between tradition and the modern situation*. On one end, new contextual experiences help cast a fresh look at the tradition. On the other, this tradition, as the ever-renewing interpretation of experiences, renders perspectives that add a Christian dimension to this modern context. The result is a real and up-to-date Christian belief in which the present-day situation "is an intrinsic element of the significance of the Christian message for us".[40] It is such a Christian faith that is both founded upon and a result of the fundamental Christian experience, which in its turn, precisely in relation to the new situation, acquires form and expression once again. Thus the correlation between tradition and context can with equal, or perhaps even greater right be called *a correlation of experiences* – i.e. between that of the fundamental experience handed down by tradition and the experiences of the modern human being.

Indeed, as already stated, Schillebeeckx understands tradition to be the history of both the experience and interpretation of the fundamental Christian experience. On the basis of his research in the New Testament, he discerns four constant structural principles that depict this fundamental experience and lend structure to all forthcoming interpretations: finding

---

[39] Schillebeeckx, *Theologisch testament*, 136.

[40] Schillebeeckx, *Interim Report*, 55. He continues: "It is therefore striking that the times in which men refer to their own experiences, individual and collective, with renewed emphasis, are always times of crisis in which they experience a gap between tradition and experience instead of continuity between, e.g. the Christian tradition of experience and their contemporary experience. Of course even old experiences have power to make men question and transform; the four structural principles mentioned above remain a critical reminder of that [for these principles, see further in our text]. But even new experiences have their own productive and critical force; otherwise, a reference to 'interpretative elements' of old experiences would do not more than solidify and hold back our ongoing history."

salvation in God is to become fully human; Jesus is the definitive mediation of this; by means of passing on his story in the Church through its
retelling, we also are invited to enter into this story; and, this salvation
embraces, but also extends beyond, history.[41] Correlated to the current situation these structural principles acquire a concrete form in so far as the
Christian faith, with respect to the new ethical sense of values in the modern context, is able "to understand the impulses of living, struggling and
praying mankind, to find here echoes of its own Christian impulses and
then to show solidarity on the basis of the belief that God does not [want]
that mankind should suffer; on the contrary".[42] The Christian message of
salvation is the full restoration of the human person and also implies an
ecological, social and political praxis. It is in this praxis, in the actual
engagement with the suffering, that the fundamental Christian basic experience can once again acquire form. This is the contemporary locus of
*religious experience, the privileged place where God's commitment to
the human person can be experienced*, in the opposition to suffering and
injustice. Christianity today is a matter of politics and mysticism bound
together.[43]

d. The Primacy of Experience over Interpretation, in Its Very Indissolu-
   ble Bond to It.

In *Church* Schillebeeckx stresses more explicitly that all experience is in
fact *irreducibly interwoven or inextricably linked to interpretation*. This
applies all the more to religious experiences, and definitely to Christian
religious experiences. Both are intrinsically experienced in and through
particular human experiences, "though with the illumination and help of
a particular religious tradition in which people stand and which is thus
influential as an interpretative framework which provides meaning".[43a]

---

[41] Cf. Schillebeeckx, *Interim Report*, 51-54.
[42] Schillebeeckx, *Interim Report*, 58.
[43] "This radical concern for human society indicates a special presence of God. If living man is the fundamental symbol of God, i.e. 'the image of God', then the place where
people are dishonoured, oppressed and enslaved, both in their own hearts and in society,
is at the same time *the privileged place where religious experience becomes possible* in
and through a life-style which seeks to give form to that symbol, to achieve wholeness and
liberation. Thus real liberation, redemption and salvation always diverge into mysticism,
because for religious people, the ultimate source and foundation for the healing and salvation of mankind, living and dead, is to be found in God" (Schillebeeckx, *Interim Report*,
59-60 – italics mine).
[43a] Schillebeeckx, *Church*, 24-25.

For Christians this illumination is offered by "the faith content of the Christian tradition of experience".[44] He also accentuates the *reflexive* character of experiences: experiences are not so much concerned with unmediated 'sensations' or 'affections', but rather with interpretation and reflection.

Nevertheless this does not undo the *pre-linguistic*, or *pre-reflexive*, aspect or even the 'original' *transparency of experience towards universal significance*, even though these are unattainable without interpretation. Inasmuch as experiences are 'revelation of reality, of that which is not produced or thought of by human beings', they have a cognitive, critical and liberating power. They teach us something about the human search for truth, goodness and righteousness, and happiness. The same is true for the Christian "offer of revelation with its non-objectifiable meaning and content" that is "to be found only in the believing interpretations of men and women in a particular social and cultural context.[45] For although the pre-linguistic experiential moment cannot be distilled as such from the accompanying interpretative moments, this does not imply that at its core the Christian revelation is empty. On the contrary, it "provides its own *direction* of interpretation, as the normative basis of our non-arbitrary interpretation of faith".[46] Further on in *Church* Schillebeeckx states more explicitly that Christians can legitimate their faith because it concerns a fundamental, thoroughly human experience. All human beings share such experience. It does not necessarily require a religious interpretation, although for every human being it is related to the deepest meaning of life. Such a fundamental experience, nevertheless, "is helped in the understanding of this fundamental character, which so deeply affects human existence, by the word of God".[46a] Schillebeeckx adds: "I say, 'is helped'; not 'gives a better understanding of' this experience than the agnostic explanation", and further: "So I am talking about universally shared experiences which are fundamental to any human existence, which by the introduction of belief in God's saving presence manifest a distinctive comprehensibility which can be understood by others (even if they do not accept them), which is not present in other interpretations in which belief in God is not expressed."[47]

[44] Schillebeeckx, *Church*, 24-25.
[45] Schillebeeckx, *Church*, 42-43.
[46] Schillebeeckx, *Church*, 38.
[46a] Schillebeeckx, *Church*, 84.
[47] Schillebeeckx, *Church*, 84.

The inextricable link between experience and interpretation also makes Schillebeeckx wonder about the concept of 'correlation' because of which he seems to *(slightly?) radicalise his hermeneutical position*, without relativising its universalistic dimension. As already mentioned, in *Tussentijds verhaal* (*Interim Report*, 1978) Schillebeeckx describes the critical correlation theory, as consisting of three steps: first, the tracing of constant structures of the Christian foundational experience within the New Testament and the tradition; second, the analysis of the present-day world of experience, in a general-cultural and a Christian-specific sense; and third, the critical correlation or confrontation of both sources of theology. Schillebeeckx will later, however, prefer to use the term *'interrelation' instead of 'correlation'*. In his valedictory lecture in Nijmegen in 1983, Schillebeeckx even states that 'correlation' is a misleading term, because it would suggest only a harmonious relationship between tradition and situation, whereas for Schillebeeckx the intrinsically necessary link between tradition and situation includes a whole range of possible relations, from identity (Dutch *het klikt*) to non-identity (Dutch *het botst*), from harmony and correlation to conflict and confrontation.[48] Authentic theologising, he writes, takes place in "two phases that nevertheless together form a dialectical whole … We after all only understand the Christian tradition out of the questions handed to us from the present situation wherein we live; the understanding of the past already implies an interpretation of the present. And the other way round, our understanding of the present stands itself under the historical influence of the Christian tradition."[49]

It remains a question however, as to whether there is already the presumption of a more fundamental continuity and harmony, underlying the very structure of Schillebeeckx's interrelation-concept, which would unmask this as essentially correlation. This would (at least in my opinion) become apparent in his continuous reference to a pre-linguistic and thus pre-reflexive element in experiences, secular as well as religious, and the way in which he profiles the relationship Christian faith has (or should

---

[48] Schillebeeckx, *Theologisch geloofsverstaan anno 1983*, 9-10.

[49] Schillebeeckx, *Theologisch geloofsverstaan anno 1983*, 12. But, as a matter of fact, already in *Gerechtigheid en liefde* (*Christ*, 1977), he employed the category of interrelation: "Christian theology in particular is concerned with an interrelationship [Dutch original: *interrelatie*] between an 'analysis of the present' on the one hand and an analysis of the historical experience of Christian life and hermeneutical reflection on this life on the other. Its concern is to distil from this totality a direction which Christians can responsibly take in the process of living towards the future" (*Christ*, 72).

have) with this element.[50] In summary: because it concerns essentially the 'same' experience that is shared by believers as well as non (or other) believers, despite the diversity of often incompatible interpretations in which this experience is expressed, it is possible for Christians to affirm the plausibility and relevance of their faith in relation to today's modern context and its standards of rationality and humaneness.

e. The Lessons of Edward Schillebeeckx

The lessons to be learned from Edward Schillebeeckx are thus clear:
– There can be no faith without experience. Faith is not about acceptance of doctrines stemming from the past but rather actual lived and reflected upon faith experience. Faith has to do with life. Indeed a faith that cannot be actually experienced is not worth believing.
– To this Schillebeeckx adds that just as such experiences are always contextually situated, the universal significance of the Christian message (the 'offer of revelation') continually manifests itself in concrete particular forms. This was the case with Jesus, and this is once again the case when the narrative of Jesus's life and death 'fits' (or does not 'fit'!) in with our own life experiences.
– Consequently, Schillebeeckx can affirm that, for a Christian, a properly understood pursuit of an ethical and just society has an affinity with following Jesus's example in working for the kingdom of God. For the modern Christian there is an intrinsic bond between both. Precisely because of this, there is a '(co)relation' possible between the experiences of the first disciples with Jesus and the deep-seated contemporary human experiences of Christians today in their modern context (with a privileged role for experiences of suffering). Interpreted against the background of the Christian tradition it is essentially the same fundamental basic experience: God is committed to human beings and their salvation. The project of the human being is the project of God: "Christianity has to do with the integration of being human in and through a source experience in which people, confronted with the man Jesus, connect the world, society and the individual with the absolute ground, the living God, our salvation".[51]

---

[50] For a similar analysis of Schillebeeckx approach, see my: "The Sacramental Interruption of Rituals of Life," *Heythrop Journal* 44 (2003) 401-417.
[51] Schillebeeckx, *Christ*, 62.

– Finally, *the particularity of the Christian tradition* therefore in no way
threatens the plausibility and relevance of Christian faith in a modern
context and its standards of rationality and humaneness, and thus *its universal significance*. On the one hand, in the words of the *Interim Report*:
"Christians find the most adequate expression of the depth-dimension
harboured in all our everyday human experiences – what can be rightly
called a primal trust or a fundamental belief – in Jesus Christ. For precisely that reason, in Jesus individual, historically unique originality and
human universality go hand in hand."[52] On the other hand, inversely, as
stated in *Erfahrung und Glaube*, the question for meaning and truth is
a question only to be solved in concrete praxis in which – for Christians
– today's actual experiences of meaning and truth are addressed in the
Christian experience tradition as a practical anticipation of universal
meaning (the praxis of the Reign of God) and as the historical mediation of the manifestation of universal truth, both standing under the crit-
ical-cognitive and liberating power of the histories of suffering.[53]

f. Experience between Particularity and Universality: Two Critiques of Schillebeeckx's Position

Schillebeeckx has been criticised for his concept of experience from two
perspectives. After having analysed the way in which Schillebeeckx uses
human (religious) experience, Leo Apostel, a prominent Flemish atheist
philosopher, observes that Schillebeeckx from beginning to end *still presupposes a Christian horizon of understanding*, and never really succeeds
in getting out of it. On the one hand, Schillebeeckx defines religious experience in as undetermined a way as possible, but on the other, he binds it
very stringently (or wishes to do so) to tradition. According to Apostel,
that is why Schillebeeckx is caught up in a thinking pattern in which what
is, generally speaking, human ultimately only can be fulfilled by integrating it into a Christian perspective.[54] "If he would have defined religious

---

[52] Schillebeeckx, *Interim Report*, 61. The quote goes further: "Just as a unique, utterly
original loving relationship between two people is a matter of universal experience, so too
the original, specific and historical career of Jesus also discloses possibilities for all men.
Historical particularity does not away with universality, but manifests it. That is why the
Christian encounter of a number of people with Jesus could become a world religion with
a message that can be addressed to all men."

[53] Cf. Schillebeeckx, "Erfahrung und Glaube," 108.

[54] Leo Apostel, "Religieuze ervaring bij Edward Schillebeeckx," *Volgens Edward
Schillebeeckx,* ed. E. Kuypers, Rondom filosofen, 3 (Leuven and Apeldoorn: Garant, 1991)

experience in itself (and in a quality of its own), then he would have found it again (in a diversity of modalities) in the different religions, and, at least as far as the experience of global meaning is concerned, also with non-religious people. This would have made possible a real dialogue. And this is in fact what Schillebeeckx wanted. But by binding the description of experience so closely to the framework of interpretation, he did not allow himself to reach his goal".[55] It would have been better to stress "the autonomy of the pre-linguistic moment in religious experience",[56] before linking it to interpretation. In the same way Jaak Vandenbulcke accentuates the autonomous character of religious experience. Vandenbulcke pleads for acknowledging a pre-linguistic, profoundly human experience of reality, in which in principle universality precedes all interpretations (religions) and likewise is constitutive of them. Even more: the relation to this experience is the criterion to evaluate the truth claims of a particular religion.[57]

The psychologist, philosopher and theologian, Antoon Vergote, on the other hand, *criticises the too facile appeal to (religious) experience in faith and theology* (and Schillebeeckx is considered one of the accused).[58] Vergote sharply distinguishes between 'faith on the basis of experience' ('ervaringsgeloof') and 'having experience of faith' or 'experienced faith' ('geloofservaring'). In the first case people start from the profoundly human experiences of love, of a mysterious power, and link to it in a second move the name of God. God, then, would seem to be an adjective: something is divine for me, "*the* mysterious, *the* profound, ... that is God for me".[59] Such fundamental experiences do not so much concern Christian faith, but rather a general, basic, human disposition, a kind of general

91-131. Cf. p. 118: "According to Schillebeeckx the struggle against alienation and for ultimate meaning is present in as complete and as authentic with atheists (be it more heroic and without hope) as well as with Christians. Immediately, however, he adds such restrictions to this that only in the Christian struggle for ultimate meaning ... the really liberating struggle is engaged in." (The translation of this and following quotations is mine.)

[55] Apostel, "Religieuze ervaring bij Edward Schillebeeckx," 118.

[56] Apostel, "Religieuze ervaring bij Edward Schillebeeckx," 118.

[57] Cf. J. Vandenbulcke, "Geloof op basis van ervaring: Naar aanleiding van A. Vergote's 'Cultuur, Religie, Geloof'," *Tijdschrift voor theologie* 29 (1989) 270-278. See also his "Geloof en ervaring," *Streven* 57 (1990) 196-198; and "God ervaren, wat betekent dat?" *Sacerdos* 58 (1991) 127-144.

[58] A. Vergote, "Ervaringsgeloof en geloofservaring," *Streven* 52 (1985) 891-903. Published again in A. Vergote, *Het meerstemmige leven: Gedachten over mens en religie* (Kapellen: DNB and Pelckmans, 1987) 16-30. We have used this last version.

[59] Vergote, *Het meerstemmige leven*, 17.

[59a] Vergote, *Het meerstemmige leven*, 28-29.

faith or basic trust, which is part of being a human being as such. Accentuating the role of experience in faith, therefore, runs the risk of *reducing Christian faith to a kind of general human faith*. It is even a mistake to try to solve the crisis of Christianity in Western Europe by appealing to 'faith on the basis of experience'. For faith is something in its own right, not a product of experience. There is nothing in Christianity that would compel people to believe. For non-engaged observers, Christianity is only the accidental product of a series of contingent, historical events, which in no way can place any claim on this history. 'Having experience of faith', on the contrary, is not primary, but can only be acquired through engaging in Christian faith, in taking the leap of faith, which one ventures in the confession that God has become present in history through Jesus Christ. Experienced faith, therefore, concerns having the experience of what it is to be in faith. Not experience produces faith, but faith, experience. According to Vergote this happens when people succeed in perceiving their own lives and understanding of reality in connection to the message of the Christian faith. This involves an integration of faith and life, through which life begins to speak about faith; and concerns "a concrete living of faith which interprets and values the world and the being a human being from the perspective of faith".[59a] This necessitates the construction of a specific culture of faith, learning to read with the eyes of faith. Because without this "one has no more than words, words words ... words *without* experienced reality".[60]

These reactions to Schillebeeckx's appeal to experience bear witness to the modern epistemological problem of relating the particularity of Christianity to the universality of general human truth, in order to validate Christianity's truth claims. All three are answers to the question as to how Christian faith fits into a context in which secular rational and epistemological criteria reign, a position all three take for granted. The answer of *Apostel*, like that of Vandenbulcke, is very similar to one of the positions of the so-called pluralistic theology of religions. All religions would seem to be partial, incomplete cultural mediations or expressions of a universally shared (mystical) experience. This implies that the truth of religions can only be accounted for in relation to this experience. To the extent no religion is able to completely express this experience, no religion can claim absolute truth. In other words: the particularity of religion is relative in terms of the universality of the (mystical) experience. Schillebeeckx is not

---

[60] Vergote, *Het meerstemmige leven*, 28-29.
[61] Schillebeeckx in fact maintains an inclusivist position: in the end the Christian truth

ready to go that far, and does not want to go that far.[61] This explains the ambiguity at which Apostel and Vandenbulcke hint. Even if Schillebeeckx in principle holds to a universal pre-linguistic element in experience, shared by all human beings as a fundamental basic experience, he nevertheless remains *de facto* within a Christian framework of interpretation. This relativises (at least somewhat) the factual distance between Vergote and Schillebeeckx, although it does not do away with it. In reflecting on the particularity of Christianity *Vergote* makes a move opposite that of Apostel and Vandenbulcke, and stresses this particularity by distinguishing it from a general human basic trust or faith. The truth of Christianity cannot be founded on the latter, but must be sought in the specificity of Christian faith, in particular, the faith option itself. One might imagine that Vergote's position does not satisfy Schillebeeckx on two counts. First, he would criticise Vergote for undervaluing the need for a rational legitimating of Christian faith (even if the latter never can be stringently conclusive), and second, he would regret that with his criticism of the appeal to experience in faith and theology, Vergote also wipes out the internal theological hermeneutical dynamics of tradition criticism and tradition development, to which the continuous interplay between (Christian) experience and Christian interpretation gives rise.

g. Towards a Theology of Experience in a Postmodern Context

From a contemporary perspective, one could judge all three of these positions to be modern to the extent that they relate the question of Christian particularity and truth to a modern (secular) epistemological framework. But one could legitimately ask what the consequences are when one takes into account the postmodern criticism of such epistemology[62] and of the secularisation thesis, which is conceived in relation to it.[63] It seems indeed that a contextual shift occurred, through which plurality and difference are

claim is the criterion for all other truth claims. See e.g. his "Identiteit, eigenheid en universaliteit van Gods heil in Jezus," *Tijdschrift voor theologie* 30 (1990) 259-275.

[62] See e.g. my "Critical Consciousness in the Postmodern Condition: A New Opportunity for Theology?," *Philosophy and Theology* 10 (1997) 449-468.

[63] For the latter, see e.g. Harvey Cox, "The Myth of the Twentieth Century: The Rise and Fall of 'Secularisation'," *The Twentieth Century: A Theological Overview*, ed. G. Baum (New York, NY: Orbis, 1999) 135-143; Peter Berger, "The Desecularisation of the World: A Global Overview," *The Desecularisation of the World: Resurgent Religion and World Politics*, ed. Peter Berger (Grand Rapids, MI: W.B. Eerdmans, 1999) 1-18.

[64] I developed this thesis at the Catholic Theological Society of America (CTSA)-con-

conceived as irreducible, and all claims to universality are regarded with suspicion. Regarding secularisation, it would seem that de-traditionalisation (rather than secularisation) does not result in a religion-free, general, human, secular discourse about the meaning of life, but on the contrary, results in a plurality of approaches, religious or not, dealing with these questions, the relativist position being only one. In such a context of de-traditionalisation and pluralisation, Schillebeeckx's project of correlation, because of its modern presuppositions (continuity), necessarily meets its own limits. It is my conviction that precisely the contact that Christian tradition and theology has with the current context forces theology to become post-correlational, not by giving up the dialogue with the context, but by reconceiving its conditions and presuppositions.[64]

In a context of irreducible plurality, the particularity of Christianity becomes constitutive of Christianity's meaning and truth, which has to be conceived in relation to the meaning and truth claims of other religions and worldviews without relativising one's own claims (or the other's) and this plurality from the very outset. Christian experience then does not bear within itself a pre-linguistic element to relativise Christianity's particularity, but reveals this particularity to itself as inescapable. It is what differentiates Christians and their tradition of experience from others, and constitutes the very point of departure for a dialogue, that is, a confrontation between different religions and worldviews. More generally, it is clear that what people initially seem to have in common (i.e. questions and answers for ultimate meaning), differentiates them the most. Experience interrupts accounts of continuity that are too facile, let alone harmony. Only the one who is able to live with difference and to think from it would seem not to lapse into hegemonic and totalitarian master narratives excluding plurality and otherness.

At the same time, within Christianity itself the Christian experience interrupts accounts of continuity and harmony that are too facile. The God of Christian faith does not coincide with tradition and interpretation. As the Other of the Christian tradition, God in principle withdraws from it, even when it remains true that only through and in this tradition God reveals God's self, i.e. can be discussed. The God who has everything to do with this tradition cannot be contained in it, but questions from the inside the tradition itself, interrupts it, makes it confront its own limits,

---

vention in New Orleans, 2002: "Postmodern Theology between Secularity and Plurality: Some Western-European Methodological Considerations."
    [65] I have elaborated further on these too brief clues for a reconceptualisation of the the-

urging it to develop and renew itself. Only to the extent that this interrupting aspect of a God, who cannot be reduced to the particular Christian narrative about God (although inconceivable without it and outside of
it) is part of the Christian experience can tradition development be theologically thought of and legitimised today.[65]

4. Conclusion

Schillebeeckx's theology is indeed a theology of experience, a hermeneutical reflection on the experiences of Christians of the past and Christians
living in a modern context, in relation to this context. To conclude this
contribution I would like to offer a schematic presentation of Schillebeeckx's hermeneutical theology, highlighting the epistemological role
of experience.

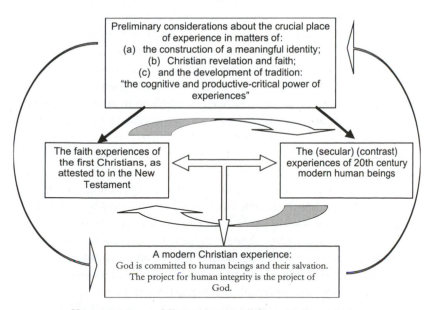

Hermeneutics and Experience: a Schematic Presentation

ological-epistemological role of religious experience in the Fourth International LEST-
conference on Religious Experience and Theological Epistemology, Leuven, November
2003. The proceedings of this conference will appear in BETL, Peeters, 2005.

It is certainly not an exaggeration to affirm that Schillebeeckx's *theo-logical epistemology* is as much an explanation of the correlation efforts he deems of theological necessity for a responsible and plausible con-temporary theological reflection as it is its first product. Stressing the role of *experience* in theological epistemology as a key element for doing the-ology in the second half of the Twentieth century is already the result of the integration of modern sensibilities in theological methodology. In this way the *hermeneutical circle* is already operative on the level of the texts in which Schillebeeckx is explaining its function in the development of tradition and theology. This holds true for the concept of *correlation* itself, which presupposes a universally acknowledgeable underlying con-sensus or continuity between the best of humanity and the Christian mes-sage. The experience of being a Christian in a modern context, apprecia-tive of the gains of modernity but also critical, with modernity's critics, of its failures, causing suffering and injustice, leads to a modern theol-ogy in which Christians are profiled as at least as modern as anybody else (especially modern agnostics or atheists). Christianity therefore is not a hindrance to human development, but may well offer a surplus of opportunities to sustain human striving for a just and humane society.

In this way, the category of experience serves at least two purposes. First, it makes it possible to describe in a new and dynamic way the *very particularity of Christian faith*, which is embedded in an ongoing history of interpretation and experience, of concrete liberating praxis, in which God, in the history of Israel and most particularly in Jesus Christ, has revealed God's self as a God of human beings. Remarkably, the notion of experience is at the same time responsible for the difference between Christian faith expressions as well as for the fundamental continuity between them: although the interpretative elements may vary, even to a point that they are incompatible with each other, Schillebeeckx claims that there is an experiential element qualified through a specific 'direc-tion of interpretation', which in the end founds and guarantees the unity of the Christian tradition (albeit in a diversity of expressions).

Second, through the notion of the contrast-experience, the category of experience serves as an instrument to sustain or to found the *universal truth and meaning claims of Christianity*. Because Christian experience has an intrinsic link with what is at the core of all human experience, what is the experiential element in all human experience – the desire for human integrity – there are good rational grounds to be or to remain a Christian. Also here the structure of experience provides the instruments to account for the difference between human interpretations and theories, e.g. between a Marxist and a Christian striving for justice, as well as for the fundamental continuity which ultimately is the driving force for all forms of resisting inhumanity and injustice, and the longing for emancipation and liberation.

GLORIA: THE ULTIMATE EXPERIENCE?
THE THEOLOGICAL AESTHETICS OF HANS URS VON BALTHASAR

YVES DE MAESENEER[1]

Not a few readers of Hans Urs von Balthasar's *The Glory of the Lord* are deterred by his theological language which sounds completely at odds with our thoroughly secularised experience.[2] The central concept of *gloria* itself has disappeared out of our contemporary discourse – the original German title '*Herrlichkeit*' rings even more archaicly. One of the rare times I encountered this word outside von Balthasar's universe was on a billboard advertising the newest Cacharel perfume. The subtitle under the picture of a woman miming an ecstatic state, somewhere between eroticism and a religious ecstasy, promised 'the ultimate experience', *gloria*. That this theological notion survives in the perfume industry ironically coincides with one of the idiosyncrasies of von Balthasar's writings, i.e., the recurrence of the metaphor of odour.

Not only perfume merchandisers seem to be grateful users of the theological heritage,[3] another cherished theme of von Balthasar's recently provided material for a horror film.[4] The film *Stigmata* (1999) tells the story of a young woman, who is working in a beauty shop in the American city of Pittsburgh. All of a sudden, after she received a rosary from her mother, an explicitly atheist woman starts to experience the stigmata,

---

[1] I would like to thank Paul Da Ponte, Lieven Boeve, Johan Ardui, and Maria Duffy for their critical comments.

[2] References to von Balthasar's work and translated version will be abbreviated: *H* I = Hans Urs von Balthasar, *Herrlichkeit: Eine theologische Ästhetik*. I: *Schau der Gestalt* (Einsiedeln: Johannes Verlag, 1961); ET: *GL* I = *The Glory of the Lord: A Theological Aesthetics*. I: *Seeing the Form*: trans. Erasmo Leiva-Merikakis (Edinburgh: T. & T. Clark, 1982).

[3] See some other recent perfumes: *Angel, J'adore, Eternity, Miracle*.

[4] This positively charged theme appears repeatedly in his theological aesthetics: see below. A more systematic approach can be found in von Balthasar's essay on Bonaventure: *Herrlichkeit: Eine theologische Ästhetik*. II, 1: *Fächer der Stile: Klerikale Stile* (Einsiedeln: Johannes Verlag, 1962) 265-361; ET: *The Glory of the Lord: A Theological Aesthetics. II: Studies in Theological Style: Clerical Styles* (Edinburgh: T. & T. Clark, 1984) 260-362. He relates that his mystical friend Adrienne von Speyr regularly bore the stigmata. See Hans Urs von Balthasar, *Erster Blick auf Adrienne von Speyr* (Einsiedeln: Johannes Verlag, 1968) 31; ET: *First Glance at Adrienne von Speyr* (San Francisco, CA: Ignatius Press, 1981).

the wounds of Christ: they occur as an irresistible reflex provoked by the accidental sight of a crucifix.[5] When the Vatican learns about these unusual experiences, a priest is sent who works for the Vatican's *Congregation for the Causes of Saints* as a kind of clerical private-eye. His mission consists in debunking false claims to miraculous experiences. The Curia's only aim is to protect the Church's monopoly of spiritual power against whatever outside sources of experience. Any messenger who could threaten the institutional status quo has to be rendered harmless.

As the priest discovers, the young woman is possessed by the spirit of a certain Father Alameida, which is transmitted by the rosary she received from her mother. Father Alameida, a devout and recently deceased priest, was a translator of ancient languages, and a member of the Pontifical Biblical Commission. He was involved in an ecclesial power game concerning the 'lost gospel' of St. Thomas. In order to control the truth and prevent the authentic words of Jesus from being revealed, he was murdered by the Curia. However, by means of the experiences of the young, stigmatized woman, the truth breaks out. Possessed, she starts talking Aramaic, and even writes an exact copy of the Aramaic manuscript of the Gospel on the wall of her room.

Some could be disturbed by the simplistic representation of the institutional Church as a kind of Mafia and the cheap exploitation of a spectacular aspect of Roman Catholic spirituality. *Stigmata* delivers a sample of today's stereotypical representations of the Christian experience, if not of the religious experience in general – there is a strong thematic resemblance between the film and James Redfield's New-Age bestseller *The Celestine Prophecy* (1993), which is also based on the fictive discovery of an ancient Aramaic manuscript containing mystical messages that are violently suppressed by the Roman Catholic Church. As such it evokes part of the context against which any contemporary interpretation of von Balthasar's theological aesthetics has to articulate itself.

1. The Aesthetic Experience as Analogy of Christian Experience

In 1961 the Swiss Roman Catholic theologian Hans Urs von Balthasar published the first volume of *Herrlichkeit: Eine theologische Ästhetik*

---

[5] Theologians may enjoy the exciting way in which the film director mixes flashy rock video style sequences – e.g., a live crucifixion in a disco with a soundtrack of Billy Corgan – with literal references to the lives of stigmatised saints – the woman smells of flowers (the smell of holiness), doves come and eat out of her hands and so forth.

(*The Glory of the Lord: A Theological Aesthetics*). In the foreword of this first part of a fifteen-volume magnum opus, von Balthasar presents his project of a theological aesthetics: it aims to counter the impoverishment within theology which is the result of the loss of the aesthetic dimension (*Entästhetisierung*). This impoverishment implies not least a poverty of experience. After an historical introduction, the first book consists of two parts, entitled 'The Subjective Evidence' and 'The Objective Evidence', which discuss respectively the subjective and objective structure of theological knowledge, or, in von Balthasar's aesthetic reconceptualisation of this question, the subjective and objective side of 'seeing the form of Christ'. Significantly, the main part of 'The Subjective Evidence' – two hundred pages, almost one-third of the whole book – treats the subject of experience. [6]

In line with his methodological claim that fundamental theology and dogmatics cannot be clearly distinguished,[8] von Balthasar does not have a separate treatment of 'experience in general': he immediately begins discussing 'the experience of faith'. It is from a theological point of view that he introduces, by means of analogy, 'worldly' notions of 'experience' and 'aesthetic experience'. In the following paragraphs we will attempt to articulate those notions in order to demonstrate the specificity of his theological construction.[9] Special attention has to be given to the categories

---

[6] See *H* I, 211-410; *GL* I, 219-425. Aidan Nichols reminds us of the fact that 'experience' was considered a suspicious subject in the mainstream Catholic theology of that period: it was associated with Protestant and Modernist thinking. See Aidan Nichols, *The Word Has Been Abroad: A Guide Through Balthasar's Aesthetics* (Edinburgh: T. & T. Clark, 1998) 32. In spite of von Balthasar's extensive exposition, there is surprisingly little attention to the notion of experience in the recent reception of his work. As far as I know, no recent article has been published on this topic. If we restrict our focus to the recent publications in English, we do not find any explicit elucidation of the theme in excellent von Balthasar studies like, e.g., Lucy Gardner *et al.*, *Balthasar at the End of Modernity* (Edinburgh: T. & T. Clark, 1999); Kevin Mongrain, *The Systematic Thought of Hans Urs von Balthasar: An Irenaean Retrieval* (New York, NY: Crossroad Publishing Company, 2002); David L. Schindler, *Heart of the World, Center of the Church: Communio Ecclesiology, Liberalism, and Liberation* (Edinburgh: T. & T. Clark and Grand Rapids, MI: W.B. Eerdmans, 1996). On the one hand, this lacuna can be linked with the fact that von Balthasar's writings are often mobilised in a strategy to counter modern theologies, which legitimated themselves precisely in the name of 'experience'. On the other, the absence of the theme is the logical consequence of a certain self-defeating character of von Balthasar's concept of experience.

[8] Von Balthasar strongly relativises the distinction between fundamental theology ('the apologetics') which is usually considered as the treatment of the preliminary and methodological questions on the conditions of possibility of faith, and dogmatic theology which explicitly deals with the contents of faith. See *H* I, 9-11; *GL* I, 13-15. As he polemically states: "The saint is the apology for the Christian religion." (*GL* I, 229; *H* I, 221: "Der Heilige ist die Apologie der christlichen Religion.")

of space, time and form (*Gestalt*).[10] More than just key concepts, they provide the metaphorical patterns and the material of the morphological and etymological operations that structure the text.[11] In his synthesis on the experience of faith these three components (space, time and form) are embraced in a fourth term, 'attunement' (*Stimmung*).

a. Experience: Time and Space

Von Balthasar develops an 'holistic' notion of experience: experience involves the human being as a whole, body and soul, intellect, will and feeling. This is stressed against two reductionist tendencies. On the one hand, there is a dualist vision, which can be found in both mainstream pre-modern theologies and 'heterodox' gnostic thinking that time and again expose 'platonising' features.[12] Experience is spiritualised, becoming a question of moving beyond the sensible appearances up to the essence, the world of ideas. This philosophical view neglects that the human being is an indissoluble unity of body and soul.[13] Von Balthasar refers here to the biblical notion of 'the 'heart' and even the 'bowels' (*splángchna*), from which is derived *splangchnízesthai*, 'to have mercy') as the seat both of man's deepest personal reactions and of God's own most profound attitude with regard to the world'.[14] Experience is always embodied: it can never place sensibility in brackets. On the other hand, von Balthasar's notion of experience is also explicitly directed against the reductionist concept which he considers the root of many aberrations in modern theologies of experience.[15] Modern thinkers associate experience too exclusively with 'feeling' (*Gefühl*), understood in a narrow sense

---

[9] Our article is meant as a critical reading of von Balthasar's section on the experience of faith (*H* I, 211-410; *GL* I, 219-425). In particular we will focus on the first chapter, entitled 'Experience and Mediation' (*Erfahrung und Vermittlung*) (*H* I, 211-290; *GL* I, 219-301).

[10] Although Von Balthasar's term *Gestalt* has some different connotations, we will translate *Gestalt* as 'form'.

[11] Time and again von Balthasar makes these linguistic processes explicit. We will point to the role of etymology in his argument. On the morphological level, he engages the morphemes 'form' (*-gestalt-*) and 'space' (*-raum-*) in numerous wordplays. He consciously adds a temporal dimension to them by verbalising them (e.g. *gestalten*), and deploys many compounds by means of spatio-temporal prefixes (e.g. *eingestalten*).

[12] See *H* I, 282-283.290.302-305.311.327.367.373.401; *GL* I, 293-294.302.313-317.323.380.386.416.

[13] See *H* I, 238 (*Leibseeleeinheit*); *GL* I, 248.

[14] *GL* I, 243; *H* I, 235: "das 'Herz', ja die 'Eingeweide' (*splángchna*, davon *splangchnízesthai*, sich erbarmen) als Sitz der tiefsten personalen Reaktionen des Menschen und Gottes selbst der Welt gegenüber."

[15] See *H* I, 236; *GL* I, 245.

as the realm of emotions, affectivity and irrationality. Interiorised as a psychological phenomenon, experience is restricted to an isolated dimension of the human person. For von Balthasar experience is more fundamental: it involves the totality of human life and reality – it is the basic 'attunement' of human existence.

In one of the many etymological steppingstones that guide von Balthasar's explorations, the sense of experience – as *er-fahren* – is explained as "insight acquired by travelling to a place".[16] The metaphor of travelling stresses that experience is not conceived of as an inner mental state, but as a dynamic event through time and space. It is a going out of self, an entering into reality (*einfahren*), the going through. To experience is to enter into the space of time. In a certain way, experience *is* the condition of humanity. It is to get in touch with reality as such, to realise its existence. Experience is to do the experiment of human life, '*experimentum*' in both senses of the word:[17] the 'test of endurance' and the 'proof'. As such it involves human suffering and the final experience of death – in clear distinction to the classical notion that situated the ideal experience in the transcendence of the passions into a state of *apatheia*. "Experience is ... the result of having lived long or suffered intensely."[18]

b. Aesthetic Experience: An Objectivism of the Form

Von Balthasar's preference for the aesthetic experience as the best analogy for the experience of faith is not self-evident. The entire 'platonising' theological tradition – according to von Balthasar, almost the whole of the theological tradition exposes more or less this 'anti-incarnational'[19] tendency – seems to interpret religious experience in terms of *anaisthêsia*:[20] experience, even aesthetic experience, has to be purified from all sensible, material forms which are held to be illusory. The risk of such a turn towards contemplation beyond the form is that it can lead

---

[16] *GL* I, 228; *H* I, 220: "Einsicht durch Fahrt". By splitting up the word *erfahren* (to experience) von Balthasar exposes the root *-fahren*, which means 'to travel'.

[17] See *H* I, 217; *GL* I, 225.

[18] *GL* I, 265; *H* I, 252: "Erfahrung ist ... Ergebnis langen oder intensiven Gelebt- oder Gelittenhabens. Wissend ist nur, wer etwas mitgemacht hat, er hat gelernt, was die Wirklichkeit ist." In this context von Balthasar refers to the Greek word play which linked *máthos* and *páthos* – learning through suffering.

[19] *GL* I, 315; *H* I, 303: "anti-inkarnatorisch".

[20] See *H* I, 257; *GL* I, 267.

easily to "a sophisticated practice of self-observation and experimentation with oneself".[21] Experience is reduced to experience of the self;
experience has become only a function of the self, instead of the
encounter with real otherness. In order to counter the self-referential tendency of this kind of theology of experience, von Balthasar wants to
rediscover the genuine aesthetic experience as distinct from the modern
'devalued'[22] concept of aesthetic experience which suffers a similar subjectivist reduction as the modern concept of experience in general. For
von Balthasar "the aesthetic experience is the union of the greatest possible concreteness of the individual form and the greatest possible universality of its meaning or of the epiphany within it of the mystery of
Being."[23] This may sound like Hegel's dialectical thinking, but the difference is that the concrete form cannot be sublimated into an absolute
knowing beyond the form.[24] Important here is that the aesthetic is radically embodied: the moment of epiphany is inextricably bound up with
a concrete form, with a singular place and time.

As we have just seen, besides all the differences between classical and
modern notions of aesthetic experience, von Balthasar diagnoses a general
tendency of subjectivisation at work. Experience risks being reduced to the
experience of the self; experience has become only a function of the self,
instead of the encounter with real otherness. Employing the binary terms
that characterise classical aesthetics, 'light' and 'form' (*lumen et species*),
von Balthasar claims that the moment of light, defined as formless, infinite, interior, and spiritual, has been overemphasised, while it is precisely
the moment of form which brings to the fore the objective component of
experience, implying exteriority, concrete materiality and sensibility, the
finite, incarnation.[25] At the end of his history and criticism of patristic and
medieval theologies of experience, he concludes:

> A Platonising theology of experience has the tendency to make the objec-
> tive image of God's appearance in salvation-history, with Christ as its cen-
> tre, become too quickly a transparency of the 'formless' light of divine
> glory; it has the tendency to dwell too much on the interior experience of
> how the Holy Spirit takes over command in one's own spirit and to pay too

---

[21] *GL* I, 269; *H* I, 257: "zu einer geradezu raffinierten Selbstbeobachtung und Experi-
mentierung mit sich selber".

[22] *GL* I, 233; *H* I, 224: "modern-abgewertet".

[23] *GL* I, 234; *H* I, 225: "Die ästhetische Erfahrung ist die Einheit einer grösstmöglichen
Konkretheit der Einzelgestalt mit der grösstmöglichen Allgemeinheit ihrer Bedeutung oder
der Epiphanie des Seinsgeheimnisses in ihr."

[24] See *H* I, 222; *GL* I, 235.

[25] See *H* I, 207-210; *GL* I, 215-218.

little attention to the historical form of God's glory, on which every interior spirit remains dependent.[26]

By stressing the indissoluble exterior moment of form, von Balthasar's aesthetics is a plea for an 'objectivist' aesthetics.[27] Form can never be given up. Even more: the objective form plays such a determining role that even the light in which the subject is beholding a form is internally determined by its object. In the aesthetic experience the light is not formless, but intrinsically configured by the form.

How form is constitutive for the aesthetic experience, is described by means of sophisticated spatial metaphors:

> All our senses are engaged when the interior space (*innere Raum*) of a beautiful musical composition or painting opens itself to us and captivates us: the whole person then enters into a state of vibration and becomes responsive space (*antwortenden Raum*), the 'sounding box' of the event of beauty occurring within him.[28]

In that experience we make room in ourselves (*Raum einräumen*) in order to correspond to the form that exacts imitation. In the enrapturing experience of beauty, a self-surrender takes place in service of the beautiful. Von Balthasar stresses that we give up our absolute autonomy in order to obey the law of the beautiful form: the aesthetic experience is in the first place an act of passivity. Beauty is said to be 'literally 'trans-porting'':[29]

> Before the beautiful – no, not really *before* but *within* the beautiful – the whole person quivers. He not only 'finds' the beautiful moving; he experiences himself as being moved and possessed by it. ... Such a person has been taken up wholesale into the reality of the beautiful and is now fully subordinate to it, determined by it, animated by it.[30]

---

[26] *GL* I, 293-294; *H* I, 282-283: "Zudem hat platonisierende Erfahrungstheologie die Tendenz, das objektive Erscheinungsbild Gottes in der Heilsgeschichte, zentral in Christus zu rasch durchsichtig werden zu lassen auf das 'formlose' göttliche Herrlichkeitslicht, zusehr bei der innern Erfahrung des Überhandnehmens des Heiligen Geistes im eigenen Geist zu verweilen, zu wenig auf die geschichtliche Herrlichkeitsgestalt Gottes, von der aller innerer Geist abhängig bleibt, zu achten."

[27] Von Balthasar introduces the term *Objektivismus* to indicate his position at following places: see *H* I, 174.208.248; *GL* I, 181.216.259.

[28] *GL* I, 220; *H* I, 212: "Schliesslich sind wir doch 'mit allen Sinnen' dabei, wenn sich der innere Raum einer schönen Musik oder Malerei uns auftut und uns gefangennimmt, der ganze Mensch gerät in Vibration und wird zum antwortenden Raum und 'Resonanzkasten' des sich in ihm ereignenden Schönen."

[29] *GL* I, 221; *H* I, 213: "buchstäblich hin-reissenden Schönheit".

[30] *GL* I, 247; *H* I, 238: "Vor dem Schönen – ja nicht eigentlich vor ihm, sondern in ihm – vibriert der Gesamtmensch. Er 'findet' es nicht nur ergreifend, sondern erfährt sich als davon ergriffen und in Besitz genommen. ... in der Wirklichkeit des Schönen gesamthaft entrückt und ihr hintergegeben, von ihr bestimmt, durch sie begeistet."

Aesthetic experience is not only travelling to a place, it is also being assumed, taken up in a space, participating in a transcending whole.

The great work of art is 'a dangerous locus', 'a moment of fear':[31] in the worldly aesthetic experience the person who contemplates the beautiful form experiences eternity in time:

> In the experience of worldly beauty the moment is eternity. ... Nevertheless, the 'sorrow of the gods' (*Göttertrauer*) wafts about the beautiful form, for it must die, and the state of being blissfully enraptured always includes a knowledge of its tragic contradiction: both the act and the object contain within themselves the death that contradicts their very content.[32]

Being a genuine experience of the eternal – of the gods – the aesthetic experience is at the same time always determined by an awareness of loss, of the inevitable mortality of time. All beauty must die. At the place of beauty there is inevitably melancholy and infinite sadness.

The natural reaction to this contradictory character of the aesthetic is to try to transcend it into a purely spiritual realm. Von Balthasar claims that the Christian form of revelation, on the contrary, offers an alternative which does not abolish the worldly aesthetics but brings it to perfection:

> The whole mystery of Christianity, that which distinguishes it radically from every other religious project, is that the form does not stand in opposition to infinite light, for the reason that God has himself instituted and confirmed such form. And although, being finite and worldly, this form must die just as every other beautiful thing on earth must die, nevertheless it does not go down into the realm of formlessness, leaving behind an infinite tragic longing, but, rather, it rises up to God *as form*, as the form which now, in God himself, has definitively become one with the divine Word and Light which God has intended for and bestowed upon the world. The form itself must participate in the process of death and resurrection, and thus it becomes coextensive with God's Light-Word. This makes the Christian principle the superabundant and unsurpassable principle of every aesthetics; Christianity becomes *the* aesthetic religion *par excellence*.[33]

---

[31] *GL* I, 321; *H* I, 309: "der gefährliche Ort"; "Furchtmoment".

[32] *GL* I, 237; *H* I, 229: "In der Erfahrung des welthaft Schönen ist der Augenblick Ewigkeit .... Dennoch umweht die schöne Gestalt eine 'Göttertrauer'. Sie muss sterben, und der Zustand des Selig-entrückten weiss sich selbst als tragischen Widerspruch: Akt und Gegenstand schliessen beide den ihrem Gehalt widersprechenden Tod in sich."

[33] This quote illustrates von Balthasar's theological method of analogy. At first sight, the way we presented his thinking up until now seems to force his meandering writing into a scheme which describes a worldly (aesthetic) experience apart from the experience of faith. The point, however, is not that von Balthasar would negate the distinction between these notions. The point is that his method takes its starting-point from within the experience of faith, which has become the principle of the worldly (aesthetic) experience – his method can be called 'descending analogy'. (On this 'katalogical analogy' see Wolfgang

More than the incarnation, the theological ground for the choice of an objectivist aesthetics is the resurrection, which is the resurrection of the form.

c. The Experience of Faith: Attunement and Transformation

As in this radical affirmation of the form against any attempt of one-sided
spiritualisation, the divine glory appeared in the flesh, the human response
to this revelation has to be faith that becomes experience. In order to synthesise the theological and aesthetic account of the Christian experience,
von Balthasar introduces the acoustic metaphor of 'tuning' (Stimmung).[35]
First of all, this allows von Balthasar to stress once again the holistic character of the encounter which determines the experience of faith: unlike the
traditional metaphor of 'hearing' (fides ex auditu) which refers to a specific,
isolated human act, 'tuning' compares the believer with a musical instrument concording as a whole with a certain pitch. Experience is situated at
a more fundamental level than the distinct faculties and acts. Theology situates this Christian 'attunement' to (Einstimmung auf) or 'consonance'
(Gestimmtheit) with God at the ontological level where the human being
as a whole is attuned to reality. Experience as 'attunement' is not the psychological part of faith, not restricted to the emotional, affective, irrational
side of human existence, but involves the human person as a whole.

It is impossible to translate the acrobatic conceptualisation of experience
along the lines of the German word Stimmung. In a concatenation of forms
of the verb -stimmen[36] von Balthasar plays with different prefixes which

Klaghofer-Treitler, Gotteswort im Menschenwort: Inhalt und Form von Theologie nach
Hans Urs von Balthasar (Innsbruck and Wien: Tyrolia-Verlag, 1992) 385-432.) The reason we first elaborated on worldly aesthetics was that we do not want to present a theological debate with some aesthetic footnotes – as not a few of the theologically skilled readers of Von Balthasar's theological aesthetics do –, but really want to respect von Balthasar's
aesthetic perspective. GL I, 216; H I, 208: "Das ganze Geheimnis des Christentums, worin
es sich radikal von jedem andern Religionsentwurf unterscheidet, ist, dass die Gestalt, weil
sie von Gott her gesetzt und bejaht wird, nicht im Gegensatz steht zum unendlichen Licht,
und, obwohl sie als endliche und weltliche Gestalt sterben muss, wie alles Schöne sterben
muss auf Erden, dennoch nicht ins Gestaltlose untergeht, eine unendliche tragische Sehn-
sucht hinterlassend, sondern zu Gott hin als Gestalt aufersteht, als die Gestalt, die nun
endgültig in Gott selber eins geworden ist mit dem göttlichen Wort und Licht, das Gott
der Welt zugedacht und geschenkt hat. Die Gestalt selbst macht den Prozess von Tod und
Auferstehung mit, und wird so koextensiv dem Licht-Wort-Gottes. Darin wird das
Christliche zum überschwenglichen und durch nichts einzuholenden Prinzip jeder Ästhetik,
es wird zur schlechthin ästhetische Religion überhaupt."

[35] See H I, 233-247; GL I, 241-257.

[36] On the fifteen pages of the German text under the heading Christliche Einstimmung
("Christian Attunement"), there occur fourty-three (43!) forms that contain the morpheme
'-stimm-'. See H I, 233-247.

relate to a decentering movement: *ein-, zu-, bei* involve the connotations of 'in', 'to', 'for', 'into', 'with'. The resonance to and for God (*Einge-stimmtsein*) involves a primordial passivity, an openness, active receptivity (*Zustimmung*) towards the divine initiative: the human person has to be the "womb for the conception"[37] of the inspiration. The Holy Spirit is attuning (*stimmt*) the believer, who receives a sensation of God: "The love which is infused in man by the Holy Spirit present within him bestows on man the sensorium with which to perceive God, bestows also the taste for God and, so to speak, an understanding for God's own taste."[38] This sensorium given enables the believer to 'consonate' (*ein-stimmen*) with God. The Christian attunement exists in "the participation of man's entire sensitivity in the manner in which God himself experiences the divine".[39]

This Christian sensorium is forever connected with the historical form of the revelation: experience as attunement is not only to God, but inevitably to Jesus Christ, and His Body, the Church. This double mediation is articulated by means of an aesthetic elaboration of the traditional notion of the imitation of Christ. The experience of faith finds its model in Jesus Christ. In an exegesis of Paul's letters, von Balthasar develops the notion of Christian experience in line with the aesthetic experience as

> the progressive growth of one's own existence into Christ's existence, on the basis of Christ's continuing action in taking shape (*Sicheingestalten Christi*) in the believer: "until Christ has taken shape (*Gestalt*) in you" (Gal 4:19).[40]

The German notion *Eingestaltung* is hard to translate: it is *in*-formation, literally understood as the impressing of a form into somebody, but it also refers to the entering of someone into a form. It is a process of a *trans*-formation: the transfer of a form, and the transport into a form. This presupposes a fundamental receptivity, a primal passivity, openness for an active form. By making room for the form of Christ within oneself, the believer is letting Christ take shape in herself, up to the Pauline "It is not I that live, but Christ lives in me."[41] In this movement of being expropriated

---

[37] *GL* I, 251; *H* I, 241: "Schoss für die 'Konzeption'".

[38] *GL* I, 249; *H* I, 240: "Die vom gegenwärtigen Heiligen Geist dem Menschen einge-flösste Liebe schenkt ihm das Sensorium für Gott, den Geschmack an ihm und sozusagen das Verständnis für Gottes Geschmack."

[39] *GL* I, 249; *H* I, 240: "Teilnahme des Gesamtfühlens des Menschen an der Weise, wie Gott selber das Göttliche erfährt." Von Balthasar refers to Aquinas's notion of con-naturality: see *H* I, 239; *GL* I, 248.

[40] *GL* I, 224; *H* I, 216: "das Hineinwachsen der eigenen Existenz in die Existenz Christi auf der Grundlage des wachsenden Sicheingestaltens Christi in den Glaubenden: 'bis dass Christus in euch Gestalt gewonnen hat' (Gal 4:19)".

[41] *GL* I, 227; *H* I, 219: "Nicht ich lebe, Christus lebt in mir".

for God, of surrender in faith, the believer finds herself already being grasped by Christ. Experience is "entering (*einfahren*) into the Son of God, Christ Jesus".[42]

Through this imitation of Christ the believer participates in His life. By "the transport of a divine *sum-pátheia*, effected and given shape by God'"[43]: the Christian *sym-pathises* – shares the *pathos*, the love, the pain – with Christ, in body and soul. Again von Balthasar quotes Paul:

> That I may know him and [experience in myself] the power of *his* resurrection and become a partaker in *his* body, receiving the very form of *his* death, and if ... possible I may attain the resurrection from the dead (Phil 3:10-11).[44]

The Christian experience receives a "christological measure, as given by Paul: *Hoc sentite in vobis quod et in Christo Jesu*"[45]. The fundamental pitch of the Christian experience is the tune of Christ. Feeling the same as Jesus Christ is to attune (*sich-einstimmen*) oneself deliberately to "the accord (*stimmen*) between Christ and the mandate from the Father": "we speak, therefore, primarily of an empathy (*mitfühlen*) with the Son who renounces the form of God and chooses the form of humiliation; we speak of a sense for the path taken by Christ which leads him to the Cross; we speak of a sensorium for Christ's 'instinct of obedience'."[46] The fundamental experience, the disposition (*Stimmung*) of the Christian, is to become expropriated for God and for man. This kenotic tune is mediated by the Church, especially "in Mary, in the saints, in all those in which 'the being-in-God of our substance occurs in the form of Christ, and the realisation of this reciprocal indwelling is the holiness of the Church that has become a reality and the transformation of the individual soul into an *anima ecclesiastica*."[46a] In this expropriation to the Church and through it to the world the Christian experience is brought to the test: the love of the neighbour.

---

[42] *GL* I, 222; *H* I, 214: "das Einfahren ... in den ... Gottessohn Jesus Christ".

[43] *GL* I, 220; *H* I, 212: "[Schwingungen] einer göttlichen, von Gott her erwirkten und gestalteten *sum-pátheia*."

[44] *GL* I, 227; *H* I, 219: "Ihn will ich erkennen und [an mir erfahren] die Kraft *seiner* Auferstehung und die Anteilnahme an *seinem* Leib, indem ich mit-gleichgeformt werde *seinem* Sterben, um etwa ... hinzugelangen zur Auferstehung von den Toten" (Phil 3:10-12).

[45] *GL* I, 253; *H* I, 243. As often, von Balthasar quotes a Latin version of a biblical verse. (Translation: "Feel the same within yourself as what is in Christ Jesus.")

[46] *GL* I, 253; *H* I, 243: "Es ist deshalb primär ein Mitfühlen mit dem auf die Gottgestalt verzichtenden und die Niedrigkeitsgestalt wählenden Sohn, ein Gespür für die Richtung, die er einschlägt, und die ihn ans Kreuz führt, ein Sensorium für seinen 'Instinkt des Gehorsams'."

[46a] *GL* I, 256; *H* I, 246.

This exegesis of the Pauline experience delivers the paradigm of Christian experience as *trans*formation: "Constant contemplation of the whole Christ, through the Holy Spirit, transforms the beholder as a whole into the image of Christ (2 Cor 3:18)."[47] As von Balthasar repetitively notes, a radical realization of this process can be found in the stigmatisation of a saint, the literal sharing in the wounds of Christ – to a certain extent this specific charisma of stigmatisation seems the best illustration of the structure that von Balthasar evokes.[48] Like Mary, the Mother of the Church, who physically bore the Son of God, stigmatisation highlights the specifically Christian aspect that religious experience is not only a matter of the spiritual, but is also connected with the organic and the corporeal, and as such perfecting the divine work of creation.[49]

2. The Locus of Experience

Von Balthasar leaves no doubt: for Christianity, *the* aesthetic religion, experience matters. From the outset experience is integrated in a theological framework. If we ask for the role of experience in his theological aesthetics, the question is not about what an autonomous human experience could bring to theology, but about the function of an already dogmatically determined notion of experience. This implies a position which gains its relevance in contravention to those modern theologies of experience that situate the question of experience rather in the sphere of fundamental theology. Von Balthasar's fascinating reworking of forgotten traditional material confronts twentieth century theologies of experience with aspects that have remained unthought.

a. The Body of Revelation: Experience as Transformation

Besides a few allusions to modern theology, von Balthasar's major target in his section on experience seems the 'platonising' – 'gnosticising', 'anti-incarnational' – tendency within pre-modern theological traditions.[50]

---

[47] *GL* I, 242; *H* I, 233: "Die dauernden Kontemplation des ganzen Christus verwandelt die Schauenden durch den Heiligen Geist als ganze in das Bild Christi (2 Kor 3, 18)."

[48] See *H* I, 233.261.399.409; *GL* I, 242.271.413.424.

[49] See *H* I, 238; *GL* I, 247-248.

[50] Even if von Balthasar himself is using a lot of platonic terminology. See Noel D. O'Donoghue, "Appendix: Do We Get Beyond Plato? A Critical Appreciation of the Theological Aesthetics," *The Beauty of Christ: An Introduction to the Theology of Hans Urs von Balthasar*, ed. Bede McGregor and Thomas Norris (Edinburgh: T. & T. Clark, 1994) 253-266.

This can be understood as a response to the criticism that Christianity had become a dualist denial of life. Von Balthasar's notion of experience involves a plea for a more sensible theology. In particular, his theological-aesthetic perspective aims at the traditional suspicion of any form of corporeal experience.[51]

Forty years later, after the theological reception of Nietzsche and feminism, the rediscovery of the body is taken for granted. Von Balthasar even seems to present a kind of straw target argument: while he is fighting against '(neo)platonism' and 'gnosticism', his agenda is to overcome the modern impasse within theology. At certain points he makes explicit how his critique includes modern theologies, in which he discerns the same 'anti-incarnational' tendency: "From Valentinus to Bultmann this flesh and blood has been spiritualised and demythologised."[52] The modern demythologising of all sensible biblical experience of God took the place of the gnostic de-fantasising of faith.[53] With regard to experience, this spiritualisation, which implies a turning away from the concrete form, involves a loss of objectivity. Experience becomes subjectivised, a function of the self. The neglect of the corporeal and historical event finds its roots in the

> próton pseudos, the 'primal lie', of theology and spirituality ... the naive or reflected equation (or confusion) of the human 'spirit' with the Holy Spirit, of 'abstraction' with the resurrection of the flesh, which corresponds to the tendency in Alexandrian theology to identify the Biblical 'flesh' with the Platonic 'body'.[54]

The extent to which this anti-platonic/anti-gnostic argument is applicable to the modern corpus needs further elaboration.[55] As we have seen above, von Balthasar criticises a logic of identity which, more or less subtly, risks negating the moment of otherness within experience, by confronting it with the theological notion of an objectivist aesthetic experience. The stress on the irreducibility of the form functions as a warrant for difference.

---

[51] This becomes manifest in his approach to the spiritual senses, which concludes his section on experience. See *H* I, 352-393; *GL* I, 365-425. See Stephen Fields, "Balthasar and Rahner on the Spiritual Senses," *Theological Studies* 57 (1996) 224-241.

[52] *GL* I, 314; *H* I, 302: "Von Valentin bis Bultmann wird dieses Fleisch und Blut spiritualisiert und entmythisiert."

[53] *GL* I, 316; *H* I, 304: "Ent-phantasierung", "Entmythisierung".

[54] *GL* I, 316; *H* I, 305: "Das proton pseudos der Theologie und Spiritualität ist die naïve oder reflektierte Gleichsetzung (oder Verwechslung) zwischen menschlichen 'Geist' und Heiligem Geist, zwischen 'Abstraktion' und Auferstehung des Fleisches, wie der Alexandrismus entsprechend die Neigung hatte, das biblische 'Fleisch' mit dem platonischen 'Leib' zusammenzulegen."

[55] See Mongrain, *The Systematic Thought of Hans Urs von Balthasar*.

The form in its corporality bears witness to an objectivity that cannot be subjectivised. Christian revelation does not abolish this structure of (aesthetic) experience, but on the contrary makes the Christian experience forever dependant on the form of the "historical Christ, dead and risen".[56] As von Balthasar emphasises the constitutive role of the form in the experience of the historical body of revelation, he links up the experience of faith with revelation, in a more explicit way than do most modern theologies of experience. Von Balthasar states polemically that the experience of faith is "not at all a psychological experience (in the sense of liberal or modernistic theology), but one which is a 'dogmatic' experience from the outset".[57] Von Balthasar urges us to think about the 'dogmatic' character of every experience of faith: experience is always experience in and through the dogma of Jesus Christ.

b. Inverted Experience: Revelation as God's Experience

The radicality of the decentering in the *trans*formation process comes to the fore in von Balthasar's recurrent objection against the 'psychologising' of the experience of faith.[58] This 'psychologising' subsists in the appropriation of the experience by the experiencing subject.[59] An objectivist theological aesthetics, on the contrary, consists in a fundamental expropriation (*Entselbstung*) that allows to say that "the believer can have 'objective' experiences in Christ and in the Church which need not be consciously perceived by him in a subjective and psychological sense".[60] This is not meant as a consolation for the people who are not yet experienced. Precisely the believers who have the deepest experience of faith become aware that the subject of experience is always 'incorporated' (*eingegliedert*)[61] in the subjectivity of the Son and the Church. Von Balthasar's analogy here is the lover who "in all things renounces what

---

[56] *GL* I, 231; *H* I, 223: "immer die Abhängigkeit vom historischen, gestorbenen und auferstandenen Christus".

[57] *GL* I, 231; *H* I, 222: "keine psychologische Erfahrung ist (im Sinn liberaler oder modernistischer Theologie), sondern eine von vornherein 'dogmatische'."

[58] See *H* I, 244-249.280-283.328-329.353; *GL* I, 253-259.291-294.341-343.366-367.

[59] Actually von Balthasar is transposing the theological tradition which states that the believer can never know about her or his own faith. See *H* I, 214-216; *GL* I, 222-224.

[60] *GL* I, 258; *H* I, 248: "der Glaubende 'objektive' Erfahrungen in Christus und in der Kirche machen kann, die ihm nicht subjektiv-psychologisch als bewusste fassbar zu sein brauchen".

[61] *GL* I, 258; *H* I, 248. The metaphor of incorporation often appears on these pages. See *H* I, 241.244.245.246.

is his own and desires to clear all available space [*Raum einräumen*] in himself for the beloved; the lover therefore embraces as his own the experience which is the beloved's, and, on the contrary, he no longer desires to have *within himself* what a non-lover would call 'his own experience', but to have it only *in the beloved*."[62]

Human experience of faith as imitation of Christ is always a participation in the *experientia Dei incarnati*[63] – the experience of the Incarnate God being the subject and the object of experience.[64] The ultimate argument against a psychologising of the experience of faith is that Christ Himself is the 'primary subject' of experience.[65] At this point von Balthasar introduces the notion "inverted experience".[66] In the Christian sense the notion of experience undergoes an inversion: it is no longer in the first place the question 'how does humankind experience God?', but it starts with the revelation of a God experiencing humankind:

> Christ, the full and perfect man, has in his own totality the experience of what God is. He is, with body and soul, the embodiment of this experience. And, as God-become-man who reveals God to man, Christ, even as God, has the experience of what man is.[67]

As such, experience is a crucial category of revelation. If experience is to enter into space and time, revelation is God's experience of the human world: it is the Word turned into Experience. Experience is a kenotic

---

[62] *GL* I, 258; *H* I, 248: "Der Liebende, in allem auf das Eigene verzichtend, dem Geliebten in sich jeden Raum einräumen will, daher auch die Erfahrung, die der Geliebte macht und hat, als siene eigene Erfahrung hinnimmt, hingegen das, was ein Nichtliebender seine 'eigene Erfahrung' nennt, nicht mehr in sich selbst, sondern einzig im Geliebten machen will."

[63] See *H* I, 313: "Die Identität dieser beiden Aspekte der christologischen Gotterfahrung – experientia Dei incarnati als genitivus subjectivus und deshalb nachfolgend objectivus – ist ein Geheimnis der hypostatischen Union, auf dem aber als auf ihrem letzten Offenbarungsfundament alle davon abkünftige Gotterfahrung und aller Offenbarungsglaube beruhen." (*GL* I, 324-325: "The christological experience of God thus presents two aspects: the *experientia Dei incarnati* as a subjective genitive, and therefore posteriorly as an objective genitive. And the identity of these two aspects is a mystery of the hypostatic union: on this mystery, as on the ultimate foundation of revelation, rest all experiences of God derived from it and all faith in revelation.")

[64] Cf. the article on Aquinas in this book: Laurence Paul Hemming, "The Experience of God."

[65] *GL* I, 264; *H* I, 254: "Primärsubjekt".

[66] *GL* I, 263 ('reversed' – we opt for an alternative translation); *H* I, 253: "umgekehrter Erfahrung".

[67] *GL* I, 304; *H* I, 292: "Christus, der volle and vollendete Mensch, macht als ganzer die Erfahrung dessen, was Gott ist. Er ist mit Leib und Seele die Verkörperung dieser Erfahrung. Christus als der menschgewordene Gott aber, der dem Menschen Gott offenbart, macht auch als Gott die Erfahrung dessen, was Mensch ist."

movement, God expropriating Godself out of love. This experience is formulated in the 'Theopaschitic formula' "One of the Trinity has suffered".[68]

c. Echoes of Christ: The Space of Experience

Von Balthasar's 'objectivist' account of experience highlights the bond
between experience and revelation. This certainly has a corrective potential insofar as the notion of 'experience' risks drifting away from revelation. On the other hand, von Balthasar's perspective has important and
often ambiguous consequences. The notion of inverted experience we
just developed, understood as the grounding of experience in the trinitarian life itself, illustrates this ambivalence. On the one hand, it seems
to involve the highest possible recognition of experience; on the other
hand, such a trinitarian perfection of experience risks accomplishing a
'trinitarian reduction'.[69] Experience risks being reduced to the sphere of
the Trinity. If one stresses too strongly that experience is always already
"incorporated by God himself into the image of the man Christ",[70] there
is no real experience left outside the Trinity. At the end of the chapter
on the experience of faith, as von Balthasar himself admits with regards
to the parallel chapter on the light of faith, "the reader will ask himself
the question whether we have confined ourselves to our theme or whether
we have not, rather, anticipated our later theme concerning the object of
faith in a way which raises serious questions".[71] Indeed, in a section on
the subjective structure of his theological aesthetics, the polemical emphasis on the "objective, trinitarian reality of God"[72] too easily overshadows
the role of the human subject.[73] In his introduction to the chapter on experience von Balthasar stresses the vital importance of the theme of experience for his theological aesthetics.[74] The question is the survival probability

---

[68] *GL* I, 304 n. 121; *H* I, 292. n. 1: "die sog. 'theopaschistische Formel': 'Einer aus
der Dreifaltigkeit hat gelitten'".

[69] See Georges de Schrijver's criticism of von Balthasar's *Theodramatik*: "Hans Urs
von Balthasars Christologie in der Theodramatik: Trinitarische Engführung als Methode,"
Bijdragen 59 (1998) 141-153.

[70] *GL* I, 222; *H* I, 214: "ja bereits von Gott selber im Bild des Menschen Christus in
Beschlag genommen".

[71] *GL* I, 215; *H* I, 207: "Wird den Leser sich die Frage stellen, ob wir beim Thema
geblieben, oder nicht vielmehr auf bedenkliche Weise das spätere Thema vom Glaubens-
gegenstand vorweggenommen haben."

[72] *GL* I, 229; *H* I, 220-221: "die objektive, trinitarische Wirklichkeit des Gottes".

[73] On the contrary, the centrality of the notion of experience within modern theology
precisely aimed at guaranteeing a space for human freedom.

[74] See *H* I, 211-212; *GL* I, 220.

of a concept of experience without a positively developed notion of human subjectivity.

To experience is to become the body of revelation, to change into Christ's body. Experience is realized revelation, is Christ's experience realizing itself in the believer. Against the tenacious phantasm of immediate experience, von Balthasar's theological-aesthetic view stresses the importance of the form, of the mediation. Against immediateness von Balthasar wants to open an interspace of mediation which allows for genuine experience, an "insight acquired by travelling to a place".[74a] His aesthetics seems to create this space of experience: a close reading brings to the light an omnipresence of the spatial metaphor. In this space the form may 'trans-port' us. The problem of his aesthetics of *trans*formation, however, is that it surreptitiously seems to close this interspace down, in the very combination of space and form, as this is articulated in the metaphor of tuning (-*stimmen*). When we read for example that "all our senses are engaged when the interior space of a beautiful musical composition or painting opens itself to us and captivates us: the whole person then enters into a state of vibration and becomes responsive space, the 'sounding box' of the event of beauty occurring within him",[75] we can imagine how within this kind of aesthetic framework, space and time, the very conditions of possibility of Christian experience – experience as a movement of going out, through, into – can be, as it were, short-circuited in the form of Christ. The christological concentration of the experience risks narrowing the space between experience and revelation up to an identification of both terms. Experience is then reduced to the 'sounding box' of revelation.[76] In its attempt to escape the subjectivist "equation (or confusion) of the human 'spirit' with the Holy Spirit",[77] von Balthasar's objectivism ends up in a kind of 'inverted equation'. As he writes by way of conclusion about the 'Christian attunement', in the experience of faith "an existence is envisaged which is like an instrument tuned (*gestimmte*) by the Spirit: at the breath of the Spirit, the instrument like the Aeolian harp rings out in tune".[78] The Holy Spirit instrumentalises the human spirit. In this theological attunement, the own

---

[74a] See above: p. 230 (note 16).

[75] *GL* I, 220; *H* I, 212. See quote above: p. 232 (note 28).

[76] Note that the notion of revelation undergoes a reduction as well. On von Balthasar's concept of revelation, see Peter Eicher, *Offenbarung: Prinzip neuzeitlicher Theologie* (München: Kösel, 1977) 293-343, esp. 339-343 (*Eidetische Reduktion?*).

[77] *GL* I, 316; *H* I, 305. See quote above: p. 238 (note 54).

[78] *GL* I, 251; *H* I, 241-242: "Es ist Dasein als vom Geist gestimmtes Instrument, das (als Äolsharfe) unter dem Wehen des Geistes auf die rechte Weise ertönt."

human voice (*Stimme*)[79] ends up as an 'echo'.[80]

Post Scriptum: The Corpse of Experience

I did not want to suggest that von Balthasar's expropriated self, analogous to the violin which receives in a radical passivity the touch of the divine bow,[81] stands not that far from the possessed girl becoming the 'sounding box' of the Gospel of Thomas.[82] The resemblance between both the film *Stigmata* and von Balthasar's theological aesthetics rather resides in a common lacuna in their respective presentation of experience. What is absent in both works is the notion of translation. Or, better, the moment of interpretation in it is concealed. Possessed by the spirit of a murdered translator, the girl in *Stigmata* in no way actively interprets the Gospel. As a passive medium, a girl who does not speak a word of Aramaic reproduces the exact verses of the Gospel in Jesus's own language. Writing becomes a direct, automatic process of transcription. A similar covering up of the moment of interpretative mediation is at work in von Balthasar's writings. In spite of his recurrent emphasis on the irreducible principle of mediation, the occasional articulations of these mediations are formulated in terms of transparency.[83] In this regard, it is interesting to remark how

[79] The German word *Stimme* is absent in a text which contains an overflow of words based on the root -*stimm*-. (Outside of the section on experience, the word occurs only once, with regards to the Incarnate: see *H* I, 457. This corresponds with a christological appropriation of the metaphor of attunement (*Stimmung*) in this section on 'objective evidence': see *H* I, 450-451; *GL* I, 468-469.)

[80] The metaphor of the echo explicitly returns to denote the human reaction on God's revealing initiative: see *H* I, 210.317.353; *GL* I, 218.329.366.

[81] See *H* I, 212: "den ganzen Menschen zu einem antwortenden Raum auf den göttlichen Klang einzustimmen ... ihn zur Geige für diesen Bogenstrich [zu machen]." (*GL* I, 220: "to make the whole man a space that responds to the divine content. Faith attunes man to this sound; ... preparing him to be a violin that receives just this touch of the bow.")

[82] See *GL* I, 247; *H* I, 237 (quoted above: p. 232 (note 30)). In the English version the translation of *in Besitz genommen* ('appropriated') as 'possessed' could strengthen this suggestion. However, although there is certainly a downplaying of the human subject at work, von Balthasar does not completely cancel its role. Note the nuance in the following comment on the paradigmatic believer Paul: "to be sure, it is 'he' who still lives, but he is no longer an autonomous ego since Christ has begun to live in him" (*GL* I, 254; *H* I, 245: "zwar lebt 'er' noch, aber er ist kein selbständiges Ich mehr, seit Christus in ihm lebt"). See *H* I, 222. 241 as well. On the other hand there remain many passages that are more ambiguous in this respect: see above; p. 241-243; *H* I, 398.400.)

[83] E.g. when he writes about the mediation of the Church, see *H* I, 245-246; *GL* I, 255-256. (See the paragraph 'Form and Transparency' (*Gestalt und Transparenz*), esp. *GL* I, 560-564; *H* I, 538-541.)

the process of reading is stripped from its hermeneutical toughness. On the rhetorical level, von Balthasar's multiple etymological operations, often combined with excursions on the translation of Greek or Latin words,[84] seem to function as a device to overcome the semiotic perplexity which obstructs every process of reading: etymology is used as a source of evidence, a way of making words transparent. This procedure resonates with his presentation of experience, i.e., of the 'reading of the form' (*Gestaltlesen*),[85] not as a process of interpretation, but as imitation, as *trans*formation in the sense of the imprint of the form. Significantly, von Balthasar equals the "form of revelation" (*Offenbarungsgestalt*) with a "revelation-body" (*Offenbarungsleib*).[86] To link the form (*Gestalt*) with a body, and not with a sign, suggests that the form is in the first place an object of perception, which is more directly accessible than a semiotic object which involves the endless mediations of interpretation.[87]

The presentation of a transfer of meaning as a transport of a corporeal form, recalls a medieval sense of *translatio*. *Translatio* denoted the triumphal processional transport of the corpus of a saint or candidate for sainthood, with regards to which the historian Richard C. Trexler reconstructed an intriguing story.[88] On 25 May 1230 the body of St. Francis

---

[84] The number of translations contrasts with the fact that in the whole section on the experience of faith, the concept of translation appears only once: with regards to Christ and the Father, von Balthasar compares the obedience of the Son to an "exact translation" (*genaue Übersetzung*). See *GL* I, 253; *H* I, 243.

[85] See our account of this process above p. 234-237. Strikingly, the metaphor of the 'reading of the form', which repetitively occurs in the rest of the book, disappears in the section on experience, which precisely copes with the subjective side of this process of reading. See *H* I, 198.416.462; *GL* I, 205.432.481.

[86] See *H* I, 416-417.507-511; *GL* I, 432-433.528-532. One should remember that von Balthasar's notion of form (*Gestalt*) is explicitly developed in line with an organic paradigm that he found in Goethe's (pseudo-) biological writings on the morphology of plants (*Die Metamorphose der Pflanzen*). See e.g. *H* I, 430; *GL* I, 447. On the notion of *Gestalt* see Pascal Ide, *Être et mystère: La philosophie de Hans Urs von Balthasar* (Brussels: Culture et Vérité, 1995) 177-180.

[87] In a lucid comment on von Balthasar's aesthetics, Vincent Holzer has formulated a parallel remark. Holzer claims that there is a conflict between von Balthasar's principal emphasis on mediation and the concrete way in which he develops an aesthetic framework in terms of perception. The concept of perception with its connotation of direct, sensible contact with the object excludes a truly hermeneutical perspective, which would be aware of the complex processes of mediation. See Vincent Holzer, "L'esthétique théologique comme esthétique fondamentale chez Hans Urs von Balthasar," *Recherches de science religieuse* 85 (1997) 557-588. Holzer speaks of a "strange and redoubtable fascination", a kind of "hyperempirical" tendency (p. 582).

[88] See Richard C. Trexler, "The Stigmatized Body of Francis of Assisi: Conceived, Processed, Disappeared," *Frömmigkeit im Mittelalter*, ed. Klaus Schreiner and Marc Müntz (Berlin: Fink Verlag, 2002) 463-497.

had to be transported from the church of San Giorgio to the new built basilica of Assisi. As at that time the coffin would be open, people were curious to check the stories about his stigmatised and post-mortem transfigured body – as such Francis embodied the perfect imitation of Christ. However, a scandal occurred. In an unexpected act of protectionism, religious and worldly authorities kept the sarcophagus closed. Even worse: in the tumult of that day, the body of the saint disappeared. (Some suggest that Assisi wanted to protect the monopoly on the relics, which were a crucial element in the merchandising of the new saint. Others suspect the Franciscan Elias, in that he wanted to cover up the lies his order had spread about the miraculous state of Francis's body.) Understandably, this fraud story is not mentioned in the official hagiography. Too easy a theological answer, however, would be to blame the hagiographical amnesia that covered up the *non habeas corpus* which would bear witness to the lack of a direct access to the 'body of revelation'.[89] Rather, the recalcitrance of the fantasy, as it manifests itself from the popular film industry to the work of a sophisticated theologian, points symptomatically to a not yet elucidated inevitability of the *corpus* in the notion of experience.[90] A theology of experience should reflect upon that fiction, and on the most astonishing fact that one of the major centres of Christian experience is a 'burial church', without anyone knowing where the body of the saint is actually located.[91]

[89] Just as a standard theological criticism of the film *Stigmata* would expose the didactic epilogue, which is presented as the ultimate moment of truth, as containing the primal lie of any work of art. At the end, the film claims that the Gospel of Thomas contains the authentic words of Christ – sharing with *The Celestine Prophecy* the same fantasy of the discovery of an original (Aramaic!) script that is not spoiled by mediatory instances. It is striking that the allegedly pure, non-manipulated verse, which they quote as being the truth of the Gospel, actually is a free translation that perfectly serves the contents of the film.

[90] A deeper investigation into the subtleties of the metaphor of the body within von Balthasar's text will probably bring to the fore that von Balthasar himself can deliver a deeper insight in the ambiguities at stake here. Especially the section on the 'Objective Evidence' contains many passages that need to be reread. (See *H* I, 507-511.520-521; *GL* I, 528-532. 541-543.) It could turn out that the suggestions in our postscript are precipitate.

[91] Until 1818 there was no body at all. In that year a skeleton was discovered in the basilica of Assisi. But about the authenticity of the bones there is a great deal of scepticism. See Trexler, "The Stigmatized Body," 493-494.

THE TRUTH NARRATED: RICŒUR ON RELIGIOUS EXPERIENCE

CHRISTOPHE BRABANT

POETRY

And it was at that age...
Poetry arrived in search of me
…
I did not know what to say,
my mouth had no way with names
my eyes were blind,
and something started in my soul,
fever or forgotten wings,
and I made my own way,
deciphering that fire
and I wrote the first faint line,
faint, without substance, pure
nonsense, pure wisdom
of someone who knows nothing,
and suddenly I saw
the heavens
unfastened and open,
planets, palpitating planations,
shadow perforated,
riddled with arrows, fire and flowers,
the winding night, the universe.

And I, infinitesmal being,
drunk with the great starry void,
likeness, image of mystery,
I felt myself a pure part
of the abyss,
I wheeled with the stars,
my heart broke free on the open sky.

Pablo Neruda[1]

---

[1] Translation found on http://www-personal.umich.edu/~agreene/Neruda.html (29 January 2004). Original text: Pablo Neruda, *Obras Competas. II* (Buenos Aires: Editorial Losada S.A., 1973) 1034-1035.

1. Introduction

In his own words, Pablo Neruda describes the experience of the muse seeking him out. His poetic vocation appears as a moment of being on fire and of deciphering what it means to burn in this way. What Neruda describes as the experience of poetic vocation is analogous to what Ricœur could have said of religious experience. I deliberately say 'could', in view of Ricœur's own resistance to the term 'religious experience'. In a lengthy interview he comments on the idea of religious experience as follows: "I have vigorously resisted the word 'experience' throughout my career, out of a distrust of immediacy, effusiveness, intuitionism: I always favoured, on the contrary, the mediation of language and scripture."[2] Ricœur resists use of the word 'experience' because of the immediacy that it implies and the importance of language and the symbolic order that is ignored.[3] Ricœur is deeply convinced of the impossibility of a direct access to God, to the world and to ourselves. Such an access is always mediated by symbols, signs, texts, and stories. Ricœur speaks of this mediation as a detour.

This article attempts to explore religious experience according to the thinking of Ricœur. Crucial in his thinking is this detour, in which the facility of putting into words is effected and in which experience becomes religious. In conclusion, we will suggest that 'experience' appears again in its etymological originality. With Ricœur we shall define religious experience as 'going through the text', that is, as a process of receiving meaning and of interpreting, with the interpretative self as what is at stake.

---

[2] Paul Ricœur, *Critique et conviction: Entretien avec François Azouvi et Marc de Launay* (Paris: Hachette Litératures, 2001) 211; English translation: *Critique and Conviction: Conversations with François Azouvi and Marc de Launay* (New York, NY: Columbia University Press, 1998).

[3] Here Ricœur is in agreement with Levinas: "The relation with infinity cannot, to be sure, be stated in terms of experience." Emmanuel Levinas, *Totality and Infinity: An Essay on Exteriority* (The Hague: Martinus Nijhoff Publishers, 1979) 25; see also Kevin Hart, "The Experience of God," *The Religious*, ed. John D. Caputo (Malden, MA: Blackwell, 2002) 164-165.

2. The Hermeneutic Circle as Structure

This article is divided into two parts because of the caesura we wish to indicate between the thinking of the symbol on the one hand and narrativity on the other. In the first part we discuss the meaning of the symbol. In the symbolic order and especially in language we are cut off from the immediate experience of reality. The second part will bring us closer to the consequences of the linguistic characteristic of human existence and its potential to transform reality.

a. Symbols of Culpability

Ricœur originally came to a study of religious symbols because of his desire to write a 'philosophy of the will'.[4] To the will there is no immediate access. Only through symbols, images, signs, and myths are we able to approach the will. Given his Protestant background, Ricœur's attention is attracted by the symbols of culpability.

In the second part of his second volume of his philosophy of will, entitled *The Symbolism of Evil*, Ricœur analyses three symbols of guilt.[5] What Ricœur has in mind is an experience of culpability 'as such' (*an sich*) in the Kantian sense of that which is inaccessible, unknowable, and full of ambiguity. The experience as such is 'not without' meaning.[6] The experience of evil is marked by a vagueness and a lack of clarity and interpretation.[7] The symbol limits the initial ambiguity and interprets it in a

---

[4] Paul Ricœur, *Philosophie de la volonté. 1: Le volontaire et l'involontaire* (Paris: Aubier, 1950); English translation: *Freedom and Nature: The Voluntary and the Involuntary*, Northwestern University Studies in Phenomenology and Existential Philosophy (Evanston, IL: Northwestern University Press, 1966).

[5] Paul Ricœur, *Philosophie de la volonté. 2: Finitude et culpabilité. 2: La symbolique du mal* (Paris: Aubier, 1960); English translation: *The Symbolism of Evil* (New York, NY and Evanston, IL: Harper Row, 1967) and *The Symbolism of Evil* (Boston, MA: Beacon Press, 1969). Ricœur summarizes the insights of *The Symbolism of Evil* in Paul Ricœur, "Herméneutique des symboles et réflexion philosophique," *Le conflit des interprétations: Essais d'herméneutique* (Paris: Éditions du Seuil, 1969) 283-310; English translation: "The Hermeneutics of Symbols and Philosophical Reflection: I & II," *Conflict of Interpretations: Essays in Hermeneutics* (Evanston, IL: Northwestern University Press, 1974) 287-334.

[6] Cf. Rudi Visker, *Truth and Singularity: Taking Foucault into Phenomenology*, Phaenomenologica, 155 (Dordrecht: Kluwer Academic Publishers, 1999) 17.

[7] "Ce language de l'aveu est la contrepartie du triple caractère de l'expérience qu'il porte au jour: cécité, équivocité, scandale." Ricœur, *Finitude et culpabilité*, 170.

defined way by which it gains in significance. The symbol functions as a category whose role consists in interpreting the experience.[8] The impenetrability of the experience is partly taken away at the moment it is brought into language. This happens at the moment that a fault is confessed. Confession is the opposite of the experience confessed because it brings to light what initially shuns the daylight. The gain in clarity involves a loss of immediacy.

The phenomenological rule that unconcealedness goes together with concealing holds true for language as well. Typical for thinkers of the twentieth century who stand in the 'linguistic turn' is that significance is only possible through the symbolic order that includes language. Entry into the linguistic order implies a loss of immediacy. Ricœur gives three examples of experiences of the phenomenon of guilt in which the consciousness of culpability is mediated by language.

The first paradigm that Ricœur describes as the experience of culpability is the stain (*la souillure*). It is the most archaic experience of culpability, in which culpability is understood *as* something material.[9] The stain is fatal because it happens to man. The stain sticks to the person like dirt does. Nevertheless, the stain is from the outset symbolic. With the 'as' the continuity with immediacy is broken and the way to a symbolic dimension lies open. The materiality is the first and literal significance of the stain that is overcome in the symbol towards a second symbolic meaning. However the literal meaning is never entirely exceeded.

Sin (*le péché*) is the second paradigm in which the experience of guilt is primarily a religious one. Whereas the stain is characterised by an experience of exteriority – the subject is in the power of external forces – sin is characterized by the fact that the subject experiences evil as a rupture in the relationship with God.[10]

The 'feeling of guilt' (*la culpabilité*) is the third paradigm of the experience of culpability.[11] The feeling of guilt is in the first instance the experience of unworthiness towards oneself. The subject has become the standard of morality. Therefore, guilt is no longer experienced in relation to another, but turns into an alienation from the self. Failure in one's duty towards oneself is the characteristic of the last symbol of evil.

---

[8] Cf. Ricœur, *Finitude et culpabilité*, 172.
[9] Cf. Ricœur, *Finitude et culpabilité*, 188.
[10] Cf. Ricœur, *Finitude et culpabilité*, 208.
[11] Ricœur, *Finitude et culpabilité*, 255.

b. The Symbol: a Definition

Symbols are signs, and signs presuppose a rupture with the immediacy to which they refer. Not all signs are symbols in the way Ricœur understands them. A sign becomes a symbol when there is a double rupture – besides the rupture with immediacy, in addition the symbol requires a rupture with the first intention of the sign. By living the first meaning we are carried to the second and latent dimension.[12] The first and literal dimension of the symbol cannot be loosed from the second and symbolic dimension. Because the first intention always already refers to a second, Ricœur labels the symbol as 'giving'.[13] Because of the relatedness of the first and second intention in the symbol, it can never be completely arbitrary.[14] In other words, symbols have roots because they take into account the pre-linguistic dimension of reality.[15]

The mediation by the symbol that structures the experience of culpability is significant for the three regimes we have traced: stain, sin and culpability. The structure of referring by a first literal significance towards a second is characteristic of the three paradigms, but is most evident in the paradigm of the stain. The impurity of the stain is symbolic because it is something *like* a stain.[16] The reference that is present in the 'like' can never adequately be determined, because the symbol is opaque. This opaqueness is the depth of the symbol. The opaque reference of the symbol is the reason why it is impossible to grasp and formulate the full meaning of it.[17] The symbol that always carries on 'referring' can never be exhaustively translated into language.

c. The Hermeneutic Circle

Within the symbol there is an offer of sense or meaning.[18] In the present context where philosophers of suspicion like Nietzsche, Marx, and Freud exert their influence it has become impossible to accept this "giving of meaning" (*donation de sens*) in an uncritical way.[19] In the postmodern

---

[12] Cf. Ricœur, *Finitude et culpabilité*, 178.

[13] Cf. Ricœur, *Finitude et culpabilité*, 178-179.

[14] Paul Ricœur, *Le conflit des interprétations,* 314.

[15] Paul Ricœur, *Interpretation Theory: Discourse and the Surplus of Meaning* (Fort Worth, TA: The Texas Christian University Press, 1976) 69.

[16] Cf. Ricœur, *Finitude et culpabilité*, 178.

[17] Cf. Ricœur, *Finitude et culpabilité*, 178.

[18] Cf. Ricœur, *Finitude et culpabilité*, 182.

[19] Ricœur, *Critique et conviction*, 221.

context we would add to this first group thinkers like Derrida and Rorty. Their critical attitude is an external viewpoint distinct from the involved point of view from within the perspective of meaning. Ricœur's aim is to integrate an external critical viewpoint into his theory of symbols as an answer to his critics and in order to assert the rediscovery of a sense of meaning in the symbol. Consequently, the acceptance of meaning offered in the symbol has to be accompanied by a critical thinking that not only integrates an external critical viewpoint, but also a consciousness of plurality.

This intuition is the ground for the religious epistemology that Ricœur expresses in the formulation of the hermeneutic circle: "We must understand in order to believe, but we must believe in order to understand."[20] On the one hand thinking requires a commitment. On the other, we need a critical distance from the position. Critique and conviction form the structure of religious truth in Ricœur's thinking of the symbol.

In this context, Ricœur discusses three distinct aspects of the symbol. The first consists in the offer of meaning that is in the symbol. To disclose meaning, the symbol must be situated in its context. Symbols do not function as standalones. They function against the background of myth. Myth is a further explication of the symbol and can be seen as a "developed symbol".[21] The symbol presupposes a form of life in which it is embedded.

The second aspect consists in the acceptance of the offer of meaning. In this assumption, thinking is given to itself because it is challenged to involve itself in a wager (*le pari*).[22] The thinking that accepts the advancement of sense that is offered in the symbol engages itself in the way that it can advance towards the truths of the symbol.[23] This engagement installs the hermeneutic circle. The thinking that refuses to risk itself in the proposition of sense will not be able to disclose the truth of the symbol. The truth of faith that is unveiled by reason will suppose a conviction or an engagement. On the other hand, a critical distance has to be left open.

Critical distance is the third aspect to which the symbol invites us. This is the proper philosophical moment in which reason will essentially be "demythologising".[24] For instance, to be a symbol of the Saint, the symbol

---

[20] "Il faut comprendre pour croire, mais il faut croire pour comprendre." Ricœur, *Finitude et culpabilité*, 482; also Ricœur, *Le conflit des interprétations*, 294.

[21] Cf. Ricœur, *Finitude et culpabilité*, 181.

[22] Ricœur, *Finitude et culpabilité*, 481.

[23] Cf. Ricœur, *Le conflit des interprétations*, 293-294.

[24] "La pensée comme *réflexion* est essentiellement 'démythologisante'." Ricœur, *Le conflit des interprétations*, 296. Ricœur's italics.

has continuously to invite a demythologising attitude for it is only able to respect transcendence when it continues referring and refuses to omit the distance between finite and the Infinite. This deconstructive moment is the necessary reverse side of every hermeneutics of retrieval that is directed towards rediscovering meaning in the symbol.[25]

An ordinary hermeneutics will not suffice to indicate a renewed sense of the symbol. A primordial naiveté, or immediacy, as an uncritical dealing with the symbol, is out of the question. A 'second naiveté' will only be possible when the hermeneutic is accompanied by a critical viewpoint, without losing sight of the conviction. The thinking that accepts this wager engages itself by setting out on its reflexive work from a particular perspective of sense.

d. Symbol and Particularity

With his study on the symbolism of evil, Ricœur presumed he had worked out a general theory of symbols. His claim to universality need not surprise us if we take into account that he stands in a philosophical tradition that links him with an idealism that considers autonomy and purity to be of paramount importance. We see that his thinking on symbols is also rooted in his familiarity with Protestant thinking.[26]

This makes his thoughts significant theologically even though Ricœur explicitly stresses that he is doing philosophy and has no intention of exceeding the limits of philosophy. He halts at the gates of theology. However, it could well be argued that his thinking is less theologically neutral than at first sight it seems.

For the theologian in search of philosophical foundations, Ricœur is an appropriate companion. The seeds for his philosophical thought at least originate in part from theological soil. The conviction that the words of human beings are preceded by a Word that makes sense, his choice of Christian symbolism, and his concept of the subject, all indicate the particular theological rootedness of Ricœur's thinking.[27] This sheds light on the particularity of Ricœur's thinking, thinking that is embedded in the

[25] Cf. Ricœur, *Le conflit des interprétations*, 329.

[26] Cf. Paul Ricœur, *Réflection faite: Autobiographie intellectuelle* (Paris: Éditions Esprit, 1995) 14; English translation: *Intellectual Autobiography: The Philosophy of Paul Ricœur*, ed. Lewis Edwin Hahn, The Library of Living Philosophers, 22 (Chicago, IL: Open Court, 1995).

[27] Cf. Ricœur, *Réflection faite*, 14.

Western tradition and that commences with a Christian view of guilt and sin. As result of this, his theory of the symbol is less universal than it appears. This need not detract from the meaningfulness of his project, rather it places in perspective the universal legitimacy of his claims by indicating how his thinking is particular, since his fundamental convictions rely on a core of Christian belief. A religious epistemology in which sense emerges from commitment and critical distance should be considered as the result of an encounter between thinking rooted in Greek philosophy and the Judaeo-Christian tradition. Consequently, it need not astonish us that his thinking relates easily to theology.

e. Symbol of the Sacred

As already mentioned, one of Ricœur's most profoundly held convictions is that the words of human beings are preceded by the Word of God. It is a fundamental presupposition that cannot be proved, and is one of the axioms of his thought. That the symbol mediates the sacred is an axiom to which we can only assent, so that we can say that God is symbolically represented. This shows not only the particularity of Ricœur's thinking, but also the particularity of the symbol. What is described is not the symbol in general, but the symbol as part of Christian tradition. Dealing with the symbol according to the thinking of Ricœur cannot bring one to a general religious experience. Just as we only can deal with language in a concrete way by investigating a particular tongue, so too can we can only describe religious experience in general from the perspective of a particular religion.[28]

Typical of the Judaeo-Christian tradition is its emphasis on the transcendence of God as wholly other. Nevertheless, God discarded this radical otherness to reveal God to humans.[29] The revealed Word of God is accessible through the Scriptures that are the reflections of human experience articulated in witness, stories, parables etc.[30] In this we discover again the principle of the hermeneutic circle. The presence of the Word

---

[28] Cf. Paul Ricœur, *Lectures 3: Aux frontières de la philosophie* (Paris: Éditions du Seuil, 1994) 266.

[29] Cf. Paul Ricœur, *De l'interprétation: Essai sur Freud* (Paris: Éditions du Seuil, 1965) 504; English translation: *Freud and Philosophy: An Essay on Interpretation* (New Haven, CT: Yale University Press, 1970).

[30] Cf. Ricœur, *Essai sur Freud*, 505; Paul Ricœur, "Expérience et langage dans le discours religieux," *Phénoménologie et théologie*, ed. Jean-François Courtine (Paris: Critérion, 1992) 21-22.

of God in Scripture is the axiom upon which the community who receives the Word is based. Inversely, the Word only reveals itself by way of a community of faith who read and interpret Scripture. That this hermeneutic circle is not a vicious one will become obvious when we speak about the transforming ability of texts.

f. Towards a Second Naiveté or a Second Immediacy

The conclusion of Ricœur's study of symbols leads to a restorative hermeneutics that is able to reveal anew the meaning of the Christian symbol in faith. Because of the critique of the philosophers of suspicion, the symbol lost its first naiveté. By means of integrating their demythologising critique, Ricœur starts to develop the basis for an epistemology of religious experience.

For Ricœur, the symbol can only remain a sign of God's transcendence when it reinforces its referring ability. Because of the impossibility for the symbol to grasp God in an adequate way, it should always refer by indicating its own failure to do justice to God's transcendence. The restoration of the meaning of the symbol will only be possible by examining the offer of sense and preserving a critical distance. The mediation of God takes place when the symbol in its signification is interpreted in a critical way. Consequently, this excludes an uncritical first naiveté and the idea of an unmediated experience and it brings us to a religious experience as a being on the way to a second naiveté. This 'second immediacy' includes a critical consciousness that operates in a demythologising way.

The detour of the symbol in bringing experience to language has brought with it clarity. Phenomenological unveiling implies that clarity is accompanied by concealment. In the case of the symbol, what is inaccessible is experience as such.[31] Because of the continuous interaction of demythologising critical distance with the restoration of meaning, this immediacy will never be definitively achieved. Consequently, the grammar of faith will always signify 'being on the way' to this second immediacy.

3. The Hermeneutical Structure as Dynamic

With an analysis of the symbol that brings experience to language, the hermeneutic circle is brought to light. In his earlier work Ricœur describes

[31] Ricœur, Le conflit des interprétations, 294.

this circle rather as a structure in which experience is mediated by language. Later he says that the hermeneutic circle remains a central concept, but he emphasises more strongly the importance of dialectic with respect to the symbol. The interaction of experience and its formulation are emphasised more in the sense that the interaction of both is considered more fully. This shift in attention signifies a switch in Ricœur's thinking whereby the importance of the transforming force of language and experience becomes more apparent.

a. The Force of Metaphor: Seeing as, Being as

For Ricœur the study of metaphor represents an important moment in the exploration of the transforming force of language. He is inspired by Aristotle's definition of metaphor as "the transfer of a word to a being that in the first instance defined another thing".[32] For Aristotle, metaphor belongs to rhetoric, in which its most significant characteristic is to "set the scene before our eyes".[33] Metaphor possesses a disclosing force to bring reality to light. But metaphor also belongs to poetics, in which its most important characteristic is to organise. It is closely connected to *muthos,* often translated as story or fable.[34] Significant for *muthos* is its capacity to organise and structure.[35] Disclosing and structuring are the most important characteristics of metaphor.

The transfer of meaning that is operated by metaphor is a kind of 'seeing as'. Conceiving a camel as 'the ship of the desert' transfers the sense of ship to camel. In this 'metaphorical view' attention is directed toward the resemblance in spite of the difference. And yet, the difference is not ignored because the metaphor utters 'is not' in a literal way and 'is as' only figuratively.[36] The metaphorical transfer of the meaning of one word to another is more than just a simple shift. The metaphorical view is at the same time also a redescription of reality. 'Seeing as' is not limited to an uncomplicated 'perceiving as', but tugs at the ontological strings of our

---

[32] Cf. Paul Ricœur, *La métaphore vive* (Paris: Éditions du Seuil, 1975) 19; English translation: *The Rule of Metaphor: Multi-Disciplinary Studies of the Creation of Meaning in Language* (Toronto: University of Toronto Press, 1977 - London: Routledge and Kegan Paul, 1978).

[33] Cf. Ricœur, *La métaphore vive,* 49.

[34] Cf. Ricœur, *La métaphore vive,* 52.

[35] Cf. Ricœur, *La métaphore vive,* 56.

[36] Cf. Paul Ricœur, *L'herméneutique biblique* (Paris: Éditions du Cerf, 2001) 201.

existence. The truth of metaphor is that the 'seeing as' becomes 'being as'. The capacity of metaphor turns out to be the redescription of reality.

Ricœur gives as an example the way in which parables in the Scripture have the capacity to redescribe reality through use of metaphor.[37] We can think of how the parable of the Good Samaritan reconfigures a fellow human being into a neighbour in need of help and, at the same time, situates us as those who receive the appeal the Samaritan represents. This capacity to reinterpret reality is also epistemologically relevant. The interaction of metaphor and reality results in a redescription that results in new insights.[38]

With this the *Rule of Metaphor* represents a part of the 'linguistic turn' in philosophy that can be said to have occurred in the twentieth century. The linguistic turn is the realisation in philosophical thinking of the impact of language on numerous domains. In Ricœur's thought it is the paradigm of metaphor which illustrates that language is more than just the mirror of a pre-linguistic reality. In organising and structuring, language creates reality. Obviously, language has to take into account the stubborn character of pre-linguistic reality in this creative figuration. However, the characteristic of language is that it founds reality.

b. Towards a Hermeneutical Ontology

With the *Rule of Metaphor* we become conscious of the metaphorisation of being.[39] The 'seeing as' of metaphor is the basis for the 'being as' which implies that language brings about reality. This is the impulse to reformulate ontology into a hermeneutical ontology. This hermeneutic presupposes the conclusions of Heidegger's *Being and Time*, namely the interwovenness of being and time.[40] It is to Heidegger's credit that he disclosed how being is situated in the horizon of time and what its consequences are. One of these consequences is that the essence of our being is not pre-given, but that being is in search of significance, a task needing completion, an answer to be given.

---

[37] Cf. Ricœur, *L'herméneutique biblique*, 145-277.

[38] Cf. Ricœur, *L'herméneutique biblique*, 198.

[39] Cf. Paul Ricœur, *Temps et récit*, t. I (Paris: Éditions du Seuil, 1983) 121; English translation: *Time and Narrative*, vol. I (Chicago, IL: The University of Chicago Press, 1984).

[40] Martin Heidegger, *Sein und Zeit* (Tübingen: Max Niemeyer Verlag, [1927] 1993).

Furthermore a hermeneutical ontology takes into account the importance of symbolic systems and the mediation of language that are an attempt to shape reality. The symbolic order is not neutral towards being but in fact creates reality. This ontology not only discounts historical consciousness, but also the linguistic turn.[41]

An ontology that emerges from this insight cannot be disconnected from interpretation.[42] Being is situated in the hermeneutic circle. Consequently our being is always an interpretative existence. Furthermore, the approach of being is interpretative, which means that being is always interpreted being. Interpretation includes ambiguity, which implies that every ontology should be open to reinterpretation and to a plurality of interpretations. The title of Ricœur's book, *The Conflict of Interpretations*, is an indication of the inevitable ruptures that can occur among these interpretations.

Analogous to his concept of the subject as the 'shattered Cogito' (a subject that is not, and cannot be, immediately accessible to itself) we speak of a 'shattered ontology' by which we mean that there is no immediate transparency of being.[43] All access to being is mediated by interpretation, which results in the conclusion that we can never utter the final word on it. It is for this reason that Ricœur remarks that a hermeneutic philosophy that is explicating its ontology and is conscious of its linguistic character is on the way to the Promised Land like Moses was with the Jews.[44] Moses could only see it from a distance, but never reach it. In a similar way, we never reach a final, all-embracing ontology.

c. Mimêsis *and* muthos

The innovative character of metaphor to transform reality is essentially situated on the semantic level of words and sentences. After reflecting on the rule of metaphor Ricœur dedicated a study to the innovative power of narrative (*récit*).[45] Narrative has the capacity to transform reality as well, but does so on a broader level than metaphor. In its capacity as synthesising, narrativity structures and reorganises reality. Expressions like the 'line of history', the 'sense of life', and others presuppose a paradigm

---

[41] Cf. Ricœur, *La métaphore vive*, 291.
[42] Cf. Ricœur, *Le conflit des interprétations*, 26.
[43] Cf. Ricœur, *Le conflit des interprétations*, 23.
[44] Cf. Ricœur, *Le conflit des interprétations*, 28.
[45] Cf. Ricœur, *Temps et récit*, 1:11.

or a horizon in which being is disclosed in an intelligible way. Narrative
has an important role to play in the organisation of the vision of time and
history.

The fundamental hypothesis of his three-volume work *Time and Narrative*, in which Ricœur develops his insights on the paradigm of narrative, is the rootedness of our existence in time and narrative. Reality
seems to be formed out of both.[46] Reality takes shape when time is
brought to language and narrative. With this operation a perspective is
given to reality in terms of a plot (*mise en intrigue*).[47] Consequently life
is imprinted with a coherence that makes significance and sense possible, and not without risk of the loss of meaning. The term Ricœur uses
for this shaping activity is *mimesis*, a concept borrowed from Aristotle.[48]
In general it indicates the linguistic shaping act in which an event is represented. Conceiving mimesis as 'imitation' or as 'representation', as
though it occurred in the past, is however too weak. It gives insufficient
expression to the creative capacity of mimesis. For Ricœur mimesis is
linked to muthos, that is, it signifies the articulated and structured representation of facts and events. The outcome of this creative activity is
on the one hand distinct from the unarticulated and pre-linguistic experience: the pre-linguistic level remains inaccessible as long as it is not
brought into language. On the other hand, mimesis as coherence is
distinct from the reflection upon it. That is eventually the task of the
sciences.

The structuring of reality by mimesis forms an in-between level on
which experiences and events are lived in a coherent way. Together with
this coherence, there emerges something of a 'line' in time and history.
There is a beginning, a middle and an end.[49] This distinction brings a
perspective into the whole. In other words, the human person who nar-
rates his story, organizes and structures his world, from whence perspective emerges. It is from this background that man derives meaning
and sense for his daily actions.

---

[46] Cf. Ricœur, *Temps et récit* 1:13.

[47] Cf. Paul Ricœur, *Du texte à l'action: Essais d'herméneutique*, vol. II (Paris, Éditions
du Seuil, 1986) 12; English translation: *From Text to Action: Essays in Hermeneutics*,
vol. II (London: The Athlone Press, 1991).

[48] Cf. Ricœur, *Temps et récit*, 1:57-58.

[49] Cf. Ricœur, *Du texte à l'action*, 13.

d. Time and Narrative

Ricœur says: "Time becomes human time to the extent that it is organized after the manner of a narrative."[50] The narration of stories, histories, and so on, is essential in human existence. Experience needs to be formulated and articulated in order for it to come to itself.[51] This hypothesis indicates that there is a strong connection between time, narrative, and experience. Ricœur distances himself from the ideal of immediacy that is situated outside language. The detour of articulation and narrativity is not an alternative to a possible immediate access to experience, time and life. The structuring mimesis is not limited to a part of human existence, but regards the whole of our life.

In *Time and Narrative*, Ricœur provides a general theory of the coherence of being and time on the one hand, and narrativity on the other. However this disclosed structure is only one key with which reality can be interpreted. It is this category that Ricœur uses. Thus Ricœur gives us his general theory of mimesis as if it were a universal perspective. However his conclusions are the outcome of a long reflection that is itself part and parcel of a particular history of thinking. Consequently, his own viewpoint is also a particular vantage point for seeing this. Furthermore, the position from which he judges and that he has attained after a long series of reflections can be determined as 'hermeneutic access to universality', which means that the access to it is a hermeneutical one.

Phenomenology not only teaches us that unveiling is always coupled with veiling, but also what is disclosed is always accessed from a specific point of view. The anamorphotic object is a good illustration of this. It is only from a very specific position that the distorted figure appears as a recognisable form. Similarly, every consideration is linked to the position in which it occurs. This particularisation places Ricœur's claim to be announcing a general theory in perspective.

Ricœur's considerations concerning mediated experience and the critical remarks we have added can be applied to the prospect of religious experience. Life too becomes Christian to the extent that it is brought into language in a Christian way by a form of mimesis. Elements of the Christian tradition such as symbols, the gospel, etc. assist in understanding experience in a Christian way. In late modernity or postmodernity

[50] "Le temps devient temps humain dans la mesure où il est articulé de manière narrative." Ricœur, *Temps et récit,* 1:17.

[51] Cf. Ricœur, *Du texte à l'action,* 56.

this understanding is not possible unless from a critical perspective. By this critical distance we are cut off from a first naiveté and forced to search for the meaning of the symbols that are beyond the first naiveté. This results in a faith that is on the way to a second naiveté. In a late-modern or postmodern context this critical consciousness cannot be eliminated from the whole of the detour. Therefore the tension between a perspective from within and a perspective from without must always co-exist.

The reader will perceive that religious experience understood as detour, which we are trying to develop by means of the concept mimesis, is not monolithic. Several aspects play a role in its elaboration. It is our intention now to systematize the various aspects that Ricœur has distinguished.

e. Prefiguration, Configuration and Refiguration

In psychoanalysis, it is common to think of a trauma as an event with at least two distinct moments.[52] Freud, and with him many others, identified the first moment of shock with something strange and inconceivable that troubles the subject. In a second moment signification attaches itself retroactively to the shock of the first moment and traumatises the subject. Consequently, the trauma is an event extended in time and is constituted of two moments, which are superimposed. The parallel with religious experience is that the 'ontological material' of our experiences is time, and it is extended through a time consisting in several moments.

According to Ricœur, experience is the temporal aspect of our life that is organised like a narrative. To analyse this process of temporalisation becoming narrative he uses the concept of mimesis. To understand how reality takes shape when time is expressed in narrative he distinguishes between "three moments" of mimesis: prefiguration, configuration, and refiguration.[53] Strictly speaking, Ricœur only applies mimesis to analyse how it is that time becomes human time. Precisely because religious experience too is extended through time, we are justified in seeking to understand it through mimesis. His distinction will help us to understand religious experience as a dynamic through which life becomes religious as it is organised in the manner of a narrative. As in our earlier analysis in the description of the symbol, the formulation is a necessary element in

---

[52] Cf. Rudolf Bernet, "The Traumatized Subject," *Research in Phenomenology*, vol. XXX, 2000, 160-179, esp. 162-163.

[53] Ricœur, *Temps et récit*, 1:86.

gaining access to the meaning of experience. It is Ricœur's profound conviction that bringing experience "into language is not to change it into something else, but, in articulating and developing it, to make it become itself".[54] Consequently with Ricœur we consider religious experience to be a process of the formulation and structuring of life in a narrative way so that it refers to transcendence. The concept of mimesis will help us to understand the distinguished moments of this dynamic in which life becomes mediated symbolically.

The first moment of mimesis is prefiguration (hereafter: mimesis$_1$). The coherence that emerges from mimesis is not a creation *ex nihilo*. There is a prefiguration of reality that precedes all interpretation. This pre-comprehension of reality is the horizon in which established experience is present. Before our experience leaves traces in this world, we meet the traces of the experience of others before us; and before we speak, there is already something spoken.

Acts, experiences, narratives, etc. are not independent objects but are always situated in the context of a history that precedes them. Consequently, before we start writing our own history, we are already in history. This mimesis$_1$ is the pre-comprehension of the realm of sense and historicity. Prefiguration together with refiguration constitute the two sides (*l'amont et l'aval*) of the configuration of our experience.[55]

In general, mimesis$_1$ means that all acts will refer to structural elements that precede them, like motives, interaction, suppositions, etc. The same is true for the formulation of experience. In bringing experience to language, models, codes and styles will be used as mediation. Without the first mimesis as a pre-comprehension, experience as well as its formulation would not be possible. For Christian experience this is especially recognisable because this presupposes each time a specific tradition to which reference is either implicitly or explicitly being made.

Mimesis$_2$, therefore, is a transforming activity in its proper sense, also described as configuration.[56] Ricœur, in speaking of mimesis$_2$ as the realm of the 'as if', explicitly refers to his work on the rule of metaphor. The capacity of metaphor to transform reality by means of 'seeing as' returns to the level of narrativity. The process of configuration is the proper moment of creating a plot (*mise en intrigue*) in which an experience, an event, or a story is given shape. Telling a story, writing a history, etc. –

---

[54] Cf. Ricœur, *Du texte à l'action*, 56; see also: Ricœur, *Interpretation Theory*, 20-21.
[55] Ricœur, *Temps et récit*, 1:86.
[56] Cf. Ricœur, *Temps et récit,* 1:101-109.

in other words, the completion of this mimesis – is making an end of (literally, finishing) something. By refiguring time in a creative manner, we also bring it to a unity, which means that it receives contours and becomes 'closed' in a certain way. This closing moment constitutes identity and realises the plot.

For the sake of convenience, the result of configuration is 'text'. This text is not limited to descriptions of reality alone, but includes different kinds of formulations of our being-in-the-world. The text expresses the plot (*mise-en-intrigue*) of our understanding of time. This renewed understanding of being appears in different sorts 'texts'. Strictly speaking, this should not be limited to texts in a literal sense. Ricœur, for his part, only analyses literary products – but in the same way art could also be construed as an expression of the formulation of an understanding of time and being.

With the configuration of mimesis$_2$ we situate ourselves between prefiguration (mimesis$_1$) and refiguration (or mimesis$_3$). It is in the tension between prefiguration and our own experience that a new configuration can arise. This is formulated in a 'text' in which time, experience, event, etc. are brought together into a coherent whole. We are not destined endlessly to repeat a prefigured pre-comprehension that comes to us in the context we live in. In this renewed understanding, a critical consciousness can be introduced, in the way that we suggested and described earlier. The tension between conviction and critique forms the basis for a 'second naiveté', in which we surpass the literal meaning of the expressions of faith in search of their deeper sense.

Besides a prefiguration that influences the reformulation of the understanding of time (configuration) there is also a 'downstream'. This is the third mimesis that is situated in the intersection of the world of the text and the receiver.[57] The third type of mimesis (mimesis$_3$ or refiguration) can be considered as the completion of the configuration that shapes reality because the vision that is formulated in mimesis$_2$ will now be translated into action. Consequently, our acting will transform the world in view of configuration. Finally, it is praxis that gives rise to a new being-in-the-world and becomes once again a pre-comprehension of the world.

Thus, the event of mimesis is also characterised by the hermeneutic circle. Action always presupposes a meaningful world that constitutes the background to our acting and speaking. In this world experience prefigures and is set down in the pre-comprehension. New experience will break

---

[57] Cf. Ricœur, *Temps et récit*, 1:109-129.

open this understanding and aims for a new configuration. By means of text, the innovated understanding penetrates the world of action. Consequently, mimesis is not a vicious circle, but a hermeneutic circle that leaves space for newness and alterity. The first prefiguration does not equate with the following because of the transformation that took place. Ultimately, the newness – as result of the configuration (*mise en intrigue*) that reshapes reality – also affects the ontological depths of our existence.

f. The Referent of the Text

This renewed understanding through mimesis$_2$ which we have just described emerges in a 'text'. I have already explained that a text 'refers' to something – a manner we must now investigate in greater detail. In this section we will examine the referent of the text as it is important for the concept of religious experience. We will also indicate the specificity of the referent and so open up its place in a hermeneutic of Christian texts.

Nowadays we consider Dilthey as one of the influential thinkers in the development of hermeneutics. According to Dilthey a text is the expression of a lived experience or the meaning of the author.[58] The task of hermeneutics consisted in getting 'behind' the text to reveal this 'implied author' and to gain access to the meaning or experience of its author. Ricœur, in commenting on the development of hermeneutics, suggests another possibility. Instead of looking for an implied author 'behind' the text, we should interpret and make explicit the implied being-in-the-world that appears in the encounter with the text.[59] Just as words have a referent, so too can texts. This referent consists in a being-in-the-world and is a relation, commitment, or involvement, rather than an object. The revealing of the 'referentiality' to another possible being-in-the-world has the capacity of a transformation of the world because of the confrontation of the lived and the possible being-in-the-world.[60] Ricœur employs Gadamer's terminology of the 'matter of the text' to refer to the referent of the text.[61]

The referent is not an objective or autonomous item present in the text. The unfolding of the referent has to be distinguished in the different

---

[58] Cf. Ricœur, *Du texte à l'action*, 144; see also: Paul Ricœur, *Temps et récit. Tome 3: Le temps raconté* (Paris: Éditions du Seuil, 1985) 228-263; English translation: *Time and Narrative*, vol. 3 (Chicago, IL: The University of Chicago Press, 1988).

[59] Cf. Ricœur, *Du texte à l'action*, 114.

[60] Ricœur, *L'herméneutique biblique*, 143.

[61] Cf. Ricœur, *Du texte à l'action*, 99.

'moments'.[62] These are not three separate moments in the developing of the process, but rather three aspects that are inseparable, yet distinct at the same time. First is that of the encounter of the world of the text and the world of the reader/receiver. The referent is unfolded in the encounter of the (fictive) world that is in the text and of the (actual) world of the reader.[63] This supposes not only the text and the receiver, but also the act of receiving the text. Because of this our being-in-the-world can be called a being-before-the-text.

A second aspect in the developing of the referent is the 'following' of a story. The event of following stimulates the creative and productive capacity of the imagination that is part of the configuration. Imagination is an essential moment in the transformation of the world. Consequently, not all literature will be suitable to stimulate this transformation. For Ricœur the royal path to redescription of the world is fiction, because it activates the 'seeing as'.[64] By this metaphorical seeing, reality appears in the light of a new configuration: actual being-in-the-world contrasts with the being-in-the-world that is unfolded in the encounter with the text. In the difference between similarity ('as …') and contrast ('is not as …') there originates something like a basis – Ricœur speaks of a vector – upon which the redescription of reality is based. The 'following' of the fiction is the discovery of a direction along which the referent of the text is to be sought out.

The third aspect is the referent of the text itself. In the encounter of reader/receiver and text there is 'communication'.[65] According to the reading of the text and what the reader himself brings to the text, he receives a proposition of a world, a 'pro-ject' that opens new perspectives.

g. The Referent of the Bible

The idea of a referent of the world of the text as discussed in the previous paragraph will allow us to understand why being Christian is inseparably connected to narrativity and the reading of particular texts.

The referent of Scripture is at least twofold, inasmuch as it refers both to human experience and to God. The possible being-in-the-world that is

---

[62] Cf. Ricœur, *L'herméneutique biblique*, 140-144.
[63] Cf. Ricœur, *Temps et récit*, 3:231.
[64] Cf. Ricœur, *Du texte à l'action*, 115.
[65] Cf. Ricœur, *L'herméneutique biblique*, 143.

unfolded in the encounter of text and reader refers in the first instance to human experience.[66] Further, this being-in-the-world should be understood from the relatedness of the signifier 'God' which receives its contours and interpretation from the Scriptures. The reference to God occurs by means of a mediation which refers first of all to an immanent transcendence in the form of a Christian being-in-the-world. This in turn refers to God's transcendence because it is structured and organised around the signifier 'God'.

God, who holds together the heterogeneity of all Bible texts, is not only the common reference. God is the direction in which reference is made, but also what remains transcendent to all. In order to be a mediation of God, each symbol, sign, narrative should refer intrinsically to the transcendent character of God. 'Referring' in this context means witnessing to God's ineffable transcendence.

The specificity of Christianity is situated in the direction that is unfolded by which the Transcendent Other has to be sought. Understanding what is meant by the signifier 'God' means following the direction to which the word points and is revealed in the encounter of text and reader as described earlier.[67] In Christianity these are the Scriptures and the faithful community that is assembled around the Word. Scripture and community stand in this hermeneutic circle.[68] Scripture reveals because the community receives the Word and reads it. At the same time the community is founded on the Word of God. This shows how closely connected Christianity is to its narrative tradition. It is the referent of the text itself (i.e. God) who relates the narrativity and the kerygmatic dimension in such a way that they cannot be separated. The Christian God reveals who God is by 'following' the Scriptures in the direction of their referent, a referent unfolded in the encounter with the community of faith with its experience and understanding of time and of the Word that is addressed to it. From this we may conclude that the narrativity of Scripture is an essential stepping stone on the way to faith.

---

[66] Cf. Ricœur, *L'herméneutique biblique*, 211.
[67] Cf. Ricœur, *Du texte à l'action*, 129.
[68] Cf. Ricœur, "Expérience et langage dans le discours religieux," 21-22.

4. Religious Experience

a. Religious Experience as Experience of Limit

The commitment which religious language invites us to make is characterised by an all-encompassing engagement. On the one hand religious
language challenges us to engage ourselves in the totality of our person:
"You shall love the Lord our God with all your heart, and with all your
soul, and with all your mind" (Mt 22:37). On the other hand, religious
language is concerned with life in its totality. Because this totality can
never be realised, the experience attains the characteristic of referentiality. We are always *on the way* to a complete transformation of our existence from a Christian perspective.

In the first instance, the referent of religious language is human experience. However, since religious experience is a strongly qualified language, it does not refer to human experience alone. In this, Ricœur pays
tribute to Ramsey when he reflects on the revealing capacity of a quali-
fying word (*qualificateur/qualifier*).[69] The defining term makes religious
speech special, because there is a descendent movement towards experience. Myths, stories, parables, etc. interpret and shape our experience.
Through this, the experience refers to what transcends man and inversely,
it emphasizes human finitude.[70] Hence the 'experience of limit' emerges.
Limit in religious experience is related to whatever is never adequately
given in experience. Ricœur speaks of this 'always beyond' as the most
specific feature in the aim of religious language.[71] Consequently, religious experience will always have the characteristic of 'non-experience'.
God will never be accessible in God's omnipresence. At best, God can
be rendered present in the 'here and now' by the symbolic order, by
which, at the same time, God can remain transcendent.

In this way, the symbolic system of Christianity structures our existence
by a semantic modelling of experience. The volitional and involuntariness
in this are part of human experience. The involuntariness lies in the fundamental conviction that our speaking is preceded by a Word that comes
from beyond – deeper and higher than ourselves.[72] This givenness (*donation de sens*) is involuntary because it sets us in the accusative.[73] The

---

[69] Cf. Ricœur, *L'herméneutique biblique*, 233.
[70] Cf. Ricœur, *L'herméneutique biblique*, 232.
[71] Ricœur, *L'herméneutique biblique*, 234.
[72] Cf. Ricœur, *Critique et conviction*, 219.
[73] "cette donation de sens" Ricœur, *Critique et conviction*, 221.

nature of the originality of this Word is not causal as in the case of the first of a series, but its nature is fundamental. The offer of meaning of this Word is heteronomous but access to this Word is always mediated by the words, testimonies and narratives of human beings. The responsibility for accepting this Word and for transforming it into a destination by a specific choice lies in the hands of human beings.[74] Autonomy and heteronomy are intertwined in an inseparable way, and can barely be distinguished at best.

b. Religious Experience as Being in Search of...

Pablo Neruda poetically evokes the experience of 'having been touched by something' which he seeks to interpret as having been burnt (literally, having had a burn or *quemadura*) at the start of his writing, since the experience is not accessible in its immediacy.[75] By means of metaphors he seeks to come nearer to his poetic vocation. However, every step nearer draws him away from the point he turns to. The process of formulating and the metaphor of approaching, open a yawning abyss between language and the nakedness of the experience.[76] Although language may be responsible for the gap and the impossibility of immediate access to the experience, it offers at the same time the capacity to bring it to words and to deepen the abyss through which we indirectly trace the contours of what is inaccessible in its immediacy.

Analogous to the assertion that time becomes human when it is formulated narratively, experience becomes Christian experience in the manner of its meaning and formulation. This leads us to a Christian hermeneutic circle. It is in the experience in front of the text and the relatedness to it that religious experience emerges. The Christian experience of God is not possible without the particularity of Scripture and the contexts in which it has its home.

The Word of God directed to humanity is accessible in Scripture in the manner that it is witnessed to by them. The Word is revealing by being the application of itself to a place or context. In this hermeneutic circle the specificity of the Bible arises, while in the same moment it becomes

---

[74] Cf. Ricœur, *Critique et conviction*, 221; see also Ricœur, *Lectures 3*, 271.

[75] Cf. Ricœur, *Lectures 3*, 266.

[76] "Pérégrination et narration sont fondées dans une approximation de l'éternité par le temps, laquelle, loin d'abolir la différence, ne cesse de la creuser." Ricœur, *Temps et récit*, 1:52.

clear what the 'proper place' of God in it is.[77] Religious language does have God as referent, but rather we must always realise that God transcends speaking. To understand what is meant by God means to grasp in what direction the grounding text of Christianity points to.[78] This direction only becomes apparent in the involving encounter with the text.

It is in this event of receiving the Word and the attempt to understand it that religious experience is shaped. Experience in search of language, and language generating experience, is the interaction we described by means of prefiguration, configuration and refiguration (the three aspects of mimesis). Through these, 'experience' (*er-fahren, er-varen, ex-perior, ex-perience*) regains its etymological originality of being-passed-through. Ricœur is influenced by psychoanalysis and he has in mind the analytical labour (*Durcharbeitung*) which the analysand has to undergo in order to discover the hidden meaning that is present in his dreams. The mediation of Christian experience requires an analogous labour.

The emphasis on the hermeneutical might lead us to conclude wrongly that God is a construct of our interpretation. It is true that the symbolic order is simultaneous with human beings. It is even true that symbols are, to a certain extent, also constructs, but they are not this solely and there is no religious experience without interpretation, just as there is no interpretation without experience.[79] However, on the basis of the mediation of the symbolic with the Sacred lies the fundamental conviction that the answer of humanity is preceded by the addressed word that comes "from beyond and above".[80] This is the theological axiom that there can be alterity. It is related to the mystery of our life and with this mystery we are at stake. With the acceptance of this alterity, we are involved and positioned within the hermeneutic circle.

This Word by which humanity is preceded, 'makes the difference'. But what precisely this difference is remains a quest. Together with the referent of the text and the experience of limit, this means that religious experience will always have the characteristic of a search for the meaning of this difference. This search implies that experience is epistemologically relevant since it is an essential element in the indication of the direction. God and religion would lose their meaning if there were no openness towards new experiences and interpretations. The accomplished

---

[77] Cf. Ricœur, *Du texte à l'action*, 128-129.

[78] "Comprendre le mot 'Dieu', c'est suivre la flèche de sens de ce mot." Ricœur, *Du texte à l'action*, 129.

[79] Cf. Ricœur, *Du texte à l'action*, 114.

[80] Ricœur, *Critique et conviction*, 219.

unity of the prefiguration is broken open by life itself as the 'discordant' of human experience.[81] The interruption here is not the nakedness of immediate experience but human experience as a 'world of text'. Religious experience here is a kind of contrasting being-in-the-world, a 'project' or a "pro-position of a mode of being in the world".[82] We can refer here to the concept of contrast-experience developed by Edward Schillebeeckx.[83] This experience would be a universal experience when it is equated to a naked experience as such. Such contrasting experience, however, is interrupting and meaningful because it applies the narrative material of the Christian tradition in order to reformulate the perspective from which it is understood. By interpreting the suffering of humanity in view of Jesus's option for the poor and the weak, it becomes an interruption 'in God's name'. And because it is already interpreted experience, it breaks open the pre-comprehensive understanding of world and time in view of a more dignified humanity. This fits well the creative capacity to re-configure reality that we described above.

In view of this, 'religious experience' is not so much the experience of a moment or an immediacy, but rather the process or the event of interpretation in which experience and narrativity become related and intertwined. By means of this the signifier 'God' is given reference and the meaning of it can, in a mimetical operation, give perspective to our life. In this respect we cannot speak of religious experience as an immediacy but, instead, as the event of an encounter between two worlds which give rise to a 'referent'. This process of 'religious experience' is combined with a consciousness which Ricœur calls a second naiveté. Understood in this way, religious experience is the process, or the 'passing through' that organises our time and our experiences after the manner of a narrative. In this becoming a Christian narrative of our experience, a viewpoint of a critical, exterior perspective can be incorporated.

---

[81] Cf. Ricœur, *Temps et récit*, 1:72.

[82] Ricœur, *Interpretation Theory*, 94.

[83] Edward Schillebeeckx, *Mensen als verhaal van God* (Baarn: Nelissen, 1989) esp. 24-26 and 47-49; English translation: *Church: The Human Story of God* (London: SCM Press, 1990). The contrast experience is described by Edward Schillebeeckx in *Christ: The Experience of Jesus as Lord* (New York, NY: Crossroad, 1980), and also used effectively throughout *Church: The Human Story of God*.

INDEX NOMINUM

LIST OF CONTRIBUTORS

Frederick Christian Bauerschmidt is associate professor at the Faculty of Theology, Loyola College in Maryland. In 2001-2003 he served as the director of the Loyola International Nachbar House in Leuven, and was a guest professor in the Department of Church History at K.U.Leuven.

Lieven Boeve is professor of fundamental theology, K.U.Leuven. He is also the coordinator of the Research Group 'Theology in a Postmodern Context' and co-promoter of the GOA research project 'Orthodoxy: Process and Product', sponsored by the Research Fund K.U.Leuven.

Christophe Brabant is a junior research fellow in the Research Group 'Theology in a Postmodern Context', working on the project 'Theology of Religious Experience', sponsored by the Fund for Scientific Research – Flanders (FWO).

Yves De Maeseneer is an aspirant reseach fellow of the Fund for Scientific Research – Flanders (FWO), associated with the Research Group 'Theology in a Postmodern Context'.

Annekatrien Depoorter is a junior research fellow in the Research Group 'Theology in a Postmodern Context', assigned to the project 'Theology of Interruption', Research Fund, K.U.Leuven.

Marc Dumas is professor of theology at the Faculté de théologie, d'éthique et de philosophy, Université de Sherbrooke, Quebec, Canada. During the academic year 2002-2003 he joined the Research Group to spend his sabbatical leave at K.U.Leuven, and was appointed guest professor for the same period.

Joris Geldhof is an aspirant research fellow of the Fund for Scientific Research – Flanders (FWO), associated with the Department of Dogmatic Theology, K.U.Leuven.

Hans Geybels is a junior research fellow in the Research Group 'Theology in a Postmodern Context', working on the projects 'Theology of Religious Experience', sponsored by the Fund for Scientific Research – Flanders (FWO), and 'Theology of Interruption', Research Fund, K.U.Leuven.

Jacques Haers, s.j., is professor of dogmatic theology and director of the Centre for Liberation Theologies, K.U.Leuven.

Laurence Paul Hemming is Head of Research at Heythrop College, University of London. From October 2002 to December 2003 he served as a guest professor at K.U.Leuven. From April 2002 he also held a postdoctoral research fellowship in the Research Group, granted by the Fund for Scientific Research – Flanders (FWO) and the K.U.Leuven Research Fund.

Terrence Merrigan is professor and chair of the Department of Dogmatic Theology, K.U.Leuven. He is also co-promoter of the GOA research project 'Orthodoxy: Process and Product'.

Stijn Vanden Bossche is assistant professor of dogmatic theology at the Katholieke Theologische Universiteit, in Utrecht (The Netherlands), and guest professor at K.U.Leuven. He also serves as a postdoctoral research fellow in the GOA research project 'Orthodoxy: Process and Product'.

PRINTED ON PERMANENT PAPER • IMPRIME SUR PAPIER PERMANENT • GEDRUKT OP DUURZAAM PAPIER - ISO 9706

N.V. PEETERS S.A., WAROTSTRAAT 50, B-3020 HERENT